SAMPSON TECHNICAL INSTITUTE

REVERSE DISCRIMINATION

REVERSE DISCRIMINATION

edited by BARRY R. GROSS

℞ Prometheus Books
Buffalo, New York 14215

Published 1977 by Prometheus Books
1203 Kensington Avenue, Buffalo, New York 14215

Library of Congress Catalog Number: 76-53643
ISBN 0-87975-083-9

Printed in the United States of America

Contents

Preface

I have striven for balance in this collection of writings and aimed to present as many interesting and opposed points of view as possible in that weighing of argument in moral reasoning which Aristotle tells us is the best for which we can hope. If the reader finds a section inclined to one side of the issue, I hope he will find another inclined to the opposite.

There is material enough for a collection much larger than this one. Considerations of space and reprint rights have worked to constrain that material to the size here presented. I have cut some selections where the views presented overlapped with others in the collection, but I have tried to maintain the essential integrity of the piece in each case.

I have to thank James Nickel and Miro Todorovich for many helpful insights, references, and for much bibliography. The Honorable James J. Oakes drew my attention to the article by Terrance Sandalow. My thanks are due especially to Sidney Hook for his constant encouragement of this project.

Barry Gross
New York, N.Y.
January 1977

1

General Introduction

As a working definition we can say that reverse discrimination is giving special or preferred treatment to persons who are members of racial or religious or ethnic groups or a sex against whose membership generally unjust discrimination was or is being practiced. The original discrimination must have been unjust, for there are many kinds of discrimination that may be practiced that do not involve justice at all; and if no injustice was done, there is no immoral harm that needs rectification. Without this dimension of morality, the notion of reverse discrimination we are trying to capture does not exist.

Those who favor reverse discrimination of one or another sort usually single out blacks, Chicanos, and women as deserving of it. Because they restrict themselves to these groups and their members, we can deduce that previous unjust discrimination is only a necessary condition of being eligible for reverse discrimination. But it is not sufficient. More must be required, since these are not the only groups whose members were or are unjustly discriminated against. Friends of reverse discrimination usually claim that the members of the groups singled out do not have a fair or acceptable level of income, or education, or social status, and that this is due solely or in large measure to the effect of past or present unjust discrimination against the group. So the three conditions that together are held necessary and suffi-

3

cient for society to practice and members of some groups to receive reverse discrimination are: past and/or present unjust discrimination against a group, currently lowered status or expectations, and a causal connection between the two.

If we should try to discover what sorts of questions are raised by a serious consideration of reverse discrimination, we would find that they fall into three groups: fact, law, and value. Obviously, if someone claims that we ought to practice reverse discrimination, we shall at the least want to know whether the groups he has in mind fit the criteria or rationale outlined. So we must ask whether there was or is unjust discrimination, what the current status of the group is, and whether or not, when it is low, one can attribute that to the unjust discrimination. This makes for a rather lively debate. Virtually no one questions that past discrimination against the named groups existed. But some do question whether all the groups seriously discriminated against have been mentioned on the list, whether all of the groups mentioned are on the same footing, and whether all of them have been discriminated against in the same way and to the same degree. And always in the background is the question of what ought to be done about it. More arguments arise when we come to assess the current status of these groups; for it's rather hard to measure, and few opponents or proponents have bothered to do it comprehensively. The debate often relies on casual surveys and common sense. Finally, there will be argument over the connection between past discrimination and current status. Certainly it is clear that past discrimination has not always led to lowered current status, nor has its absence led to higher status.

Regardless of the answers to these questions, we must inquire what the law says. Whatever the current status of minority groups, we could not practice reverse discrimination if the law enjoined it, and we could not frame laws permitting it if the Constitution forbade it. The legal and constitutional questions, being raised at a greater level of generality, are more abstract than the factual ones. They are also more technical because the law is technical and involves many questions of interpretation. For example, neither the Founding Fathers nor the framers of the Fourteenth Amendment, which contains a clause forbidding denial of equal protection of the law to anyone, could have foreseen that reverse discrimination would come to exist and that it would be a problem. No specific mention is made of it. Constitutional experts, and ultimately the Supreme Court, will have to decide whether and on what grounds the Constitution permits it. But an examination of the legal issues and challenges will show that there are many ways of practicing reverse discrimination and many rationales for it. Judges tend to rule on as narrow grounds as possible and so a decision in one case will not settle the issue once and for all.

Among other things, we shall want to know whether or not the Constitution permits or enjoins racial reference and whether or not there is a constitutional distinction between benign and invidious racial discrimination and its inverse. Again, the law often supplies the means to remedy bad laws or policies. Does or should it supply remedies also when what we normally think of as good or even exemplary laws and policies lead, in some cases, to results similar to those we had tried to avoid by changing bad laws? For example, when people are discriminated against de jure resulting in, say, lowered employment prospects, we intervene to change or to strike down the laws enjoining this. But suppose for one or another group, lowered employment prospects existed merely de facto as a result of some contingent trait of the group or of society as a whole. Should the law intervene? On what scale? Should it do so if it would have to discriminate against others? What arguments can be brought for or against intervention?

At this point we begin to discuss values and find ourselves in the third area, at a still higher level of abstraction. These values exist at a higher level of abstraction because it is in terms of the values we wish to achieve in society that we frame our laws. Here questions of consistency, fairness, and justice arise, and we must decide in what direction we wish to aim for solutions to them. Such decisions are logically prior to the framing of our laws, though they are not always explicitly articulated. They are continually being made, remade, and refined as our consensus about values evolves. Indeed, some of the fundamental questions are precisely about this evolution of social values. For in a democracy how far ahead of a national consensus can a moralist be and remain either right or effective? And is one obliged to take a moral position to which he has no hope of bringing a considerable body of public opinion?

From another point of view, if a position is theoretically morally correct while its implementation in practice is so flawed as to bring into doubt whether the desired ends may be secured, what shall we do? Shall we stand aside from it or shall we implement away, shutting our eyes to the consequences. And how is moral correctness assessed?

So, from the purely philosophic point of view we may inquire whether and when reverse discrimination is justified or just. And we may ask in whose favor ought it to be practiced. Do we practice it in favor of groups or of individuals only? If of individuals, then how does it differ from ordinary compensation or reparations where mere group membership fails to qualify one for an award and direct injury must be shown? If we must practice it in favor of groups, then how can it be just to favor any member of the group who has received no injury, though the members of the group generally have been injured by discrimination against the group itself?

In the selections that follow many such questions are raised and answers given. It is the virtue and the vice of inquiry that answers given to questions raise new ones and cause us to reformulate the old. The reader should bear that in mind as he turns to the articles which follow.

One: Facts and Polemics

Introduction

The correspondence between Miro Todorovich and Howard Glickstein is a perfect introduction to the web of problems surrounding reverse discrimination. It ranges over most of the issues and attitudes, extending even to that testiness and ascerbity so characteristic of the debate. Its points are not easily summed up, though they are easily understood, and may best be left to the reader, who will capture for himself both the substance and the flavor of the disagreement.

J. Stanley Pottinger is head of the Office of Civil Rights of the Department of Health, Education, and Welfare. It was under his direction that the affirmative-action programs concerning colleges and universities got their start, and he has himself taken considerable fire from critics who alternately charge that HEW has done too little and too much. In his essay he defends his division's enforcement of its policies and the necessity for them, especially goals and timetables, and he analyzes what he claims is an overreaction by university administrators and others, which he holds is due in part to a bit of misunderstanding and in part to a bit of bad faith.

Lee Nisbet tells briefly of his own experience in being "reverse discriminated" out of a job, and comments upon letters he received after his story appeared in print. In his view many of those calling themselves liberals have shifted from the traditional liberal concern with individual rights to a

9

concern with abstract groups and their purported rights. He argues that such persons should reconsider both their concerns and their appellation.

F. K. Barasch argues that there is an abundant supply of women qualified for high university positions and that any lack of them there is due to discrimination. At present they tend to be concentrated at the lower end in rank and salary, and, where they *have* attained high rank, it is in rather less prestigious departments. Not quotas, but good-faith efforts are needed to give women a fair chance. The reader should compare this analysis with that of Thomas Sowell.

R. M. O'Neil puts an eloquent case for the preferential admission of minorities to law schools. Among his reasons, he cites the fact that minorities are presently unlikely to meet the stringent requirements for admission, and he holds it desirable that the number of minority lawyers be increased because their lack has harmful side effects: lowered minority income, insufficient legal services for minorities, and lack of self-respect. He also holds that the standard entrance tests and requirements are not good enough predictors for us to rely solely upon them in the case of minority candidates. Preferential admissions can also serve in part as reparations for prior discrimination and will aid in making the law school a microcosm of society as a whole.

The two pieces by Sidney Hook deal respectively with quotas and with Professor Richard Lester's book *Anti-Bias Regulation of Universities*. Professor Hook charges that those in the Office of Civil Rights advocating and enforcing "goals" are ignorant both of statistical analysis and the purpose and mission a university. Goals are no more than another name for quotas, and quotas based upon the proportional representation of various groups in society are a sociological absurdity. They pose a danger in that the demand for them erodes the quality of a faculty, which is the only legitimate demand that can be made for one. By their constant reference to race, goals or quotas promote racism, not equality.

Professor Hook brings out the sharpness of Lester's statistical analysis of the use of women and minorities in higher education, showing how the relevant contrast is not with their percentage of the general population but rather with that segment of the population fully qualified for academic positions. He also commends Lester for his strong emphasis on the unique character of educational institutions.

In a very lively outline of the question of HEW's role in the university Paul Seabury encapsulates some of the history of civil-rights legislation and its ironies. He outlines the peculiar vulnerability of universities to attack from government bureaucracies that have great power over budgets and hence over their very existence. The burden of proof is shifted from HEW, which does not have to prove discrimination, to the universities, which have to prove their innocence. HEW accuses, prosecutes, judges, and passes sentence. He defends the merit system as basically fair and workable. The reader may wish to compare his analysis with those of O'Neil, Archibald Cox in the Harvard *amicus curie* brief (in Section 2), and Hardy Jones (in Section 3), who disagree with him.

In a recent and influential article Thomas Sowell subjects the statistics of minority and female employment to a sophisticated analysis in an attempt to take the emotion from the issue. He admits that at least several decades ago discrimination was prevalent in the university, but he argues that it covered others as well as those now classed as minorities. His argument is that the various affirmative-action programs were begun before any analysis of minority positions in academia had been made and that such analysis reveals that minority-group members had made considerable progress *before* affirmative action but very little after. He concludes that when internal factors are taken into account, they provide an explanation for the current position of minority and female academics, which is relatively very good and absolutely far better than portrayed in popular accounts. In his view affirmative-action programs were unnecessary to begin with and are unlikely to have much good effect now.

Nathan Glazer provides us with a rather different view of American society. He argues that it has developed as a nation of minorities, each of which is accepted as a social entity but none of which has been accorded legal status or recognition. The popular picture of the country as composed of a large and monolithic majority, which tolerates some and opposes other minorities is therefore false. In governmental plans like affirmative action he sees a threat to the relative stability of this balance of minorities, not merely because some will be favored over others but rather because this favoritism and the defining characteristics of the favored will be given that legal status which none was before accorded. He underscores the irony that just at the moment when the nation seemed to decide once and for all to do away with racial prejudice it implemented plans whose outcome was to reenforce it.

Miro M. Todorovich
and Howard A. Glickstein

Discrimination in Higher Education
A Debate on Faculty Employment

The exchange of letters which follows was published in Civil Rights Digest *in the spring of 1975 because it illuminates, in an interesting as well as informative fashion, the controversy surrounding affirmative action in higher education. The first letter was written by Miro Todorovich, coordinator of the Committee on Academic Nondiscrimination and Integrity. The Committee is a nontax-exempt organization closely related to the University Centers for Rational Alternatives. Mr. Todorovich addressed his letter to Dr. Richard A. Lamanna, Department of Sociology, University of Notre Dame, who turned it over to Howard Glickstein, director of the Center for Civil Rights at the same university. Mr. Glickstein, formerly staff director of the U.S. Commission on Civil Rights, then responded to Mr. Todorovich—Editor.*

Source: Civil Rights Digest (*Spring 1975*).

December 11, 1973

Dear Dr. Lamanna:

The recent contacts of our Committee with members of Congress indicate that there is a growing interest on Capitol Hill in matters of affirmative action in general and discrimination in reverse in particular. We found, however, that there is regrettably little hard information presently in the hands of our elected representatives.

As a first corrective step, I would suggest the writing of letters expressing our concern to senators and congressmen of your local area.

The letters could reflect (depending on the situation in any one particular area) concern that the goal-setting timetables containing affirmative-action plans demanded by federal agencies are introducing de facto quotas in educational hiring; concern about administrative interference in educational matters, difficulties in finding employment for well-qualified graduating candidates who do not fit a particular description of "affected minorities" and women, diversion of educational resources and structures into noneducational endeavors, and invasion of privacy and of confidential data; concern about the promotion of color- and sex-related criteria in hiring, student admission, and the like, erosion of institutional and departmental autonomies, and the undermining of the peer-judgment principle.

In addition, one should point out that all these activities have been generated by the Office of Federal Contract Compliance, HEW, Equal Employment Opportunity Commission, and other federal agencies without the proof of need, any hard data, any adequate analysis, without any hearings or any consultation with the affected institutions and professors.

You may wish to cite the following provisions of Title VII of the Civil Rights Act of 1964:

> Sec. 703 (a) It should be an unlawful employment practice for an employer . . . to limit, segregate, or classify his employees in any way which would deprive or tend to deprive any individual of employment opportunities or otherwise adversely affect his status as an employee because of such individual's race, color, religion, sex, or national origin.
>
> (j) Nothing contained in this title shall be interpreted to require any employer . . . to grant preferential treatment to any individual or to any group because of race, color, religion, sex or national origin of such individual or group on account of an imbalance which may exist with respect to the total number or percentage of persons of any race, color, religion, sex, or national origin employed by any employer.

You may also find useful the quotes from the Executive Order 11246 [issued] by President Johnson. This order, which is allegedly the basis for the various departmental orders and guidelines demanding the establishment of affirmative-action programs, has quite an unambiguous language:

> (1) The contractor will not discriminate against any employee or applicant for employment because of race, color, religion, sex, or national origin.
>
> The contractor will take affirmative action to ensure that applicants are employed, and that employees are treated during employment, without regard to their race, color, religion, sex, or national origin. Such action shall include, but not be limited to the following: employment, upgrading, demotion, or transfer; recruitment or recruitment advertising; layoff or termination; rates of pay or other forms of compensation, and selection for training, including apprenticeship. The contractor agrees to post in conspicuous places, available to employees and applicants for employment, notices to be provided by the contracting officer setting forth the provisions of this nondiscrimination clause.
>
> (2) The contractor will, in all solicitations or advertisements for employees placed by or on behalf of the contractor, state that all qualified applicants will receive consideration for employment without regard to race, color, religion, sex, or national origin.

All these clear provisions have been in one way or another violated by the various affirmative-action programs, which treat Americans *with* regard to race, color, and sex.

We feel that congressional action is needed to stop rampant violation by the nonelected and nonaccountable federal bureaucrats of antidiscrimination statutes and orders. I hope that you and many of your colleagues will bring to the attention of your elected representatives the magnitude of the problem and your views on the matter.

Miro M. Todorovich, Coordinator
Committee on Academic
Nondiscrimination and Integrity

May 29, 1974

Dear Mr. Todorovich:

A copy of your December 11, 1973, letter to Dr. Richard A. Lamanna of this university has come to my attention. The letter lists certain alleged abuses of affirmative-action programs and cites a provision of the Civil

Rights Act of 1964 which prohibits preferential treatment because of race, color, religion, sex, or national origin, and a provision of Executive Order 11246 requiring affirmative action, which provides that employees be treated during employment "without regard to their race, color, religion, sex, or national origin." The letter goes on to claim that "these clear provisions have been in one way or another violated by the various affirmative-action programs, which treat Americans with regard to race, color, and sex," and concludes by urging action to influence legislation.

I find your letter shockingly misleading and deceptive. The language from Title VII and Executive Order 11246 which is cited has been interpreted consistently by the courts to permit affirmative-action plans and policies which are designed to remedy the present effects of past discrimination. Merely citing the language of a statute or executive order tells only part of the story; it is essential that the purpose and judicial interpretations of the language in question also be considered. I presume that you are not a lawyer—if you are, God help the legal profession—but there are lawyers on your steering committee who must bear responsibility for such a disingenuous letter.

Let me first turn to Section 703(j) of the Civil Rights Act of 1964—the so-called ban against "preferential treatment" in employment. The meaning of that provision was considered by the Court of Appeals for the Sixth Circuit in *United States* v. *IBEW Local 38,* where the court said:

> When the stated purposes of the act and the broad affirmative relief authorization (42 U.S.C. Sec. 2000e-6) are read in context with Sec. 2000e-2(j), we believe that section cannot be construed as a ban on affirmative relief against continuation of effects of past discrimination resulting from present practices (neutral on their face) which have the practical effect of continuing past injustices. Any other interpretation would allow complete nullification of the stated purposes of the Civil Rights Act of 1964.

A similar result was reached by the Court of Appeals for the Ninth Circuit. In *United States v. Iron-workers Local 86,* the court ordered the union to offer immediate job referrals to previous discriminatees, and ordered the union's apprenticeship and training committee to select and indenture sufficient black applicants to overcome past discrimination. The order also included judicially imposed ceiling requirements for apprenticeship-program participation of minorities. On appeal, the union argued that this order was in violation of Sec. 703(j). The union condemned the order as "racial quotas" and "racial preferences." The court rejected this argument, stating: "There can be little doubt that where a violation of Title VII is found, the court is vested with broad remedial power to remove the vestiges of past discrimination and eliminate present and assure the nonexistence of future barriers to the full enjoyment of equal job opportunities by qualified black workers."

The court went on to say that: "Without such powers, the district court would be unable to effectuate the desire of Congress to eliminate all forms of discrimination."

(See also *United States v. Wood, Wire and Metal Lathers International Union No. 46:* "While quotas merely to attain racial balance in employment are forbidden by the Civil Rights Act of 1964, quotas to correct past discriminatory practices are not"; *Carter v. Gallagher:* "(T)he antipreference treatment section of the new Civil Rights Act of 1964 does not limit the power of a court to order affirmative relief to correct the effects of past unlawful practices"; *Stamps v. Detroit Edison*: "Having found a pattern of discriminatory exclusion in hiring and assignments, this court has wide discretion in ordering such affirmative action, including the accelerated hiring and assignment of blacks in an effort to meet goals established for the purpose of overcoming the past patterns of racial exclusion"; *Heat and Frost Workers, Local 53 v. Volger;* and *United States v. Sheet Metal Workers International Association*).

At the time Congress amended Title VII in 1972, it considered various amendments which would have modified the judicial construction of Section 703(j). The fate of these amendments was described by the Court of Appeals for the Sixth Circuit in *United States v. Local Union No. 212, International Brotherhood of Electrical Workers:* "It also appears from the legislative history of certain proposed amendments to 42 U.S.C. Sec. 2000e-2(j) that it is not the intent of Congress to forbid remedies of the kind used in this case (a black membership quota was imposed on the union)."

Plainly, as recently as 1972, Congress was fully appraised of what you call "rampant violation by the nonelected and nonaccountable federal bureaucrats of antidiscrimination statutes and others." Yet Congress chose to take no action and, in fact, rejected efforts to curb the practices about which you complain. Congress, fortunately, has the good sense to recognize that it is necessary to be "color conscious to prevent discrimination being perpetuated and to undo the effects of past discrimination."

You are equally misinformed about the meaning of the affirmative-action provisions of Executive Order 11246 which prohibit all contractors or subcontractors on federally financed projects from discriminating in their employment practices. Cases arising under that order have upheld plans which take race into account and which establish racial quotas.

For example, the Court of Appeals for the Third Circuit upheld the Philadelphia Plan, which required that contractors obligate themselves to achievement of minority manpower goals or quotas if they wished to participate in federal construction projects or federally assisted construction of $500,000 or more (*Contractors Association of Eastern Pennsylvania v. Secretary of Labor*). That plan, promulgated under the authority of Executive Order No. 11246, provided for annually increased manpower utilization goals to raise minority employment in selected construction trades.

In *Southern Illinois Builders Association v. Ogilvie,* the court recognized that quotas are a logical part of an affirmative-action plan formulated pursuant to Executive Order No. 11246, and said:

> Basic self-interests of the individual must be balanced with social interests, and in circumstances where blacks have been discriminated against for years, there is no alternative but to require that certain minorities be taken into consideration with respect to the specific minority percentage of the population in a given area in order to provide a starting point for equal employment opportunities. In this regard, it is the feeling of this Court that minimum ratios, where *de jure* or *de facto*, based upon race are constitutional and valid when adopted for the purpose of implementing affirmative action to achieve equal employment opportunities.

Most recently, in *Associated General Contractors of Massachusetts, Inc. v. Altshuler,* the court upheld a state affirmative-action plan, which was more stringent than the federal plan, which was formulated pursuant to Executive Order No. 11246. The "Boston Plan" case involved an action by construction contractors, each a prospective bidder for state contracts, challenging contract provisions requiring contractors to employ a stated percentage of minority workers.

The court upheld the use of these racial criteria and stated:

> It is by now well understood, however, that our society cannot be completely color-blind in the short term if we are to have a color-blind society in the long term. After centuries of viewing through colored lenses, eyes do not quickly adjust when the lenses are removed. Discrimination has a way of perpetuating itself, albeit unintentionally, because the resulting inequalities make new opportunities less accessible. Preferential treatment is one partial prescription to remedy our society's most intransigent and deeply rooted inequalities.

In addition to my complete disagreement with your statement of the law, I also believe you grossly exaggerate the nature and extent of abuses connected with affirmative-action programs. Perhaps there has been overzealousness on some occasions, but that problem pales into insignificance when compared to the shameful injustices toward which affirmative-action programs are directed.

I can, nevertheless, understand and respect sincere differences of opinion over the implementation and consequences of affirmative-action programs. But I cannot understand an organization presumably dedicated to academic integrity sending out a letter which displays such complete ignorance of the subject with which it purports to deal.

Howard A. Glickstein, Director
Center for Civil Rights, University of Notre Dame

July 18, 1974

Dear Dr. Glickstein:

Thank you for your lengthy communication of May 29. Serious dialogue on a topic shrouded by fear and passion is sorely needed. It is thus unfortunate that your missive is composed chiefly of misapplied and irrelevant judicial citations, garnished with gratuitous insult.

You choose, I note, to focus on the fact that in my December 11 letter I cited the clear language of the Civil Rights Act of 1964 and Executive Order 11246 as amended, both of which explicitly forbid preferential treatment on the grounds of race or sex. You then quote certain lower-court decisions which interpret this to mean that where previous discrimination had been proved, race may be taken into account in establishing nondiscrimination.

However, you disregard entirely the sentence in my letter which points out that no proof of need or statistical data was presented to justify instituting these programs in the field of higher education, with which the Committee on Academic Nondiscrimination and Integrity concerns itself. In other words, there was no showing of prior discrimination. This fact is undisputed and of decisive importance. There was no sizable pool of unemployed minority Ph.D. holders when the affirmative-action programs were set loose on the colleges. The great upswing of minority undergraduate admissions preceded the institution of affirmative-action programs. In fact, the HEW guidelines do not even presume to speak of the correction of discrimination through "numerical goals" and "precise timetables." As you no doubt know well, the guidelines seek to alleviate "underutilization." In that light, all your citations which depend on a showing of previous discrimination are simply irrelevant. What is more, one of them points clearly to the impermissibility of the programs you defend. "While quotas merely to attain racial balance in employment are forbidden by the Civil Rights Act of 1964, quotas to correct past discriminatory practices are not," says the decision (*United States v. Wood, Wire, and Metal Lathers International Union No.* 46). One wonders what possibly could be meant by a quota "merely to attain racial balance," if it did not include in its meaning a correction of statistical imbalance without a showing of discrimination.

Yet it is not enough to say that your citations miss the point. They also tend to obscure it by implying that the law, as interpreted by the courts, uniformly justifies preferential treatment for social ends. For a man who is as ready as you to hurl charges of ignorance, deception, and disingenuousness, it seems downright imprudent not to have mentioned in your letter that Justice Douglas' seminal comments on the *DeFunis* case fundamentally support the principle that equal treatment under the laws means equal treatment for individuals and not groups. Thus, he wrote, "the consideration of race as a measure of an applicant's qualifications normally introduces a capricious and irrelevant factor working an invidious discrimination. . . . " According to the Justice, the states "may not proceed by racial classifications to force strict population equivalencies for every group in every occupation, overriding individual preferences. The Equal Protection Clause commands the elimination of racial barriers, not their creation, in order to satisfy our theory as to how society ought to be organized."

While you quote from lower-court decisions that do not even lie in the field of higher education, you fail to cite the words of a Supreme Court Justice on the one case that does lie in the higher-education area. Shall we take a leaf from your rhetorical book and attribute this to either ignorance or disingenuousness? And if you feel that a dissent in a moot case is unworthy of your attention, why did you neglect Chief Justice Burger's clear formulation in the *Griggs* case: "discriminatory preference for any group, minority or majority, is precisely and only what Congress has proscribed"?

Were the law as clear as you seem, somewhat contemptuously, to think, there would have been no need for the *DeFunis* case and for the Court's action in vacating the Washington State decision while declaring the case moot. Nor, more importantly, would there be any reason for the HEW guidelines to deny, as vigorously as they do, that they involve any preferential treatment whatever. Nor would HEW officials have found it necessary to disguise their quota requirements with the sophistry and euphemism of calling them "goals." Your frankness is useful in laying bare the real issue; your shamelessness in avowing your love of preferential treatment is, however, not shared by most government officials.

Yet even if the courts could be understood as interpreting "without regard to race" to mean "with regard to race," your indignation at CANI's presumption in questioning this miracle of dialectic would still be out of place. Though I am indeed not a lawyer (and it seems to me that the Deity has his hands quite full enough with the legal profession today), I do believe that there are precedents in American history for attempts to change the understanding of certain laws and constitutional provisions. I wonder if you had quite the same awe for the sanctity of *Plessy v. Ferguson* in 1953 as you have today for certain lower-court decisions. Perhaps you did. If so, let me remind you that Abraham Lincoln did not share this reverential view and spoke openly in his debates with Stephen A. Douglas of his total opposition to the Dred Scott decision and his determination to reverse it by legal means. No doubt there was some antebellum Glickstein on hand to accuse him of ignorance and disingenuousness.

You say, in your letter, that the language of a statute tells only part of the story and that one needs to consult the purpose as well. Had you taken the advice you so graciously proffered me, you might have discovered, by consulting the *Congressional Record* on the debates on the Civil Rights Act of 1964, that the proponents of the bill laughed off as imaginary horribles the very interpretations you so piously defend. I refer you in particular to Dr. Paul Seabury's article in *Commentary* of February 1972. Nor does the 1972 Equal Employment Opportunity Act in any way, either by language or intent, justify discriminatory racial quotas.

Perhaps the most disturbing aspect of your letter is the facility with which you skate over the substantive questions. You "believe" that I grossly exaggerate the nature and extent of abuses connected with affirmative-action programs. You will go so far as to concede that "perhaps" there has been overzealousness on some occasions, but you cheerfully maintain that the problem "pales into insignificance when compared to the shameful injustices towards which affirmative-action programs are directed." Might I ask on what you base your belief that I grossly exaggerate?

At CANI we can and have documented the charge that there is widespread discriminatory recruitment in academia, brought on by the demand of federal agencies for "proper representation." We can and have documented the charge that the majority of the male and female staff professors of sociology engaged in hiring, when polled, avowed the belief that affirmative action requires discrimination on the basis of sex and race and not of merit. We can and have documented the charge that there is under way a thoroughgoing exclusion of qualified white teachers of Afro-American history and black studies. We can and have documented the charge that federal officials have sought to intimidate universities and even to enter into the sphere of the disposition of the curriculum in order to attain what they conceive to be the ends of affirmative action. Yet you believe I exaggerate.

I refer you, for example, to the April 1973 issue of *Measure*, a publication of the University Centers for Rational Alternatives, of which our Committee is an offshoot. It gives the detailed factual account of the travails of one Martin Goldman, a qualified professor of Afro-American history, who had, in the year before the advent of the affirmative-action programs, received several offers of academic employment. Because of his race he now cannot find academic work. I can assure you that his case is not an exception. Paul Lammermeier, another specialist in Afro-American history, now works as a short-order cook in Mentor, Ohio, because his skin is the wrong color for a professor of his specialty today. Yet you believe I exaggerate.

If you are unwilling to lend credence to evidence that comes from me, perhaps you might listen to Dr. Richard Lester of Princeton University, formerly vice-chairman of President Kennedy's Commission on the Status of Women. In his book *Anti-Bias Regulations of Universities: Faculty Problems and Their Solutions*, Dr. Lester offers a powerful array of factual evidence which proves that the affirmative-action programs you defend not only commit injustice through preferential treatment—which apparently causes you no concern—and destroy academic standards and autonomy—which may not disturb you in the slightest—but also are wholly ineffective in obtaining their own intended purposes of increasing the number of women and minority-group members in faculty positions.

Professor Lester shows that the need to fulfill utterly unrealistic quotas, under the threat of loss of federal funds, leads to an undignified and essentially pointless game of musical chairs, in which blacks and women are lured from one place to the next by offers of higher salary and greater prestige, but which does not markedly increase the actual numbers in circulation. Thus quotas and timetables merely distract from the problem, which is mainly one of supply, by making the fallacious assumption that it is essentially one of demand, hampered by discrimination. Thus, Dr. Clark Kerr, in his introduction to the book, points out that Dr. Lester "stresses the fact that current faculty members favor such an increase [in minority members and women] but warns that many of the action programs prescribed to achieve it fail to take into consideration either the inadequate supply of qualified people among these groups currently underrepresented on our faculties or the characteristics of academic employment that distinguish it from employment in industry." Speaking for himself, Dr. Kerr continues: "At stake is not only an equitable system of academic employment, but also loss of financial support as governments apply economic sanctions to achieve numerical hiring goals that often have little relevance to the character and mission of universities." Yet you believe I "grossly exaggerate" the abuses of affirmative action.

Under the circumstances, is it really too much to ask of a man who accuses others of deception and ignorance that he substantiate his allegations with more than his "belief," or, one might uncharitably say, his gall? I cannot, however, merely leave the question at this point. You should consider the logical form of your argument. You say that existing abuses pale by comparison with the injustices that affirmative-action programs are directed toward. Apparently then, because the program's aims are noble, their evils are insignificant. I trust I need not remind you of the kind of politician and demagogue who uses this sophism to justify misdeeds by good intentions. Why then do you make such an argument?

In fact, whether you are willing to believe it or not, nondiscrimination is CANI's most cherished goal. Our members have shown a lifelong commitment to equality and fairness and have been in the forefront of actions fought for the disadvantaged. However, we do not see how you can possibly hope to create color-blindness out of color consciousness, and nondiscrimination out of preferential treatment. Those who suffer discrimination today in order to "compensate" the children of those who suffered it yesterday will someday have children who will in turn have a claim to "compensation." How shall it all end except in a policy of true nondiscrimination which looks to individual merit and not to race, class, sex, or religion?

I do not deny that you and many others have shown a remarkable ingenuity in discovering ways in which "without regard" can be interpreted to mean "with regard." Such ingenuity would be laudable if it were applied to making real nondiscrimination a working reality. You delude yourself if you believe that "preferential treatment is one partial prescription to remedy our society's most intransigent and deeply rooted inequalities." In fact, preferential treatment is a wholly adequate prescription for the perpetuation of preferential treatment, which is, you may recall, what caused those intransigent and deeply rooted inequalities in the first place.

Miro M. Todorovich

November 13, 1974

Dear Professor Todorovich:

I appreciated receiving your letter of July 18, 1974, and read it with great interest. Please forgive my delay in responding.

I have spent most of my professional career in activities seeking to achieve racial justice in this country, and frequently feel a deep sense of frustration about the limited progress we have achieved. I acknowledge, nevertheless, the appropriateness of your suggestion that "serious dialogue on a topic shrouded by fear and passion is sorely needed." Accordingly, let me attempt to define our points of difference in as dispassionate a way as possible.

Perhaps we differ most fundamentally over the extent of discrimination in employment in higher education. You believe that institutions of higher learning are being subjected to a burden without "proof of need or statistical data." I believe that there is ample proof. It is for that reason that I relied on cases that assumed the existence of discrimination. What is that proof?

As you know, educational institutions were not covered by Title VII, the fair-employment title of the Civil Rights Act of 1964. The 1972 amendments to Title VII, however, extended coverage to educational institutions. Congress acted only after extensive proof that there was a severe problem which required that educational institutions be subjected to the provisions of Title VII. The House Committee Report underscored the scope of the problem:

> Discrimination against minorities and women in the field of education is as pervasive as discrimination in any other area of employment. In the field of higher education, the fact that black scholars have been generally relegated to all-black institutions or have been restricted to lesser academic positions when they have been permitted entry into white institutions is common knowledge.
>
> Similarly, in the area of sex discrimination, women have long been invited to participate as students in the academic process, but without the prospect of

gaining employment as serious scholars.

. . . . The committee feels that discrimination in educational institutions is especially critical. The committee can not imagine a more sensitive area than educational institutions where the Nation's youth are exposed to a multitude of ideas that will strongly influence their future development. To permit discrimination here would, more than in any other area, tend to promote misconceptions leading to future patterns of discrimination. Accordingly, the committee feels that educational institutions, like other employers in the Nation, should report their activities to the [Equal Employment Opportunity Commission] and should be subject to the provisions of the Act. (House Committee on Education and Labor, *Equal Employment Opportunities Enforcement Act of 1971*).

Similar views were expressed in the Senate Committee Report:

The presence of discrimination in the Nation's educational institutions is no secret. Many of the most famous and best remembered civil rights cases have involved discrimination in education. This discrimination, however, is not limited to the students alone. Discriminatory practices against faculty, staff, and other employees are also common. The practices complained of parallel the same kinds of illegal actions which are encountered in other sectors of business, and include illegal hiring policies, testing provisions which tend to perpetuate racial imbalances, and discriminatory promotion and certification techniques.

As in other areas of employment, statistics for educational institutions indicate that minorities and women are precluded from the most prestigious and higher-paying positions, and are relegated to the more menial and lower-paying jobs. . . . The Committee believes that it is essential that these employees be given the same opportunity to redress their grievances as are available to other employees in the other sectors of business. . . . There is nothing in the legislative background of Title VII, nor does any national policy suggest itself, to support the present exemption.

In fact, the Committee believes that the existence of discrimination in educational institutions is particularly critical. It is difficult to imagine a more sensitive area than educational institutions, where the youth of the Nation are exposed to a multitude of ideas and impressions that will strongly influence their future development. To permit discrimination here would, more than in any other areas, tend to promote existing misconceptions and stereotypical categorizations which in turn would lead to future patterns of discrimination. (Senate Committee on Labor and Public Welfare, *Equal Employment Opportunities Enforcement Act of 1971*).

The need for the inclusion of institutions of higher education within the coverage of Title VII is illustrated further by the extent to which charges of discrimination have been filed with the Equal Employment Opportunity Commission. Since 1972, 1,600 charges of job discrimination by post-secondary institutions have been filed. In 1973, approximately one out of four

EEOC charges involved higher education. Seventy-nine percent were against public institutions, 21 percent against private. Forty-four percent of the charges involved sex discrimination; 39 percent race or ethnic discrimination; 4 percent religious discrimination; and 13 percent of the charges constitute multiple allegations.

While a charge is not proof or an adjudication, I believe that the large number of charges filed against educational institutions in the short time they have been covered by the act is indicative of a widespread problem.

The extensive number of charges of discrimination that continue to be filed by members of minority groups and women also argues strongly against your assertion that affirmative-action programs are being abused and that there is "widespread discriminatory recruitment in academia." This certainly could not be proven by the results. The increase in blacks and women on the faculties of previously white and male schools has been infinitesimal.

If we were doing so well in implementing goals and timetables—or giving preferences or imposing quotas—the EEOC would be inundated with charges from white males, not minorities and women. It is difficult for me to accept the argument that affirmative-action programs have been abused, that is, have discriminated against white males, when I see so little evidence of increased numbers of minorities and women on university faculties. John H. Powell, Jr., as chairman of the Equal Employment Opportunity Commission, stated: "We must look beyond the rhetoric . . . and look at the facts. Any sort of preliminary analysis of the facts will show that blacks are not displacing white males, that women are not displacing males, and I think that it is terribly important in this area, an area subject to so much misunderstanding, for us to tell it like it is and not necessarily respond to the rhetoric."

Nor do I find in Richard Lester's recent book any proof that affirmative-action programs have been abused. The book differs sharply from its press releases and the exaggerated newspaper stories that preceded its release. Contrary to your claim, it does not offer a "powerful array of factual evidence" of anything. It only suggests, without proving, that affirmative-action programs are ill-suited to university faculty-hiring practices. Lester's book is more a theoretical analysis of why "affirmative action" plans for the recruitment and hiring of women and minority-group members by major government contractors, while possibly effective in the construction and manufacturing industries, are not well suited to the professional recruitment and hiring of university faculty members.

The basic tenet of this thesis is that faculty-hiring practices are a delicate and sensitive matter among high-level professional scholars, which cannot be understood by those outside the academic community and therefore should not be interfered with. Lester's book does not purport to be a comprehensive study of "abuses" that have occurred in requiring affirmative action in the hiring of university faculty. He cites some examples of such abuses, but what he has undertaken is an academic analysis of a program, and not a field study of its application.

My understanding of the situation convinces me that discrimination in higher education is more the rule than the exception. Accordingly, I felt that your December 11, 1973, letter was misleading because it concentrated almost entirely on a simple recitation of the language of laws prohibiting "preferential treatment" without also warning that those provisions were not applicable if there were a showing of past discrimination. To be sure, you mentioned that affirmative-action programs were instituted in higher education without proof of need—an assertion which I am convinced is inaccurate—but you failed to point out that the general language of Title VII and Executive Order 11246 had to be interpreted in the light of a particular institution's past practices.

In other words, I felt your letter left the impression that in all cases involving institutions of higher education "preferential treatment" was prohibited. I think it would have been more accurate to advise your constituency that if there were no past record of discrimination, if an adequate affirmative-action program were being made toward increasing the representation of minorities and women on faculties, it probably would be possible to avoid a governmentally imposed hiring program.

While I take you to task for assuming there has been no discrimination, you fault the cases I cite on the ground they apply only where previous discrimination has been proven. As I already indicated, my letter proceeded on the assumption that discrimination does exist. In addition to the evidence of discrimination relied on by Congress in extending Title VII to institutions of higher education, it is now well accepted that a statistical showing of underrepresentation is sufficient to establish a prima facie case of discrimination. (See *United States v. Ironworkers Local 86; United States v. Hayes International Corp.; United States v. United Brotherhood of Carpenters and Joiners.*) It then becomes the burden of the person or institution accused of discrimination to convince the court that minorities or women are underrepresented for reasons other than discrimination (*U.S. v. Ironworkers Local 86*).

My own experience with the recruiting and hiring procedures of institutions of higher education convinces me that this would be a burden that few institutions could sustain. Nor is it enough that a university demonstrate that it has not itself engaged in overt discrimination. A university's compliance with the law is not adequate unless it takes into account "broader patterns of exclusion and discrimination practiced by third parties and fostered by the whole environment in which most minorities must live" (*Johnson v. Pike Corporation of America*). Yes, Professor Todorovich, it is appropriate to ask universities to examine "external problems" and not at all unreasonable to require a public university, such as the University of Connecticut, to study the feasibility of "improving transportation between Hartford and Storrs."

But whatever the necessity under Title VII to prove past discrimination before a race-conscious remedy will be required, such a necessity does not exist under Order 11246. In *Contractor's Association of Eastern Pennsylvania v. Secretary of Labor,* the Court upheld the Philadelphia Plan and said:

> The absence of a judicial finding of past discrimination is also legally irrelevant. The Assistant Secretary (of Labor) acted not pursuant to Title VII but pursuant to the Executive Order. Regardless of the cause, exclusion from the available labor pool of minority tradesmen is likely to have an adverse effect upon the cost and completion of construction projects in which the Federal Government is interested.
>
> Even absent a finding that the situation found to exist in the five-county area was the result of deliberate past discrimination, the Federal interest in improving the availability of key tradesmen in the labor pool would be the same. While a court must find intentional past discrimination before it can require affirmative action under 42 U.S. 2000 e-5 (g), that section imposes no restraint upon the measures which the President may require of the beneficiaries of Federal assistance. The decision of his designees as to the specific affirmative action which would satisfy the local situation did not violate the National Labor Relations Act and was not prohibited by 42 U.S. 2000 e-5 (g).

Since most major colleges and universities are government contractors, there is no need to prove an actual case of discrimination before requiring that such institutions adopt and implement affirmative-action plans.

Unfortunately, I am not sure that my efforts to cite precedent or to distinguish the cases you rely on, or your efforts similarly directed at me, really will get us very far in bridging the differences that separate us.* Those differences are bottomed on our respective notions of what must be done to eradi-

---

* For example, you fault me for relying on decisions that do not even lie in the field of higher education while overlooking the one case—the DeFunis case—that does lie in the higher education area. But your objection seems misplaced to me. DeFunis dealt

cate and overcome the generations of discrimination suffered by blacks, Chicanos, and women. Similar differences also accounted for the sides taken by the many parties who filed *amicus* briefs in the *DeFunis* case. On both sides of that case there were well-intentioned individuals and organizations all equally committed to our constitutional principles and the concept of equal opportunity. Yet one group regarded the treatment of Mr. DeFunis as a violation of the Constitution and the other group discerned no such violation. To my mind, the basic question separating these groups—and us—is the question of whether our nation is prepared to tolerate short-range, temporary disadvantages for white males in order to overcome our racist and sexist past.

I have enormous empathy for Martin Goldman (and I am glad to see that he has been compensated for the discrimination he believes he has suffered) and Paul Lammermeier, whose cases you cite in your letter, but at the same time I realize that the process of correcting past injustices cannot be totally painless. In the past, many Martin Goldmans and Paul Lammermeiers were able to obtain prestigious positions because they were protected from the competition of blacks and women. For every Paul Lammermeier working as a short-order cook today there probably were 1,000 blacks with college degrees or better who worked at the post office or as Pullman porters in the past.

It would be nice if we could make up for the disadvantages that some groups have suffered without any inconveniences to the advantaged group. I doubt whether this is possible, however. Undoubtedly, there are many individuals who feel that they have been disadvantaged because of the preferences we give to our veterans. But the sacrifices made by veterans, as a group,

---

with the student-admission process and not with employment. Almost without exception, the cases I cited dealt with employment discrimination—the matter at issue between us.

Your criticism, however, is very revealing. It suggests a belief that there is something special about higher education. This seems to be a common problem among those working in higher education. As Chairman Powell has stated: "The concept that institutions of higher education are 'above,' or at least not in the same relationship to the rest of society, is shared by a larger segment of the population, and by most institutions of higher learning as well. This view is frequently held, notwithstanding glaring realities to the contrary."

It is not readily perceived that the same principles of nondiscrimination that apply to plumbers, policemen, and sheet-metal workers also apply to professors. It is with a sense of déjà vu that I listen to fellow faculty members tell me about the delicate, complicated issues involved in making decisions about academic competence. This was the same rationalization used by officials of plumbers unions to explain to the U.S. Commission on Civil Rights why there were so few black plumbers.

justify according them preferences, as a group. Similarly, our laws contain numerous examples of preferences for Indians, including preferences in employment, but because of the cruelty this group has suffered such preferences have been allowed.

When a society has committed past injustices or when historically disadvantaged groups exist side by side with more advantaged groups, it simply is not possible to achieve equality and fairness by applying neutral principles.* This has been recognized by India, whose laws accord many preferences to "scheduled castes." This has been recognized by Israel, where so-called "colored Jews" receive preferred treatment. It is not pure fantasy, therefore, to believe that it is possible to "create color blindness out of color consciousness, and nondiscrimination out of preferential treatment."

Just a few months ago, the Court of Appeals for the Fifth Circuit upheld a lower-court order which required the Alabama Department of Public Safety to hire one qualified black trooper or support person for each white so hired until approximately 25 percent of both the state troopers and support-personnel force was comprised of blacks. Judge Coleman's reasoning is equally applicable to the situation we are discussing.

> ... the affirmative hiring relief instituted ... [here] fails to transgress either the letter or the spirit of the Fourteenth Amendment. . . . No one is denied any right conferred by the Constitution. It is the collective interest, governmental as well as social, in effectively ending unconstitutional racial discrimination, that justifies temporary carefully circumscribed resort to racial criteria, whenever the chancellor determines that it represents the only rational, nonarbitrary means of eradicating past evils.

---

* I confess my love for preferential treatment and believe such policies are supported by the law. I do not believe, however, that it is because HEW officials are less frank than I am or less shameless than I am that they deny that their policies involve preferential treatment. I believe there is a vast difference between the "goals and timetables" program and a program that directly embraces quotas or preferential treatment. A demonstration of "good faith" is sufficient to excuse meeting a goal. If university officials sincerely believe they have undertaken good-faith efforts to hire minorities, let them stand up to HEW and demonstrate their good faith—in court, if necessary.

As the attorney general said in upholding the legality of the Philadelphia Plan, "If unfairness in the administration of the Plan should develop, it cannot be doubted that judicial remedies are available." The problem is that the self-righteousness of so many academic people completely blinds their ability to engage in good-faith efforts. If the energy expended attacking HEW was instead devoted to implementing affirmative-action programs vigorously, I am sure there would be few difficulties in demonstrating good faith.

By mandating the hiring of those who have been the object of discrimination, quota relief promptly operates to change the outward and visible signs of yesterday's racial distinctions and thus, to provide an impetus to the process of dismantling the barriers, psychological or otherwise, erected by past practices. It is a temporary remedy that seeks to spend itself as promptly as it can by creating a climate in which objective, neutral employment criteria can successfully operate to select public employees solely on the basis of job-related merit. For once an environment where merit can prevail exists, equality of access satisfies the demand of the Constitution. (*NAACP v. Allen.*)

In addition to our differences over what must be done to overcome the effects of past discrimination, I imagine we differ on what constitutes "merit" and "competence." Many of those who oppose affirmative-action efforts argue that such efforts will upset systems that have been run strictly on the basis of merit and competence. They suggest that in the past the rule has been "may the best man (and I use the word intentionally) win" and that advocates of affirmative action are intent on destroying this principle.

Aside from the fact that in so many instances the only ones allowed to demonstrate their "merit" were white males, I do not believe that even within that limited category merit and competence were generally the decisive factors. We paid lip-service to merit and competence, but so many hiring decisions are made on the basis of extraneous factors. If there were some foolproof litmus test for determining merit, perhaps I would be fearful of tampering with the system. But the rules have been so rubbery in the past that I become a bit suspicious when a new rigidity is demanded as women and minorities appear at the gates.

Nor, I suspect, do we agree on who is "competent" to be a teacher. I have known all too many persons, as I am sure you have, with a string of degrees who did not have the vaguest idea of what he or she was doing in the classroom. The conventional badges of accomplishment in terms of certificates, diplomas, and degrees are not necessarily what we should be looking for to provide the best teachers for young Americans. Perhaps our efforts to insure that women and minorities have greater access to academic positions will force us to reevaluate our standards for determining competence.

We still have a long road to travel to achieve "an environment where merit can prevail." It is plain to me that we cannot achieve such an environment merely by requiring nondiscrimination. Such a policy was first imposed on government contractors in 1941, yet today—over thirty years later—we see daily examples of extensive patterns of discrimination. It is not mere whim motivating those who advocate strong affirmative-action programs. Rather, it is a realization that other approaches to equal opportunity—approaches that have been given fair chances to prove themselves—have not worked.

The programs currently being pursued by HEW—not nearly as vigorously or effectively as I would like—were developed slowly and carefully over a period of years to meet a proven need. It is not that the type of "affirmative efforts" advocated by CANI never have been tried. They have been tried and been found wanting. After years of frustrating efforts to integrate the schools in the South, the Supreme Court finally ordered the adoption of plans that "promise(s) realistically to work, and promise(s) realistically to work now." It is precisely such programs that we need in higher education.

In the late 1950s and early 1960s, those who advocated the enfranchisement of black citizens and the desegregation of schools and public accommodations were told by Southerners that they were embarked on a program that would destroy the fabric of Southern society and would result in chaos or disorder. Governor Wallace, in fact, warned that any effort to desegregate places of public accommodation would require the use of all the troops the country had—including our forces in Europe and Asia. These dire warnings did not come true, and the society is a lot better for the dramatic changes that have taken place in the South.

Similarly, I do not think our present programs to open up academic positions to women and minorities threaten academic integrity. Rather, if you accept the definition of *integrity* as "the state of being whole, entire, or undiminished," I do not see how we can claim to have academic integrity, how we can claim to be "whole," until all segments of our population are fairly represented in a profession that has such a basic and fundamental impact on the lives of young Americans.

Howard A. Glickstein

April 18, 1975

Dear Dr. Glickstein:

Please forgive the delay in responding to your letter of November 13, 1974. I feel that certain of the points you raise are well worth pursuing a bit further. But I would first like to remark that I respect and applaud your lifelong efforts on behalf of racial justice in this country.

Most of my own professional career has been spent, here and abroad, seeking to advance the content of higher learning as well as improve the means of disseminating that content. It is thus quite natural that I am highly sensitive to actions which I find detrimental to the activity of higher learning or to the fairness of the procedures by which it operates and which determine its quality. My commitment, needless to say, is rooted in my belief that learning is one of the best tools for the betterment of the lot of individuals, as well as of entire societies.

While, as I say, I respect your commitment, I must question both the choice of your targets and the selection of weapons for hitting the set mark. Let us begin by looking more closely at the actual figures behind the rhetorical use of statistics, since only then can the issues that divide us appear in their proper factual proportions.

At the end of the last decade about 1 percent of the Ph.D.'s in this country were black. This was at a time when many federal officials engaged in vigorous arm-twisting in order to force colleges and universities to incorporate goals for hiring black faculty far in excess of the 1 percent availability level into their affirmative-action plans. The result of such pressures could have been predicted and was. The continuous threat of loss of federal funds led to bidding wars and a musical-chairs game for existing black faculty; extraordinarily high salaries for black appointees; and even a few cases of one professor holding several jobs, sometimes illegally, to satisfy the unappeasable demand.

But did this effort lead to its desired end of increasing black participation in higher education? According to just-published data for the 1972-73 academic year, only about 4,000 of 33,000 American doctorates went to members of minority groups. Of those 4,000 only 975 were black, and only 37 percent were U.S. citizens. Thus, approximately 330 black American citizens received a doctorate. Once more, 1 percent, and therefore 1 percent of the newly available supply.

This is the factual basis on which our discussion must take place. We at CANI share with you a deep sense of frustration about these facts. But we feel they must be recognized if we are to find a way to change them. Comforting oneself with the thought that it is all the fault of evildoers merely disguises the real problems and make them harder to solve. This, I feel, is one of our fundamental differences. We would wish to try a variety of approaches both to increase the supply and to see justice done speedily for all individuals who may have suffered from discrimination. You, and several other groups and institutions whose views you so eloquently present, seem to desire to stick doggedly to plans and programs which have not produced positive results but have created much ill will, cynicism, and no little injustice of their own.

In turning to the main argument, you distinguish properly between the quotas imposed by courts in cases where specific acts of discrimination have been proved, and the affirmative-action programs required of higher-education institutions under Executive Order 11246 in their role as federal contractors. In making this distinction, you direct our discussion away from the general question of the justice, prudence, and propriety of preferential treatment to the more specific question of whether, as you and HEW officials claim, there is a "vast difference" between "numerical goals and precise timetables" and preferential treatment through quotas. This area is foggy with deceptive rhetoric and undocumented assumptions. Only after dealing with those can we return to the basic issue which divides us: whether racial or sexual discrimination is always or only sometimes wrong.

You argue that goals are not quotas because they only involve a "demonstration of 'good faith.'" Here it is necessary to clear up an ambiguity. If by *good faith* you mean good faith in fulfilling the goal, come what else may, such good faith could only be measured by numbers of positions offered and could not be distinguished from good-faith efforts to achieve a quota. Under this reading then, goals would be indistinguishable from quotas since they would require good-faith efforts to achieve quotas.

If, on the other hand, by *good faith* you mean good-faith efforts to hire the best-qualified candidate, then an admission that such good faith can be measured aside from the fulfillment of goals is also a tacit admission that the goals are not necessary, since affirmative action can be both pursued and judged without reference to their existence. HEW continues to say publicly that this latter kind of good faith is the sort it requires, but contradicts itself by demanding goals. In fact, of course, what this amounts to is requiring quotas, but using the words *good faith* to present a respectable public face which denies their existence. Everyone knows that numerical goals are set for a reason, and that reason is that they be met.

You also seek to deny the existence of reverse discrimination by arguing that if it did occur, "it cannot be doubted that judicial remedies are available." In the abstract of course, it cannot be doubted. In reality, however, the possible complainant who would make use of the judicial remedy would have to be the university itself. And the university is precisely in the position of having to placate federal officials who can cut off federal contracts usually vital to a university's quality, if not its very survival, with a single telephone call. The bureaucracy's power as judge, jury, accuser, and patron combined makes it downright impossible for universities to avail themselves of such judicial remedies.

This has led, as we all know, to university administrators complaining in private about the folly and unfairness of affirmative-action plans, while speaking in public only of their eagerness to comply with whatever the government wants. Testimony before this past fall's hearings of the House Special Subcommittee on Education gave evidence of the real attitudes of university administrators. Thus, President Hester of New York University testified that if many aspects of the regulations are meant to be taken at face value and their five- or ten-year deadlines enforced, "it will be disastrous."

If, on the other hand, a particular individual who has suffered reverse discrimination seeks to use a judicial remedy, he or she finds that though one may get some redress from the university, one cannot get at the real culprit who encouraged and incited the university to commit discrimination. The federal government washes its hands of the university and proclaims the usual pieties about how reverse discrimination is not its policy. It is thus in the advantageous position of an individual who tells another to leap out of a fifteenth-story window, but sternly forbids incurring any injury on landing. I agree wholly with former Congresswoman Edith Green, who like you has spent most of her professional career in activities seeking to achieve justice for minorities and women in this country. In a recent speech she said: "I consider the rhetoric of some in saying, 'we don't require quotas, we require goals,' as nothing more than a game of semantics."

You seek furthermore to deny the seriousness of reverse discrimination by citing the number of complaints of discrimination brought before EEOC by women and members of minorities, while contrasting them to the lack of complaints of reverse discrimination brought before that body. You thus give the often cited figure of 1,600 discrimination complaints in the field of higher education. One should note that these are but a small part of the overall EEOC backlog of about 100,000 cases. What is more, not all—perhaps only 900 cases—relate directly to instructional personnel (others may involve clerical, janitorial, or other staff).

Also, as you note, charges are not proof of the truth of charges. It is thus interesting that, according to President Hester's congressional testimony, of forty-three charges against NYU on grounds of discrimination, at the time of his statement thirty-four had been dismissed, withdrawn, or settled in favor of the university, while nine were still pending. Furthermore, those 900 cases should be contrasted with the number of 2,686 institutions of higher learning in the United States. That is, the order of magnitude is one complaint for every three institutions.

Now I would like very much to see the adjudication of this backlog. It would not only give us some real insight into the nature of the problem (as it stands now the EEOC figures may reasonably represent or hopelessly distort the reality of discrimination in higher education), but it would enable justice to be done, which I am sure we would both applaud.

For this reason, in my testimony in the name of CANI before the O'Hara subcommittee, I proposed a number of steps that, contrary to your letter, have not been tried before in higher education, and that would use the expertise residing in those 2,686 schools in the form of arbitration panels, both within particular schools and drawn, at the appellate level, from pools established by the professional associations, in order to deal expeditiously with complaints, whatever their origin, and in order, by resolving cases, to set examples and broadcast warnings.

Given the woeful record of the EEOC in dealing with individual complaints, it is hard to see why anyone would object to an effort to provide justice speedily for those deprived of it. Yet, in the paradoxical manner I have alluded to before, our critics seem so enamored of group proportionality, which is to be achieved by bureaucratic compulsion, that they seem willing to see individual complaints go unresolved for years to come. Achieving such proportionality may make the bureaucrats happy whose task it was to achieve it, but it is not justice, which, as I understand it, is expected ultimately to bend to the level of concern for individual citizens and their rights.

As for the few complaints of reverse discrimination before the EEOC: this is hardly surprising, in view both of the EEOC's well-documented weakness in dealing with anybody's complaints and of comments by the former chairman, one of which you cite, which deny the reality of reverse discrimination itself. One could imagine more sympathetic forums.

But there are other reasons as well. First, many victims of reverse discrimination feel disinclined to make a fight of it precisely because they do not want to seem to be standing in the way of women and blacks. Second, and most important, practitioners of reverse discrimination have gotten much better at it since those naive early days when messages were sent out informing candidates that they were the wrong color. Reverse discriminators have now learned the use of code words long known to previous practitioners of the more genteel forms of discrimination. "Women and minority candidates especially welcome to apply," seems to be a current favorite. Thus, most victims of reverse discrimination never find out what happened. In a market where there are often two hundred applicants for a single job, excellent candidates are often rejected and can thus not conclude from that fact that something might be amiss.

Finally, you cite former EEOC Chairman Powell to the effect that since women and blacks are not displacing whites and men, there can be no reverse discrimination. As I argued above, one would think that the failure of supposedly "result-oriented" programs would give their supporters some pause. Apparently, however, just as in certain military adventures, failure seems to be merely an argument for more of the same thing that has failed. But there is more to it than that and distinctions must be made. The facts about black employment have been cited already; it is clearly and preeminently a problem of supply. What figures we have, such as in the field of political science, show that hiring rates for black Ph.D.'s far outstrip those for whites.

With women, the supply is increasing and the percentage of those hired as compared with men is more than keeping pace. Again in political science, the percentage of women hired is significantly greater than that of men in recent years, most clearly in the ranks of those who have yet to finish their doctoral dissertations. Scattered indications in the field of history show the same phenomenon. The reason blacks and women are not pushing whites out of faculty positions in dramatic numbers is that there is little new hiring going on. Still, if you compare the chances of a new Ph.D. just entering the job market, you will see that it is good to be black, valuable to be a woman, and bad luck to be both white and male.

Goals and timetables are an engine which creates preferential treatment on grounds of race and sex. There is not much fuel in the engine now, due to the economic situation, but to the extent that it works, it works to produce discrimination. I am willing to concede that the harm goals and timetables do in the form of cynicism about the meaning of equal opportunity, selfishness for one's own interest, willingness to obtain advantage through doing injustice rather than suffering it, far outweigh their actual numerical results. Even so, enough cases of individuals who, through the incaution of potential employers, learned of their victimization and made complaints of reverse discrimination now exist and have been accepted as valid by government officials reluctant enough to do so, that we can safely claim that widespread patterns of reverse discrimination do exist today and that they are caused by federal requirements to fill "numerical goals and precise timetables."

We now must return to the general question. In conceding, and at the same time seeking to justify or extenuate the existence of reverse discrimination, you state: "The basic question [is] . . . whether our nation is prepared to tolerate some short-range, temporary disadvantages for white males in order to overcome our racist and sexist past." I would interpret this to mean that whereas we believe that all discrimination is equally bad, you do not.

Actually, I would suggest that the question is not whether our nation will tolerate discrimination, but whether it should. I would also suggest that it is not the "nation" which tolerates disadvantages to individuals, but the individuals who suffer them. I would suggest that what may be a temporary and short-range disadvantage when viewed from the comfortably Olympian perspective of the "nation" is a permanent and long-range disadvantage to the individual whose career is closed to him or her because of having the wrong skin color or sex.

I would suggest that I can see no principled difference between the question you ask and another question which is asked: whether the nation is willing to tolerate temporary and short-range disadvantages to black citizens in order to calm social turmoil. Different policies, same argument. I cannot bring myself to believe, and find it hard to comprehend that you believe, that fundamental constitutional rights may be made to yield to social policies, however fervently maintained.

But even from the perspective of the nation I believe you err. The example of India which you yourself cite indicates that group privileges are not, once allotted, a temporary and short-range matter. All that is temporary is their limitation to the original beneficiaries. Special privileges, granted either by custom or law, are tenaciously defended. As I pointed out before, why do you think it is so hard to create nondiscrimination where discrimination was once the rule? It is extremely hazardous to take one's chances on an equal basis with strangers in civil society, and we tend, therefore, to be reluctant to do it. Thus, the desire for special breaks or preferential treatment is perpetual and must always be kept in check.

The belief that discrimination can be administered to the body politic in judicious doses in order to create nondiscrimination is akin to the medical wisdom of curing an alcoholic with whiskey. Discrimination is addictive. To think that its use can be precisely controlled reveals the same naive belief in the perfect wisdom and manipulative abilities of social engineers that has characterized much of the worst (and most disastrous) in our recent foreign and domestic policy.

It should be understood that men and women in this nation are not mere passive recipients of the decisions of others; they have minds of their own and an ability to reason from principle and precedent. They are also, like most of us, biased in their own favor. Jusifying discrimination in favor of those who have been historically wronged may not mean in principle to you discrimination in favor of everyone who claims to have suffered historical wrongs. But it will to those who claim it; that is, it will to almost all of us. Already Italian, Jewish, Japanese, and other groups are beginning, for reasons that seem good and sufficient to them, to claim the same "right" to favored treatment that women and blacks seem to them already to have won.

You err as well, I believe, in imagining that one discrimination can compensate for another. Discrimination causes individuals to suffer. If they can be individually compensated, well and good. But compensating their grandchildren at the cost of discriminating against someone else does not compensate them in the slightest. It does replace private discrimination (or at least supplement it) with public, government discrimination, sanctioned by the laws. It also sets up another imaginary debt for the social engineer, whose successors will one day have to compensate the grandchild of the one victimized today, at the expense of the grandchild of one benefitted today—that is, if moral consistency can be expected.

Put it this way. We object to discrimination against a class of people because it unjustly hurts individual members of that class. If now we argue that it is all right to discriminate against members of other classes in order to compensate the first group, we shall have destroyed the basis of our objection to the very discrimination we sought thereby to eliminate. Justifying group discrimination depends on the notion of historical guilt which is to be borne by individuals of the stigmatized group. It is a notion far from the spirit of our laws, of our Constitution, and of the Declaration of Independence, which argue that governments are created to assure individuals (not groups) the retention of their inalienable natural rights, one of which is the pursuit of happiness.

Please understand: this is not an abstract or academic argument. Legal principles do have political results. The lesson you wish to teach is that discrimination against blacks and women is so bad that any means, even discrimination, is permissible to eradicate it. The lesson you actually teach though, is that discrimination against others is a permissible tool to remedy or avenge wrongs you believe you have suffered.

Two other points. You seek to justify preferential treatment in academic hiring on the ground that considerations were never based on merit in the past. It is true that judging standards of merit in higher education is difficult (a fact that you seem to wish to deny in your comparisons to sheetmetal workers and policemen), precisely because the standards of merit in every academic field change in accordance with advances in scholarship, while there is usually not universal agreement at any moment on what the advances are and what are the false trails. This fact does not, however, justify putting a rigid fix into the system which would guarantee that hiring would be carried on without regard to merit.

If anything, this flexibility has always been the greatest asset in the quest for knowledge. Einstein's chair at Princeton is today surely occupied by someone whose attainments would suffer if brutally measured by the yard-stick of Einstein's genius. Yet we can legitimately hope that someday another Einstein will be able to find his way to Princeton, unimpeded by its affirm-ative-action requirements.

Likewise, you are of course correct in assuming the existence of bad teachers with many credentials. How this leads to justifying the use of race or sex as a criterion in hiring (or in credentialling) is beyond me. All that that can possibly accomplish, as such scholars as Thomas Sowell and Walter E. Williams have pointed out, is to guarantee that there will be more bad teachers, doctors, and lawyers inflicted on minority communities.

As one black professor said in refusing the request of a black student that he be given a B in a course he had earned a D for, on the grounds that he wanted to teach in Watts: "You want to be one more p--- poor teacher in Watts. If you'd said the San Fernando Valley, I'd have given you the B." The problem is to increase the role that merit plays in hiring, not to find excuses for dispensing with merit altogether.

Finally, I would like to clarify once more the point on which this dia-logue originated. For your belief that there is "ample proof" of widespread discrimination in higher education, you cite general statements from House and Senate committee reports. We share Professor Eugene Rostow's view, imparted to you in a letter, a copy of which he sent us, of the relative reliability of such general comments.

In fact, widespread programs were instituted without the least statistical knowledge of the actual size of disproportions, which were, however, assumed to be immense. The fact that such data were simply not available, has not, to my knowledge, been questioned. Now, as the facts come gradually to light, it has become clear that the disproportions, where they existed at all, were small. The new Berkeley plan graphically shows the triviality of the dis-proportions.

But even were the disproportions greater, such general evidence would still not satisfy the conditions justifying imposing quota programs on an individual college. As Congressman James G. O'Hara remarked in a speech made shortly after the conclusion of the hearings on this issue over which he presided: "We have developed over the centuries a few principles related to law enforcement that may be of some value to us. . . . One of them is the proposition—constitutionally of equal importance with the principle of nondiscrimination—that we don't expect a person suspected of a crime to prove that he has not committed it."

I objected, and still object, to the practice of moving from general assumptions to the affixing of the burden of proof of innocence on an individual person or institution. When the assumptions are not based on much general statistical knowledge, it is all the worse; however, the assumption of individual participation in group guilt is particularly obnoxious.

We shall have to agree to disagree. But I greatly fear that you will be among those most chagrined and disappointed in the final results, if you succeed in prescribing the nostrum of discrimination as an alleged cure for itself. Like the heroin cure for morphine addiction once popular among medical specialists, the discrimination cure for discrimination will undo much of the good work that has been done and create much fresh evil of its own.

Miro M. Todorovich

J. Stanley Pottinger

The Drive Toward Equality

About two years ago, a previously unnoticed executive order prohibiting employment discrimination by federal contractors (which includes most universities) was discovered by women's organizations and minority groups on a few East Coast campuses. Soon afterwards, the volume of formal complaints of sex and race employment discrimination in institutions of higher education rose sharply, and the Office for Civil Rights began constructing a systematic program of enforcement. During the early stages of this process, as the office struggled to define law and policy and to obtain staff, the attention and support of women's and civil-rights groups increased, while the higher-education establishment remained unruffled.

When the office made its presence on campuses felt, however—by deferring payment of some twenty-three million dollars in federal contracts to various universities pending compliance with the order—it began to raise the academic community's eyebrows. Today a significant and vocal segment of that community is actively challenging HEW's enforcement of Executive Order 11246 and the policies upon which it is based.

The reasons for this challenge are, as one might expect, more complex

Source: Change 4, no. 8 *(Oct. 1972). Reprinted with permission from* Change Magazine, *NBW Tower, New Rochelle, New York.*

than the current dialogue on the subject would suggest. But every crusade must have its simplistic side—a galvanizing symbol, a bogeyman, a rallying cry. The word *quotas* serves these rhetorical purposes in the present case. Since quotas are not required or permitted by the executive order, they are for the most part a phony issue, but very much an issue nevertheless.

To understand the quotas issue one must first understand what the executive order is all about. In attempting to deal with employment inequities, Executive Order 11246 embodies two concepts: nondiscrimination and affirmative action.

Nondiscrimination means the elimination of all existing discriminatory treatment of present and potential employees. University officials are required under this concept to ensure that their employment policies do not, if followed as stated, operate to the detriment of any persons on grounds of race, color, religion, sex, or national origin. Typically, this means eliminating officially sanctioned quotas restricting women and minorities, antinepotism policies that operate to deny equal opportunities to women, recruitment procedures that tend exclusively to reach white males, and the like. In addition, the university must examine the practices of its decision-makers to ensure that nondiscriminatory policies are in fact implemented in a nondiscriminatory way. This may require warning or firing personnel who, for example, reject women's applications not on the basis of merit, but (as we have found) with a cursory note that "we have enough of these" or "sorry but we have filled our women's quota"—despite the fact that quotas or discriminatory policies are not official policy.

1

The concept of affirmative action requires more than mere neutrality on race and sex. It requires the university to determine whether it has failed to recruit, employ, and promote women and minorities commensurate with their availability, even if this failure cannot be traced to specific acts of discrimination by university officials. Where women and minorities are not represented on a university's rolls, despite their availability (that is, where they are "underutilized") the university has an obligation to initiate affirmative efforts to recruit and hire them. The premise of this obligation is that systemic forms of exclusion, inattention, and discrimination cannot be remedied in any meaningful way, in any reasonable length of time, simply by ensuring a future benign neutrality with regard to race and sex. This would perpetuate indefinitely the grossest inequities of past discrimination. Thus there must be some form of positive action, along with a schedule for how such actions are to take place, and an honest appraisal of what the plan is likely to yield—an appraisal that the regulations call a "goal."

It is at this point that the issue of "quotas" rears its ugly head. What is a quota, and what is wrong with it? What is a goal, and what is right about it?

Historically, hiring quotas have been rigid numerical ceilings on the number of persons of a given racial, ethnic, religious, or sex group who could be employed by (or admitted to) an academic institution. If quotas were required or permitted by the executive order, they would operate as levels of employment that must be fulfilled if the university is to remain eligible for federal contracts.

Some critics have assumed that the government is arguing that rigid numerical requirements would not constitute quotas under the executive order since, unlike traditional quotas, they would operate in favor of minorities and women rather than against them. But obviously, where the number of jobs is finite, as is true in all universities, a numerical requirement in favor of any group becomes by definition a restrictive ceiling or quota for all others. No one in the government is making an argument that any requirements in the form of quotas—for or against a defined class—are legitimate.

Once it is assumed that quotas are required, of course, there is no end to the horrors and hysteria that can be generated. University officials, it is said, will be obliged to hire regardless of merit or capability. Standards of excellence will crumble. Existing faculty will be fired and replaced wholesale. And if there are not enough qualified women engineers to fill the Engineering Department's quota, never mind; the positions will be filled with female home-economics teachers (a favorite stereotype), and don't blame the university if the country's next suspension bridge looks like a plate of spaghetti. If there are not enough black surgeons to teach surgery, no matter; they'll be hired anyway, and when scores of hapless patients (hopefully Office for Civil Rights personnel) are left bleeding on the table, don't come to the universities for so much as a Band-Aid. If there are not enough qualified Chicano professors of Latin and Greek to fill their quotas, Latin and Greek can be dropped from the curriculum, and don't blame the universities for the fall of Western civilization.

2

Perhaps those charges would be worthy of debate if quotas were required. But they are not. Department of Labor guidelines state that goals "may not be rigid and inflexible quotas that must be met." HEW directives reflect the same policy. Furthermore, the executive order is a *presidential* directive, and the President's prohibition of quotas is clear: "With respect to ... Affirmative Action programs, I agree that numerical goals, although an important and useful tool to measure progress which remedies the effect of past discrimination, must not be allowed to be applied in such a fashion as to, in fact, result in the imposition of quotas ... "

What is required by the executive order is evidence of good faith and a positive effort to recruit and hire women and minorities. Since the road to exclusive white male faculties is paved with good intentions, however, we ask for something more than the mere promise of good behavior. Universities are required to commit themselves to defined, specific steps that will bring the university into contact with qualified women and minorities and that will ensure that in the selection process they will be judged fairly on the basis of their capabilities. Universities are also required to make an honest prediction of what these efforts are likely to yield over a given period of time, assuming that the availability of women and minorities is accurately approximated, and assuming that the procedures for recruitment and selection are actually followed.

This predictive aspect of affirmative action could be called any number of things: "level of expectancy"; "honest guesses"; "targets." They happen to be called "goals." The important point is not the term, but how it functions. Unlike quotas, goals are not the sole measure of a contractor's compliance. Good-faith efforts and adherence to procedures that are likely to yield results remain the test of compliance. A university, in other words, would be required to make precisely the same level of effort, set and adhere to the same procedures, and take the same steps to correct the lack of women and minorities resulting from former exclusion, even if goals and timetables did not exist at all.

If goals are not designed to warp affirmative action toward quotas, what is the purpose of requiring them at all? There are two reasons:

First, since a university cannot predict employment results in the form of goals without first analyzing its deficiencies and determining what steps are likely to remedy them, the setting of goals serves as an inducement to lay the analytical foundation necessary to guarantee nondiscrimination and the affirmative efforts required by the executive order.

Second, goals serve as one way of measuring a university's level of effort, even if not the only way. If a university falls short of its goals at the end of a given period, that failure in itself does not require a conclusion of noncompliance(as would be the case if quotas were in use). It does, however, signal to the university that something has gone awry, and that reasons for the failure should be examined. If it appears, for example, that the cause for failure was not a lack of defined effort or adherence to fair procedures, then we regard compliance to have taken place. Perhaps the university's original goals were unrealistically high in light of later job-market conditions. Or perhaps it faced an unforeseen contraction of its employment positions, or similar conditions beyond its control. On the other hand, if the failure to reach goals was clearly a failure to abide by the affirmative-action program set by the university, compliance is an issue, and a hearing is likely to ensue.

3

Once it is understood that there is nothing in the executive order that requires quotas, it should be equally clear that there is nothing that requires their undesirable side-effects either. White males or other allegedly "over-represented" groups should not be fired in order to permit goal fulfillment; indeed, to do so would constitute a violation of law. Standards of performance and qualifications that are not themselves discriminatory need not be abandoned nor compromised in order to hire unqualified women and minorities. (The argument frequently advanced by university officials that there are virtually no qualified women and minorities simply does not stand up, particularly when advanced by universities that have failed even to canvass the market.) Nothing in the affirmative-action concept infringes on "academic freedom" or the university's right to teach, research, or publish whatever it wishes, in whatever forum it desires—whether the classroom, the laboratory, the campus, the press, or elsewhere.

If goals are not quotas, and quotas really are not required, why the current fuss and confusion?

The Office for Civil Rights must share some of the blame for not getting the distinction between quotas and goals firmly and early implanted in the higher-education community. But such efforts have not been lacking in the last year. The distinction has been drawn repeatedly in press releases, speeches, letters to editors, articles, compliance reviews, and negotiations. Indeed, the effort has been so substantial that a cynical observer might be inclined to conclude that at least some of the academic community, priding itself as it does on careful research and the intellectual ability to comprehend important distinctions, hears us loud and clear but simply doesn't want to understand. At any rate, comprehensive guidelines are presently in draft form and, when issued, should resolve the quota controversy once and for all.

Some critics object to goals, not because they fail to understand how they differ from quotas, nor because they secretly want to throttle effort-oriented affirmative action. They object to the use of goals because of their fear that sound conceptual distinctions will be lost, and in actual practice, goals will be used as quotas, regardless of the law.

In confirmation of this fear, such evidence as a university official's letter is cited (but not condoned) by John Bunzel, the distinguished president of California State University at San Jose.

No one would agree more quickly than I that any form of "Affirmative Action-with-a-vengeance" is an outrageous and illegal form of reverse bias. I am not ready to agree, however, that blame for this petulant behavior must be laid to goals, or that valid distinctions between goals and quotas are too elusive for university officials to follow if they are sharply interested in equal opportunity.

More than once, we have discovered that what appears to be reverse discrimination born of a confusion about quotas is really nothing more than avoidance of a decision on the merits. A white male, like the person who received the letter quoted by Dr. Bunzel, is told that he was the "top candidate" for the job, when in fact that is not the truth. The personnel officer, lacking the fortitude to reject the applicant honestly, and shaking his head in mock sympathetic disgust, conveniently delivers the bad news as "federally-required reverse discrimination."

But even if some employment decision-makers engage in reverse discrimination out of an honest mistake about what is required, the concept of goals should not be abandoned by way of overreaction, at least not while so many questions remain unanswered. When reverse discrimination is discovered on the campus, why should the academic community immediately assume that the federal government is the villain? The Office for Civil Rights is remote from the actual hiring process, and rightly so, while the university department head is right where the action is. The scant efforts by top university officials to correct abuses or to educate their colleagues to the real issues at stake in carrying out affirmative action cast doubt on the credibility of their protestations.

One also needs to ask just how widespread reverse discrimination really is. Evidence suggests that there may be some loosening of high-school academic achievement scores with regard to the admission of disadvantaged students to undergraduate colleges. The merits of this policy aside, it has nothing to do with *employment* standards under the executive order, and there is no clear evidence that goals or affirmative-action requirements are prompting widespread abuses in the employment processes.

But even if the problem is widespread, or likely to become so, assuming that goals are the problem still misses the point. If, as our critics seem to imply, numbers of faculty and administrators are truly incapable of understanding and adhering to the distinction between a goal and a quota, or willfully commit reverse discrimination, are we ready to believe that these people will behave differently if goals are removed? To make the point that goals cannot operate in the real world without becoming quotas, critics must characterize university officials generally as ignorant, as spiteful, as unconcerned about merit, or as weaklings ready to collapse in the face of supposed whispered directions "from upstairs" to hire unqualified women and minorities because that is the easiest way to ensure a flow of federal dollars. It is an unconscionable argument and an unfair condemnation of the academics' intelligence and integrity.

4

There is yet another fear: even if goals are not converted to quotas by university officials, they may be by the government. As a prominent newspaper editor said recently, "The distinction between goals and quotas may be sound today, but how do we know that in the future a different Director of Civil Rights will not tack goals to the university door and proclaim them to be quotas?" The short answer is that we don't know. No one can guarantee today that tomorrow's government officials will never exceed the bounds of good policy or legitimate discretion. This possibility exists in virtually every government program, but we also enjoy adequate due process safeguards in the courts, as well as a consistent vigilance by the Congress and the president.

Hindsight has shown on more than one occasion that an unsuccessful program that seemed right at its inception should never have been launched. But it is equally true that most policies that turn out to have dealt successfully with controversial issues also faced extinction at the outset because of someone's fear that they might "get out of hand" and should therefore be "nipped in the bud." The historical observation that these possibilities exist lends little help in determining whether abuses are so widespread that the policy in question presents a greater evil than the one to be cured.

Unfortunately, it is my impression that some critics who argue that goals are quotas are really not arguing against quotas at all. They understand that one need not inevitably become the other. Their insistence on crying "quota" to every discussion on affirmative action and their refusal to accompany their arguments with any alternatives that would appear to guarantee affirmative action without goals, lead to the conclusion that their real target is affirmative action itself.

Too many university spokesmen are in this position today. A university's salary analysis, for instance, may reveal significant discrepancies in pay to white men, minority men, white women, and minority women in the same job classification, doing the same work. The issue has nothing to do with quotas, yet the university refuses to make the analysis or salary adjustments without a protracted struggle with HEW, running the risk of deferring important contracts.

Attention to such matters as fair and adequate grievance procedures, antinepotism regulations, salary reviews and adjustments, training for non-academic personnel, safeguards against "clustering" or segregation of women, Chicanos, Jews, or others, guarantees of nondiscriminatory leave policies between men and women—these and other requirements have no bearing on hiring or promotion policies, goals, or quotas. Yet too many institutions are still failing to deal with them voluntarily. Instead, facile objections are raised to all affirmative action as constituting reverse discrimination and preferential treatment. And since these phrases ordinarily imply the evils of "quotas," the criticisms, no matter how simplistic or irrelevant, slide easily into a rhetorically appealing "anti-quota" posture.

5

The pathetic irony about those who say "never" to employment policy changes is the certainty with which they are inviting the very federal policies which they and their colleagues deplore. Historically, universities throughout the country have understandably resisted government intervention over even the most trivial aspects of university life, to keep out influence over their teaching, research, publication, and curricula. At the same time, however, there cannot be a university or college anywhere in the country today that does not know that where basic grievances exist, those who are aggrieved will turn to every available source for redress, including the federal government. And surely they must know that if the university does not *voluntarily* deal with the issue, a vacuum is created which the government, like nature, abhors. Knowing this, it is deeply troubling to see the lethargy and paralysis with which so many universities have responded to even the most fundamental grievances presented.

For those who agree that affirmative action is necessary and appropriate and that goals are conceptually consistent with that approach, what is needed desperately today is an effort at the university level to make affirmative action work. If this occurs, both the universities and the government can make sure that affirmative action remains within boundaries that preclude quotas and reverse discrimination.

All of us must recognize that, ultimately, the success of any continuing struggle for equal opportunity depends heavily upon the devotion of our great institutions of higher learning to the protection and extension of human rights and opportunities to everyone. Whether this is recognized as a morally compelling argument or as a way to avoid the potentially corrosive effects of federal involvement matters little as long as the result is to deal with the problems of exclusion and discrimination which even our critics do not deny. Let us move to a mature recognition of the talent of all persons in society, thereby enriching their lives and that of the university community as well.

Lee Nisbet

Affirmative Action—
A Liberal Program?

A short article on reverse discrimination, authored by myself appeared recently in *The Humanist* magazine. The reaction it provoked provides the opportunity to reflect not only on affirmative action but on some disturbing trends in contemporary "liberal" or "progressive" thinking.

The article, entitled "Reverse Discrimination—A Personal Encounter," said the following:

> Fair-minded persons applaud all efforts to make equal-employment opportunities a reality. Affirmative-action programs that contain racial, ethnic, or sex quotas or goals end up, however, in denying such opportunity. Consider as evidence excerpts from the following letter that I received last spring from a department chairman at the University of North Carolina at Asheville, "It is with considerable regret that I have to let you know that we are not offering you the position in our department. As you know, there is considerable pressure from HEW to hire members of minority groups. We have offered the place to [Ms. ——], the one who was here just a few days before you arrived.
>
> "We all felt, of all the candidates we had checked into, you and [Ms.——] were at the top of the list. You have had more experience in teaching and

Source: This is an original paper.

already have your doctoral degree in hand. Her teaching experience is rather limited, and she will not get her degree until sometime this fall. Yet, under the circumstances, it was thought wise to offer her the position."

At the bottom of the page was inscribed: "An Equal Opportunity Employer."

The irony and hypocrisy of the message hardly needs comment. Appeals to HEW, articles carried in the *New York Times* and *Change* magazine by sympathetic scholars come to nought. This affair suggests that the principle of justice on which this social order *operates* is: When one group is unfairly treated, remedy the situation by unfairly treating another group. The new victim need not, however, have been the actual offender. White male graduate students looking for positions played no part in formulating university hiring practices, but they suffer sanctimonious punishment from the very academicians who did. If faculties are going to support quotas, it would seem only fair that *they* resign and search for minority candidates to replace themselves. Widespread support for this idea among academics has not yet been heard.

We might pursue irony a bit further. HEW's affirmative-action program, at least as it works at the University of North Carolina at Asheville, is sexism par excellence. A working assumption of the program is that if a person is a woman she is not as competent as a male. Hiring a less qualified person *because* of their sex implies that this sex is weaker. Paternalistic administrators therefore must intervene to protect women from more competent males. What self-respecting woman would accept a position on these grounds? I have not yet heard widespread support for this argument from feminists.

The consequences of reverse discrimination touch not only employer and potential employees, but also the many students who will be denied the attention of a better qualified educator. Worse yet are the political and social implications of official sanction of reverse discrimination. Creative, work-oriented individuals can hardly be willing to sacrifice themselves for injustices they did not perpetrate. Sympathy for the just grievances of individuals discriminated against in the past and present will vanish if it becomes clear that these persons are advancing themselves unfairly. If the movement for political and social reforms shows itself *in practice* to be perpetrating further injustice, this social order is in for some very nasty times. In sum, it is not clear that affirmative action affirms much that is worth affirming.

A substantial number of letters to the editor followed. *All* of the correspondents were critical, some were outraged. Consider these excerpts from representative letters:

[A woman] . . . There is no "fair" way to bring about (relatively) equal opportunity in the short run, but if it is to be accomplished in the long run there is no way to avoid some injustice now. Or does Mr. Nisbet prefer to ignore three hundred years of injustice and not try to correct it? . . . Until we can gainfully employ everyone who wishes to work, some device—call it affirmative action, reparations, or anything else—is going to have to be used to distribute slices of the pie more equitably."

[A man] If discrimination were directed only against isolated individuals, then the problem would be much simpler. Mr. Nisbet ignores the fact that, in social situations, no one is truly innocent. How many of the white male graduate students who are now having to bear this burden are the direct or indirect beneficiaries of racist, sexist, or classist social policies? . . . What then is, or should be, the goal of a government sponsored equal-opportunity and affirmative-action program? In part, it is to provide relief from injustice to those individuals who have suffered discriminatory treatment. In the short run it can help to insure that all members of society have an equal chance at job and promotion opportunities. But such justifications fail to address the real problem, to provide a solution that will, ultimately, obviate the need for affirmative action. Such a solution requires that one not think just in terms of individuals, but that one have an awareness of the importance of class or group membership. Affirmative action, to be worth the trouble and effort that it requires, must be dedicated to creating a social setting where the power of the white, middle-class male is broken. . . . When those who are now the victims of the social order have their fair share of power—and power is the name of the game—then we will have moved closer to a just social arrangement. It is true that those who are the beneficiaries of an unjust social order will consider its alteration to be yet another injustice from the personal point of view, but this cannot be helped.

In other letters, males proclaimed readiness to sacrifice career aspirations to women and white women professed willingness to do the same for blacks—all in the name of reparations for past injustice. Besides letters, disapproval was expressed in more direct ways. Many of my friends, comrades in political philosophy and causes, expressed surprise and dismay over my new found "conservatism." The entire affair provoked the following reflections.

Too much of so-called liberal or progressive thinking today is in fact illiberal, unprogressive, and unintelligent. The essence of liberalism has always been concern with the welfare, rights and responsibilities of *individuals qua individuals*, not the masses or classes or other such linguistic abstractions. Furthermore, although there has been disagreement among liberals as to what social arrangements might best liberate individual capacities, no disagreement exists with the thesis that illiberal means, means that impose *avoidable* injustices on individuals, cannot achieve just ends.

Therefore, when my letter-writing liberal or radical critics and friends explain that "in social situations no one is truly innocent" or that "power is the name of the game" or that in effect, if one is a white male he is "guilty" of job discrimination because other white males have so discriminated and therefore "reparations" are justified and required—something seems peculiar. We find here no concern for the individual. What the person *did* as a person is irrelevant. His gender and race in some mysterious way render him guilty of offenses and deserving of admittedly unfair treatment. It hardly needs to be said that such proposals are neither liberal nor intelligent much less morally intelligible.

Commonsensically, racial, ethnic, or sexual classes do not seek employment; individuals do. Commonsensically, discrimination is making racial, ethnic, or sexual classifications relevant criteria for jobs in which such criteria are clearly irrelevant to performing the task. As we know, the consequences of making such classifications conditions for employment have been amply and notoriously experienced by individuals who are black, female, Mexican-American, or other. To claim now that these criteria *are* relevant to employment when used to even the score for the "good guys" is literally doublethink. The proposal that such doublethink can serve as a principle of social and economic justice is a classic example of the foolish attempt to secure just ends (equal job opportunity) through unjust means (reverse discrimination). Yet, now we face the specter of a government-administered program trying to accomplish this impossible feat and thereby perpetuating the very abuses that genuinely progressive people have labored so long to eliminate.

I conclude therefore, that labeling support of Affirmative-Action programs of the sort discussed "liberal" or "progressive," is not only mistaken, but slanderous.

F. K. Barasch

HEW, The University, and Women

Over the past few years the Department of Health, Education, and Welfare (HEW) and the academic establishment have been engaged in a contest over equal-employment opportunities for university women. In October 1967, Executive Order 11246, as amended by 11375, extended equal-employment rights to women in universities holding federal contracts. Under this order, academic women alleging discrimination could file complaints with the Office of Civil Rights, directed by J. Stanley Pottinger. If noncompliance was found with the terms of federal contracts, Mr. Pottinger could recommend contract cancellations to the Department of Labor.

In 1969 it seemed that the status of women could be improved if statistical information was presented showing patterns of discrimination in colleges. Once employment data were available, university officials conceded the point; there was discrimination against women. They argued, however, that the situation could not be corrected because there were no able candidates. More data were then compiled, demonstrating the extent of available competent women. University officials now requested guidelines for imple-

Source: Dissent (*Summer 1973*). *Reprinted by permission of the author and publisher.*

menting the order.

In October 1972, the guidelines were issued. Secretary Elliot Richardson reported satisfactory progress. In November, however, Pottinger left the Syracuse Conference for Affirmative Action in exasperation, saying that the government's program was "losing ground . . . to a growing rhetorical backlash from male faculty members and administrations." He added that the myth persists that goals are thinly disguised quotas. "All we can do is keep repeating what everybody should know by now, that you can't redress discrimination against some people by practicing it against others." (*New York Times,* November 30, 1972)

The arguments for improving the status of university women bear repeating. Many critics, such as President Bunzel of California State University at San Jose, claim that few women have been hired or promoted simply because few are qualified under the guidelines of "academic judgment." Yet the data collected by professional organizations in the past few years challenge this assumption and establish realistic bases for reasonable affirmative-action goals in hiring qualified women.

Among the universities required to reassess its assumptions about women was the University of Wisconsin. A fact-finding study commissioned by the university's chancellor produced notable results. In the sciences, it was found, the percentages of qualified women in 1967-69 were far greater than was generally supposed and far higher than the employment rate of women in academic science departments. For example, the percentages of women among all those holding Ph.D.'s in those years were 26.1 in psychology; 20-20.5 in molecular biology; 21.4 in biochemistry; 22.6 in bacteriology; 23.0 in anatomy and histology; 18.9 in anesthesiology; 13.4 in botany; 13.4 in psychiatry.[1] In 1969, women constituted somewhere between 18 and 22 percent of the total faculty in higher education, with a large proportion concentrated in the lower ranks. It becomes clear, then, that there were proportionately more trained, qualified women in the sciences than were employed even in *all* fields of higher education—and thereby the gap in the sciences between qualified women and women in high-level jobs is greater still. These are facts that should explode the myth that women and science do not mix.

By contrast, the Wisconsin report found the percentage of women who had earned the highest degrees in mathematics in the top graduate departments was remarkably low—only 5.5 percent. The figure reflects recent findings that girls are conditioned to avoid success in "male" subjects when they are at an especially impressionable age in high school. Until their junior year, girls do as well as boys in mathematics, sometimes better. After that, they show a sharp decline in their scholarly achievement and a growing interest in social affairs. By the end of high school, women are at an "enormous" disadvantage. Studies by David Riesman, Ellen and Kenneth Keniston, and Patricia Graham demonstrate these patterns.

With the Wisconsin data, one may begin to understand the impetus behind the professional-women's movement. In January 1970 the Women's Equity Action League (WEAL) filed the first complaint against a university to be made under Executive Order 11375. Since then, the National Organization of Women (NOW) and the Professional Women's Caucus (PWC) have filed over three hundred fifty complaints against colleges and universities. Women at a number of colleges are forming new groups in order to build strong and valid cases. For example, the Association of Women in Science was chartered recently by a number of scientists, which include Gertrude Shloer, a microbiologist at Mt. Sinai School of Medicine. CUNY women are becoming more and more aware of the extent of discrimination against them, as Bernice Sandler reported to members at the October convention of the American Association of Colleges, and angry women are filing suits in increasing numbers. In the sciences alone, seven organizations of 30,000 women are suing the National Health Institutes for appointments.

Similar studies in other disciplines support the Wisconsin report's findings in the sciences, maintaining that more qualified women are available for most academic jobs than male incumbents would like to believe. In 1972, the American Psychological Association (APA) surveyed nearly 5,100 women members; of this sample 57 percent (2,903) held Ph.D.'s, and 8 percent (425) held Ed.D.'s. A job survey of this group revealed that only 5 percent (283) were employed in basic research; the largest group, 28 percent (1,451) were employed as clinical psychologists; the second largest, 24 percent (1,248) were teachers. Almost all were concentrated in low-prestige occupations and positions. Only three-quarters of the APA women responded to the questionnaire, and not every woman psychologist is an APA member. Thus, the number of qualified women who are potentially available for academic work or upgrading is over 3,000 at a minimum—and the employment figures of women on the faculties of academic psychology departments do not reflect these figures.

In the field of sociology, according to Alice Rossi's 1970 report to the American Sociological Association, 2,345 men were employed full time in 180 sociology departments, compared with 300 full-time women. Of the full-time women, 27 percent were full-time lecturers and instructors, 14 percent assistant professors, 9 percent associates, and 4 percent full professors. As in the national pattern of distribution, women faculty members in sociology were concentrated at the lowest, most undesirable levels, including women with Ph.D.'s and ten or more years of experience. High attrition rates among women students in graduate sociology departments were attributed to "the negative influence of the structure of typical graduate schools."[2]

The Rossis mention other discriminatory practices in sociology that keep women "underqualified." Those employed on subprofessional levels, **even** with a Ph.D. and years of experience, cannot apply for grants as sole principal investigators, while an assistant professor with a new Ph.D and no prior research can do so.

Women are concentrated in social work, but even there only a small percentage rise in rank. At the University of Chicago, for example, only 2 percent of all professors in a 1968-69 survey were women; more than one-half of this total were in social work; that is, six of the eleven women professors at Chicago were concentrated in sociology's low-prestige department. Formerly, in schools of social work, as in schools of education, women were deans. In administration in both fields, however, recent trends have been to replace women with men.[3]

In social work, education, and nursing, and in the modern-language departments, too, a greater number of women are found than in other academic disciplines. In 1969, 37 percent of the modern-language faculties in the United States were women. However, of these only 33 percent worked full time, which means that two-thirds of the women then employed in modern-language departments were theoretically available for more desirable, full-time jobs.

Of those women employed full time in modern language, most held lower ranks than men and taught on the lower levels. In this group, 39 percent of the women were in the community colleges, sometimes comprising half the modern-language faculty in a single two-year school. By contrast, on graduate faculties merely 12 percent of the national total were women, and only 8 percent of the total number taught graduate courses exclusively.

It may seem that 37 percent is a high rate of employment in modern languages, considering the present low status of women in higher education. In this field, however, it is not. Because of the large number of women potentially available for appointment in the field, the low rate of employment is more destructive than in most other disciplines. Among graduate students, according to James A. Davis,[4] the figure for women studying modern languages in the early 1960s was 69 percent, of which 65 percent were in English. By 1969, Florence Howe (MLA) reported that only 55 percent of the graduate students in modern language were women and even fewer in Ph.D. programs. Many were "cooled out" before entering a long training program with no hope of a job at the end of the line. Others gave way under a pattern of discouragement by male professors. The testimony of many women bears witness to this pattern. Professor Howe maintained that the high percentage of male professors in graduate schools indicates to female students that women cannot "make it" to the top.

The concentration of women in the lower academic ranks at lower salaries is a serious economic aspect of discrimination against academic women. A pattern of nonpromotion and slow promotion is revealed in the 1969 data of the American Council on Education (ACE), which reported that *63 percent of all faculty women earned less than $10,000 while only 28 percent of all faculty men were in that bracket.* Another study of 1969 salaries showed that female instructors earned $410 less than men, and female professors earned $1,119 less than their male colleagues.[5] In the ACE study of the ranks, 21.9 percent of the male respondents were associate professors, while 15 percent of the female respondents were associate professors; 24 percent of the males and only 9 percent of the females were full professors. The percentage for tenured women in all ranks was 38 percent in contrast to 49 percent for males. At Berkeley in 1970, for example, only 2 percent of all full professors were women.

Assuming a women is able to find a job, she starts on a more or less equal footing with men. However, more men are promoted than women, and many women spend their entire careers in the bottom ranks, no matter what their professional contributions. Professor Sidney Hook, one of the more outspoken critics of "affirmative action," claimed that HEW enforcement agents did not understand how the university merit system worked. He explained that individuals are promoted by recommendation of their peers, and for a variety of reasons, sometimes for administrative service. Hook was especially troubled by the government's lack of understanding that in some situations a merit raise due to a woman might instead be offered to a man, who could threaten to leave for a better-paying position. Professor Hook would have us believe that women who do not engage in academic pressure or cannot readily leave a location are not as worthy of merit raises and promotions as men—even if those women serve loyally, publish regularly, receive prestigious fellowships, and administrative posts.

Other academics would have us believe that promotions are always based on academic merit and that, because women raise families they do not stay on jobs long enough for promotion. Still others claim women do not publish enough or do not measure up in other ways. These critics fail to take into account that many women who found jobs before having children have been forced out by punitive maternity-leave regulations. Some untenured women, as in the case of a Brooklyn College woman, are demoted on their return to work. At New York Community College, a woman returning to her previous job level had to begin earning tenure credit all over again. These practices are now illegal, but the superstitions about women that engendered them are still widely held.

A national study on the job drop-out rates of women Ph.D.'s and their publications records, conducted by Helen Astin, answers the conventional objection about women. Astin proved that women's lack of job continuity and professional contributions has been grossly exaggerated. She showed, in fact that, as job candidates, women have more stability and promise than men. In *The Woman Doctorate in America*,[6] she demonstrated that of the group of women Ph.D.'s studied, 91 percent were still working eight or more years after receiving their Ph.D., 81 percent worked full time, and 79 percent had worked without interruption. Almost half were still on their first jobs, and 30 percent had changed jobs only once. As for publication, 75 percent had published, and 10 percent published considerably. The percentages for women in all categories were better than those for men.

Helen Astin's study also cleared the married woman with a Ph.D. of the charge of her alleged irresponsibility; "married women Ph.D.'s who were employed full time published slightly more than either men Ph.D.'s or unmarried Ph.D.'s." More than half the women studied by Astin were married and had families, though the percentage of childless women was twice that of the general population.

These national studies, many of them published in professional journals, unfortunately do not reach the average male professor or the general reader, who insists on perpetuating antique myths—that qualified women are not available in the academic labor force, will not remain on their jobs owing to marriage of family obligations, and do not publish. Within the academy, many dismiss such evidence on the ground that national statistics do not prove that, in individual departments in specific universities, qualified women in general or individual women with appropriate credentials have been victimized by sex discrimination. A number of these critics demand that, before they will be stirred into action, individual cases of discrimination must be proved. But the problem is that proof requires specific data, which many of these critics interpret and control.

Evaluation of a candidate's experience, to determine entry-level salaries, is almost exclusively subject to male judgments. In last year's job market, for example, a women's dossier contained this statement: "Mrs.——, though a woman and older, should be as well received as a younger man." But "the dossier of a forty-year-old man asserted that one should hire this man; his distinguished career record (army, public relations) 'has been a better preparation for the university than uninterrupted schooling could have been'" (*MLA Newsletter*, September 1972). Salary records are closely guarded secrets in most universities, but even when discrepancies between men's and women's salaries are revealed, authorities insist that *their* estimates of merit are the only legitimate ones.

While national statistics demonstrate that patterns of discrimination against women are a national practice, the data required by HEW to develop specific corrective programs in individual colleges have been withheld by university officers. With the threat of cancellation of federal contracts and as a result of political pressures, such universities as Harvard, Michigan, Columbia, and Cornell have moved toward compliance over the protests of their faculties and are now developing techniques for assembling the information on hiring and personnel practices.

Over a twenty-month period, the City University of New York refused to submit voluntarily full information and affirmative-action programs. Recently, however, agreement was reached that CUNY would supply information, provided the names of individual staff members remained anonymous. HEW will no longer act on individual CUNY cases, which are now to be handled by the Equal Employment Opportunity Commission (EEOC).

Meanwhile at CUNY, the Advisory Committee on the Status of Women, appointed by the university's chancellor, amassed data for the preparation of two reports. The reports, one assumes, will lead to an internal corrective program. Although the first report, in open hearings that were held last spring, has been released, the second, which contains exact data and recommendations, seems to be reserved for exclusive circulation. Its contents, according to Project Director Katherine Klotzburger, demonstrate discrepancies in hiring practices in a number of disciplines and departments. The patterns at CUNY, she maintained (in a speech, November 18, 1972, before the Women's City Club), are those of the nation. She referred to patterns of keeping women at bottom ranks; of concentrating women in community colleges, women's and former women's colleges, or in "women's disciplines"; of offering lower salaries to women than to men for similar job functions; and of limiting women's advancement opportunities. Yet, so far, no corrective program has been announced.

The CUNY Women's Coalition (CWC), an organization of about seven hundred women representing sixteen campuses, anticipating a compromise between HEW and CUNY officials in the matter of enforcement, has assembled data from college catalogues, personnel printouts, faculty lists, and other published materials. With these data, and with the full understanding that catalogues and lists are often inaccurate, CWC filed charges against CUNY with the Equal Employment Opportunity Commission (EEOC). Knowledgeable interpretations based on first-hand experiences of department practices accompanied these data.

Not surprisingly, the CWC data reveal the same patterns of discrimination found in the report of the chancellor's committee and in various national surveys. In some cases, however, the picture may be far more grim. New York is a city of graduate schools, where the number of qualified women is higher than elsewhere in the country and interviews with graduating students are more easily arranged. Yet discrepancies between male and female appointments, ranks, and unit distribution, even within the same discipline, are more glaring in New York than on the national scene as a whole.

For example, the visibility of women in different English departments within the university differs widely from one unit to another. Yet all CUNY units have access to the same graduate labor pools, to the same bank of lecturers and part-time women with Ph.D.'s currently employed in CUNY English departments, and to the same national organizations and universities where local and out-of-town recruitments are made. One cannot account for the disparate treatment of women at different CUNY units on the ground that qualified women are "unavailable." For example, at Bernard M. Baruch College, which is a four-year school where the Ph.D. is required of women for positions with rank, more women, both in number and in percentage, are employed in the English department than at Bronx Community College, a two-year school that has lower job requirements.

This is not to say that the record of Baruch College is a good one. In 1971 its English department (formerly a part of CCNY's English department) employed a total of thirty-nine women; only two were tenured, and only one had earned all tenure credits at Baruch, facts that reflect the history of prejudice against women at both CCNY and Baruch until 1965. Of the thirty-nine women in Baruch's English department, approximately twelve worked full time during the 1971 period studied. There were no women professors or associates; the twelve full-time women were assistant professors or lecturers. Thus, with a total staff of about eighty, nearly half of whom were women, about 15 percent were full time, about 2.5 percent were tenured, and none had obtained senior rank.

At CCNY the English department reflects the same tradition of discrimination that has prevailed at Baruch. Although female students began to attend City College during World War II (when there were not sufficient male students), the department has maintained its discriminatory policy with few exceptions. CCNY statistics for 1971 showed a department of one hundred four members, twenty-two of whom were male full professors, seventeen male associates, and twenty-four male assistants. In contrast, no woman was a full professor, four were associates (the only tenured women in the department), and eleven relative newcomers were assistants. Since 1968, only one woman (in remedial English) had earned tenure in the department, for although new women are hired each year, none is retained long enough to gain tenure. Thus, according to the study conducted by the CUNY Women's Coalition (CWC), fifteen women of one hundred four faculty members held professorial ranks, yielding a percentage of 14.4—less than half of the modern languages' national average of available women. CCNY not only reflects historical patterns of discrimination but persists in the discriminatory practices of its founders.

According to national patterns, Bronx Community College should show better rates of hiring than senior units of CUNY, but it does not. In 1971-72, according to the CWC study, there was a total full-time faculty of thirty-nine. Of these, fourteen were women, distributed by rank in the usual pattern; one professor, no associates, five assistants, eight lecturers. Thus, at Bronx Community, women comprised only about 15 percent of the English faculty, and all but one were employed at the bottom ranks.

The Brooklyn College English department is nearly as bad. A coeducational senior college since its inception in the 1930s, Brooklyn College employed in its English department in 1971 a total faculty of one hundred forty-seven. The women's number in professional ranks had a pinhead and bulging midriff; three professors, nine associates, and seven assistant professors. A total of nineteen women were in the professional ranks, in contrast to forty men. Only 27.5 percent of the total staff were women, of whom approximately one out of four was a full professor and one out of two an associate. Compared with national availability averages, Bronx Community, Baruch, CCNY, and Brooklyn nearly break the record for overt discrimination, both in numbers hired and retained in their English departments.

The evidence for prejudicial hiring and promotion practices in the English departments under examination should be conclusive. Yet some members argue it is not. They imagine that the large numbers of low-ranking women in community colleges, in former women's colleges, and new colleges somehow exonerate them of charges of discrimination. One is hard put to understand the logic of those who espouse equality of opportunity for qualified candidates, abstractly, but feel it need not be offered everywhere.

After months of negotiations with women of the Professional Staff Congress (CUNY's bargaining agent), and in the face of HEW's noncompliance finding of November 1970 and its finding for a Brooklyn College woman in 1971, CUNY officials shrugged their shoulders and kept their hands in their pockets. In June 1972, HEW gave CUNY ten days' notice to comply with employment information. CUNY refused, offering to surrender its government contracts rather than reveal confidential employment records. By the end of the summer, however, CUNY came to terms with HEW.

Universities will have at least five years to fulfill affirmative-action goals. A show of "good faith," not actual recruitments of large numbers, will suffice to keep universities supplied with federal contracts—and a reasonable number of female appointees. But qualified women will be "unavailable" if universities continue to keep openings secret or pick their candidates before interviews begin. Under the watchful eyes of academic women, the "good faith" of university men may have a chance to show itself. Without pressure, however, present practice forecasts the future; one need only cite the case of Joe Porter and Mary Gardner, told in *Newsweek*, May 17, 1971. Young marrieds who had met in graduate school, the Porters had studied the same subjects, earned the same degree, and applied for jobs with the same qualifications, except that Mary was somewhat the better student. Joe received numerous offers—Mary received none.

What is needed for the improvement in the status of women is a fair chance for qualified women, not a system of quotas but supervised demonstrations of "good faith" in recruitment: positions announced, job descriptions and qualifications stipulated, papers and documents presented for applications, interviews—and reasons for hiring decisions filed for HEW's inspection and held to answer possible complaints from men or women who feel abused by "discrimination," or "reverse discrimination," both of which are illegal.

I have faith in the studies that prove women make good candidates, and I believe it is time the competition was opened to public inspection, with impartial judges watching the match. I have no faith in the judgment of chairmen who recently have been writing rejection letters to male candidates, blaming their rejections on HEW's requirement that women be hired. I believe that women and men recently hired won their jobs on the basis of equal qualifications.

It is to be expected in any era of change that those who must reconsider past practices will be troubled and will attack the instrument of change. It is understandable that HEW's desire for goals should be misinterpreted as quotas; for many university men still remember unfair quotas against Jews in recent decades. They do not remember, because they never noticed, that many academic women suffered from those old quotas, too, as well as from the new "backlash." But I have heard of no case in any university in which men were dismissed in order to make way for women. As a recruit, no man is owed the position he seeks; male candidates cannot "lose" positions they do not have. I do not believe that critics such as Sidney Hook or the Cornell professors who protested affirmative action in the *New York Times* (November 5, 1971, and January 6, 1972) fear displacement by women. I believe, as Alan Pifer does, that fantastic charges are "trotted out by the male academic simply to cover up his deep-seated aversion to having women as equal colleagues, as competition, and possibly even as superiors" (in a speech delivered November 29, 1971).

Despite HEW's efforts to show university men that "goals may not be rigid and inflexible quotas,"[7] the critics continue to claim that they are. The concept of quotas is abhorrent to qualified academic women who have long been victims of that system. The Women's Equity Action League, women of the Professional Staff Congress (CUNY), and every professional women's committee, from MLA to ASA have spoken for high standards and fair hiring practices, goals, and timetables—not quotas. Such goals may be contrasted with actual quota systems developed for women students at such universities as New York University (University Heights campus), Yale, and other private as well as state institutions. Under those systems, the number of women admitted to coeducational programs is fixed and inflexible. A limited number of two hundred first-rate women students each year were granted admission at NYU (University Heights campus), skimmed from the top of high-school classes so that underqualified male applicants could be screened out. Although the purpose of coeducation was to upgrade the college where standards had been slipping for some time, the NYU quota system was designed to favor men rather than to assure the admission of the "best." Most critics of affirmative action have not been notable for opposition to sex quotas and to double standards in college admissions, despite the inequities revealed annually in American Council on Education surveys and despite the protests of women student groups and professional women who have repeatedly urged reforms.

Under an ideal affirmative-action plan, the competition for each position would be equal each time; qualified women want that 50-50 chance. Pottinger agrees: corrective action means "men will simply be asked by their universities to compete fairly on the basis of merit, not fraternity; on demonstrated capability, not assumed superiority" (*New York Times,* December 18, 1971).

Assuming fair recruitment procedures are practiced according to HEW guidelines, there is, finally, the problem of choosing the best candidate among male and female applicants. How are we to know when a women is better qualified than a man in question? Is it facetious to inquire how we have ever known a man was the better one? Eventually, women will sit on selection committees, and their opinions will be sought and valued. Meanwhile, men of good faith must learn from women. In the September 1972 issue of the *MLA Newsletter*, Professor Nancy Hoffman of MIT offered guidelines to men for recommending and evaluating women: avoid comments on her physical appearance, her marital status, and her feminist activities, if any. These guidelines can help those who wish to be helped. For the rest, Nancy Hoffman's conclusion is the most significant and the most difficult to achieve: "The need for consciousness-raising and for change should by now be apparent."

NOTES

1. Material distributed by Bernice Sandler, executive associate, Project on the Status of Women, American Association of Colleges.

2. Alice S. Rossi, "The Status of Women in Graduate Departments of Sociology, 1968-69," paper delivered on September 3, 1969, before the American Sociological Association; quoted by Peter Rossi in "Statement and Resolutions of the Women's Caucus," *American Sociologist,* February 1970.

3. E. Alden Dunhan, *Colleges of the Forgotten American* (New York: McGraw-Hill, 1970); Alan Pifer speech, November 29, 1971.

4. J. A. Davis, *Great Aspirations: The Graduate School Plans of American College Seniors* (Chicago: Aldine, 1964).

5. U.S. Department of Labor, *Handbook on Women Workers* (Washington, D.C.: U.S. Government Printing Office, 1969).

6. Helen Astin, *The Woman Doctorate in America* (New York: Basic Books, 1970).

7. Executive Order 11246 as amended, Title 41, December 1971.

R. M. O'Neil

The Case for Preferential Admissions

In the fall of 1968 a black law student at UCLA was recalling his own educational background to a faculty group. He had grown up in Watts, attended entirely black schools and lived most of his life in the ghetto. Of his high-school class of several hundred, only three graduates went on to college. At that time there were no nearby junior or community colleges, and higher education was simply out of the question for most people in that part of Los Angeles. Of the three who had gone to college, all graduated with high distinction. One was now a fourth-year medical student at USC, the speaker was in his final year of law school, and the third was about to receive his Ph.D. in political science, also at UCLA. This remarkable account tells several things about the higher education of minority students in the period before preferential-admission policies were adopted. First, the barriers (both educational and financial) to matriculation were so high that very few students from the ghetto or barrio even began college; most of the small minority population on white-Anglo campuses came from middle-class backgrounds.

Source: Chapter 5 of Discriminating Against Discrimination: Preferential Admissions in the DeFunis Case *by Robert M. O'Neil, Copyright © 1975 by Indiana University Press. Reprinted by permission of the publisher.*

Second, those who did make it into college from severely disadvantaged backgrounds were extremely good risks and were likely not only to survive but to distinguish themselves. (In the late 1960s, a survey of attrition rates at the medical school of a midwestern state university showed that the dropout rate for white-Anglo students was almost ten times that of minority students; the number in the latter group was pitifully small, but those who managed to get that far stuck it out.) The third lesson that emerges from the UCLA student's experience brings us to the central focus of preferential admissions: without some selective consideration of the special backgrounds, needs, and potential of disadvantaged minority students, no substantial increase in their numbers is likely to occur. The essence of the case in favor of preferential admission is that little would have happened without such policies. But the matter is obviously much more complex than that and deserves a chapter of its own.

THE EFFECTS OF MINORITY UNDERREPRESENTATION

We discussed earlier in some detail the historic exclusion of minorities from higher education and particularly from graduate and professional programs. This condition by itself would not be a cause of national concern if it did not have harmful collateral effects. Education is, after all, not an end in itself. Indeed, we learned from the recent student protests that many young people have attended college who should have done something else. A national television documentary (entitled "Higher Education—Who Needs It?") raised the most basic doubts about the value of the general baccalaureate degree. Many of the new jobs anticipated within the next decade will demand technical skills rather than liberal education. Thus it is fair to question whether mere underrepresentation of minorities in higher education is a critical problem.

While the United States is far short of having universal higher education (matriculation seems to have peaked at about 50 percent of high-school graduates), both the college experience and the baccalaureate degree remain vital for many reasons. Christopher Jencks and David Riesman, wise commentators on American higher education, have observed that "the bulk of the American intelligentsia now depends upon universities for a livelihood and virtually every would-be member of the upper-middle class thinks he needs some university's imprimatur, at least in the form of a B.A. and preferably in the form of a graduate degree or professional degree as well." What is true for the majority is especially true for the minority. Much as with immigrant groups earlier in the century, upward mobility almost demands higher education, whatever may be the intrinsic merit of a liberal-arts degree.

Even if a college degree were simply window dressing, the collateral effects of restricted minority access would be disturbing. Persons with college degrees do enjoy earning capacity far above non-degree holders; the ratio which obtains in this regard for the population as a whole also exists in the minority community, although the income figures are lower. Access to graduate and professional schools (and of course to the professions they serve) are effectively limited to college graduates. As we have seen earlier, the percentage of minority students in the graduate schools is lower than the corresponding undergraduate percentage. The number of minority persons holding graduate and professional degrees is not only lower than the proportion for the entire population; graduate-undergraduate ratios are substantially lower *within* the minority sector of the academic community, a fact which reduces the prospects for increases in minority-group teachers and professional practitioners. Indeed, it seems that even an arithmetic expansion of minority participation in the learned professions would require an almost geometric increase in the number of minority undergraduates.

The nature of the underrepresentation and its effects can best be understood by taking the legal profession as a microcosm. Today there is roughly one white attorney for every 630 persons, but only one black attorney for every 6,000 black citizens. Despite the vigorous recruitment efforts and the substantially increased number of minority students, not more than 2 percent of the American bar is black. Minority representation in the legal "establishment" is even less substantial. A 1973 survey of the seventeen largest law firms in Chicago reveals that of 1,364 attorneys, there are but one black partner, thirteen black associates, and eight Spanish-surnamed persons (of whom seven are in a single firm with a substantial Latin-American clientele.) These results are especially depressing because of the large and increasingly well-educated black population in Chicago, and the special efforts (and monetary contributions) of the Chicago bar to support minority legal education.

The situation in particular regions is even more extreme than the national averages suggest. Several years ago there were only seventeen black lawyers in Mississippi to serve a black population of nearly a million. Today there are forty-nine black attorneys admitted to practice in the state—an improvement, but still a rato of 1:16,000 compared to 1:450 for white lawyers to white Mississippians. In Georgia, the situation is superficially somewhat better than in Mississippi. But since about one-third of the black attorneys in Georgia work for the federal, state, or local governments, the number actually available for private clients is smaller than the total lawyer population would indicate.

Moving to the opposite corner of the country, the situation in the state of Washington is illustrative. One of the groups supporting Marco DeFunis argued there was no need for preferential admission because the percentage of black students in the law school (2.2 percent) at the time the program was adopted matched the racial makeup of the state. The relevant comparison, of course, should be to the minority representation in the bar, which presents quite a different picture. According to 1970 census figures, there is one white lawyer for every 720 white Washingtonians; one black lawyer for every 4,195 blacks, one Indian attorney for every 6,677 Indians, and at most one Mexican-American lawyer for every 35,000 Chicanos.

As the Washington-state data suggest, other minority groups are even less well-represented than blacks. Take the case of the Spanish-speaking population in California, the state's largest minority group. The ratio of lawyers to clients for California as a whole is 1:530. In the Mexican-American community, however, there is but one attorney for every 9,482 persons. Across the country, a similar situation exists for the Puerto Rican population of New Jersey; the state appears to have only three Spanish-speaking lawyers for a population of some 300,000.

Figures for the medical profession show a similar, if slightly less acute, underrepresentation. At last count there was one white physician for every 750 persons in the general population, but only one black doctor for every 3,500 black citizens. There appear to be only 250 Mexican-American and 56 American Indian physicians in the entire United States. Thus the extent of the underrepresentation in the professions seems beyond dispute.

The cold statistics do not, however, tell the whole story. Much more significant in terms of governmental interest are the social, psychological, and economic effects of underrepresentation. The correlation between income and education seems obvious. The significance of this factor has been heightened by recent economic trends. During the 1960s the gap between incomes for blacks and whites narrowed, and at one point the black median was 61 percent of the white median. During the 1970s the gap has begun to widen again, moving back by 1973 to the ratio of 1966. Meanwhile, the Spanish-speaking community has fared no better. Recent Census Bureau data show that Spanish-speaking groups have been losing ground in purchasing power vis-à-vis the general population, and that educational attainment for this group is even lower than for blacks. (Of Mexican-Americans, 27.8 percent have finished high school, a figure slightly better than the 26 percent of Puerto Ricans.) The pressures of inflation which have pressed all groups have hit the minority community particularly savagely. Savings are lower there and unemployment (even in good times) is higher. Thus the consequences of lower levels of educational attainment and opportunity are felt with particular force by minority groups.

Socioeconomic status is by no means the only collateral value. Professional status is a vitally important factor in shaping minority-group self-respect and capacity for effective civic participation and self-government. There have, to be sure, been dramatic strides in black political involvement and participation. By 1974 there were just short of 3,000 black elected office-holders in the country. But this figure is still less than 1 percent of all elected officials in the country. It is only in the federal and state civil service that blacks begin to be represented meaningfully, though even there at typically lower salaries and classifications. Obviously not all elected officials are lawyers, and a law degree is no prerequisite to political success. But lawyers are disproportionately represented at all levels of public life, and exert legislative power even beyond their numbers. Thus, in the most direct sense, the underrepresentation of minorities in the professions impairs the capacity for civic involvement and self-government.

Minority professionals and educators also serve a vital function as role models for younger members of the community. Success and achievement suggest to minority youths that there are ways of "making it" within the system that do not require resort to self-help or more drastic means. Such sanguine prospects might profoundly reduce the high-school attrition of minority students, despite the segregation and overcrowding which will probably persist in the inner-city schools for some time. The promise of success through higher education may also have a salutary effect on crime and violence in the minority community, where the principal victims of lawlessness are the members of those communities themselves. Conversely, there is little question that the closing off of opportunities will breed frustration, resentment, and anger at the predominantly white-Anglo society. Columbia University political scientist Charles V. Hamilton has shown that a major cause of urban violence is the exclusion of minority groups from the decision-making process. "People do not," he observed, "blow up or burn down what they feel they are a legitimate part of."

Let us take a closer look at the effects of minority underrepresentation in the legal profession. Clearly the bar as presently structured does not fully meet the needs of the poor and especially of the minority poor. "Legal services are still the preserve of middle and upper incomes," notes Virginia law professor Ernest Gellhorn, one of the earliest proponents of increased opportunity for minorities in law. "Government sponsored and voluntary legal services programs, while expanding, do not fill the need. They are not available in all parts of the country, are limited by an inability-to-pay test, and do not provide representation in all types of cases." Superficially it might appear that this need could be met simply by expanding the number of white-Anglo lawyers with a commitment to serve the poor. That is, however, only partially accurate.

While many white lawyers do admirably serve the minority community, there are certain things they cannot do as well as a person who comes from that community. Supreme Court Justice William J. Brennan once observed that black lawyers "most clearly understand the problems and difficulties found by members of the Negro community." The director of the southern regional office of the American Civil Liberties Union believes that many racially oppressive practices would have gone unchallenged but for the presence of native southern black lawyers; even highly competent and committed white attorneys "would not have understood or would not have raised the racial issues."

What is true of the black community is even more true in the Spanish-speaking community. New Mexico Governor Roberto Mondragon has written eloquently of that special need from his own Chicano background:

> When these people are forced to resort to Anglo law and counsel, the language and cultural differences result in the most difficult communication imaginable. In cases where the Spanish-speaking American resorts to Anglo counsel, the Spanish-speaking, because of his suspicion of the Anglo value-oriented legal system, will relay only that information which he feels is relevant to his case and withhold all other information which may indeed be vital. Despite any good faith representation by the Anglo attorney, lack of information will in many cases result in the loss of the suit. This in turn escalates and deepens the fear of the Spanish-speaking American in the legal process. . . .
>
> To carry the situation one step further, the prevailing feeling in the barrio and the pueblos is that the courts are insensitive to their social and cultural values. To them the legal system is used to perpetuate injustices rather than to protect their legal rights. This feeling is reinforced by many very unfavorable contacts that these people have with the courts and law enforcement agencies.
>
> The legal profession itself has closed the door to the Spanish-speaking and Native American. In many cases the legal rights of these people go unprotected because attorneys are unwilling to represent them either because their cases are so controversial or because they are unable to pay the high cost of legal assistance. Furthermore, until recently, the legal profession has for the most part been indifferent in protecting the civil rights of these people.

If there remains any doubt about the importance of getting more minority students into college, there should be little doubt about the need to get more of them out and into those professions where they can play a unique role. In short, there does seem to be a substantial governmental interest in increasing the number of minority students and graduates because of the intrinsic value of having more and better educated members of the minority community. This is the first and undoubtedly the most obvious interest underlying preferential admission policies in higher education. It is not, however, the only argument a college or university might advance for giving special consideration to minority-group members. We now turn to several other possible governmental interests.

THE EFFECTS OF TRADITIONAL ENTRANCE CRITERIA

The causes of minority underrepresentation are more complex than the consequences. There has been extensive debate about the fairness of standardized tests such as the Law School Admission Test. The Educational Testing Service and its various branches have conducted considerable research on this subject. What emerges from these studies is a set of beguilingly simple propositions that set the stage for this discussion: First, that the use of standardized tests (and grades) has served to exclude disproportionate numbers of minority applicants, who have lower-than-average scores and grades. Second, however, standardized tests do not underpredict the performance of minority students, and may in fact slightly *overpredict* the performance of minority persons. Third, such tests appear valid and reasonable criteria for selecting among nonminority applicants; while they do not correlate perfectly with later performance, their record is sufficiently good to warrant their retention for most groups. Obviously the juxtaposition of these three propositions creates a paradox for the admissions officer who wants to be both fair and rational in selecting among applicants.

The issue before us is not whether admissions should be based *solely* on grades and test scores. No responsible institution, no matter how large the applicant group, would invoke exclusively quantitative measures in this sensitive area. While mathematical factors may operate at the high and low ends of the scale, hard choices in the middle range must be resolved with the help of other factors. The question here is whether a college or university may validly take race or ethnic status into account in deciding what weight to give the grades and test scores—or possibly to adjust the resulting performance predictor on the basis of race. The real issue is therefore much narrower than the question many people associate with *DeFunis*—whether the numerical rank ordering can be varied or departed from at all. . . . All sorts of exceptions and variations have long been recognized for reasons that have nothing to do with race. The issue now before us is only whether race can be added to the list.

If we agree that standardized tests (1) exclude disproportionate numbers of minority students, but (2) neither have inherently biased content nor are unfair as predictors, how do we resolve the paradox? It is relevant first to note that the organizations which devise and administer the tests and report the results have not only cautioned against excessive reliance on test scores but have suggested that race or ethnic status might properly be weighed along with numerical indices. The Law School Admission Council filed a most significant brief in the *DeFunis* case, supporting the University of Washington's preferential policies. The brief reviewed the growing concern of the Council over the underrepresentation of minority students, despite its confidence in the accuracy and fairness of the LSAT for the general run of students. Particularly in a time of rising applications for professional study, the Council recognized the need to temper the admissions decision with non-quantitative factors. With particular reference to the use of standardized test scores the brief urged:

> The handicaps visited on members of minority groups bear directly on the appraisal of their pre-law educational attainments. . . . A proven capacity to catch up in learning, and the distance between where he started and where he now stands, may be more important to prediction than a comparison of his present level of attainment with that of others who had no headwind to overcome. Standardized testing is not so familiar in segregated or vocational schools, where college preparation is not emphasized, and the verbal abilities measured by such tests—and by the law school examinations—are seldom developed in such an environment.

The LSAC also argued that "predictions based on test scores and college grades must be ameliorated for minority backgrounds which restrict opportunities to acquire or to demonstrate academic abilities."

It would be ironic if a court were to insist that a law school give greater weight to test scores than the organization reporting those scores believed was warranted. In addition, much experience with preferential programs confirms that many applicants who would have been excluded by rigid adherence to numerical ranking are in fact well qualified and will succeed if given the chance. (In the very class of which Marco DeFunis was a member at the

University of Washington, for example, the attrition rate for minority students—all of whom were preferentially admitted—was virtually identical to the attrition of nonminority students, most of whom were admitted on the basis of more traditional criteria.) Thus the denial of infallibility to the tests accords not only with the convictions of admissions officers, but with recent practical educational experience as well.

It is important to note that we are dealing here with two quite distinct theories that may lead to the same conclusion. The view of the testing experts is that race should be taken into account in an "ameliorative" way even though the tests are fair to, or even slightly favorable to, minority groups. The other theory, reflected in Mr. Justice Douglas' *DeFunis* opinion, is that such tests should be disregarded for minorities (or even for all applicants) because they are culture-bound, biased, or whatever. Douglas' sweeping view on this issue is revealing: "Insofar as LSAT test reflect the dimensions and orientation of the Organization Man they do a disservice to minorities. . . . My reaction is that the presence of an LSAT test is sufficient warrant for a school to put racial minorities in a separate class in order better to probe their capacities and potentials."

Neither theory really expains the paradox—that standardized tests exclude disproportionate numbers of minority applicants and thus should be weighted differently even though their content may not be racially biased and even though they may predict academic performance about as well for minority and majority students. Several factors offer hope for reconciliation. First, a negative correlation between test scores and law school or college performance would be surprising in view of their symbiotic development and validation. Professors David Kirp and Mark Yudoff have recently written: "That standardized test scores and higher education performance are highly correlated is unsurprising, for the tests are meant to mirror institutional requirements. They stress the very linguistic and logical skills the university prizes."

A negative correlation would be most puzzling in view of the homogeneity of the factors being compared—traditional admission standards and traditional grading policies and curricula. Both curricula and grading standards have been designed to deal with a predominantly white-Anglo, middle-class student population whom the traditional admission tests have brought to American campuses. As the students change, the curricula will presumably change in some degree, and the correlation of performance with admission standards should also change. Where curricula and evaluation procedures have been redesigned to reflect the special needs and interests of minority students, rather different correlations seem probable—that is, standardized test scores might be found to be underpredictive for minority applicants.

Second, most of the validation studies involve freshmen or first-year grades rather than total performances. Adjustment to the strange and sometimes hostile environment of a white campus takes longer for the minority than the majority student. The freshman year is undoubtedly traumatic for many students, but is especially so for students from the ghetto or barrio. Correlations which stop with freshman-year grades may thus in fact be biased in a rather subtle but damaging way.

Third, the populations being compared in most validation studies are simply not comparable. When one contrasts the performance of all minority students in a class with that of all other students, the pairing is superficially sound. In fact, however, a much higher percentage of the minority students come from inadequate elementary and secondary schools; many more are poor and must work at outside jobs; a far higher proportion will either have heavy and time-consuming family responsibilities or will lack the reinforcement and support that white students typically derive from stable home environments. Thus a fairer comparison would be between minority students and similarly disadvantaged white students, of whom there are in fact far too few on most campuses. The critical issue would be how well the test-performance correlation for poor black students from, say, Cleveland's East Side compares with the same data for children of poor Czech steelworkers from the West Side—not whether blacks do better or worse than Shaker Heights graduates with the same predicted first-year averages. Until we have comparisons of truly comparable samples, the issues must remain conjectural.

Finally, the validation studies have dealt almost entirely with blacks, who are, after all, English-speaking minority students. Even if heavily verbal standardized tests are completely fair for these students, their application to students who grew up speaking Spanish or an Indian tribal tongue may be quite different. In recognition of that difference, several courts have held that Spanish-speaking children may not be classified as "educationally mentally retarded" on the basis of English-language tests, because of the linguistic bias. (San Francisco school officials acknowledged a while ago that when a group of Chicano children who had been so classified were retested in Spanish, 45 percent of them showed average or above-average intelligence.)

Special consideration of the test scores of minority applicants would be warranted, however, only if there are reasons—unrelated to ability or college potential—why all or most minority students tend to score lower. In the case of students from non-English-speaking backgrounds (Chicanos, Indians, and some Asians), the explanation seems obvious. The tests are in English, and rely rather heavily on facility in our native tongue. In the case of black students, the explanation is more elusive. There are variations in vernacular language, to be sure, and cultural differences between black and white community life are significant. But black children surely have an advantage in this regard over their Spanish-speaking counterparts, and the pervasive effect of television has also blurred the differences. In the case of blacks there is a different factor: the deplorable condition of the urban ghetto public schools, which within the last decade have become increasingly racially isolated despite formal attempts at desegregation. These schools are often overcrowded, housed in old and rundown plants, with equipment, programs, and extracurricular activities of a quality far below those of the middle-class and suburban schools. The rates of retention and graduation even from these schools are often much lower than for the general school population. But even graduation rates tell only part of the story. It is well known that high-school counselors and advisers tend to channel minority youth into technical and vocational tracks that may render them ineligible for college. (In New York City, about one-quarter of the students graduating from eight high schools in the most depressed areas of the city received "academic" or college preparatory diplomas in 1957. A decade later the percentage of academic diplomas in the same schools had fallen to 13.)

Experience in taking standardized tests (and the likelihood of success on them) varies inversely with such conditions endemic to the ghetto or barrio school. Students in non-college-bound classes obviously will not practice on college-board exams. At a higher level, postsecondary students in technical and vocational programs will have far less experience in writing essay examinations than their contemporaries in liberal-arts and sciences programs. Since the general condition of minority education militates against the experience that helps middle-class, white-Anglo students perform well on such tests, a different weighting of the scores seems entirely appropriate.

This last point suggests that the use of standardized tests which exclude disproportionate numbers of minority applicants may even be constitutionally vulnerable. Many recent decisions have invalidated the use of such tests in employment, where minority groups have been underrepresented in the workforce. The Supreme Court several years ago held that when such a condition exists, "if an employment practice which operates to exclude Negroes cannot be shown to be related to job performance, the practice is prohibited." At least one lower court has extended this theory to school testing. In that case, in which the use of tests was attacked because a disproportionate number of minority students ended up in the educationally mentally retarded track, the court required the school authorities to demonstrate the educational relevance of the tests, which they were unable to do. The failure of such justification rendered the continued use of such tests unconstitutional in this context.

The case that is most nearly in point leans the other way, however. San Francisco has one highly selective, city-wide college-preparatory school, Lowell High School. Admission to Lowell from other schools is based on grades in four college preparatory subjects. The proportion of minority students entering Lowell is considerably lower than minority enrollment throughout the district. A group of parents brought suit to challenge this procedure, claiming that the Lowell admission (or transfer) policy denied them equal protection. The federal court of appeals in the summer of 1974 rejected the claim and upheld the use of grades, despite the tendency to exclude larger numbers of minorities. The court found it conclusive that "conditioning admission to Lowell upon the level of past academic achievement substantially furthers the district's purpose of operating an academic high school." Moreover, the students excluded from Lowell were not denied a quality, or even college-preparatory, education elsewhere in the San Francisco system. (The effect of the policy was in fact mitigated by a preferential minority-transfer policy adopted about the time the suit was brought. While this program played no part in the holding, the court may have been influenced by the voluntary steps already taken to diversify the Lowell student body.)

Despite the paucity of pertinent court cases, an argument can be made for the unconstitutionality of entrance criteria which disproportionately exclude minority applicants. The parallel issue in employment has countless times been resolved against the maintenance of racially or ethnically detrimental criteria that are not clearly job-related. Perhaps it would be easier to prove the "education-relatedness" of grade-point averages and standardized tests in college admissions, as the Lowell case suggests. It is one thing to require a college degree of one who seeks to become a lawyer or a physician; it is another to require a candidate for a police- or fire-department job to be versed in Shakespeare and Mozart. In any case, the time is not far off when courts will call upon colleges and universities to justify in educational terms any entrance standards which disfavor minority groups.

To summarize this discussion of the effect and validity of standardized tests: Even if traditional entrance and admissions criteria are not *discriminatory* (that is, biased in content), there is little question they are *exclusionary* to minority groups. This fact alone suggests that colleges and universities have a valid interest in weighting test scores differently for members of these excluded groups, even without finding the tests themselves invalid. Substantial numbers of minority students will not be enrolled at predominantly white campuses unless one (or more) of the following changes occur: (1) the quality of secondary education for minority students improves dramatically; (2) financial and social barriers that now impede advancement of minority students are dramatically reduced; (3) alternative tests and predictive measures are developed that do not disproportionately exclude minority applicants; or (4) the use of traditional admissions criteria is adjusted to overcome the effects of their uniform application. Of these possibilities, the fourth appears the only one immediately attainable. Thus there appears to be a strong state interest in doing precisely what the Law School Admission Council and other groups suggest—taking race or ethnic status into account in the use of test scores and grades.

COMPENSATION FOR THE EFFECTS OF PAST DISCRIMINATION AND SEGREGATION

A third and quite distinct governmental interest in preferential-admission policies derives from educational history. There is little question that past racial segregation partially explains the present minority underrepresentation. Higher education in many states has been until quite recently organized along explicitly racial lines. In fact, "dual" higher-education systems in the southern and several border states remained segregated far longer than the elementary and secondary systems. Racially divided public-college systems are not unique to the South. In addition to states like Missouri, West Virginia, and Kentucky, publicly supported black colleges persist in such states as Pennsylvania (Cheyney and Lincoln) and Ohio (Central State). While many blacks have pursued higher education only because these colleges existed, the range of offerings, quality of faculties and facilities, and extracurricular opportunities typically do not match those of the major white institutions. The potential effect of total desegregation upon these colleges and their students is problematic; some black students would undoubtedly benefit from the dismantling of these dual systems, while others would be effectively denied even the quality of higher education now available to them through the black colleges.

Quite apart from the perpetuation of segregated public systems, blacks have until recently been denied graduate and professional opportunities that exist only in predominantly white institutions. It was only twenty-five years ago that the United States Supreme Court struck down racial segregation in legal education, requiring the University of Texas at Austin to admit its first black student. James Meredith's battle with the University of Mississippi Law School—then completely white—goes back only a little over a decade. Well into the 1960s some private university law schools still excluded blacks, and at least two institutions had to go to court to nullify racial restrictions in their charters or endowments. Thus if higher education now wishes to remedy the lingering effects of a condition for which it was at least partly responsible, that goal would appear to constitute a valid and substantial state interest.

Even if the academic community had been blameless for the racial imbalances which exist, consideration of race in the admissions process would seem a permissible remedy. As we suggested earlier, it would be anomalous if universities that had once discriminated on grounds of race could now use race preferentially, while newer institutions in the same state could not do so. So long as it is the same evil or condition to which the admissions policy is addressed, the corrective should be equally available. "Just as the race of students must be considered in determining whether a constitutional violation has occurred," the Supreme Court has said, "so also race must be considered in formulating a remedy."

Regardless of past wrongs, a college or university might well regard race-conscious admissions as a key element in an affirmative-action plan. Institutions which receive federal funds (as almost all colleges and universities do) face a serious dilemma under current federal guidelines. On the one hand they must take positive steps to identify, evaluate, and recruit more women and minorities at all levels; on the other hand they may not "discriminate" in doing so. Federal officials have already taken several academic institutions to task for announcing or using too explicit a racial preference in hiring or admission. The case of the University of Washington poignantly illustrates the dilemma: At the very time the university was fighting Marco DeFunis in the courts to continue to be able to consider race in admissions, federal officials were pressing in hard on the other side and threatening to cut off funds to the university unless it formulated a bolder affirmative-action plan for minority recruitment and advancement. For a court to preclude any consideration of race or ethnic status at the admissions level would virtually cripple many affirmative-action programs. Surely the right hand cannot so stay the left.

REPRESENTATION OF THE LARGER SOCIETY: THE UNIVERSITY AS MICROCOSM

There is a fourth interest underlying preferential admissions which relates only indirectly to the needs of minority students. A major function of higher education must be to prepare students for responsible and meaningful citizenship in the larger society. In certain respects, of course, the campus is appropriately cloistered and insulated from practical and political demands. Academic freedom must, for example, be protected in ways that are neither necessary nor appropriate in other kinds of institutions. But when it comes to the makeup of the student body, there is neither need nor justification for failure to reflect the general condition of society. If education is to be more than simply book learning and sterile research, groups present in the total community must also be present in the academic community. Thus a college or university may seek more minority students as much to provide a more realistic learning and extracurricular environment for its white-Anglo students as to improve opportunities for minorities.

The goal of diversity and representation has been recognized by the United States Supreme Court as a valid governmental interest at the elementary and secondary level. In holding that race could constitutionally be considered in the framing of remedies for past segregation, the Court has said: "School authorites . . . might well conclude . . . that in order to prepare students to live in a pluralistic society each school should have a prescribed ratio of Negro to White students reflecting the proportion for the district as a whole. To do this as an educational policy is within the broad discretionary powers of school authorities."

The same reasoning has also been applied at the graduate and professional level. A quarter-century ago, the Supreme Court held that the University of Texas could not constitutionally exclude black students from its law school. While this decision preceded *Brown v. Board of Education* by four years, and paid lip-service to the waning "separate but equal" philosophy, the Court did indicate the positive value of integration: "Few students and no one who has practiced law would choose to study in an academic vacuum, removed from the interplay of ideas and exchange of views with which the law is concerned. . . . With such a substantial segment of society excluded . . .

we cannot conclude that the education offered . . . is substantially equal."

While the Court's immediate concern was the effect of isolation on the excluded black, precisely the same argument could be made for the white students on a campus that was demographically unrepresentative of the larger society. In its *DeFunis* brief, the Association of American Law Schools amplified the argument along these lines:

> The quality of legal education parallels student understanding of the ways in which law relates to society. Student perception of legal situations is conditioned by the prior experience, training, background, culture, race and sex of the student body members. A White student from a "good" undergraduate school, amply funded by a well-to-do family, views law and society differently from the way a Black student would with a similar, or different background. . . . Diversity in the law school student body achieves another important interest for state law schools. Law schools serve as the source of training of a bar which must satisfy the legal needs of a heterogenous society.

There are other institutional interests that reinforce the case for preferential consideration of minority applicants. When a selective institution decides to admit a qualified Chicano or black or American Indian student instead of a superficially better qualified white-Anglo, the person thus displaced was not expected to excel. Had the class been a bit smaller, or had the number of returning veterans been slightly larger, or had more first-choice admittees decided to accept, and so forth, the rejected applicant would not have got in anyway. The minority student admitted in his place may well have a lower predicted first-year average, and may actually do less good academic work. But if the preferred minority student does graduate, the chances are somewhat greater that he will distinguish both himself and his alma mater in later life. Moreover, the prospects for attending graduate school now appear higher (as a result of preferential policies, admittedly) for the minority student who survives than for the white applicant who is supposed to get by with a gentleman's C and does only that. Thus the preference for the minority student may be justified in institutional as well as individual terms.

Minority students may also supply a catalyst for beneficial change. One of the most frequent demands from minority students has been for special ethnic-studies programs. Black or Afro-American programs and departments are now widespread. Puerto Rican or Borricua studies and Chicano programs are less common but flourish in the relevant regions. There has been much debate about the quality of these programs and their value for *minority* students. Their greatest ultimate impact, however, may be on the majority students who are enrolling in such courses in increasing numbers. Even those who question the worth of ethnic programs generally accept Kenneth B. Clark's view that "it is whites who need a program of black studies most of all." Without the minority students, it is doubtful that pressure for such programs would ever have existed at all.

There is also a substantial interest in the production and recruitment of minority faculty—an interest which is now heavily undergirded by federal affirmative-action requirements. There can be no major expansion of the black and Spanish-speaking professoriate until graduate schools turn out many more minority scholars and teachers. Given the competition from other professions, a geometric expansion of minority graduate enrollments may be required to increase minority faculty even arithmetically—at least without decimating the black-college staffs. There is a related if subtler factor: The black or Chicano Ph.D. has a broad range of options these days and faces a difficult career choice. Other institutional variables being at all constant, he will probably seek evidence of commitment to equality of educational opportunity and will be most likely to find that commitment in a vigorous minority-recruitment program.

Finally, the effectiveness of a minority-student program may depend in part upon its scope. In the 1960s, a number of smaller institutions—especially those in rural areas like Cornell and Wisconsin at Oshkosh—had disastrous experiences with black-student protests. In most cases the student dissatisfaction could be traced simply to isolation and fear. A tiny band of black students in a rural northern community is not likely to feel very comfortable. When issues arose—like the burning of a cross in front of the black-women's dormitory at Cornell in 1969—already tense feelings could surface and violence ensue. The program will succeed only when there is a large enough group of minority students—a "critical mass" as some have called it—to provide a community and a source of strength and confidence for the members of the group. James McPherson, a black graduate of the Harvard Law School and a distinguished poet and teacher of creative writing, has observed that the anxiety of black students at predominantly white institutions "can be reduced only when there are enough blacks on white campuses to establish an interdependent, self-sufficient black community."

These latter interests relate mainly to the college or university and to its majority-student population. There seems no reason why, from a constitutional point of view, the desire to make the campus a more representative and realistic environment may not stand equal to the goals of overcoming past discrimination or increasing minority participation in the mainstream of American life. In fact these interests are quite closely and logically related; the future of opportunities for minorities depends in large part upon the majority of our society for the foreseeable future. Thus, in some respects the desire to improve the educational experience for the present generation of white-Anglo students may really be the most substantial interest of all.

Sidney Hook

Discrimination, Color Blindness, and the Quota System

Every humane and fair-minded person must approve of the presidential executive order of 1965, which forbade discrimination with respect to race, religion, national origin or sex by any organization or group that receives financial support from the government in the course of fulfilling its contractual
obligations with it. The difficulties in enforcing this order flow not from its
ethical motivation and intent, but in establishing the criteria of evidence that
discrimination has been practiced. Very rarely are the inequities explicitly
expressed in the provisions guiding or regulating employment. They must be
inferred. But they cannot be correctly inferred from the actual figures of
employment independently of the *availability* of different minority groups,
their *willingness* to accept employment, and the objective *qualifications* of
those able and willing to apply. To be sure, the bigoted and prejudiced can
distort these considerations in order to cover up flagrant discriminatory
practices. But only the foolish and unperceptive will dismiss these considerations as irrelevant and assume that reference to them is an obvious sign
of prejudice.

Source: Measure, *no. 30 (Summer 1974). Reprinted by permission of the author and
University Centers for Rational Alternatives.*

There is, unfortunately, evidence that some foolish and unperceptive persons in the Office of Civil Rights of the Department of Health, Education, and Welfare are disregarding these considerations and mechanically inferring from the actual figures of academic employment in institutions of higher learning the existence of discriminatory practices. What is worse, they are threatening to cancel federal financial support, without which many universities cannot survive, unless, within a certain period of time, the proportion of members of minorities on the teaching and research staff of universities approximate their proportion in the general population. Further, with respect to women, since it is manifestly absurd to expect that universities be staffed in an equal sexual ratio in all departments, the presence of discrimination against them is to be inferred if the composition of the teaching and research staffs does not correspond to the proportion of *applicants*— independently of the qualifications of the applicants.

In the light of this evidence, a persuasive case can be made that those who have issued these guidelines and ultimata to universities, whether they are male or female, black or white, Catholic, Jewish, or Protestant are unqualified for the offices they hold and therefore unable to properly enforce the presidential executive order. For they are guilty of fostering the very racialism and discrimination an executive order was issued to correct and forestall.

It is not hard to demonstrate the utter absurdity of the directives issued by the Office of Civil Rights of the Department of Health, Education, and Welfare. I shall use two simple instances. A few years ago, it was established that more than 80 percent of the captains of tugboats in the New York Harbor were Swedish. None were black. None were Jewish. And this in a community in which blacks and Jews outnumbered Swedes by more than a hundred to one. If one were to construe these figures along the lines laid down by the office of Civil Rights of HEW, this would be presumptive proof of crass discrimination against Negroes and Jews. But it is nothing of the sort. Negroes and Jews, for complex reasons we need not here explore, have never been interested in navigating tugboats. They have not applied for the positions. They have therefore never been rejected.

The faculties of many Negro colleges are overwhelmingly black out of all proportion to their numbers in the country, state, or even local community. It would be a grim jest therefore to tax them with discriminatory practices. Until recently, they have been pathetically eager to employ qualified white teachers, but they have been unable to attract them.

The fact that HEW makes a distinction between women and minorities, judging sexual discrimination not by simple proportion of women teachers and researchers in universities to their proportion in the general population, but only to their proportion among *applicants,* shows that it has a dim understanding of the relevant issue. There are obviously various occupational fields—military, mining, aeronautical, and so forth, for which women have, until now, shown little inclination. Neither the school nor the department can be faulted for the scarcity of female applications. But the main point is this: no matter how many applicants there are for a post, whether they are male or female, the only relevant criterion is whether or not they are qualified. Only when there is antecedent determination that the applicants, with respect to the job or post specifications are equally or even roughly equally qualified, and there is a marked and continued disparity in the relative numbers employed, is there legitimate ground for suspicion and inquiry.

The effect of the ultimata to universities to hire blacks and women under threat of losing crucial financial support is to compel them to hire *unqualified* Negroes and women, and to discriminate *against* qualified nonblacks and men. This is just as much a manifestation of racism, even if originally unintended, as the racism the original presidential directive was designed to correct. Intelligent, self-respecting Negroes and women would scorn such preferential treatment. The consequences of imposing any criterion other than that of qualified talent on our educational establishments are sure to be disastrous on the quest for new knowledge and truth as well as subversive of the democratic ethos. Its logic points to the introduction of a quota system, of the notorious *numerus clausus* of repressive regimes of the past. If blacks are to be hired merely on the basis of their color and women merely on the basis of their sex, because they are *under*represented in the faculties of our universities, before long the demand will be made that Jews or men should be fired or dismissed or not hired as Jews or men, no matter how well qualified, because they are *over*represented in our faculties.

The universities should not yield to the illiberal ultimata of the Office of Civil Rights of HEW. There is sufficient work for it to do in enforcing the presidental directive in areas where minorities are obviously qualified and are obviously suffering from unfair discrimination. It undoubtedly is true, as some members of UCRA who have long been active in the field of civil rights have long pointed out, that some educational institutions or their departments have been guilty of obvious religious and racial discrimination. The evidence of this was flagrant and open and required no elaborate questionnaires to establish. The Office of Civil Rights could cooperate with the Department of Justice here. Currently, its activities in the field of higher education are not only wasting time, effort, and the taxpayer's money but debasing educational standards as well. It is bringing confusion and conflict into an area where, prior to its intervention, the issues were well understood and where voluntary efforts to hire qualified women and members of minorities were being made with increasing success.

Sidney Hook

The Bias in Anti-Bias Regulations

Although the writings of those who have sought to arouse the academic community against the preferential-hiring practices resulting from the HEW *Guidelines on Affirmative Action* have often been attacked, their arguments have not been adequately met. Instead, their intellectual integrity has been impugned and they have been represented as racists and/or sexists, defenders of the status quo and of the practices of discrimination that have developed over the years.

The basic truth is that almost every academic critic of the HEW Guidelines has been a strong supporter of the Executive Order 11246 as amended, which outlaws, on pain of forfeiting federal contract awards, employment practices that discriminate on the basis of membership in any racial, religious, sexual or national group. The gravamen of their criticism has been that the provision of "numerical goals" and "precise timetables," mandated by HEW and the Office of Federal Contract Compliance, violates the principles of the executive order. Evidence and argument have established that despite the frantic denials and semantic evasions of HEW and its academic

Source: Measure, *no. 14 (Oct. 1971). Reprinted by permission of the author and University Centers for Rational Alternatives.*

apologists, their Guidelines require "good-faith efforts" on the part of universities to adopt a quota system. The critics of a quota system in all its disguises have opposed a program that would result in the hiring either of unqualified members of minority groups or women or of persons who were not the best qualified. Instead they have advocated the adoption of all effective measures that would increase the qualified supply of minorities and women.

Enormous damage has already been done from which universities and students will suffer for a very long time. Even greater damage is in the offing as HEW moves to enforce its demands that minority members and women be hired in proportion to their alleged availability, on the level of *individual departments.*

In the struggle to preserve the intellectual integrity of the university, the appearance of Richard A. Lester's *Anti-Bias Regulation of the Universities: Faculty Problems and Their Solutions* (New York: McGraw-Hill, 1974) should prove a boon. It is sponsored by the Carnegie Commission on Higher Education, which, however, takes no responsibility for any of its opinions or conclusions. It starts from the same premise that has inspired the University Centers for Rational Alternatives, the Committee on Academic Nondiscrimination and Integrity, the Anti-Defamation League and other critics of the governmental affirmative-action program as implemented by HEW, namely, that invidious discrimination or prejudice in employment "is destructive of democratic values and violates the principle of appointment and promotion on merit." It reviews the first five years of the program, marshalls the criticisms that have been made against it, differentiates between its legitimate and illegitimate purposes, and analyzes some of the assumptions and thought-ways that have misled the zealots.

One must distinguish between two questions. (1) What is the degree of discrimination against minorities and women in higher education, and the nature of the evidence for it? (2) What can be done to remedy discrimination wherever it exists?

That discrimination has existed against members of minorities and women in higher education and still lingers under various disguises, no critic of HEW's affirmative-action program denies. What has been questioned is the validity of the inferences drawn from superficial, raw and uninterpreted statistical data about the relative distribution of members of minorities and women, concerning the existence of a definite policy of discrimination. A disproportionate number of members of minorities and women teaching at universities *may* reflect a deliberate policy of exclusion, both with respect to admission of such students to graduate study and to their employment. On the other hand, it may show nothing of the sort. The small number of black graduate students, for example, may reflect not an anti-black policy but the lack of equitable social, economic, and educational stimuli or opportunities, for which the entire community must accept the blame, that resulted in the absence of qualified black students for admission to graduate schools. The disproportion in the numbers of men and women graduate students may be evidence not of bias against women but primarily of the pervasive effect of social attitudes concerning sex-oriented careers.

In any case, where a specific charge of overt discrimination against members of minorities or women is made it must be buttressed by specific case evidence in a manner comparable to establishing that the provisions of the Fair Housing Act have been violated. Because no member of a certain ethnic group lives in an apartment house is *by itself* not evidence of discrimination. But when a specific violation has been established, the statistical fact becomes relevant. Similarly, the overrepresentation of a certain group is by itself not a proof of favorable discrimination: no one would seriously accuse the Metropolitan Opera of past discrimination in favor of tenor singers from the Mediterranean area or blame tugboat operators in New York Harbor for hiring predominantly male captains of Scandinavian ancestry. It would first have to be shown that some equally qualified tenors from other regions and equally qualified men or women navigators of other ethnic groups were denied employment.

Very illuminating is Professor Lester's discussion of alleged discrimination against blacks in higher education. The issue is of particular importance because the entire early federal affirmative-action drive was motivated and stimulated by the history of three hundred years of injustice against blacks. Only after the argument for reparation to blacks had prevailed as the single determining factor of overriding importance in justifying a temporary preferential treatment of aggrieved groups, were the programs for minorities implemented. Women were added later. Dr. Lester shows that present-day efforts of institutions of higher education to hire blacks are so strenuous that blacks often receive many more offers from white colleges than equally qualified whites do. One study reveals that, "Blacks with doctorates from high-quality schools who have published, report jobs by invitation almost four times as often as whites with the same excellent credentials." It is no secret today that many universities are offering appointments to black faculty at salaries much higher than those offered to their white colleagues with equivalent and sometimes better qualifications. It is not unusual for associate professorships to be offered to blacks just completing their Ph.D. How avid the pursuit is may be inferred from the recent case of a black assistant professor of philosophy at Yale earning a salary of $13,000 on full-time who was discovered to have also a full-time *tenure* appointment at New York State University at Stony Brook at $26,000. (Yale objected to this, not SUNY.)

The fact that only 1 percent of university faculties and 5.4 percent of four-year college faculties are black is no evidence that today active discrimination against qualified blacks exists, and that it is five times as strong in the universities as in the colleges. And yet some statistical illiterates still hurl charges of overt discrimination and racism at universities merely because blacks are underrepresented. A flyer recently circulated at New York University by three faculty members denounces NYU for racism because blacks constitute 2.1 percent of the full-time faculty which, incidentally, is more than twice the national average. It goes on to assert: "As a matter of simple justice and in order to reflect the population of which NYU is a part, the number of full-time black faculty should be perhaps ten times this number— 2.1 percent full-time black faculty now versus 21.2 percent black population in New York City.

Even if the number of qualified black applicants for college and university positions *were* equal to their proportion in the general population, the argument of McCauly et al. would still be fallacious: one cannot ask schools in New York City and Washington, D.C., to increase their black academic percentages to those of the surrounding population and *at the same time* support HEW officials who ask universities in North Dakota and Oregon to increase *their* percentages to the *national* average.

But why should we assume that the number of blacks in university teaching or any other area or profession in New York City must equal 21.2 percent of the population? Does this mean that blacks on the professional basketball and baseball teams of New York City are discriminatorily *over*-represented? Even if complete equality of educational opportunity exists, the vocational distribution of different groups will depend on so many variables —traditions, shifting social values, wars and unemployment, and so forth— that it is completely unreasonable to assume that the ratios in employment will necessarily reflect the ratios in the general population. To impose them is to impose a straitjacket incompatible with the slightest respect for the principle of individual justice and merit. This straitjacket becomes even more intolerable—and ludicrous—when imposed on college departments with tenured faculty or with so few members that statistical laws cease to have any meaning. It is one thing to expect general-population ratios in setting up classes or groups that would normally reflect the community's racial or sexual makeup, such as jury rolls. It is altogether different when we are setting up groups, admission to which is based upon merit selection, whether it is a mathematics department or a varsity basketball team.

That factors other than overt discrimination have accounted for certain disproportions in graduate study emerges very clearly from Professor Lester's study. In particular, he discusses the disproportions between the numbers of men and women in graduate schools. He shows, for example, that the percentage of all Ph.D. degrees received by women between 1920 and 1929 was much higher than between 1950 and 1959. To infer from this that discrimination against accepting women for graduate school and accrediting them had markedly *increased* during the fifties from what it was in the twenties would be absurd. But this is just the kind of inference that the originators of, and apologists for, bureaucratic affirmative action draw from statistical tables. Lester, who is professor of economics at Princeton University, argues persuasively that fluctuations in the number of women attending graduate school are more significantly correlated with fluctuations in the attitudes of society and of women to *themselves*, with respect to the desirability of family and children *or* a career, than with changes in men's bias against women.

> "The 1950s and early 1960s were years of 'the baby boom.' Between 1940 and 1965, the proportion of married women in the female population rose significantly, and the percentage of married women in the age group 25 to 35 who had children under six years of age also increased markedly. These developments helped to cause the labor force participation rates of these women to decline appreciably and to limit their career ambitions. A result was that in the 1950s and early 1960s a much smaller percentage of women prepared themselves with Ph.D. training and drove hard to 'reach the top of their profession.' "

One can find corroborative evidence of . . . [Lester's] conclusion from other sources, particularly the memoirs of women writing about this period. For example, here is a gifted woman writing about her twenty-fifth Radcliffe reunion at Cambridge. "My class is full of highly intelligent and capable women. But it was graduated into the 1950s when it was fashionable to marry young, have a big family fast and settle into a house full of togetherness." (*New York Times*, June 26, 1974.)

Many other citations stressing the same point can be given.

It was this attitude that better explains the present overall disproportions among the percentage of men and women teaching in universities than male bias against women. The latter certainly exists but is peripheral, not central, statistically minor, not major. My own experience, extending almost half a century, recommending qualified young women for positions in philosophy, confirms this. I do not offer this as "proof" but as relevant evidence. Bias against women exists and there is absolutely no justification for it: where it exists, it must be eliminated, not by reverse discrimination but by a fair application of the merit principle. Nonetheless, it is wrong to exaggerate the hostility of men to women in the university or to introduce a new *numerus clausus* as the decisive yardstick for hiring.

Professor Lester has some interesting data (from Astin) on the relative strength of different factors encountered as obstacles by women, themselves already employed in academic institutions, in "developing (their) careers fully." A questionnaire sent to women at the end of 1965 who received their Ph.D. degrees in 1957 and 1958 requested that they list the career obstacles they found to be "major problems." *Only 12 percent listed "employer discrimination" as a major problem*; 88 percent listed other obstacles as major problems; for example, 18 percent "finding adequate help at home." Of the married women (50 percent), 12 percent listed "husband's job mobility," 4 percent listed "husband's negative attitude toward my working."

Some university rules adversely affected women more than men, not because they were designed to discriminate against women, but because of social attitudes towards in-group dealings, that is, the nepotism rule. The purpose was legitimate, but the nepotism rules had a blunderbuss effect that barred qualified married women. They are rapidly being abolished. Professor Lester also cites several studies that indicate that single women on university faculties "seem notably less disadvantaged" in their careers than married women. Recently, male attitudes towards the sharing of domestic duties appear to be changing, resulting in greater equality of opportunity for married women.

As we go up the academic ladder we find that the percentage of women of the total in each rank diminishes: the largest percent is found in the lowest rank—instructor and lecturer (37.6 percent)—and the smallest in the highest rank of full professors (5.2 percent). "Is this not conclusive evidence of discrimination?" ask the proponents of government-sponsored affirmative-action plans. Professor Lester firmly denies it, as well as the assumption that "equal employment opportunity would lead to the same percentage for women in each professional rank," as for men. Such an assumption is questionable since it "fails to take account of the distribution of the qualified supply of women for university appointment at particular ranks." Here too, the greater burden of home responsibilities on women may affect acquisition

of the qualifications for promotion to the upper ranks. Two additional considerations support Professor Lester's conclusions. "The distribution of single
women by faculty rank seems to resemble the distribution for men more than
it does for married women." Further, in every country for which data are
available, including the Soviet Union and the Scandinavian countries where
discrimination is allegedly less than in the U.S., "the percentages of women
become smaller as one moves up the promotional ladder, with relatively few
women at the full professor level." The statement holds true even for
countries where, due to the huge strains of World War II and the associated
extensive male casualties, the work force at the time shifted drastically in
favor of women. Marriage and motherhood seem to be career obstacles to
women universally, although there is some reason to believe that this will be
gradually less so in the future.

Professor Lester is at his best in Chapters 4 and 5, in which he offers a
devastating analysis of the specific federal guidelines for faculty employment
and the affirmative-action goals for faculty. In the course of his analysis, he
exposes the inconsistencies and inadequacies of the Report of the Committee on Discrimination of the AAUP and the uncritical endorsement by the
Carnegie Commission of numerical goals (in reality, quotas) in hiring. Both
represent scandalous capitulations to the HEW bureaucracy, whose schemes
have never received congressional consideration or approval.

Particularly noteworthy is Lester's criticism of HEW's method of cal-
culating "deficiencies" in the employment of women and minority persons,
and determing whether and when they have been "underutilized." He protests the repeated reference in the guidelines to the mere "absence of women
or minorities in an academic department" as an "'exclusion' on the part of
the institution and as a 'deficiency' (meaning discrimination by the institution) regardless of the amount of fully qualified supply of women and blacks
actually available for each of the faculty positions in that discipline or department." He shows in considerable detail the inappropriateness of the
"availability-utilization" techniques as applied to most tenure positions in
major universities.

The points Professor Lester makes are quite telling. Their importance
will be acknowledged by any person familiar with the various criteria involved in selecting teacher-scholars for a discipline that embraces many sub-
fields and areas of specialization in a well-rounded department. The authors
of the HEW Guidelines are unaware that their method of determining
"deficiencies" and "underutilization," "though perhaps usable and appropriate for jobs requiring manual qualifications and skills, is inappropriate for

quite individualized positions that require rare combinations of qualities, such as is the case for most positions at major universities."

Professor Lester has no difficulty in establishing that the numerical goals and time schedules imposed by HEW on universities lead to *inflated* goals that "can only be met by giving some women and minority-group members preference in hiring, promotion, and/or salary." The result is easy to foresee—new forms of discrimination, and a two-standard faculty: those who have made it strictly on their own, selected by their professional peers in open competition, and those who have made it by virtue of membership in some group. The erosion of the principles of merit, scholarly quality and integrity are unavoidable in such circumstances.

There is much more in Professor Lester's challenging volume that deserves evaluation. On some points, for example, the hiring of assistant professors, he seems to draw back from his own excellent principles. His book will of course become the target of enraged attack by the partisans of HEW. It cannot be recommended too strongly, especially to those who support the Civil Rights Act of 1964 whose Section 703 (j) of Title VII, explicitly forbids granting "preferential treatment to any individual or to any group because of race, color, religion, sex or national origin on account of any imbalance which may exist with respect to the total number or percentage of persons of any race, color, religion, sex, or national origin employed by an employer in comparison with the total number of percentage of such race, color, religion, sex, or national origin in any community, state, section, or other area, or in the available work force in any community, state, section or other area."

Interpreting Title VII, the Supreme Court has declared that: "Discriminatory preference for any group, minority or majority, is precisely and only what Congress has proscribed . . . Congress has not commanded that the less qualified be preferred over the better merely because of minority origins. Far from disparaging job qualifications, Congress has made such qualifications the controlling factor, so that race, religion, nationality and sex become irrelevant."

It would seem that any affirmative-action program that commands the establishment of numerical goals that can be achieved only by preferential hiring is definitely unconstitutional. It is to be hoped that the U.S. Supreme Court will soon rule to that effect.

It is not only unconstitutional, it is immoral, for it makes a mockery of the principle of desert which was the basis of denunciations of past discriminatory practices. Independently of the validity of the findings about the actual degree of discrimination that exists today in educational institutions, its elimination does not require reverse discrimination but only the establishment of equal opportunities to compete for open positions, and their award to the best qualified individual.

Many years ago the blacks were deprived of their right to vote and women were denied the right to vote. In rectifying these injustices, no one would dream of demanding that blacks and women be compensated for past discrimination by being given the right to cast an extra vote or two at the expense of their fellow citizens. Something like this demand is reflected in the view that women and members of minorities *today* receive compensatory, preferential treatment because of discrimination against their groups in the past.

Paul Seabury

HEW and the Universities

Old Howard Smith, Virginia swamp fox of the House Rules Committee, was a clever tactical fighter. When Dixiecrats in 1964 unsuccessfully tried to obstruct passage of the Civil Rights bill, Smith, in a fit of inspired raillery, devised a perverse stratagem. He proposed an amendment to the bill, to include women as an object of federal protection in employment, by adding sex to the other criteria of race, color, national origin, and religion as illegitimate grounds for discrimination in hiring. This tactical maneuver had far-reaching effects; calculated to rouse at least some Northern masculine ire against the whole bill, it backfired by eliciting a chivalrous rather than (as we now call it) sexist response: the amendment actually passed!

Smith, however, had greater things in mind for women's rights. As a fall-back strategy, they would distract federal bureaucrats from the principal object of the bill, namely, to rectify employment inequities for Negroes. In this, at least in higher education, Smith's stratagem is paying off according to expectations. The middle-range bureaucrats staffing the HEW Civil Rights office, under its director, J. Stanley Pottinger, now scent sexism more easily than racism in the crusade to purify university hiring practices. Minority-group spokesmen grumble when this powerful feminine competitor appears,

Source: Commentary *(Feb. 1972). Reprinted by permission; Copyright* © *1972 by the* American Jewish Committee. This article has been cut slightly.

to horn in. In the dynamics of competition between race and sex for scarce places on university faculties, a new hidden crisis of higher education is brewing. As universities climb out of the rubble of campus disorders of the 1960s, beset by harsh budgetary reverses, they now are required to redress national social injustices within their walls at their own expense. Compliance with demands from the federal government to do this would compel a stark remodeling of their criteria of recruitment, their ethos of professionalism, and their standards of excellence. Refusal to comply satisfactorily would risk their destruction.

The story of how this came about, and what it portends, is a complex one, so complex that it is hard to know where to begin. It is also an unpleasant tale. Only its first chapters can be written.

1

Let us begin the story, then, with a brief history of the Civil Rights Act of 1964. This act, in the view of its principal sponsors, proposed (among other things) to engage the force of the federal government in battle to diminish or to rectify discriminatory hiring practices in firms and institutions having or seeking contracts with the federal government. Title VII of the act expressly forbids discrimination by employers on grounds of race, color, religion, and national origin, either in the form of preferential hiring or advancement, or in the form of differential compensation. Contracting institutions deemed negligent in complying with these provisions could be deemed ineligible for such contracts, or their contracts could be suspended, terminated, or not renewed.

When Title VII was debated in the Senate, some opponents of it, asserting (in the words of a Washington *Star* editorial) that it was a "draftsman's nightmare," voiced alarm that it might be used for discriminatory purposes, and employers might be coerced into hiring practices which might, in fact, violate the equal-protection doctrine of the Constitution, thus perversely reversing the stated purposes of the bill. In one significant interchange, this alarm, raised by Florida's Senator Smathers, was genially dismissed by Senator Humphrey in words which bear recalling:

> MR. HUMPHREY: [T]he Senator from Florida is so convincing that when he speaks, as he does, with the ring of sincerity in his voice and heart, and says that an employee should be hired on the basis of his ability—
> MR. SMATHERS: Correct.
> MR. HUMPHREY: And that an employer should not be denied the right

to hire on the basis of ability and should not take into consideration race—how right the Senator is. . . .

But the trouble is that these idealistic pleadings are not followed by some sinful mortals. There are some who do not hire solely on the basis of ability. Doors are closed; positions are closed; unions are closed to people of color. That situation does not help America. . . .

I know that the Senator from Florida desires to help America, industry and enterprise. We ought to adopt the Smathers doctrine, which is contained in Title VII. I never realized that I would hear such an appropriate description of the philosophy behind Title VII as I have heard today.

MR. SMATHERS: Mr. President, the Senator from Minnesota has expressed my doctrine completely. . . .

The first steps in implementing the new act were based on executive orders of the President corresponding to Humphrey's Smathers Doctrine. President Johnson's Executive Order No. 11375 (1967) stated that "The contractor will not discriminate against any employee or applicant because of race, color, religion, sex, or national origin. The contractor *will take affirmative action* [italics added] to ensure that employees are treated during employment, without regard to their race, color, religion, sex, or national origin."

Under such plausible auspices, "affirmative action" was born, and with a huge federal endownment to guarantee its success in life. Since 1967, however, this child prodigy—like Charles Addams's famous nursery boy with the test tubes—has been experimenting with novel brews, so as to change both his appearance and his behavior. And it is curious to see how the single-minded pursuers of an ideal of equity can overrun and trample the ideal itself, while injuring innocent bystanders as well.

2

Affirmative action was altered by a Labor Department order (based not on the Civil Rights Act but on revised presidential directives) only months after the Johnson order was announced. This order reshaped it into a weapon for discriminatory hiring practices. If the reader will bear with a further recitation of federal prose, let me introduce Order No. 4, Department of Labor:

An affirmative-action program is a set of specific and result-oriented procedures to which a contractor commits himself to apply every good faith effort. The objective of these procedures plus such efforts is equal employment opportunity. Procedures without effort to make them work are meaningless; and effort, undirected by specific and meaningful procedures, is inadequate. An acceptable affirmative-action program must include an analysis of areas within which the contractor is deficient in the utilization of minority groups and women, and further, *goals and timetables to which the contractor's good faith efforts must be directed to correct the deficiencies and thus, to increase materially the utilization of minorities and women, at all levels and in all segments of his work force where deficiencies exist.*

This directive is now applicable through HEW enforcement procedures to universities by delegation of authority from the Labor Department. By late 1971, something of a brushfire, fanned by hard-working HEW compliance officers, had spread through American higher education, the cause of it being the demand that universities, as a condition of obtaining or retaining their federal contracts, establish hiring goals based upon race and sex.

3

Universities, for a variety of singular reasons, are extremely vulnerable to this novel attack. As President McGill of Columbia remarked recently, "We are no longer in all respects an independent private university." As early as 1967, the federal government was annually disbursing contract funds to universities at the rate of three-and-a-half billion dollars a year; recently the Carnegie Commission suggested that federal contract funding be increased by 1978 to thirteen billion dollars, if universities are to meet their educational objectives. Individual institutions, notably great and distinguished ones, already are extraordinarily dependent on continuing receipt of federal support. The University of California, for instance, currently (1970-71) depends upon federal contract funds for approximately $72 million. The University of Michigan, periodically harassed by HEW threats of contract suspension, cancellation, or nonrenewal, would stand to lose as much as $60 million per annum. The threat of permanent disqualification, if consummated, could wholly wreck a university's prospects for the future.

In November 1971, HEW's Office for Civil Rights announced its intent to institute proceedings for Columbia's permanent debarment—*even though no charges or findings of discrimination had been made.* Columbia had simply not come up with an acceptable affirmative-action program to redress inequities which had not even been found to exist. When minor officials act like Alice in Wonderland's Red Queen, using threats of decapitation for frivolous purposes, when they act as investigator, prosecutor, and judge rolled into one, there may be no cause for surprise. But one can certainly wonder how even they would dare pronounce sentence—and a sentence of death at that—even before completion of the investigatory phase. Such, however, appears to be the deadly logic of HEW procedures. As J. Stanley Pottinger, chief of HEW's office, said at a West Coast press conference recently, "We have a whale of a lot of power and we're prepared to use it if necessary." In known circumstances of its recent use, the threat resembles the development of MIRV missiles to apprehend a suspected embezzler.

4

As the federal government of the United States moves uncertainly to establish equitable racial patterns in universities and colleges, it does so with few guidelines from historical experience. The management, manipulation, and evaluation of quotas, targets, and goals for preferential hiring are certainly matters as complex as are the unusual politics which such announced policies inspire. How equitably to assuage the many group claimants for preference, context-by-context, occasion-by-occasion, and year-by-year, as these press and jostle among themselves for prior attention in preference, must by now occasion some puzzlement even among HEW bureaucrats. On a recent inspector general's tour of California, J. Stanley Pottinger found himself giving comfort to militant women at Boalt Hall Law School of the University of California; yet at Hayward State College, he was attacked by Chicanos for giving preference to blacks! Leaders of militant groups, needless to say, are less interested in the acute dilemmas posed to administrators by this adventure than in what they actually want for themselves. (When at Michigan I raised with a Women's Commission lady the question of whether an actual conflict-of-interest might exist between blacks and women, she simply dismissed the matter: that's for an administrator to figure out.) How to arrive at some distant utopian day, when "underutilization" of minorities or women has "disappeared," is as difficult to imagine as the nature of the ratios that will apply on that day.*

5

Fifteen years ago, David Riesman in his *Constraint and Variety in American Education* pointed to certain qualities which distinctively charac-

---

*When I asked an administrator at San Francisco State College what "underutilization" of minorities meant, he simply replied, "Experience will let us know."

terized avant-garde institutions of higher learning in this country. The world of scholarship, he said, "is democratic rather than aristocratic in tone, and scholars are made, not born." A "certain universalizing quality in academic life" resulted from the existence of disciplines which "can lift us out of our attachments to home and mother, to our undergraduate alma mater, too, and attach us instead to the new country of Biophysics or the old of Medieval History." In America, the relative decline of ethnic and social-class snobberies and discrimination, combined with immense expansion of the colleges, drew into scholarship a great majority whose backgrounds were distinctly unscholarly. "The advancing inner frontier of science," he wrote, had for many, taken the place which the Western frontier served for earlier pioneers. The loyalty which the new democratic scholar showed to his discipline signalled a kind of "non-territorial nationalism." In contrast to his European counterparts, the American scholar found few colleagues among the mass of undergraduates on the basis either of "a common culture or a common ideology in the political or eschatological sense." Paradoxically this democratization of the university (with its stress not on status but upon excellence in performance) had not begun in rank-and-file small colleges of the nation, which were exemplars of America's ethnic, religious, and cultural diversity. Rather it had come out of those innovating institutions which, in quest of excellence, either abandoned or transcended much of their discriminatory sociological parochialism. It was the denominational college, where deliberate discrimination according to sex, religion, color, and culture continued to be practiced in admissions and faculty recruitment, which made up the rear of the snakelike academic procession. The egalitarianism of excellence, a democracy of performance, was an ethos consummated by the avant-garde. Riesman labelled the disciplines of the great universities the "race-courses of the mind."

Felix Frankfurter, who went from CCNY to Harvard Law School, was equally impressed with how the system worked. "What mattered," he wrote, "was excellence in your profession to which your father or your face was equally irrelevant. And so rich man, poor man were just irrelevant titles to the equation of human relations. The thing that mattered was what you did professionally. . . . " As he saw the merit system, the alternative to it had to be "personal likes and dislikes, or class, or color, or religious partialities or antipathies. . . . These incommensurable things give too much room for unworthy and irrelevant biases."

The greatest boost to America's universities came in the 1930s from European emigre scholars whose powerful influence (notably in the sciences and social sciences) is still felt even today. As exemplars of learning, their impact upon young and parochial American students was profound.* Thanks in part to them, by the 1950s the great American universities attained an authentic cosmopolitanism of scholarship matched by no other university system in the world. And the outward reach of American higher education toward the best the world of scholarship could offer generated an inward magnetism, attracting to itself the most qualified students who could be found to study with these newly renowned faculties.

This system of recruitment also left a myriad of American sociological categories statistically underrepresented in the highest precincts of American higher education. Today, with respect to race and ethnicity, blacks, Irish, Italians, Greeks, Poles, and all other Slavic groups (including Slovaks, Slovenes, Serbs, Czechs, and Croatians) are underrepresented. On faculties, at least, women are underrepresented. Important religious categories are underrepresented. The great Catholic universities, until recently, have stood aside from the mainstream of secular higher education; they have been enclaves of a separated scholarship. Thus few Catholics are to be found in the roster of distinguished faculties of America's great secular universities, even though Catholics comprise perhaps 30 percent of the population. And it is interesting to note that the quest for professional excellence in some respects has militated against the achievement of group parities: among those women's colleges which had obtained by the 1950s an enviable academic status as being more than apartheid seminaries, one apparent "price" of scholarly excellence was the rapid infusion of male faculty.

And then, on the other hand, there are the Jews. For a long time, administrators of some of America's universities, aware of the powerful scholarly competition which Jewish students and scholars posed, and the social "inequities" which their admission or recruitment might pose, established protective quotas—the famous *numerus clausus*—to keep their numbers down. Yale Law School, for example, abandoned its Jewish quota for incoming students only in the 1950s. With the triumph of equal opportunity over quotas, the bastions of discrimination collapsed. It is estimated that Jews make up about 3 per cent of the population. Clearly they constitute a

---

* It is now sometimes said, on behalf of preferential recruitment of less-qualified minority faculty, that majority students require *examples* whom "their community" can respect. Whether in practice this would, as claimed, stimulate their performance, is hard to say. The most stimulating exemplary professors I encountered as a student had quite different "socio-economic" backgrounds from mine. Many were even foreigners. It seems almost foolish to have to mention this.

vastly greater proportion than that on the faculties of America's greatest universities, especially in the social sciences, mathematics, and the humanities.

One could enlarge this catalogue of statistical disparities indefinitely. Yet I must also mention the political, although it is seldom touched upon. The partisan complexion of universities is a matter which HEW does not, and cannot, attend to. Still, I would point out that the faculty of my department at Berkeley, for example, very large by any standards, had to the best of my knowledge three Republicans on it a few years ago; two have since left, one by retirement and one by resignation. There is one new convert, who switched registration to vote for Senator Kuchel in the GOP primary and against Max Rafferty and found, after conversion, that he enjoyed the notoriety which his deviance produced. So, currently we have two Republicans in a department of thirty-eight. This situation is in no way unique. Yet I doubt that even Nixon's HEW crusaders for equality of results would tread into this minefield of blatant inequity. On the other hand, one wonders whether, in White House garrets, there are not some among the President's Republican equerry who take perverse pleasure in watching academic liberals, crusaders for social justice for others, now hoist by their own petard on home territory.

6

The ironic potentials in affirmative action might have been foreseen, had American lawmakers and administrators known the results that in recent years have plagued the government of India's pursuit of a quite similar goal. Here, perhaps more clearly than in any other contemporary culture, the idea that social justice can be reached via quotas and preferences has led almost inexorably to extremes of absurdity.

Before independence, under British rule, special privileges to communities and castes were given or withheld under the British *raj* both to rectify inequities and (as in the instance of Muslims) to punish disloyalty or reward support. Commencing in legislatures as the establishment of reserved seats for privileged groups—first for Muslims, then for Anglo-Indians, then for Indian Christians—the principle of privileged representation soon spread into other sectors of public life.

When in the early 1930s B. R. Ambedkar, leader of the Untouchables, demanded that the British establish preferential electoral quotas for them, Gandhi objected, arguing that the interests of the Untouchables would better be advanced by integrating them into society than by protecting them with preferential treatment. Gandhi believed that preference would heighten identity of caste rather than diminish it, and that it further risked creating vested-interest minorities. Yet in negotiations with the British, Ambedkar won and Gandhi lost. After independence, the government of India back-tracked, abolishing preferential treatment for all groups except tribal peoples and scheduled castes (that is, Untouchables), who were accorded certain pref-erences in government recruitment and in access to educational institutions, fellowships, and admissions. Such preferences, originally instituted as temporary devices, soon became institutionalized, and again they spread. So-called "backward classes" proliferated to the point where it became necessary to be designated as "backward" in order to become privileged. And, indeed, in 1964, a "Backwardness Commission" recommended in the state of Mysore that every group except two (the Brahmins and the Lingayats) be officially designated as backward!

The Indian experience clearly shows that when access to privilege is defined on ethnic-community lines, the basic issue of individual rights is evaded; new privileges arise; caste privilege sabotages the principle of equality; the polity further fragments; and the test of performance is re-placed by the test of previous status. . . .

7

To remain eligible for federal contracts under the new procedures, uni-versities must devise package proposals, containing stated targets for pre-ferential hiring on grounds of race and sex. HEW may reject these goals, giving the university thirty-days notice for swift rectification, even though no charges of discrimination have been brought. Either innocence must be quickly proved, or acceptable means of rectification devised. But how does one *prove* innocence?

"Hiring practices" (that is, faculty recruitment procedures) are decen-tralized; they devolve chiefly upon departments. At Columbia, for instance, seventy-seven units generate proposals for recruitment. Faculties resent (most of the time quite properly) attempts of administrators to tell them whom to hire, and whom not. Departments rarely keep records of the communications and transactions which precede the making of an employ-ment offer, except as these records pertain to the individual finally selected. Still, the procedure is time-consuming and expensive. The Department of Economics of the San Diego campus of the University of California estimates that it costs twenty to forty man-hours, plus three to five hundred dollars, to screen *one* candidate sufficiently to make an offer. Typically, dozens of candidates are reviewed in earlier stages.

Compliance data thus tend to be scanty and incomplete. "Columbia's problem," President McGill recently observed, "is that it is difficult to prove what we do because it is exceedingly difficult to develop the data base on which to show, in the depth and detail demanded [by HEW], what the University's personnel activities in fact are." Yet HEW demands such data from universities on thirty-day deadlines, with contract suspension threatened. Moreover, on its finding of discrimination (usually based on statistical, not qualitative, evidence), it may demand plans for rectification which oblige the university to commit itself to abstract preferential goals without regard to the issue of individual merit.

The best universities, which also happen to be those upon which HEW has chiefly worked its knout, habitually and commonsensically recruit from other best institutions. The top universities hire the top 5 percent of graduate students in the top ten universities. This is the "skill pool" they rely upon. Some may now deem such practices archaic but they have definitely served to maintain quality. Just as definitely they have not served to obtain "equality of results" in terms of the proportional representation of sociological categories. Such equality assumes that faculties somehow must "represent" designated categories of people on grounds other than those of professional qualification. As Labor Department Order No. 4 states, special attention "should be given to academic experience and skill requirements, to ensure that the requirements in themselves do not constitute inadvertent discrimination." Indeed, according to four professors at Cornell, writing in the *Times* (Letters to the Editor, January 6, 1972), deans and department chairmen have been informed by that university's president that HEW policy means the " 'hiring of additional minority persons and females' even if 'in many instances, it may be necessary to hire unqualified or marginally qualified people.' "

If departments abandon the practice of looking to the best pools from which they can hope to draw, then quality must in fact be jeopardized. To comply with HEW orders, every department must come up not with the *best* candidate, but with the best-qualified *woman* or *non-white* candidate. For when a male or a white candidate is actually selected or recommended, it is now incumbent on both department and university to *prove* that no qualified woman or non-white was found available. Some universities already have gone so far in emulating the federal bureaucracy as to have installed their own . . . affirmative-action coordinators to screen recommendations for faculty appointments before final action is taken.

A striking contradiction exists between HEW's insistence that faculties prove they do not discriminate and its demand for goals and timetables which require discrimination to occur. For there is no reason to suppose that equitable processes in individual cases will automatically produce results which are set in the timetables and statistical goals universities are now required to develop. If all that HEW wishes is evidence that universities are bending over backward to be fair, why should it require them to have statistical goals at all? Do they know something no one else knows, about where fairness inevitably leads?

Yet another facet of HEW's procedures goes to the very heart of faculty due process: its demand of the right of access to faculty files, when searching for evidence of discrimination. Such files have always been the most sacrosanct documents of academia, and for good reason: it has been assumed that candor in the evaluation of candidates and personnel is best guaranteed by confidentiality of comment; and that evasiveness, caution, smoke-screening, and grandstanding—which would be the principal consequences of open files —would debase standards of judgment. In the past, universities have denied federal authorities—the FBI, for instance—access to these files. Now HEW demands access. And it is the recent reluctance of the Berkeley campus of the University of California to render unto this agent of Caesar what was denied to previous agents, which occasioned the HEW ultimatum of possible contract suspension: $72 million. One might imagine the faculty would be in an uproar, what with Nixon's men ransacking the inner temple. But no. In this as in other aspects of this curious story, the faculty is silent.

8

"In respect of civil rights, common to all citizens, the Constitution of the United States does not, I think, permit any public authority to know the race of those entitled to be protected in the enjoyment of such rights. . . . Our Constitution is color-blind, and neither knows nor tolerates classes among citizens." This is Justice Harlan, dissenting in *Plessy v. Ferguson* in 1896, when the Surpeme Court endorsed the "separate but equal" doctrine.

Some of us in the league of lost liberals are still wont to say that the Constitution is color-blind. Yet now under the watchful eye of federal functionaries, academic administrators are compelled to be as acutely sensitive as Kodachrome to the physical appearance of their faculty members and proposed candidates for employment. Forms supplying such information are now fed into data-processing machines; printouts supply ethnic profiles of departments, colleges, and schools, from which compliance reports may be may be sent to HEW, and university affirmative-action goals are approved or rejected.*

All of this is done in some uneasiness of mind, to put it mildly. In many states, Harlan-like blue-laws of a recent innocent epoch still expressly prohibit employers from collecting and maintaining data on prospective employees with respect to race, religion, and national origin. The crafty practices contrived to elude the intention of such laws while at the same time complying with HEW, vary from campus to campus. At the University of Michigan, the procedure entails what is known as "self-designation"—the employee indicates on a form the race or ethnic group of which he considers himself a part.† These forms are collected and grouped according to job classifications, departments, and so forth, and then they are burned, so as to disappear without a trace. Other universities, less anxious to cover their traces, simply file the forms separately from regular personnel files, without the names of the individuals concerned. In New York, the CUNY system resorts to a quite different practice invented and perfected by South African Boers: "visual identification." Affirmative-action coordinators are told to proceed as follows: "The affirmative-action inventory is to be done by a *visual* survey [italics in original]. There *should not be a notation of any kind* as to ethnic background in either personnel records or permanent files. This is against the law. . . . Identification of Italian Americans will be done visually and by name. . . . Please remember, however, that each individual is to be listed in only one ethnic group."

The number of categories established on behalf of affirmative action, though at present finite, already betrays accordion-like expansibility. The affirmative-action program at San Francisco State College, typical of most, is now confined to six racial groups: Negroes; Orientals; other Non-Whites; persons of Mexican, Central or South American ancestry ("except those who have physical characteristics of Negro, Oriental, or other Non-White races"); Native Americans (American Indians); and All Others, " . . . including those commonly designated as Caucasian or White." All but the last

* Since HEW has divulged no reliable standards of its own, the well-intentioned administrator is like a worshiper of Baal, propitiating a god who may punish or reward, but who is silent.

† Self-designation is not always reliable. At Michigan, the amused or disgusted members of one of the university's maintenance crews all self-designated themselves as American Indians (bureaucratese: Native American); their supervisor was quietly asked to redesignate them accurately.

category are eligible for discriminatory preference.*

As the CUNY memorandum signals, however, this last category of "those commonly designated as Caucasian or White" is a Pandora's box inside a Pandora's box. Now that the Italians have escaped from it in New York, the lid is open for others—all the many different groups now fashionably known as "ethnics"—to do likewise. A farseeing administrator, even as under HEW's gun he hastily devises future-oriented hiring quotas ("goals") to muffle the noise of one or two squeaky wheels, might wonder how he will be able to gratify subsequent claimants on the dwindling capital of reserved quotas still at his disposal.

Yet the administrator, in practice, has no choice but to act on the "sufficient unto the day is the evil thereof" principle. HEW ultimata, when they come, are imperious and immediate. Thirty-day rectifications are in order. At Johns Hopkins, MIT, Columbia, Michigan, and the University of California, an acute agony arises from no such philosophical long-range speculations, but from how to put together attractive compliance reports fast enough to avoid the threatened withholding of vast funds, the closing-down of whole facilities, the dismissal of thousands of staff workers, and the irreparable damage done to important ongoing research, especially to laboratory experiments. Crocodile tears do flow, from the gimlet-eyes of HEW investigators, who observe these sufferings from distant federal offices. Even J. Stanley Pottinger recently noted, in appropriate Pentagonese, that the act of contract suspension at Berkeley, for instance, might constitute "overkill." Yet no sooner had he voiced this note of sadness than his regional compliance director recommended to Washington precisely such action.

9

While deans, chancellors, and personnel officials struggle with these momentous matters; faculties and graduate students with few exceptions are silent. HEW is acting in the name of social justice. Who in the prevailing campus atmosphere would openly challenge anything done in that name? Tenured faculty perhaps consult their private interests and conclude that whatever damage the storm may do to less-protected colleagues or to their

---

* One object of current discriminatory hiring practices at San Francisco State is to make the institution's nonacademic personnel ethnically mirror the population of the Bay Area.

job-seeking students, prudence suggests a posture of silence. Others perhaps, refusing to admit that contending interests are involved, believe that affirmative action is cost-free, and that all will benefit from it in the Keynesian long run. But someone will pay: namely very large numbers of white males who are among those distinguishable as "best qualified" and who will be shunted aside in the frantic quest for "disadvantaged qualifiables."

The inequities implied in affirmative action, and the concealed but real costs to individuals, would probably have had less damaging effects upon such highly skilled graduate students had they been imposed in the early 1960s. Then, the sky was the limit on the growth and the affluence of higher education. If a pie gets bigger, so may its slices enlarge; nobody *seems* to lose. Such is today not the case. The pie now shrinks. One West Coast state college, for example, last year alone lost nearly seventy budgeted faculty positions due to financial stringency. Yet this same college has just announced the boldest affirmative-action program in California higher education. "Decided educational advantages can accrue to the college," it said, "by having its faculty as well as its student body be more representative of the minority population of the area. *It is therefore expected that a substantial majority of all new faculty appointments during the immediate academic years will be from minorities, including women, until the underutilization no longer exists*." (Italics added.) Departments which refuse to play the game will have their budgets reviewed by university officials.

It is hard to say how widely such pernicious practices have been institutionalized in other colleges and universities. But were they to be generalized across the nation, one thing is certain: either large numbers of highly qualified scholars will pay with their careers simply because they are male and white, *or*, affirmative action will have failed in its benevolent purposes.

10

It seems superfluous to end this chronicle of woe with mention of another heavy cost—one not so immediately visible—in the forceful administration of affirmative-action hiring goals. This is that men will be less able to know, much less sustain, the professional standards by which they and others judge and are judged. An enthusiastic affirmative-action administrator recently in argument with a skeptical college president said, "Let's face it —you and I know there are a lot of lousy programs and a lot of shoddiness around here. Why object to this?" By such logic, one bad turn deserves another. Since more and more less and less qualified students may enter universities, why bother too much about the quality of the new faculty hired to teach them? It is an interesting reflex habit of some federal bureaucrats and politicians (when confronted with objections that affirmative action might, for instance, discriminate against well- or better-qualified persons) to draw rhetorical analogies to confute their critics on this score. Told that affirmative action might actually discriminate against white males, J. Stanley Pottinger of HEW simply replied, "That is balderdash. That is the biggest crock I have ever heard. It is the kind of argument one expects to hear from a backwoods cracker farmer."

Indeed, backwoods cracker farmers *are* making this argument—though for reasons other than those Pottinger had in mind, and which have much to do with the things great universities require in order to survive in their greatness. Consider what a white, third-year law student at a Southern university (self-designating himself disadvantaged but according to no currently approved norms) had to say with respect to his personal situation:

> The ability to think in the abstract is hard for a person with my cultural background and economic background. My parents were WASPS whose income barely exceeded the poverty level. My father is a Southern Baptist with a third-grade education. . . . My mother is a Southern Baptist also. . . . She can read and write but my father is illiterate.
>
> In the public schools I attended, memorization was always emphasized. At ——— University . . . during my first eight quarters at this law school no one has emphasized the ability to think in abstract terms. . . . I do not know if this type of education is good or bad, but I do know that all your time is spent taking notes and that there is no time for thought. . . . Regardless, the course has made me acutely aware of how fortunate I am to be an American. In no other country would I have been able to complete the requirements for a J.D. degree. My cultural and economic background would have prevented it. . . . My background also prevents me from answering a test like this in the manner you desire. But if I must answer, then I will. . . .
>
> There is another form of discrimination of which, I believe, I am a victim. As a non-member of a minority group I feel that I . . . [am] discriminated against constantly. The same admissions standards are not applied because a certain percentage of minority students must be admitted in each class regardless of their qualifications. My test score, undergraduate record, and my family (poor white) deny me admittance to Harvard because I am white. I do not say this in bitterness, but in observation of the current status of admission practices as I perceive them. . . .

Somebody, then, has to pay, when the principle of merit is compromised or replaced by preferential ethnic and sex criteria.

Who then wins? The beneficiaries of preference? The particular institution involved? Society as a whole? One may debate the answer to each of those questions, but one thing is certain: HEW wins. It wins, as Aaron Wildavsky has pointed out, because winning can be defined by internal norms. The box-score is of its own devising. To the extent that its goals are met and the body-count proves this, it wins. But then, where have we heard *that* before?

Thomas Sowell

"Affirmative Action" Reconsidered

Images and labels have taken the place of facts in the controversies surrounding so-called affirmative-action. Words like *quota, qualified,* and *underutilization* are flung about, and defined in strange and tortuous ways; and images are conjured up of either massive benefits conferred on blacks and females at the expense of white males, or cynical evasions of affirmative-action programs by employers whose discriminatory practices are ignored by inept or cowardly government agencies. For the academic world, there is the additional image of an "old-boy network," through which professors are hired by their cronies. But despite an abundance of horror stories, there has been pathetically little analysis establishing the general conditions in the academic world before or after affirmative action.

To make these intricate and emotionally charged issues manageable, it is necessary to (1) distinguish the basic concepts and legal rationale of affirmative action from the many specific laws, regulations, and practices that have developed under that label; (2) measure in some general terms the mag-

Source: The Public Interest (*Winter 1976*). *Reprinted by permission of the publisher, with footnotes omitted. A longer, more detailed version of this article appeared as a pamphlet published by the American Enterprise Institute for Public Policy Research, Washington, D.C.*

nitude and severity of the problem that was intended to be solved or ameliorated by affirmative-action programs; (3) consider the actual results achieved and general trends set in motion by such programs; and finally (4) weigh the implications of affirmative-action policies both for those directly affected and for the general society.

UNDOING THE PAST

The general principle behind affirmative action is that a court order to cease and desist from some discriminatory practice may not be sufficient to undo the harm already done, or even to prevent additional harm as the result of a pattern of events set in motion by the prior illegal activity. This general principle goes back much further than the civil-rights legislation of the 1960s, and extends well beyond questions involving ethnic minorities or women. In 1935, the Wagner Act prescribed affirmative action as well as cease-and-desist remedies against employers whose anti-union activities had violated the law. Thus, in the landmark Jones and Laughlin Steel case, which established the constitutionality of the Act, the National Labor Relations Board ordered the company not only to stop discriminating against those of its employees who were union members, but also to post notices to that effect in conspicuous places and to reinstate unlawfully discharged workers, with back pay. Had the company merely been ordered to cease and desist from economic (and physical) retaliation against union members, the *future* effect of its *past* intimidation would have continued to inhibit the free-choice elections guaranteed by the National Labor Relations Act.

Racial discrimination is another obvious area where merely to cease and desist is not enough. If a firm has engaged in racial discrimination for years, and has an all-white work force as a result, then simply to stop explicit discrimination will mean little as long as the firm continues to hire by word-of-mouth referrals of its current employees' friends and relatives. (Many firms hire in just this way, regardless of their racial policies.) Clearly, the area of racial discrimination is one in which positive or affirmative steps of *some kind* seem reasonable—which is not to say that the particular policies actually followed make sense.

Many different policies have gone under the general label of affirmative action, and many different organizations—courts, executive agencies, and even private organizations—have got involved in formulating or interpreting the meaning of that term. The conflicting tendencies and pressures of these various institutions have shifted the meaning of affirmative action and produced inconsistent concepts at the same time. There is no way to determine *the* meaning of affirmative action. All that can be done is to examine the particulars—the concepts, intentions, and actual effects.

In a society where people come from a wide variety of backgrounds and where some backgrounds have been severely limited by past discrimination, the very definition of equality of opportunity is elusive. For example, a seniority system in a company which previously refused to hire minority individuals means that present and future discrimination occurs because of past discrimination. A Court of Appeals decision struck down such a system on the grounds of its *current* discriminatory effect. In another case, the Supreme Court struck down a mental test for voters in a community with a long history of providing segregated and inferior education for Negroes. Again, the rationale was that the case involved *present* discrimination, considering the past behavior; but this case touches the crucial question of what to do when the effects of past discrimination are incorporated in the current capabilities of individuals. Is equal opportunity itself discriminatory under such circumstances? If so, is anything more than equality of treatment justifiable under the Fourteenth Amendment and corollary statutes and court rulings? As important as the question of whether a legal basis exists for any compensatory or preferential treatment is the question of who should bear the inevitable costs of giving some citizens more than equal treatment. A question may also be raised as to whether such treatment really serves the long-run interests of the supposed beneficiaries.

The legislative history of the Civil Rights Act of 1964 shows that many of these concerns and dilemmas were present from the outset. Senator Hubert Humphrey, in helping to steer this legislation through Congress, attempted to meet criticism by pointing out that the Act "does not require an employer to achieve any kind of racial balance in his work force by giving any kind of preferential treatment to any individual or group." He said that there must be "an intention to discriminate" before an employer can be considered in violation of the law, and that the "express requirement of intent" was meant to prevent "inadvertent or accidental" conditions from leading to "court orders." Senator Joseph Clark, another supporter, made it clear that the burden of proof was to be on the Equal Employment Opportunity Commission (EEOC) to "prove by a preponderance" that a "discharge or other personnel action was because of race." Clark added flatly: "Quotas are themselves discriminatory."

Congress also faced the difficult question of what to do about groups whose historic disadvantages left them in a difficult position to compete on tests with members of the general population. Senator Tower of Texas cited, as an example of what he was opposed to, a case in Illinois where a state agency had forced a company to abandon an ability test which was considered "unfair to 'culturally deprived and disadvantaged groups.'" Senator Case replied that "no members of the Senate" disagreed with Tower concerning such examples, and Senator Humphrey affirmed that such tests "are legal unless used for the purpose of discrimination." Humphrey rejected Tower's proposed explicit amendment on this point because he considered it redundant: "These tests are legal. They do not need to be legalized a second time." Senator Case characterized the actions of the Illinois state agency as an "abuse," and said that the Civil Rights Act did not embody "anything like" the principle involved in the Illinois case. Humphrey brushed aside the Illinois case as "the tentative action of one man," which he was sure the Illinois commission as a whole would "never" accept.

THE SHIFT IN THE BURDEN OF PROOF

Despite the clear congressional intent, expressed by both supporters and opponents of the Civil Rights Act of 1964, the actual administration of that law has led precisely in the direction which its sponsors considered impossible. The burden of proof has been put on those employers whose proportional representation of employees by race or sex is not satisfactory to federal agencies administering that law. The chairman of EEOC has demanded that employer witnesses at public hearings cite "the action taken to hire more minority people." The position of EEOC is that "any discussion of equal-employment-opportunity programs is meaningful only when it includes consideration of their results—or lack of results—in terms of actual numbers of jobs for minorities and women. . . . " Numbers and percentages are repeatedly invoked to show "discrimination" without any reference to individual cases or individual qualifications—with percentages below EEOC's expectations characterized as "exclusions" or "underutilization." The notion of qualified applicants has been expanded to mean "qualified people to train"—that is, people lacking the requirements of the job, whom the employer would have to pay to train. Contrary to the congressional debates, the burden of proof has been put on the employer to show the validity of tests used, and the notion of "tests" has been expanded to include job criteria in general, whether embodied in a test or not. As for employer intentions, a poster prepared by EEOC includes among ten true-or-false questions the statement: "An employer only disobeys the Equal Employment Opportunity laws when it is acting intentionally or with ill motive"—and the answer to that question is *false*. Despite Senator Humphrey's assurances about "express requirement of intent," legal action can be taken on the basis of "inadvertent or accidental" conditions.

EEOC is only one of many federal agencies administering the Civil Rights Act in general or the "affirmative action" programs in particular. There are overlapping jurisdictions of the Labor Department, the Department of Health, Education, and Welfare (HEW), the Justice Department, the EEOC, and the federal courts. There are also regional offices of all these agencies, which vary significantly in their respective practices. Moreover, when one federal agency approves—or requires—a given practice, following such an approved course of action in no way protects an employer from being sued, on the grounds of following that very same course of action, by another federal agency or by private individuals. Indeed, federal agencies have sued one another under this Act.

Parallel to this development of the interpretation of the Civil Rights Act, and more significant for higher education, has been the elaboration of an Executive Order requiring "affirmative action" by federal contractors. This order is enforced by different federal agencies under the general supervision of the Labor Department. For higher education, the regulating agency is HEW.

The courts have not gone so far as the administrative agencies have in forcing numerical "goals and timetables" on employers. Such numerical specifications have typically been invoked by the court only where there has been demonstrable discrimination—not simply "wrong" racial proportions—by the particular employer in question: They are a "starting point in the process of shaping a remedy" for "past discriminatory hiring practices" by the employer to whom the court order applies. In the landmark *Griggs vs. Duke Power Company* case, the Supreme Court included the company's past racial discrimination as a reason that the company could not use tests which eliminated more black job applicants than white job applicants and had no demonstrated relationship to actual job performance. In general, the courts have rejected the notion that "any person be hired simply because he was formerly the subject of discrimination, or because he is a member of a minority group. . . ."

Legal remedies under the Civil Rights Act and related executive orders range from cease-and-desist orders, through individual reinstatement or group preferential hiring, to the cutting off of all federal contracts to the offending employer. The latter is a virtual sentence of death to any leading research university, whether public or private, for they are all dependent upon federal money to maintain their competitive standing, and will sustain a massive loss of top faculty without it.

DISCRIMINATION IN ACADEMIA

There is little real question that if one goes back a number of years one finds a pervasive pattern of discrimination against minorities in academic employment. This applies not only to blacks and other minorities regarded as disadvantaged, but also to Jews, who were effectively excluded from many leading university faculties before World War II. The situation with respect to women is somewhat more complicated and will be deferred for the moment. However, the question that is relevant to affirmative-action programs for both minorities and women is what the situation was at the onset of such programs and how the situation has changed since.

While colleges and universities were subject to the general provisions of the Civil Rights Act of 1964 and to subsequent executive orders authorizing cancellation of federal contracts for noncompliance, the *numerical-proportions* approach dates from the Labor Department's 1968 regulations as applied to academic institutions by HEW. More detailed requirements—including a written affirmative-action program by each institution—were added in 1971. The Revised Order No. 4 contains the crucial requirement that to be "acceptable" an institution's "affirmative action program must include an analysis of areas where the contractor is deficient in the utilization of minority groups and women" and must establish "goals and timetables" for increasing such "utilization" so as to remedy these "deficiencies."

For purposes of establishing a chronology, 1971 may be taken as the beginning of the application of numerical "goals and timetables" to the academic world. The question thus becomes: What were the conditions in academic employment, pay, and promotions as of that date? With respect to minorities in general, and blacks in particular as the largest minority, *virtually nothing* was known about these crucial matters at that point. Assumptions and impressions abounded, but the first national statistical study of black academic salaries was not published until the spring of 1974 by Professor Kent G. Mommsen of the University of Utah. *In short, affirmative-action programs were going full blast for years before anyone knew the dimensions of the problem to be solved.*

Nevertheless, it is relatively easy to find out what the situation is in academic employment, for the academic profession is unique in the mountains of statistical data that exist giving detailed information on crucial career factors for individuals. It is a relatively straightforward process to match individuals of similar characteristics—as regards degrees, research publications, experience, and so forth—and to determine what pay and promotions differences there are by race or sex. Moreover, each of the major academic fields has long-established ratings of its own departments across the country, so that the crucial *qualitative* dimension of an individual's training or of the employing department can be gauged much more easily than in most other occupations. The American Council on Education (ACE) has made massive surveys covering all these factors, with samples of more than 50,000 academics each, in 1968-69 and in 1972-73—perfect for a "before" and "after" look at the effects of employment "goals and time-tables," which were established in 1971 for colleges and universities. In addition, the National Science Foundation (NSF) and the National Academy of Sciences (NAS) have similarly massive samples of data on holders of doctoral degrees, going back for more than a decade. In short, it is easy to get the facts about academics—for those who want the facts, instead of the overheated rhetoric and indignant posturing that have become standard procedure in the controversy concerning affirmative action in academia.

THE SITUATION "BEFORE"

What was the situation in academia that the employment goals and timetables of 1971 were designed to correct? Blacks as a group earned less than whites as a group, and women as a group earned less than men as a group—and both minorities and women were a smaller percentage of the academic profession than of the general population. Thus far, everyone can agree on the facts. But when seeking *reasons* for these facts, different observers split into warring camps. But there are innumerable facts on file to permit matching individuals on the crucial variables of an academic career, in order to determine how much of the gross racial or sex differentials in employment, pay, and promotion are due to different career characteristics and how much to employer discrimination against equally qualified individuals.

A mere glance at academic career characteristics shows vast differences between blacks or women and the rest of the profession. Blacks or female academics have a Ph.D. less than half as often as the rest of the profession, publish less than half as many articles per person, and specialize in the lowest-paying fields—notably education, the social sciences, and the humanities, with very few being trained in the natural sciences, medicine, or law, or other highly paid specialties. Even if no employer had a speck of prejudice, black and female academics would still have lower pay and promotion prospects. But in the real world, where prejudice obviously exists, how much concrete difference remains when the career characteristics are the same?

Academic salaries in 1969-70 for black academics with a Ph.D. in the natural and social sciences averaged exactly $62 a year below that of all doctorates in these fields. This was before "goals and timetables" were applied to colleges and universities, and makes *no* allowance for the different distribution of black academics by field. On a field-by-field basis, black academics earned *more* than doctorates as a whole. Earlier data for doctorates in education and the humanities showed whites earning more in the former and blacks earning **more** in the latter.

Table I. *Race Differences Before Affirmative Action (1969-70 Mean Academic Year Salaries of Doctorates)*

Field	All Doctorates	Black Doctorates	Black Differential
Biological Sciences	$16,000	$16,044	+$ 44
Physical Sciences	$16,466	$16,558	+$ 92
Social Sciences	$15,440	$18,043	+$2,603
Total	$16,500	$16,438	-$ 62

Source: Kent G. Mommsen, "Black Doctorates in American Higher Education," *Journal of the Social and Behavioral Sciences*, Spring 1974, p. 106.

This does not prove the purity of the academic soul. The situation that existed just before affirmative action was the result of more than a decade of civil-rights legislation, demonstrations, and changes in American public opinion. Affirmative action, however, must be judged against the background of the situation that actually existed when numerical goals and timetables were applied to colleges and universities in 1971, not against the background of virtually total exclusion of blacks from leading academic institutions a generation earlier. Some proponents of affirmative action persistently make comparisons with that earlier era, as if all the antidiscrimination forces of the 1960s had never existed.

The issue of equal representation is a little more complicated than the issue of equal pay, and the case of women is somewhat different from that of minorities—but the end results are equally clear-cut. If representation in academic employment is measured against the qualified supply, everything depends upon how *qualified* is defined. Taking the standard academic requirement of a Ph.D. for a long-term career as a tenured professor (though non-Ph.D.'s fill many nontenured positions), both blacks and women are *over*represented among academics. Women hold about 10 percent of all Ph.D.'s, but are more than 20 percent of the academics. Blacks hold less than 1 percent of the Ph.D.'s, but are more than 2 percent of the academics. These figures are, of course, nowhere near the population proportions for either group, nor are they any reason for complacency, but they do suggest that the *cause* of underrepresentation is not necessarily employer discrimination. (The complex social processes behind the figures reach back well before the date when the statistics were collected, and extend well beyond the institution at which they were collected.)

Although minorities and women are often lumped together, it is very questionable to lump even minorities together. Orientals have very different patterns from blacks, and women are quite different from either. The crucial variable for academic women's careers is marriage. Single academic women with a Ph.D. achieve the rank of full professor more often than do other academics with similar years of experience—though married female Ph.D.'s achieve that rank far less frequently. This was true *before* affirmative action. Moreover, the average 1968-69 academic-year salary of full-time female academics who were never married was slightly *higher* than that of males who were never married (Table II). Indeed a number of measures and indicators show that the basic difference in pay and promotion was between married women and all other persons. The gross "male" versus "female" comparisons are lopsided largely because married women (and especially married women with children) drag down the averages of other women.

It is not difficult to understand why married female academics fall so far behind others. Innumerable surveys show that (1) married academic women put more time than married academic men into the home and family; (2) the geographical location of academic couples is usually determined by the husband's career prospects, with little concern for how this affects the wife's career; and (3) women interrupt their careers more often than men, usually

Table II. *Sex Differentials Before Affirmative Action (1968-69 Mean Academic-Year Salary, All Academic)*

	Male Academics	Female Academics	Female/Male Salary Percentage
Never married	$11,070	$11,523	104%
Presently married	$13,562	$10,264	76%
Divorced, widowed, etc.	$15,065	$13,176	88%

Source: American Council on Education.

for childbearing or other reasons related to the needs of others. Surveys of academics show that men and women both overwhelmingly agreed that marriage advances a man's career and retards a woman's. Income statistics confirm these beliefs: While academic women who never married have an edge over their male counterparts, married academic men have a huge advantage over married female academics. The situation averages out to a "male" advantage over "females," but this average conceals more than it reveals. What it conceals is that (1) people who are independent do about the same in the academic world, regardless of sex; (2) people with help (married men) do much better; and (3) those who are doing the helping (married women) do worst of all in their own careers. Such a situation may not be just —but it does not result, however, from employer discrimination.

There are some further indications that the location of the problem is the home rather than the workplace: low marriage rates and high divorce rates among academic women. Academic women are married less frequently than academic men and divorced several times as often. This tendency reflects more than the general problem for women of combining a career with marriage. Nonacademic female Ph.D.'s have higher marriage rates than academic female Ph.D.'s, as do women in other professions. The academic profession is unique not only in the Darconian "publish or perish" rule, which demands great amounts of time for research, but also in the geographical isolation of most top research universities. The demands of continuous research are an obvious strain on whoever assumes the primary responsibility for maintaining domestic life—the wife, in most cases. The geographical isolation is a less obvious but very potent force, as well. An academic woman whose husband teaches at Cornell will not have an equally prestigious institution available as a potential employer within a radius of two hundred miles (for UCLA the comparable figure would be four hundred miles). So her career faces a major setback, barring the happy coincidence that the same institution has an opening for her at the same time that it has one for him—unless her husband considers her career equally important in deciding where to locate, which may be an even more unlikely circumstance. If she resigns herself to working at a less prestigious institution nearby, she may be accepting not only a lower salary but also a lesser prospect of developing her own abilities in the environment that such growth requires. While Cornell or UCLA may be unusually isolated, it is rare to have several top-rated research universities within commuting distance of one another. The result is that a married academic woman, equally qualified with her husband, is going to be underutilized unless the couple agree to alternate, or somehow share, the inherent disadvantages of their professional situation—or unless a coincidence rescues them from some hard choices.

THE SITUATION "AFTER"

What drastic changes have been wrought by affirmative action in the academic world to result in the great outpourings of words and emotions? Practically none, as far as the pay, employment, or promotions of women and minorities are concerned. The ACE data show that blacks were 2.1 percent of academics in 1968-69 and 2.9 percent in 1972-73, while women were 19.1 percent in 1968-69 and 20.0 percent in 1972-73. These are hardly revolutionary changes. Later data from studies also show very little change.

Neither are there dramatic changes in the salaries of minorities or women relative to other members of the academic profession. A tabulation of ACE data shows a black/white salary differential of $640 per year for academic year 1972-73 in favor of whites ($16,677 versus $16,037); but blacks usually earn slightly more than whites on a field-by-field basis, with degrees and publications held constant. This is very similar to the statistical results before affirmative action. For women, NAS data show that full-time, continuously employed female doctorates in the natural sciences and the social sciences earn identical percentages of the incomes of male doctorates in these fields in 1970 and in 1973.

What is a drastic change is that the *process* of academic hiring has become a bureaucratic nightmare, regardless of who ends up being hired. A university's affirmative-action report to the government typically weighs several pounds—and may still be rejected for not being detailed enough! The University of Michigan spent $350,000 for compiling statistics alone. HEW prescribes elaborate and arbitrary formulas for determining the available supply of qualified applicants—formulas which defy economics, statistical theory, or logic. Moreover, the long-standing practice of having a professor's qualifications judged by other specialists in his field is increasingly being over-turned by academic administrators who now either take the decision out of the hands of academic departments or put the departments under heavy pressure to act in a way that will preserve the institution's access to federal money. This need not involve hiring a minority or female faculty member—and usually does not, as the statistics indicate—but does involve a legalistic and bureaucratic manner of recruiting, screening, and evaluating candidates in order to generate enough paperwork to show "good faith efforts" to meet numerous goals and timetables for minority and female employment. These charades take the place of meeting quotas which no one seriously expects to be met. For example, if American colleges and universities were to hire every black Ph.D. in the United States, active or retired (or indeed, living or dead)—a 100 percent drain from industry, government, and other institu-tions—the result would still be less than three black faculty members per institution. Given the hard facts of the situation, it is not surprising that colleges and universities do not fulfill their employment goals, but instead go through a costly and demoralizing process called "good-faith efforts"—a process equally embittering to supporters and opponents of affirmative action. This produces few jobs and much anguish.

An additional source of bitterness is the current academic retrenchment in hiring, brought on by financial conditions. This retrenchment means that many aspiring academics would necessarily have had their career hopes dis-appointed, regardless of affirmative action. Now, when a hundred white male applicants are rejected, they can all blame it on one or two minority or female academics who were hired—even though over 90 percent of the white males could not have been hired anyway, and there are probably ten or twenty other white males hired for the one or two "affirmative action" professors. But administrators can, of course, *tell* rejected applicants that they lost out because of affirmative action, whether it is true or not, because that may be easier than telling them the real reasons. Again, the situation has high potential for [creating] bitterness for both the supporters and the opponents of affirmative action.

QUALIFICATIONS

Among the many crudities of the affirmative-action program is the notion of "qualified" applicants. Given the enormous range of standards among the thousands of American colleges and universities, virtually anyone who has been to graduate school is "qualified" to teach somewhere, while only a small fraction of the Ph.D.'s are qualified to teach at the top institutions. In the real world, the question of qualifications is the question whether an individual's career characteristics—degrees, publications, and so forth—match those sought by the employing institution. If a university does not hire someone, that does not mean either that the candidate is "unqualified" to be in the profession or that the university is being unreasonable or discriminatory. But, obvious as this is, the government defines "underutilization" as the existence of a lower representation of a given group among employees than the representation of that same group in the "available" supply of "qualified" people. Moreover, the meaning of *qualified* has been stretched to mean "qualified to be trained," and the "available" supply includes women who no longer work (usually because of their husbands' prosperity).

The government's crude concept of a pool of "qualified" individuals overlooks the basic fact that academic departments in general do not hire faculty in general. Departments hire specialists in different areas of their respective fields. An economics department will seldom be in the market for "an economist" or even a "qualified" economist. They will be looking for an international-trade theorist familiar with econometrics, or a labor economist knowledgeable about manpower-training programs. Statistics on the racial or sex composition of the economics profession are irrelevant. Women, for example, are distributed very differently among the specialties in economics than are their male counterparts. What matters is the pool of qualitatively comparable people in the specialty, which may be only a half-dozen for any given department at a given time. Schools at the top of the prestige rankings are unlikely to have even this many candidates usually available to move at a given time—although hundreds lacking the qualifications may submit resumes if the position is advertised. Moreover, it will be virtually impossible to draw up in advance a list of vacancies to be filled in the years ahead—as the government would like—for that means predicting which members of a department are likely to leave.

THE "OLD-BOY NETWORK"

Universities have long relied on the expertise of their respective departments in gauging job qualifications, rather than have administrators pretend to be experts on every field from art to zoology. The department, in turn, often has had to canvass the opinions of trusted colleagues at other institutions to develop a balanced assessment of candidates or to suggest likely prospects. Since no one department is in touch with the thousands of other kindred departments in the country, each is limited in its information network to a relative handful of similar departments for candidates about whom it can get the kind of detailed and reliable information it wants. This situation has led to charges of an "old-boy network," through which jobs are given to cronies, and in particular to the charge that minorities and women, as outsiders, are institutionally disadvantaged by the very existence of the network. As in so much of the affirmative-action controversy, however, in this charge there is a premium on rhetoric, preconceptions, and insinuations, and a virtual moratorium on facts.

Two considerations must be separated: (1) the necessity and value of the informal communications network as a recruiting channel in general, and (2) the extent to which minorities and women are outside this network. The first is a large subject in itself. Long before affirmative action, there were numerous attempts to replace the informal networks with a more rational system of academic hiring—with *rational* being used here in the usual sense of something plausible to those unfamiliar with the intricacies of the situation. It is significant that all these attempts at rational hiring systems failed miserably, in terms of the reported dissatisfaction of both employers and employees and their observable unwillingness to continue investing time in alternative systems. The more relevant question for affirmative action is whether minority and female academics are outside the recruiting channels, which are used especially frequently by top-rated academic institutions, and which are especially important at the beginning of an individual's academic career—before there has been time to establish a scholarly reputation independent of this informal network. The fact is that women receive their Ph.D.'s at the top universities—*within* the "old-boy network"—a higher percentage of the time than men. A comprehensive survey by Professor Mommsen found the same to be true of blacks, with more than half of all black Ph.D.'s coming from just ten universities (mostly top-ranked institutions), compared to 37 percent of all white Ph.D.'s being products of the ten most frequent Ph.D.-granting institutions. The ACE sample, with different definitions, indicates that a higher percentage of white academics than of black academics received their Ph.D.'s from top-ranked institutions (29 percent versus 22 percent). In any case, the hard facts show nothing like the exclusion of women and blacks from the "old-boy network" suggested by the prevailing rhetoric. It is significant that the purveyors of such rhetoric have found it unnecessary to supply any supporting evidence.

THE PROBLEMS OF MINORITIES

With all the caveats about "qualifications," it is still useful to get a general view of the career characteristics of minorities and women. The ACE data permit the inclusion of Orientals, so that *minority* need not be synonymous with *black* as it so often is, because of relatively more abundant statistics on the black population compared with Mexican-American, Puerto Ricans, American Indians, and other ethnic minorities.

The data in Table III show both the salary edge of white academics over blacks, and also the *reason* for that edge—a different distribution among various qualification brackets, rather than an edge within those brackets themselves. Blacks, in fact, have the salary edge over whites within three out of the four brackets. These statistics also undermine the belief that "incompetent" blacks are generally earning "exorbitant" academic salaries because of affirmative action. Actually it is the most-qualified blacks who have the greatest edge over their white counterparts, while the least-qualified blacks do not earn as much as the least qualified whites. This is even more apparent when these statistics are further broken down according to publication

Table III. *Mean Academic-Year Salary (1972-73) of Full-Time Faculty*

	White Academics	Black Academics	Oriental Academics
"Distinguished" or "strong" Ph. D.	$17,991 (11%)	$20,399 (4%)	$18,235 (16%)
Lower-ranked Ph.D.	$17,414 (14%)	$19,014 (6%)	$17,035 (27%)
Unranked doctorate	$18,179 (12%)	$20,499 (8%)	$16,724 (17%)
Less than doctorate	$15,981 (62%)	$15,195 (82%)	$12,272 (41%)
All faculty	$16,677 (100%)	$16,037 (100%)	$15,419 (100%)

Source: American Council on Education.

records: Black academics who have published five or more scholarly articles average about $3,000 per year more than white academics who have published five or more scholarly articles, while black faculty who have published nothing earn slightly less than white faculty who have published nothing. Insofar as this is attributable to affirmative-action pressures, it suggests that that program has had its greatest financial impact on those blacks who needed it least.

The situation for Orientals is very different. Oriental faculty earn slightly less than black or white faculty, but are better qualified than either—whether measured by the percentage holding a Ph.D., the proportion of Ph.D.'s from top-rated departments, or the number of publications per person. More than 40 percent of all Oriental faculty had published five or more scholarly articles, compared with 31 percent for whites and 12 percent for blacks.

The case of Oriental faculty illustrates the pitfalls in trying to determine the level of discrimination from the amount of gross differentials. There are minor salary differentials among all three racial groups, but these small differentials represent substantial underpayment of Oriental faculty relative to others with the same qualifications in the same fields. Orientals are in the high-paying natural sciences to a greater extent than either blacks or whites, so that they would tend to have the highest salaries overall, if everyone were paid the same within each field. But Orientals are almost invariably the lowest paid, by two or three thousand dollars per year in every field for any given level of degree and any given number of articles published. For example, Orientals in the natural sciences with five or more articles published averaged $17,852 in salary in 1972-73, compared to $19,469 for whites and $20,640 for blacks with these same qualifications. In the humanities, Orientals with five or more articles earned nearly $2,000 a year less than blacks and nearly $4,000 a year less than whites with the same publication records. In the social sciences the Orientals with the most publications earned $4,000 per year less than whites with the same publication records. In the social sciences the Orientals with the most publications earned $4,000 per year less than whites and $8,000 less than blacks in the same category. In all three fields, Orientals had Ph.D.'s more often than blacks or whites, and had these Ph.D.'s from higher-ranked departments than the other two groups. In short, just as substantial pay differentials overall do not prove discrimination —because groups fall in different qualifications categories—so an absence of large gross differentials between groups does not prove an absence of discrimination, if one group has large unrewarded qualifications differentials.

The complications of marital status make it impossible to directly compare women with men in the same way. However, a further breakdown of the data already cited in Table II shows that "never married" women with publications earned slightly more ($293 annually) than "never-married" men in top-rated institutions, and slightly less ($114 annually) in other institutions; and "never married" women without publications in unranked institutions earned a hefty 45 percent more than "never married" men in the same category. This lends support to the belief that many able women end up in non-research institutions because they prefer teaching, and are therefore superior to the men who more often end up in such places simply beause they could not do better. It also indicates that when women do better than men, they get paid more than men.

The preference of women for teaching over research is not only significant in itself, it also highlights the crucial element of individual *choice*, which is routinely ignored in syllogistic arguments that go directly from statistical "under-representation" to "exclusion" or "discrimination." Blacks, too, exercise individual preference and choice. The Mommsen study found that black faculty were unwilling to move from their present positions— mostly in black colleges—for less than a $6,000-per-year raise. They are hardly standing with their noses pressed against the windows of universities from which they are "excluded."

THE NEGATIVE EFFECTS

If the affirmative-action program was merely inane, futile, and costly, it might deserve no more attention than other government programs of the same description. But it has side effects which are negative in the short run and perhaps poisonous in the long run. While doing little or nothing to advance the position of minorities and females, it creates the impression that the hard-won *achievements* of these groups are *conferred* benefits. Especially in the case of blacks, this means *perpetuating* racism instead of allowing it to die a natural death or to fall before the march of millions of people advancing on all economic fronts in the wake of equal-opportunity laws and changing public opinion. During the 1960s—*before* affirmative action—black incomes in the United States rose at a higher rate than white incomes. So, too did the proportion of blacks in college and in skilled and professional occupations— and along with this came a faster decline in the proportion of black families below the poverty line or living in substandard housing. When people ask why blacks cannot pull themselves up the way other oppressed minorities have in the past, many white liberals and black spokesmen fall right into the trap and rush in to offer sociological explanations. But there is nothing to explain. The fact is that blacks have pulled themselves up—from further down, against stronger opposition—and show every indication of continuing to advance.

While this advance is the product of generations of struggle, it accelerated at an unprecedented pace in the 1960s, once the worst forms of discrimination had been outlawed and stigmatized. Black income as a percentage of white income reached its peak in 1970—the year *before* numerical goals and timetables. That percentage has gone down since. What affirmative action has done is to destroy the legitimacy of what had already been achieved, by making all black achievements look like questionable accomplishments, or even outright gifts. Here and there, this program has undoubtedly caused some individuals to be hired who would otherwise not have been hired—but even that is a doubtful gain in the larger context of attaining self-respect and the respect of others.

The case of women is different in many factual respects, but the principle is the same. Unfortunately, there is much fictitious "history" used to apply the "minority" concept to women. The fact is that women were a higher proportion of college faculty, Ph.D.'s, M.D.'s, people in *Who's Who*, and so forth, generations ago than they are today—and female incomes in the nation as a whole were a higher percentage of male incomes then than they are now. While many factors may have influenced their relative decline over the decades, that long decline parallels a rise in marriage rates among educated women and a rising birth rate among women in general—the population explosion—and the recent upturn for women has followed a reversal in these trends that had tied them to domesticity. In the case of women, as in the case of minorities, this all happened *before* affirmative action and its numerical goals and timetables. Their achievements were also made to look like the government's gift.

Who were the gainers from affirmative-action quotas? Politically, the Nixon administration, which introduced the program, gained by splitting the ethnic coalition that had elected liberal Democrats for decades. Blacks and Jews, for example, were immediately at each other's throats, after having worked together for years on civil-rights legislation and other sociopolitical goals. Whether the architects of Watergate had any such Machiavellian design in mind is a question on which each can speculate for himself. Certainly, the clearest continuing beneficiaries are the bureaucrats who acquired power, appropriations, and publicity from their activities, and who have stretched the law far beyond any congressional intent. Nothing in the Civil Rights Acts or the executive orders authorizes quotas by any name, and both the congressional debates and the specific language of the law forbid them. But the boldness of the various agencies who interpret and administer affirmative action, and the reluctance of courts to overrule administrative agencies, has permitted the growth of an administrative empire serving itself in the name of serving the disadvantaged.

The semantic evasions and political zigzags which have marked the evolution of affirmative-action programs are symptomatic of the confused thinking that exists in this area. Central to this confusion is a failure to understand the tragic situation of disadvantaged groups—tragic both in the sense of involving unhappy circumstances and in the classical sense of involving a genuine conflict of rights, not merely a conflict between the "good guys" and the "bad guys."

Nathan Glazer

The Emergence of an American Ethnic Pattern

In the middle of the last decade, we in the United States seemed to have reached a national consensus as to how we should respond to the reality of racial and ethnic-group prejudice and racial and ethnic-group difference. Almost simultaneously, we began to move away from that consensus into new divisions and a new period of conflict and controversy. The consensus was marked by three major pieces of legislation: the Civil Rights Act of 1964, the Voting Rights Act of 1965, and the Immigration Act of 1965. Following the passage of the Civil Rights and Voting Rights acts, the federal government intervened firmly in the South to end the one-hundred-year resistance of the white South to full political, civil, and social equality for blacks, insofar as this resistance was embodied in law and public practice. The passage of the Immigration Act of 1965 marked the disappearance from federal law of crucial distinctions on the basis of race and national origin. The nation agreed with this act that there would be no effort to control the future ethnic and racial character of the American population and rejected the claim that some racial and ethnic groups were more suited to be Americans than others.

Source: Chapter 1 of Affirmative Discrimination: *Ethic Inequality and Public Policy.* ©*1975 by Nathan Glazer, Basic Books, Inc. Reprinted by permission of the publisher.*

In the phrase reiterated again and again in the Civil Rights Act of 1964, no distinction was to be made in the right to vote, in the provision of public services, the right to public employment, the right to public education, on the ground of "race, color, religion, or national origin." Paradoxically, we then began an extensive effort to record the race, color, and (some) national origins of just about every student and employee and recipient of government benefits or services in the nation; to require public and private employers to undertake action to benefit given groups; and school systems to assign their children on the basis of their race, color, and (some) national origins. This monumental restructuring of public policy to take into account the race, color, and national origin of individuals, it is argued by federal administrators and courts, is required to enforce the laws against discrimination on these very grounds. It is a transitional period, they say, to that condition called for in the Constitution and the laws, when no account at all is to be taken of race, color, and national origin. But others see it as a direct contradiction of the Constitution and the laws, and of the consensus that emerged after a long struggle in the middle 1960s . . . .

. . . The first step is to try to characterize and understand the consensus of the middle 1960s. This is not to be understood as an historically new response to the unprecedented events of those years—the vicious resistance in great parts of the South to the efforts of blacks to practice their political rights, the South's resistance to school desegregation, the shocking assassination of a president identified with the hopes of suppressed minority groups. It is to be understood rather as the culmination of the development of a distinctive American orientation to ethnic difference and diversity with a history of almost two hundred years. That orientation was shaped by three decisions. They were not taken all at once, or absolutely, or in full consciousness of their implications, but the major tendencies of American thought and political action have regularly given their assent to them.

The three decisions were:

First, the entire world would be allowed to enter the United States. The claim that some nations or races were to be favored in entry over others was, for a while, accepted, but it was eventually rejected. And once having entered into the United States—and whether that entry was by means of forced enslavement, free immigration, or conquest—all citizens would have equal rights. No group would be considered subordinate to another.

Second, no separate ethnic group was to be allowed to establish an independent polity in the United States. This was to be a union of states and a nation of free individuals, not a nation of politically defined ethnic groups.

Third, no group, however, would be required to give up its group character and distinctiveness as the price of full entry into the American society and polity.

There is of course an inevitable breathtaking arrogance in asserting that *this* has been *the* course of American history. It would be almost equally breathtaking to assert that *any* distinctive course can be discerned in the history of the shaping of the American people out of many different stocks. It is in part an act of faith to find any *one* course that the development of American society has in some way been reaching toward. It smacks of the unfashionable effort to give a "purpose," a direction, to history. Certainly this direction is not to be thought of as some unconscious immanent tendency continuing to reveal itself in American history. Direction in history is taken only in the concrete actions of men and of groups of men. Those actions in the United States have included—in direct conflict with the large direction I have described—the enslavement of the Negro, anti-immigrant and anti-Catholic movements that have arisen again and again in American life, the near extermination of the American Indian, the maintenance of blacks in a subordinated and degraded position for a hundred years after the Civil War, the lynching of Chinese, the exclusion of Oriental immigrants, the restriction of immigration from Southern and Eastern Europe, the relocation of the Japanese and near confiscation of their property, the resistance to school desegration, and so forth. If we are to seek a "direction" in American history that defines a distinctive approach to the relationship of the various ethnic groups that make up American society, the sequence of events just listed might well be made the central tendency of American history. Many current writers and scholars would have it so: They argue that racism defines our history—racism directed against blacks, Indians, Mexican-Americans, Puerto Ricans, Filipinos, Chinese, Japanese, and some European ethnic groups. Many would have it that even the last ten years should be interpreted as a losing battle against this racism, now evident in the fact that colleges and universities resist goals and targets for minority hiring, that preferential admissions to professional schools are fought in the courts, that the attempt to desegregate the schools in the North and West has now met a resistance extremely difficult to overcome, that housing for poor and minority groups is excluded from many suburbs.

I think this is a selective misreading of American history: that the American polity has instead been defined by a steady expansion of the definition of those who may be included in it to the point where it now includes all humanity; that the United States has become the first great nation that defines itself not in terms of ethnic origin but in terms of adherence to common rules of citizenship; that no one is now excluded from the broadest access to what the society makes possible; and that this access is combined with a considerable concern for whatever is necessary to maintain group identity and loyalty. This has not been an easy course to shape or maintain, or to understand. There have been many threats to this complex and distinctive pattern for the accommodation of group difference that has developed in American society. The chief threats in the past were, on the one hand, the danger of a permanent subordination of certain racial and ethnic groups to others, of the establishment of a caste system in the United States; and on the other hand, the demand that those accepted into American society become Americanized or assimilated, and lose any distinctive group identity. The threat of the last ten years to this distinctive American pattern, however, has been of quite another sort. The new threat that followed the most decisive public actions ever taken to overcome subordination and caste status was that the nation would, under the pressure of those recently subordinated to inferior status, be permanently sectioned on the basis of group membership and identification, and that an experiment in a new way of reconciling a national polity with group distinctiveness would have to be abandoned. Many did not and do not see this latter possibility as any threat at all, but consider it only the guarantee and fulfillment of the commitment of American society to admit all peoples into full citizenship. They see the threat to a decent multigroup society rising from quite another direction: the arrogance and anger of the American people, specifically those who are descended from colonists and earlier immigrants, aroused by the effort to achieve full equality for all individuals and all groups. The prevailing understanding of the present mood is that those who have their share—and more— want to turn their backs on the process that is necessary to dismantle a caste society in which some groups are held in permanent subordination. I think this is a radical misreading of the past few years. . . .

. . . If the history of American society in relationship to many of the groups that make it up is not a history of racism, what is it? How do we define an emergent American attitude toward the problem of the creation of one nation out of many peoples?

I have suggested there were three major decisions—decisions not taken at any single point of time, but taken again and again throughout the history —which defined this American distinctiveness. The first was that all should be welcome and that the definition of America should be a political one, defined by commitment to ideals, and by adherence to a newly created or freshly joined community defined by its ideals, rather than by ethnicity. Inevitably "American" did come to denote an "ethnicity," a "culture," something akin to other nations. A common life did create a common culture, habits, language, a commonness which parallels the commonness of other nations with their more primordial sense of commonness. But whereas all European and many Asian nations have grown out of a primordial group of long history, bound together by culture, religion, language, in the American case there was a continual struggle between the nation understood in these terms—terms akin to those in which the French, or English, or Germans understood themselves—and the nation understood in very different terms.

Yehoshua Arieli describes a number of ways in which a pattern of national identification has been achieved. In some cases, national identification is imposed by force; in others, it has grown gradually, and " . . . resulted from a long-established community of life, traditions, and institutions. . . . " But " . . . in the United States, national consciousness was shaped by social and political values which claimed universal validity and which were nevertheless the American way of life. Unlike other Western nations, America claimed to possess a 'social system' fundamentally opposed to and a real alternative to . . . "—and here I edit Arieli, but not against his meaning— " . . . [other social systems], with which it competed by claiming to represent the way to ultimate progress and a true social happiness." [1] These different terms in which American nationality defined itself consisted not only of the decisive revolutionary act of separation from England and self-definition as a separate nation. They also included for many of those who founded and helped define the nation the rejection of ethnic exclusivity.

Three writers to my mind have, in recent years, given the best definition of what it meant to found a nation in this way: Seymour Martin Lipset in *The First New Nation;* Hans Kohn in his book *American Nationalism: An Interpretive Essay;* and Yehoshua Arieli in *Individualism and Nationalism in American Ideology.*

Arieli argues forcefully that the American Revolution should *not* be seen as another uprising of an oppressed nation, but as an event whose main shapers presented it as significant for the world and all its peoples:

> All the attempts made by Americans to define the meaning of their independence and their Revolution showed an awareness that these signified more than a change in the form of government and nationality. Madison spoke of the American government as one which has "no model on the face of the globe." For Washington, the United States exhibited perhaps the first example of government erected on the simple principles of nature, and its establishment he con-

sidered as an era in human history. . . . John Adams was convinced that a greater question than that of American Independence "will never be decided among men."

For Jefferson, America was the proof that under a form of government in accordance "with the rights of mankind," self-government would close the circle of human felicity and open a "wide-spread field for the blessings of freedom and equal laws." Thomas Paine hailed the American Revolution as the beginning of the universal reformation of mankind and its society with the result "that man becomes what he ought." For Emerson, America was " . . . a last effort of the Divine Providence in behalf of the Human race."[2]

We might of course expect a second-generation sociologist, a scholar who found refuge here, and another refugee who has become a scholar in a newly founded democratic nation to respond to these claims, to reverberate to them, so to speak. We might also expect Jewish scholars to respond to these claims; for if the United States was very late in fulfilling its promise to blacks, Indians, Mexican-Americans, and others—that is, those of other races—it almost from the beginning offered an open field and freedom to those who practiced another religion. Can a more searching examination, however, sustain these claims? Could it not also be said that American independence and the establishment of a new country was little more than the assertion of the arrogance of British colonists, refusing to accept a moderate overseas government more solicitous of the rights of Indians and blacks than they were, insisting on taking the land from the Indians and on the right to import and hold black men as slaves, and eventually threatening their neighbors with imperial expansion?

Our history, indeed, included all this. Even the appropriation of the name "American" for the citizens of the United States is seen by our neighbors to the north and to the south as a symbol of arrogance. Yet other interpretations of this appropriation are possible. The Americans *did* accept as the name for themselves a name with no ethnic reference, a name even with no limited geographical reference (since the Americas include all the Western Hemisphere). One side of this self-naming may be seen as a threat to the rest of the Americas and as arrogance in ignoring their existence. But another side must also be noted: the rejection by this naming of any reference to English or British or any other ethnic or racial origins, thus emphasizing in the name itself the openness of the society to all, the fact that it was not limited to one ethnic group, one language, one religion.

Lipset argues that the American nation from the beginning established and defined its national identity on the basis of its decisive break, through revolution, with England, and, by extension, with the entire old world. This weakened the ethnic identification with England. Further, two values became dominant in American society and the shaping of American character, equality and achievement, and these values can be seen sharply marked in American society from the beginning of its independent political existence. [3] One point about these two values that I would emphasize is that, by their nature, they cannot remain ethnically exclusive. And the most far-sighted of the early leaders understood this. Thus, to quote Hans Kohn:

> Thomas Jefferson, who as a young man had opposed immigration, wished in 1817 to keep the doors of America open, "to consecrate a sanctuary for those whom the misrule of Europe may compel to seek happiness in other climes." ... This proclamation of an open port for immigrants was in keeping with Jefferson's faith in America's national mission as mankind's vanguard in the fight for individual liberty, the embodiment of the rational and humanitarian ideals of eighteenth century man.
>
> The American nation,

Hans Kohn continues, summarizing Jefferson's point of view:

> was to be a universal nation—not only in the sense that the idea which is pursued was believed to be universal and valid for the whole of mankind, but also in the sense that it was a nation composed of many ethnic strains. Such a nation, held together by liberty and diversity, had to be firmly integrated around allegiance to the American idea, an idea to which everyone could be assimilated for the very reason that it was a universal idea. To facilitate the process of integration, Jefferson strongly opposed the settlement of immigrants in compact groups, and advocated their wide distribution among the older settlers for the purpose of "quicker amalgamation." [4]

Of course, to one tradition we can oppose another. If Jefferson was positive about the immigration of other groups, Benjamin Franklin was suspicious. "For many years," Arieli writes, "he strenuously argued against the wisdom of permitting the immigration of non-English settlers, who 'will never adopt our language or customs anymore than they can acquire our complexion.'"[5] Undoubtedly, he was influenced by the substantial number of Germans in Pennsylvania, itself established as an open colony of refuge:

> This will in a few years [Franklin wrote] become a German colony: Instead of their Learning our Language, we must learn theirs, or live as in a foreign country. Already the English begin to quit particular Neighborhoods surrounded by

Dutch, being made uneasy by the Disagreeableness of dissonant Manners; and in time, Numbers will probably quit the Province for the same Reason. Besides, the Dutch under-live, and are thereby enabled to under-work and under-sell the English; who are thereby extremely incommoded, and consequently disgusted, so that there can be no cordial Affection or Unity between the two Nations.[6]

The themes are, of course, familiar ones: They were to be repeated for many groups more distant from the Anglo-American stock than the Germans, who were, after all, of related tongue and Protestant religion. And yet this was a private comment, to be set against a public one that, again to quote Kohn, "extolled Anglo-America as a place of refuge."[7]

There were two traditions from the beginning, traditions exemplified by different men and social groups, and carried in tension within the same men. Yet even to say there were two traditions makes the issue somewhat sharper than it could have been during the early history of the United States. After all, the very men who spoke about the equal rights of all men accepted slavery. If they spoke of the United States as a sanctuary for all, they clearly thought of men very like themselves who might be seeking it and were not confronted with the hard realities of men of very different culture, religion, and race taking up their offer. In addition, we must take account of the expansive rhetoric of a moment in which a nation was being founded. Yet stipulating all of these cautions, there was a development implied in the founding documents and ideas which steadily encouraged the more inclusive definitions of who was eligible to become a full participant in American life. In the Revolution and its aftermath, limitations on participation in public life by the propertyless, Catholics, and Jews were lifted. Waiting in the wings, so to speak, were other categories, implied in the founding principles. That some others waited for almost two centuries, and that their equality came not only because of founding principles but because of complex social and political developments is true; but the principles were there, exerting their steady pressure, and indeed even in 1975 much of the argument over how to define full quality for different groups revolves around a Constitution that dates to 1787.[8]

As Arieli puts it: "Whatever the impact of universal concepts on the American historical experience, the conservative and nativistic interpreters of American history, no less than their opponents, concede that American nationality has to be defined, at least to some degree, by reference to certain political and social concepts; that it is a way of life and an attitude which somehow represents ultimate social values. . . . "[9]

There is no Supreme Historian, sitting in heaven, who totes up the record and tells us which way the balance of history ran. One picks out a dominant theme, on the basis of one's experience as well as one's knowledge, and our choice is made, in part, on the basis of our hopes for the future as well as our experience. In the 1950s and 1960s men like Hans Kohn and Arieli wanted to emphasize the inclusive tradition; in the later 1960s and in the 1970s, many historians and other scholars want to show us the exclusive tradition. There is enough to choose from on both sides. We can quote Melville, writing in 1849:

> There is something in the contemplation of the mode in which America has been settled, that, in a noble breast, should forever extinguish the prejudices of national dislike. Settled by the people of all nations, all nations may claim her for their own. You cannot spill a drop of American blood without spilling the blood of the whole world. . . . We are not a narrow tribe of men with a bigoted Hebrew nationality—whose blood has been debased in the attempt to ennoble it, by maintaining an exclusive succession among ourselves. No; our blood is as the flood of the Amazon, made up of a thousand noble currents all pouring into one. We are not a nation, so much as a world. . . . On this Western Hemisphere all tribes and peoples are forming into one federal whole. . . .[10]

Or James Fenimore Cooper, writing in 1838:

> The great immigration of foreigners into the country, and the practice of remaining, or of assembling, in the large towns, renders universal suffrage doubly oppressive to the citizens of the latter. The natives of other countries bring with them the prejudices of another . . . state of society; . . . and it is a painful and humiliating fact, that several of the principal places of this country are, virtually, under the control of this class, who have few convictions of liberty. . . . Many of them cannot even speak the language of the land, and perhaps a majority of them cannot read the great social impact, by which society is held together.[11]

In certain periods, it seems clear, one voice or another was dominant. The uprising of the white South in the Civil War marked the most determined effort to change the pattern into one in which other races and groups, labeled inferior, were to be held in permanent subjection and subordination. A new justification was to be established for this "heresy," as Arieli dubs it— and in the American context, heresy it was. Justification was to be found in religion, in pragmatic necessity, in political theory, even surprisingly enough in Auguste Comte's new-founded science of sociology, which was drawn upon to show the superiority of slave labor to Northern, immigrant, free labor, and of a society founded on slavery to one founded on free immigration.[12]

> It is revealing that one great effort to avoid the conflict consisted of the rapid upsurge of the "American" party [the "Know-Nothings"] which labored to unite discordant political factions by making ethnic and religious loyalties the basis of national identification. It sought to substitute for traditional American values a nationalism of the Old World type based on common descent and religion, and thus to divert against the "foreigners" the antagonisms that existed among the native-born. Similarly, the theory of race which justified Negro slavery also aimed to create an identity between North and South on the basis of a common belief in white superiority and through territorial expansion. Yet the historical situation and the national tradition frustrated these efforts and turned the conflict between free and slaveholding states into a gigantic struggle over the nature of American social ideals.[13]

After early remarkable successes, the Know-Nothings disintegrated before the rise of the new Republican party, thus setting a pattern that other nativist movements were to follow again and again, such as the American Protective Association of the 1890s and the Ku Klux Klan of the 1920s— first a sudden upsurge that seemed to carry all before it, and then, equally suddenly, disintegration. The challenges to the central American pattern, brief and intense, were rapidly overtaken by the major tendency to a greater inclusiveness. The Know-Nothings disintegrated, and the South lost the war. The heresy was, for a while, extirpated.

In the wake of the Civil War, the great Southern heresy that had threatened the idea of American nationality as broadly inclusive seemed crushed. As John Higham writes of those postwar years:

> America had developed a fluid, variegated culture by incorporating alien peoples into its midst, and the experience had fixed in American thought a faith in the nation's capacity for assimilation. This faith, carrying with it a sense of the foreigner's essential identification with American life, expressed itself in a type of nationalism that had long offset and outweighed the defensive spirit of nativism. A cosmopolitan and democratic ideal of nationality made assimilation plausible to Americans. . . .
>
> The twin ideals of a common humanity and of equal rights continued in the 1870s and 1880s to foster faith in assimilation. Temporarily the tasks of post-war reconstruction even widened assimilationist ideals; for the Radical Republicans' effort to redeem the southern Negro, to draw him within the pale of the state, and to weld the two races into a homogeneous nationality discouraged emphasis on human differences. To James Russell Lowell, for example, just and equal treatment of black men meant simply an enlargement of the Christian mission which the United States had long performed in

bringing together the peoples of all nations in a common manhood. And Elisha Mulford, philosopher of Reconstruction, argued that the nation "is inclusive of the whole people. . . . There is no difference of wealth, or race, or physical condition, that can be made the ground of exclusion from it."[14]

But of course, new threats and new heresies were rising, and the United States was soon to enter a dark age in which the promise of an all-embracing citizenship and nationality, already a hundred years old, was, for a while, quite submerged. Indeed, the very New England elite who had refused to accept slavery and celebrated the open door themselves began to undergo a significant change as the flood of immigration poured into the country after the Civil War, a flood that became increasingly Jewish and Central and Eastern European as the century wore on. By the 1890s, a new criticism— which took many forms—of an inclusive idea of American citizenship was arising. The New England intellectuals, now displaced politically and culturally, no longer carried on the tradition of the American revolution. Having attacked the racist ideology of the South before the Civil War, many succumbed to a new, if milder, racism which placed the Anglo-Saxon or "Germanic" element of the American people at the apex of world evolution as the carriers of some special racial commitment to liberty and free government. On quite a different cultural level, waves of anti-Catholicism spread through the masses of white Protestant farmers and workers, peaking in the American Protective Association of the late 1880s and 1890s, which had as rapid a rise—and fall—as Know-Nothingism before the Civil War. Anti-Semitism for the first time appeared in the United States. Some scholars discern it in the Populist movement of the 1890s; some do not. But all recognize it in an increasing exclusivism of wealthy Eastern Americans in the same period. In the West, an anti-Chinese movement became virulent among the workingmen, and led to the first restriction of American immigration in 1882. By the end of the decade, the strongest and darkest thread of this skein of prejudice and discrimination dominated the rest as the modest gains of Reconstruction were swept aside in the South, Jim Crow laws were fastened on the free Negro, the last Negro representatives were swept from Congress, and a rigid caste system was imposed upon the black, by law in the South and custom in the North.[15]

Each thread of this complex pattern deserves full analysis, and in the present mood, in which the American past is being reviewed by scholars representing many oppressed groups, and in a time when many see the United States as the chief force of reaction in the world, each thread is receiving such analysis. For fifty years, between the 1890s and the 1930s, exclusivism was dominant. It affected many groups—blacks and Orientals, Jews and Catholics, Indians and Mexican-Americans—in many ways. One can at least explain some of the reasons for the reaction against admitting all people into the country and to full citizenship. People of position felt threatened by the incoming flood of immigrants. Workers and shopkeepers without stable positions also felt threatened, by the Chinese, the blacks, the Catholics, the immigrants, with the same fears that Franklin had expressed one hundred fifty years before over the Germans "under-living, under-selling, and under-working" the English. Those not in direct competition with the immigrant and the black felt the fears just as strongly, as we see in the case of the farmers, who tried to understand the sudden falls in price which threatened to destroy them, by resorting to a belief in dark plots by international financial forces. Fears do not justify prejudice, discrimination, and racism, but they help explain it. And the expansion of American society to include strangers from all over the world was not without its real losses as well as its imaginary fears.

Barbara Solomon has recorded the story of the New England intellectuals at the turn of the century. Earlier, they had supported free immigration as well as abolition. Thus, long before Emma Lazarus, James Russell Lowell delivered some verses quite reminiscent of her poem on the Statue of Liberty, in an ode delivered at Harvard in 1861. He spoke of the American nation as:

> She that lifts up the mankind of the poor,
> She of the open soul and open door,
> With room about her hearth for all mankind! [16]

And in an address delivered in 1878, Emerson wrote: "Opportunity of civil rights, of education, of personal power, and not less of wealth; doors wide open . . . invitation to every nation, to every race and skin, . . . hospitality of fair field and equal laws to all. Let them compete, and success to the strongest, the wisest, and the best." [17] By the end of the century, many had quite given up their faith in democracy and the equality of all peoples and had become enamored of the notion that American liberty sprang from German forests and could not be maintained by the flood of immigrants from Eastern and Southern Europe. (Of course, not all New England intellectuals took this course. Preeminently in opposition were Charles Eliot, President of Harvard—though not alas, his successor President Lowell —and William James. Eliot wrote in 1920: "I should like to be saved from loss of faith in democracy as I grow old and foolish. I should be very sorry to wind up as the three Adamses did. I shall not unless I lose my mind." [18] Essentially, what troubled the New England intellectuals who no longer followed the democratic faith of Emerson was the threat to American homogeneity, for a measure of homogeneity had indeed existed before the heavier floods of immigration had begun. In our presentday mood of easy analysis of American racism, we would argue that they were defending their economic, political, and social interests. But their economic interests were not threatened by immigration: Quite the contrary, the immigrants gave New England industry an important source of cheap labor. Their political interests were not threatened, for their local political domination had already been lost to the Irish immigrants when the flood of East Europeans and Italians began seriously to concern them in the 1890s. Indeed, these new immigrants offered them, perhaps, a chance to regain political power. Their social interests were not deeply involved, for there seemed little chance that the new immigrants would join them in polite society.

Where, then, did they feel threatened? They felt they were losing their country, that what they knew of as America was disappearing and becoming something else, and that American culture was going to be radically changed into something they would not recognize. Small-town life, country pleasures, certain forms of education, modes of recreation, characteristic tendencies in religion—this whole complex, they feared, was in danger. As we learn from Solomon's book, no crude or simple prejudice activated them. Many of the old New Englanders who favored immigration restriction were active in social work among the immigrants, and some were patrons of bright immigrant youths. But they did not want to see the American culture they knew go.

As one of them wrote, in a passage quoted by Horace M. Kallen: "We are submerged beneath a conquest so complete that the very name of us means something not ourselves. . . . I feel as I should think an Indian might feel, in the face of ourselves that were." [19] Henry James, returning to this country in 1907 after an absence of twenty-five years—he still considered himself an American—expressed this shock most vividly: "This sense of dispossession . . . haunted me so, I was to feel . . . that the art of beguiling or duping it became an art to be cultivated—though the fond alternative vision was never long to be obscured . . . of the luxury of some such close and sweet and *whole* national consciousness as that of the Switzer and the Scot." [20]

Toward the end of his life, William Dean Howells, who had enjoyed seeing French Canadians and Italians around Boston in the 1870s and had praised the Jewish immigrant writer Abraham Cahan, wrote a novel, *The Vacation of the Kelwyns,* subtitled *An Idyll of the Mid-1870s.* We are introduced to a New England landscape in the year of the centennial celebrations of 1876. Kelwyn, a university lecturer, is spending the summer with his family in a large Shaker family house, now empty. The New England countryside is slightly menacing that year with "tramps"—unemployed workers—and foreigners wander through it: a Frenchman with a trained bear, Italian organ grinders, some gypsies. Kelwyn bears no antipathy to them—quite the contrary, they enliven the scene, and, as he says, they cook better than the natives, and may help make life pleasanter. And yet, one feels an unutterable sadness over the passing of a peculiarly American civilization. The Shaker house is empty, and will never be filled again; the surviving Shakers have misguidedly furnished it for the Kelwyns with new furniture; the New England countryside is different from what it has been; and the year of the centennial—Howells seems to be saying—marks the passing of something simple and sweet in America. Indeed, the centennial itself involves deeper feeling in some of the characters in the book than we can imagine any national celebration since evoking.

In the North, exclusivism expressed itself in resistance to immigration from Eastern and Southern Europe and suspicion of immigrant settlements in the cities—of their habits, their culture, their impact on political life and on urban amenities. The Negroes were present—they always had been—but they were so few and so far down the social scale that they were scarcely seen as a threat to anything. In the South, exclusivism was directed primarily against the Negroes, though Catholics and Jews came in for their share of prejudice and, on occasion, violence. In the West, the Chinese and the Japanese were the main targets of a pervasive racism which included the Mexicans and the Indians.

The dismantling of this system of prejudice and discrimination in law and custom began in the 1930s. In the North, the ethnic groups created by the new immigration began to play a significant role in politics; and blacks, after the disenfranchisement of the 1890s, began again to appear in politics. The last mass anti-Catholic movement was the Klan's in the 1920s. It had a short life, and was in eclipse by the time Al Smith ran for president in 1928. Anti-Semitism had a longer life, but the war against Hitler ended with the surprising discovery that anti-Semitism, so strong in the thirties, was undergoing a rapid and unexpected deflation. And similarly with anti-Chinese and Japanese prejudice. The immigration restriction law of 1924 was modified to accept at least token numbers of people from all nations and races in 1952, and all elements of natural or racial preference were expunged in 1965.

Of course, the major bastion of race discrimination was the South, and the legal subordination of the Negro there remained firm throughout the 1930s and 1940s. But twenty years of liberal domination of national polities, by a coalition in which in Northern cities' blacks played an important role, finally made its effects felt in the administration of President Truman. The Armed Forces were desegregated, national demands for the enfranchisement of Southern blacks became stronger and began to receive the support of court decisions, and a major stage in the elimination of discriminatory legislation was reached with the Supreme Court decision of 1954 barring segregation in the public schools. With the Civil Rights Act of 1964 and the Voting Rights Act of 1965, the caste system of the South was dismantled. The thrust for equality now shifted from the legal position of the group to the achievement of concrete advances in economic and political strength.

Thus for the past forty years, the pattern of American political development has been to ever widen the circle of those eligible for inclusion in the American polity with full access to political rights. The circle now embraces —as premature hyperbolic statements made as long as two hundred years ago suggested it would—all humanity, without tests of race, color, national origin, religion, or language. To what extent an equalization of economic position has been associated with this political equalization is discussed in the second chapter.

Two other elements describe the American ethnic pattern, and those are not as easily marked by the processes of political decision-making, whether by court, legislature, or war. The first additional element is that the process of inclusion set limits on the extent to which different national polities could be set up on American soil. By "polity" I refer to some degree of political identity, formally recognized by public authority. Many multiethnic societies do recognize different ethnic groups as political entities. In the Soviet Union, each is formally entitled to a separate state or autonomous region (though these distinctive units exercise their powers in a state in which all individuals and subunits are rigidly controlled by a central dictatorship). Even a group dispersed throughout the Soviet Union such as the Jews is recognized as a separate nationality; and at one time, this nationality had rights, such as separate schools, publications, publishing houses. In Eastern Europe, where successor states to the German, Russian, and Austro-Hungarian Empire were set up after World War I, once again national rights were given to groups, even to such groups as the Jews, who were dispersed throughout the national terrritory. In nations that have been created by migration, such as the United States, we do not have examples of something like "national rights."

But the United States is more strict than others in preventing the possibility that subnational entities will arise. Consider the case of Canada, which is also a multiethnic society. The major minority national group, the French, is a compactly settled group which was conquered in the eighteenth century: It was not created through migration into a preexisting homogeneous or multiethnic nation. There are far more extensive national rights for the French than the United States allows for any group. Bilingualism is recognized not only in the areas of French settlement, but throughout the country. It is required of civil servants.

But what is the position of the "third element," those neither of English nor French origin? Their language has rapidly become English (except in the isolated prairie settlements of Eastern Europe farmers); nevertheless, as French rights have become more and more secured, they, too, have come to demand some special rights. In contrast with the United States, Canadian nationality is made up of *two* distinct founding ethnic groups, the French Canadians and the descendants of settlers from the original conquering power, to which have been added many ethnic groups derived from immigrants. There is a certain resistance among the third element—whether Jews in Montreal and Toronto, or Ukrainians in the West—to identifying fully with or assimilating to one or the other founding group, in part because these founding groups persist in maintaining specific ethnic characteristics of an English or French character. This is understandable: Canada was not founded in a revolutionary break from the fatherland, whether French or English, and while it is true a distinct Canadian personality and character did develop in both the French and English element, no great emphasis was placed on specifically distinguishing "Canadian" from everything "non-Canadian. "[21] This created a problem for new immigrant groups: Were they to maintain their original ethnic characteristics to the same extent that the founding groups did? And it created a problem for the polity. To what extent were the new immigrant groups to be encouraged to do so, or hindered in doing so? Thus, becoming Canadian did not imply, to the same extent that becoming American did, an abandonment, of immigrant ethnic traits and a becoming something different. And so, the assimilation of the ethnic groups in Canada did not proceed as rapidly as that of their ethnic relatives in the United States.

Among the possibilities for making political accommodation to groups of different ethnic character in a contemporary state, the United States falls near one end of the spectrum in denying formal recognition for any purpose to ethnic entities. In contrast to Canada, we do not ask for "ethnicity" in our census—though some government census sample surveys have recently done so—nor do we demand that each respondent select an ethnic origin.

Our pattern has been to resist the creation of formal political entities with ethnic characteristics. The pattern was set as early as the 1820s, when, as the historian of American immigration, Marcus Hansen, describes it, a number of European groups thought of establishing a New Germany or a New Ireland in the United States. He writes:

> The first step in any of these dreams [to establish branches of other nations on American soil] was the acquisition of land. But the government of the United States, though possessed of millions of acres, proved unwilling to give a single acre for the purpose. It expressed its opinion in unmistakeable terms in the year 1818 when the Irish societies of New York and Philadelphia, burdened with a large number of charitable cases, petitioned Congress for a land grant in the West on which to establish their dependents. Congress refused, agreeing with the report of a special committee that it would be undesirable to concentrate alien peoples geographically. If a grant were made to the Irish, the Germans would be the next, and so with other nationalities. The result would be a patchwork nation of foreign settlements. Probably no decision in the history of American immigration policy possesses more profound significance. By its terms the immigrant was to enjoy no special privileges to encourage his coming; also he was to suffer no special restrictions. His opportunities were those of the native, nothing more, nothing less.[22]

No new nations would be established on American soil. We were to be, if a federal republic, a republic of states, and even the states were not to be the carriers of an ethnic, or national pattern. Most divergent from this norm, perhaps, is New Mexico, a state created out of conquered territory with a settled population, or the special rights of the Spanish-origin settlers of the Gadsden Purchase in Arizona; but even in those states, the rights of the Spanish-speaking barely lead to the creation of an ethnic state, although some militant Chicano leaders would perhaps like to see this happen.

Finally, there was a third set of decisions that defined the American ethnic pattern: Any ethnic group could maintain itself, if it so wished, on a *voluntary* basis. It would not be hampered in maintaining its distinctive religion, in publishing newspapers or books in its own language, in establishing its own schools, and, indeed, in maintaining loyalty to its old country.

This was a policy, if one will, of "salutary neglect." If immigrants could not establish new polities, they could do just about anything else. They could establish schools in their own language. They could teach their own religion, whether it was the ancient faith of Rome or the newly founded variants of Judaism and Islam developed by American blacks. When the state of

Washington tried, in the early 1920s, to make public education a state monopoly, the Supreme Court said it could not.[23] Immigrants could establish their own churches and, under the doctrine of state-church separation, these would neither be more favored nor less favored than the churches of the original settlers which had once been established churches. They could establish their own hospitals, cemeteries, social service agencies to their own taste. All would be tax exempt: The state, in effect, respected whatever any group more or less wanted to consider education, or health and welfare, or religion, or charity. (Polygamy was one exception.) Indeed, the hospitals and social service agencies of these groups were even eligible for state funds, just as the institutions set up by the churches and groups of the early settlers had been. Immigrants could send money freely to their homelands, they could support the national movements of their various groups, and they could also, relatively easily, get tax exemption for their contributions to anything that smacked of religion, education, health and welfare, or charity.

There was no central public policy organized around the idea that the ethnic groups were a positive good, and therefore should be allowed whatever freedom they needed to maintain themselves. Policymakers generally never thought of the matter. It was, rather, that there was a *general* freedom, greater than in most other countries, to do what one willed. The mere fact that city planning and the controls associated with it were so much weaker than in other countries made it easy to set up churches, schools, and the like. In a society in which land could easily be bought and sold, fortunes easily made (and unmade), and mobility was high, there were, in effect, two sets of forces set loose: One force tended to break up the ethnic communities, for it was easy in American society to distance oneself from family and ethnic group, if one wanted to; but at the same time, and this is what is often forgotten, it was also easy to establish the institutions that one desired. This meant, of course, that every church divided again and again: The state was disinterested, and thus every variant of liberalism and orthodoxy would express itself freely in institutional form. It also meant there was no hindrance to the maintenance of what one wished to maintain.

One of the interesting general findings of ethnic research is that affluence and assimilation have double effects. On the one hand, many individuals become distant from their origins, throw themselves with enthusiasm into becoming full "Americans," and change name, language, and religion to forms that are more typical of earlier settlers. On the other hand, however, many use their increased wealth and competence in English to *strengthen* the ethnic group and its associations. It is hard to draw up a balance as to which tendency is stronger, because different people evaluate different effects differently. Thus undoubtedly, with longer residence in the United States, folk aspects of the culture weaken, and those attached to them feel that the original culture is lost. Yet associational and organizational forms of ethnicity are strengthened. For example, the one-room school, the *heder*, where Jewish children learned their letters, their prayers, and a bit of Bible under the tutelage of an Old World teacher, disappeared; so it became possible to say that the true old East European Jewish culture was gone. But regularly organized religious and Hebrew schools, with classrooms and teachers after the American pattern, increased greatly in number, and more Jewish children had some formal Jewish education under the organized system than under the folk system. Or, to take another example, undoubtedly, in 1975, the more folkish aspects of Ukrainian culture have weakened, for both pre-World War II and post-World War II immigrants. This weakening is associated with assimilation and higher income. But now there are chairs for Ukrainian studies at Harvard, supported by funds raised by Ukrainian students. It is this kind of trade-off that makes it so difficult to decide whether there is really, as Marcus Hansen suggested, a third-generation return to ethnic origins and interests. There is a return, but as is true of any return, it is to something quite different from what was there before.

In any case, whatever the character of the return, it is American freedom which makes it possible, as American freedom makes possible the maintenance and continuity and branchings out of whatever part of their ethnic heritage immigrants and their children want to pursue.

When we look now at our three sets of decisions—that all may be included in the nation, that they may not establish new nations here, and that they may, nevertheless, freely maintain whatever aspects of a national existence they are inclined to—we seem to have a classic Hegelian series of thesis, antithesis, and synthesis. The synthesis raises its own new questions, and these become steadily more sharp, to the point where many argue we must begin again with a new thesis. For the three sets of decisions create an ambiguous status for any ethnic group. The combination of first, you may become full citizens; second, you may not establish a national entity; third, you may establish most of the elements of a national entity voluntarily without hindrance, does not create an easily definable status for the ethnic group. The ethnic group is one of the building blocks of American society; politics, and economy, none of which can be fully understood without reference to ethnic group formation and maintenance, but this type of group is not given any political recognition or formal status. No one is "enrolled" in an ethnic group, except American Indians, for whom we still maintain a formally distinct political status defined by birth (but any individual Indian can give up this status). For all public purposes, everyone else is only a citizen. No one may be denied the right to political participation, to education, to jobs because of an ethnic status, nor may anyone be given better access to political appointments or election, or to jobs, or education because of ethnic status. And yet we pore over the statistics and try to estimate relative standings and movements among ethnic groups.

A distinction of great importance to our society is thus given no formal recognition and yet has great meaning in determining the individual's fate. In this sense, ethnicity is akin to "class" in a liberal society. Class does not denote any formal status in law and yet plays a great role in the life of the individual. Ethnicity shares with class—since neither has any formal public status—a vagueness of boundaries and limits and uncertainty as to the degree to which any person is associated with any grouping. No member of the upper, middle, or lower class—or choose what terms you wish—needs to act the way most other members of that class do; nothing but social pressure will hold him to any behavior. Similarly with persons whom we would consider "belonging" to ethnic groups: They may accept that belonging or reject it. Admittedly, there are some groups, marked by race, where belonging is just about imposed by the outside world, as against other less sharply marked groups. Nevertheless, the voluntary character of ethnicity is what makes it so distinctive in the American setting. It is voluntary not only in the sense that no one may be required to be part of a group and share its corporate concerns and activities; no one is impelled *not* to be a part of a group, either. Ethnicity in the United States, then, is part of the burden of freedom of all modern men who must choose what they are to be. In the United States, one is required neither to put on ethnicity nor to take it off. Certainly this contributes to our confusion and uncertainty in talking about it.

Undoubtedly, if this nation had chosen—as others have—either one of the two conflicting ideals that have been placed before us at different times, the "melting pot" or "cultural pluralism," the ambiguities of ethnic identity in the United States and the tensions it creates would be less. Under the first circumstance, we would have chosen a full assimilation to a new identity. Many nations have attempted this: some forcefully and unsuccessfully, as did Czarist Russia in relation to certain minority groups; some with a supreme self-confidence, such as France, which took it for granted that the status of the French citizen, *tout court*, should satisfy any civilized man; some, with hardly any great self-consciousness, such as Argentina, which assimilated enormous numbers of European immigrants into a new identity, one in which they seemed quite content to give up an earlier ethnic identity, such as Spanish or Italian. If a nation does choose this path of full assimilation, a clear course is set before the immigrant and his children. Similarly, if the principle is to be that of cultural pluralism, another clear course is set. We have not set either course, neither the one of eliminating all signs of ethnic identity—through force or through the attractions of assimilation—nor the other of providing the facilities for the maintenance of ethnic identity.

But our difficulties do not arise simply because of the ambiguities of personal identity. They arise because of the concrete reality that, even in a time of political equality (or as close to political equality as formal measures can ensure), ever greater attention is paid to social and economic inequality.

If we search earlier discussions of the immigrant and of ethnic groups, we will not find any sharp attention to these inequalities. It was assumed that time alone would reduce them, or that the satisfactions of political equality would be sufficient. It was assumed, perhaps, that social and economic inequalities would be seen as *individual* deprivations, not as *group* deprivations. But there was one great group whose degree of deprivation was so severe that it was clearly to be ascribed to the group's, not the individual's status. This was the Negro group. As we concentrated our attention in the 1960s on the gaps that separated Negroes from others, other groups of somewhat similar social and economic status began to draw attention to *their* situation. And as these new groups came onto the horizon of public attention, still others which had not been known previously for their self-consciousness or organization in raising forceful demands and drawing attention to their situation entered the process. What began as an effort to redress the inequality of the Negro turned into an effort to redress the inequality of all deprived groups.

But how is this to be done? And does not the effort to redress upset the basic American ethnic pattern? To redress inequalities means, first of all, to define them. It means the recording of ethnic identities, the setting of boundaries separating "affected" groups from "unaffected" groups, arguments among the as yet "unaffected" whether they, too, do not have claims to be considered "affected." It turned out that the effort to make the Negro equal to the *other* Americans raised the question of who *are* the other Americans? How many of them can define their own group as *also* deprived? The drawing of group definitions increased the possibilities of conflicts between groups and raised the serious question, what is legitimate redress for inequality?

In 1964, we declared that no account should be taken of race, color, national origin, or religion in the spheres of voting, jobs, and education (in 1968, we added housing). Yet no sooner had we made this national assertion than we entered into an unexampled recording of the records of the color, race, and national origin of every individual in every significant sphere of his life. Having placed into law the dissenting opinion of *Plessy v. Ferguson* that our Constitution is color-blind, we entered into a period of color- and group-consciousness with a vengeance.

Larger and larger areas of employment came under increasingly stringent controls so that each offer of a job, each promotion, each dismissal had to be considered in the light of its effects on group ratios in employment. Inevitably, this meant the ethnic group of each individual began to affect and, in many cases, to dominate consideration of whether that individual would be hired, promoted, or dismissed. In the public school systems, questions of student and teacher assignment became increasingly dominated by considerations of each individual's ethnic group: Children and teachers of certain races and ethnic groups could be assigned to this school but not to that one. The courts and government agencies were called upon to act with ever greater vigor to assure that, in each housing development and in each community, certain proportions of residents by race would be achieved, and a new body of law and practice began to build up which would, in this field, too, require public action on the basis of an individual's race and ethnic group. In each case, it was argued, positive public action on the basis of race and ethnicity was required to overcome a previous harmful public action on the basis of race and ethnicity.

Was it true that the only way the great national effort to overcome discrimination against groups could be carried out was by recording, fixing, and acting upon the group affiliation of every person in the country? Whether this was or was not the only way, it is the way we have taken. . . .

NOTES

1. Yehoshua Arieli, *Individualism and Nationalism in American Ideology* Cambridge, Massachusetts: Harvard University Press, 1964; (Penguin Books Edition, 1966), pp. 19-20.

2. Arieli, *op. cit.,* pp. 86-87.

3. Seymour Martin Lipset, *The First New Nation,* New York: Basic Books, 1963, esp. Chap. 2, "Formulating a National Identity," and Chap. 3, "A Changing American Character?"

4. Hans Kohn, *American Nationalism: An Interpretive Essay,* New York: Mac-

millan, 1957 (Collier Books edition, 1961, p. 144).

5. Arieli, *op. cit.*, p. 44.

6. Kohn, *op. cit.*, pp. 143-144, quoting from Max Savelle, *Seeds of Liberty: The Genesis of the American Mind,* New York: Knopf, 1948, p. 567 f.

7. Kohn, *op. cit.*, p. 143.

8. On the legal position of Jews, see Oscar and Mary F. Handlin, "The Acquisition of Political and Social Rights by the Jews in the United States," *American Jewish Year Book,* Vol. 56, New York: American Jewish Committee, 1955, and Philadelphia: The Jewish Publication Society of America, 1955, pp. 43-98. There is no equally convenient summary for the legal position of Catholics, but see Anson Phelps Stokes, *Church and States in the United States,* New York: Harper and Bros., 1950, Vol. I, Chapters V and XII.

9. Arieli, *op. cit.*, pp. 27-28.

10. From *Redburn: His First Voyage,* quoted in Kohn, *op. cit.*, pp. 153-154.

11. From *The American Democrat,* New York: Knopf, p. 135, quoted in Kohn, *op. cit.*, p. 162.

12. Arieli, *op. cit.*, pp. 293-305.

13. Arieli, *op. cit.*, p. 292.

14. John Higham, *Strangers in the Land: Patterns of American Nativism, 1860-1925,* New Brunswick, New Jersey: Rutgers University Press, 1955, pp. 20-21.

15. For this period, see Higham, *op. cit.;* Seymour Martin Lipset and Earl Raab, *The Politics of Unreason: Right-Wing Extremism in America, 1790-1970,* Chaps. 3-4, New York: Harper & Row, 1970; C. Vann Woodward, *The Strange Career of Jim Crow,* New York: Oxford University Press, 1955.

16. Kohn, *op. cit.*, p. 161.

17. Kohn, *op. cit.*, p. 143.

18. Barbara Miller Solomon, *Ancestors and Immigrants: A Changing New England Tradition,* Cambridge, Massachusetts: Harvard University Press, 1956, p. 176.

19. Horace M. Kallen, *Culture and Democracy in the United States,* New York: Boni and Liveright, 1924, p. 93. Kallen does not give the writer's name but describes him as "a great American man of letters, who has better than anyone else interpreted to the world the spirit of America as New England." The writer was probably his teacher at Harvard, to whom he dedicated this book, Barrett Wendell.

20. Henry James, *American Notes,* New York: Charles Scribner's Sons, 1946 [originally 1907], p. 86.

21. Seymour Martin Lipset analyzes the significance of the difference in the political origins of the United States and Canada in "Revolution and Counterrevolution: The United States and Canada," Chapter 2 in *Revolution and Counterrevolution: Change and Persistence in Social Structures,* New York: Basic Books, 1968.

22. Marcus Hansen, *The Immigrant in American History* (Cambridge, Massachusetts: Harvard University Press, 1940), p. 132.

23. *Pierce v. Society of Sisters,* 268 U.S. 510 (1925). Of course, as public and bureaucratic controls multiply in every part of life, this freedom is restricted, and not only for ethnic groups. It means that the establishment of church or school in a single-family house—a typical pattern—may run into zoning and planning restrictions, and often does; that the establishment of a nursery or an old-age home in less than insti-

tutional quarters fulfilling state requirements becomes almost possible. New groups suffer probably more from these restrictions than old groups. But I note that a magnificent nineteenth-century Richard Morris Hunt-designed home for the aged in New York, maintained by an old Protestant welfare agency, is to be demolished because it cannot meet state standards of "proper" facilities for the aged. All suffer from the ever-widening reach of state controls.

Two: The Law

Introduction

The questions of the constitutionality and the legality of reverse discrimination are of major importance. Unfortunately, they are also much less clear than they seem, and they raise a number of subsidiary issues as well. Thus far, we have no definitive answers to any of them. It is worth reviewing a number of decisions not here reprinted, so as to get the flavor of the issues.

In the landmark case of *Griggs v. Duke Power Company* the Supreme Court held that a practice would be invidiously discriminatory, no matter what its intention, if it both produced unequal consequences for different races and could not be shown to be justified or validated by some purpose related to the job for which it was a screening device. In that specific case it was the requirement of a high-school diploma which, though a requirement for all alike, was struck down. And in *McDonnell Douglas Corporation v. Green* the Court held that statistics could provide proof that minorities or women had been discriminated against.

Equal Employment Opportunities Commission and New York City v. Local 28, 638 Sheet Metal Workers is an illustrative case. The two locals in question were found to have engaged in discriminatory practices, since few or no minority persons had ever been admitted into the union, and jobs in the industry were open only to union members. Both individual case histories and statistical patterns provide a basis of evidence for the finding. The tests provided by the union were struck down as discriminatory under *Griggs*.

Kirkland and Hayes v. New York State Department of Correctional Services is a case where a test for corrections sergeant was struck down as discriminatory and a court order was issued to devise another. But the Appeals court refused to affirm a lower-court ruling that quotas be instituted for the promotion of minority-group members on the grounds that the issues framed in the case were of too limited a scope and that little proof was presented of past discrimination. In the view of the court, merit must be taken into account.

In *Chance and Mercado v. Board of Examiners* an appeal was granted from a lower court order that directed the New York City Board of Education to lay off supervisory personnel by racial quotas rather than seniority. The court held that a last-hired, first-fired plan does not discriminate disproportionately against the minorities affected. Special consideration was given by the court to the small number of persons in the positions affected and to the value of experience in school administration.

The settlement in the case of *Margaret Kohn v. Royall, Koegel & Wells* provides an example of a firm agreeing to certain reforms in hiring procedures without admitting to or being required to admit to any discriminatory acts or patterns. It is especially interesting to compare this well-known law firm's statement that it reaffirms a policy of seeking out and employing persons according to merit with its agreement to tender offers of positions to female graduates on a quota basis.

The Supreme Court has decided several other cases of interest recently. *Griggs* seems to have been modified by *Washington, Mayor of Washington, D.C., v. Davis* 74-1492, where the Court ruled that a law or official act is not unconstitutional solely because of any racially disproportionate effect. In *McDonald v. Sante Fe Transportation Company*, 75-260, the Court ruled that the Civil Rights Act of 1866 (Sec. 1981) prohibits racial discrimination in private employment against whites as well as blacks, and so does Title VII of the Civil Rights Act of 1964. Nor may private schools practice racial discrimination against blacks, and this prohibition does not controvene the constitutional guarantee of freedom of association (*Runyon v. McCrary*, 75-62; *Fairfax-Brewster School, Inc. v. Gonzales*, 75-66; *Southern Independent School Association v. McCrary*, 75-278; *McCrary v. Runyon*, 75-306).

Virginia Black argues that the introduction of ad hoc and contradictory legal policies like reverse discrimination over a foundation of equal liberty and justice under the rule of law, can result only in social disorder. Worse, the "success" of such policies in terms of visible changes in the social order cannot be known, even in principle. For these reasons, she holds that reverse discrimination should not be legally mandated, though curiously, she envisions the possibility of the voluntary introduction of such a policy.

Professor Cox's *amicus curiae* brief for Harvard College in the *DeFunis* case ranges over the issues raised by the case itself, general policy about law-school and college-admissions criteria, and the place of race as one of them. He argues in part that the issue is not one of quotas, but rather of the permissibility, even desirability, of using race as one among many factors for or against a candidate's admission. One may be surprised to see what is probably the nation's greatest university arguing that intellectual ability is not an overridingly desirable characteristic in its student body.

The Supreme Court took the rather unusual step of accepting the case of *DeFunis v. Odegaard,* hearing oral argument, and then declaring the case moot. In Robert O'Neil's felicitous phrase, it decided not to decide. Mr. Justice Douglas dissented. Douglas believed the Court should have decided the case on its merits. He wrote, "[a] DeFunis who is white is entitled to no advantage by reason of that fact; nor is he subject to any disability, no matter his race or color. Whatever his race, he has a constitutional right to have his application considered in its individual merits in a racially neutral manner." He went on to argue that racial preferences could only involve the Court in a morass of competing claims. While conceding that LSAT scores and other "mechanical" means were unsatisfactory and that a law school had a constitutionally wide latitude in criteria used to evaluate and admit candidates, he stops short of allowing racial preference as one of these, questioning the "compelling state interest" that might allow this. (See O'Neil, *Discriminating Against Discrimination,* chapter two for speculations about the Court's motives and Douglas' dissent.)

Alevy v. Downstate Medical Center of New York (not herein printed) is sufficiently similar to *DeFunis* in many respects to make the judge's decision of interest. Mr. Alevy's screening code for entry to the medical school was high enough so that he would have been admitted had he been a minority candidate. He argues that giving less-qualified minority candidates a greater opportunity to enter medical school because of their race violates the equal-protection clause. Judge Gabrielli's decision takes into account levels of judicial review, the notion of suspect classification, and the proposition put forward by Professor Ely later, that a majority can be trusted when it discriminates against itself. He concludes that here is a case of reverse discrimination, but that Mr. Alevy is entitled to no relief since, even had all minority candidates been excluded from consideration, he would still have been too far down the list for acceptance.

The three articles concluding this section examine the constitutional issues of racial classification and reverse discrimination in several ways. John Hart Ely treats a majority as a single entity which is self-interested enough to prevent itself from going too far in discriminating against itself. One may inquire about the logical propriety of going in this way from wholes to parts, for even if there is a majority, a view disputed by Glazer, it is always some part of that majority—some group of people—who would have to sanction discrimination against another part. Could we be sure that every possible group identified with and was protective of the other? The history of human relations, especially just before and during World War II, and contemporary events around the world does not give this view much support. Professor Ely concludes that a moral, though not necessarily a constitutional, dilemma remains that ought to be resolved by the political process.

Professor Greenawalt undertakes an analysis of levels of review appropriate when state educational agencies adopt preferential classifications for racial minorities. He argues that an intermediate level of substantial public interest should be satisfied rather than a higher level of compelling state interest or a lower one of rational relationship to the goals in question. He deals with topics such as qualifications, service to minority communities, diversity, and the like. He concludes with a much-needed plea for honesty and openness in such matters.

Terrance Sandalow casts his article in a wider, more philosophic mold, which makes it a good transition to part 3. He introduces broad questions of freedom, justice, and the philosophy of law into which, perhaps, we must embed a reading of the equal-protection clause. For him there are two different sorts of issues at stake in the preferential treatment of minorities: whether a legislature is not the proper authority to sanction them and whether in the absence of a legislative sanction a state agency may adopt them. He holds that there are good reasons for having such policies but that they are less compelling in the absence of explicit legal mandates. He takes us through a legislative history of the equal-protection clause, raises the general philosophic and legal questions about the validity of classification by involuntary characteristics, and analyzes the question of consistency in alternatively denying and applying racial status as a criterion for the distribution of benefits, along with many other questions.

Virginia Black

The Erosion of Legal Principles in the Creation of Legal Policies

1   THE PROBLEM

There is a tendency on the part of well-meaning people to rectify inequities in social life. In a democratic society, some seek to change the laws so that those who have been at a social and economic disadvantage may enjoy an enforceably favored status. The purpose of this paper is to show how certain special edicts that impose discriminatory restrictions on the formerly undiscriminated against, so that the disadvantaged may be raised to a par, create new inequities themselves and hurt those they are meant to help. I will try to show that such discriminatory edicts, sometimes called instruments of "reverse discrimination" or "preferential treatment," are counterproductive and confuse causes with effects. Instead of helping equalize persons in economic status—their professed object—they congeal and rigidify classes. Legal efforts to reduce the range of economic or educational differences impose their opposite, a class structure even more difficult to eradicate and one whose most obvious historic parallel is feudalism, a system American law was designed to eliminate. More and more, I believe, we exhibit in this coun-

Source: Ethics *84, no. 2 (Jan. 1974). Reprinted by permission of the University of Chicago Press.*

try the immoral and unjust institutions of feudalism, and much of it is due to certain unintelligent types of legislative acts.

The specific conceptual and moral conflict we shall be concerned with is the displacement in law of individual justice, wherein a designated person is held responsible for wrongs which can be laid to him, by the introduction of its opposite: collective edicts wherein an entire group is held corporately and legally responsible for past wrongs (or for current unwanted social effects) impossible to lay to any determinate individuals. A prototype is found in current legislation which proposes that certain groups, at a disadvantage in their social achievements, ought *in law* to be extended preferential and hence discriminatory treatment in order to compensate them for wrongs reputedly suffered at the hands of others more fortunate. The disadvantaged groups I especially have in mind are defined by their color (black) or by their sex (female), although other groups are also shown to be underrepresented on the statistical graphs that correlate population quotas with achievements. The mandates currently instituted by the U.S. Department of Health, Education and Welfare are exactly such displacements in law, wherein commands to discriminate are inconsistently introduced upon the foundations of a social order in which justice under the rule of law is defined as equality in rights and equality before the law.

What I shall claim is, I believe, true of all incoherent legislation. Reverse discrimination, however, because it directly contradicts justice, exhibits in sharper terms the difficulties that arise when conceptual disorders invade the society by way of legal requirements. Reverse discrimination is, moreover, current and crucial; it has been called "the most fundamental change in American history" and "an ominous reversal of an ideology." These epithets are not exaggerations.

Much has already been written on the subject of reverse discrimination, pro and con. Lectures and conferences have argued its merits. Institutions— organizations, industries, and universities—throughout the country have debated its morality, its reasonableness, and its effects, and continue to do so. For the most part, as far as I can discern, these arguments have focused upon four main areas of contention, not exclusive of each other: (1) special-interest groups contending that the compensatory legislation does or does not affect them adversely; (2) universities claiming that reverse discrimination invades, or does not invade, their historic rights of autonomy in the selection of faculty and students; and that it violates, or does not violate, the merit system which gives meaning to higher education; (3) arguments accepting or rejecting the belief that reverse discrimination is moral and/or just; and (4) a few arguments pointing at reverse discrimination as incipiently or overtly totalitarian.

My central effort here is to concentrate on two other main effects of reverse discrimination which I have not seen mentioned anywhere else. (1) As legal policy, special-treatment mandates are irrational because, while they require demonstration of their effectiveness (as indeed do all ad hoc policy programs, in contrast to what we might call laws sustaining civilly fundamental prohibitions and rights), it is *logically impossible* to provide such a demonstration. (2) The frustrations, factional disorders, and ideological chaos provoked by reverse discrimination through contradictory legislation tend to rigidify class structures, thus creating the kind of feudal society which constitutional justice helps to prevent and reverse discrimination presumes to abhor.

2   THE ILLOGIC OF LEGAL DISCRIMINATION

To justify discrimination in law, when the meaning of *law* within our legal system carries with it the moral implication of equality or nondiscrimination, requires the use of euphemisms and vindicatory rhetoric. The least offensive such rhetoric on the part of advocates of reverse discrimination seems to be *affirmative action*, which conveys the tone of enterprising loyalty to just laws of which Americans are in violation. But this is not the meaning of *affirmative action*. Affirmative action is a national discriminatory program. I shall try to show that this program cannot be known to improve the position of blacks or of women. This is because, although it implies a quota system, the quota called for cannot, in principle, stand as evidence of improvement. Behind affirmative action stands the unavoidable objective of numerical quotas, since enumeration of group members is necessary in order to know exactly when an organization is in compliance, that is, when it has reached what HEW calls "a target of expected employment." How else can a "good faith effort at recruitment" (HEW's term) be measured?

Even Modified Affirmative-Action Programs Imply Quotas. When affirmative action was first publicized, its wording was sharp and unambiguous. Terms like *quotas, timetables,* and *proportional percentage hiring* were used, and they meant just what they said, namely, that a given organization has just so much time in which to include among its membership a specified number of the disadvantaged class (blacks or women in particular). Penalties were implied. Some were enforced: there were threats, censures, fines, loss of jobs, withdrawal of federal funds. And the sanctions always required snooping and interference.

In a revisionary back-down from the explicitly discriminatory vocabulary of quotas, timetables, and percentage hiring, HEW's affirmative-action program has more recently been redrafted along new guidelines. Critical feedback has been partly responsible. Under ideological attack and attacks from institutions questioning the legal validity of the mandates, arguing their ill effects, claiming exemption, or threatening noncompliance, HEW has to an extent modified its requirements. But its voice is still very strong. The thrust now is to put pressure on institutions to demonstrate what is called a "good faith effort to redress imbalances." Conveniently obscure phrases like *goals* and *corrected imbalances* have been overtly substituted for fixed ratios and numerical quotas. Stated sanctions now are ambiguous, hinting at indirect countermeasures and veto powers instead of strict prescriptions. This is worse in a way. For it has led to confusion about what the law prescribes, an egregious error in anybody's lexicon of legal justice. Some institutions, in their fear, have overcomplied.

Before examining the logic by which compliance with legal edicts is required, let me say that I believe a qualified case can be made for discriminatory procedures *when they are voluntary*, as long as no legal threats or pressures hang over the heads of those who are trying, because they want to try, to show good faith. A homely analogy may help. Sometimes a parent makes an effort to give special care to a child who, the parent believes, needs some unusual attention in making its way. Is this prejudice? Is this unconscionably discriminatory? I believe not. There is an important difference between moral pangs, prompting a parent to favor one child over another temporarily, and legal sanctions, coercing all organizations into favoring members of certain groups over others indefinitely. A parent can observe whether his discriminatory efforts are, on the one hand, paying off in increased self-esteem and development in the child who fell behind. He can also survey the effects of discrimination on siblings and take action to remedy *their* discontent if it develops. Continual correctives can be applied as they are needed. The favors can be withdrawn for a time; the group can talk things over, and so forth. Broad-scale legal programs do not work this way. They cannot accomplish these niceties of redress to the innocent.

Voluntary compliance, in contrast to coercive compliance, yields the following social desiderata: (1) Social habits are more dependable than legal mandates or administrative orders, which can change arbitrarily with new officials or old officials with new moods. (2) Transgression of noncoercive, or strictly moral, obligations can be a social educator when individuals incur public pressure or censure; but when such transgressions are subject to legal punishment, little social benefit accrues. (3) The flexibility of such pressures and habits makes for a more stable development and continuous growth of the society toward the ideal of a gradually evolving corporate "organism." Their variability, overlap, and withdrawal make for "safe" experimentation, whereas a national experiment may have results of disastrous proportions. (4) A related point: voluntary effort by some avoids total and wide-scale destructive error, and it is self-correcting, allowing for the selection of the most effective routes to social change.

Legalized public policies are often devised with what we may call "levels of consequences." These correspond to ends, means-ends, and strictly instrumental means in the pursuit of a given society's intrinsic social values. Thus, for example, a quota of three women to one man may be said to exemplify, or stand as evidence for, a "fair employment" standard based on a quota system. But, we may ask, What does a fair employment standard stand as evidence for? Fair employment standards may be said to exemplify, or stand as evidence for, "equality in rights." Others may argue, as I would, that *equality* in rights and *fair* employment standards cannot imply a quota system. But in any case the methodology is the same. Higher-order values imply lower-order values. We may go on to ask, What does equality in rights stand as evidence for? By way of ideals that become more abstract as we justify our practices, we approach our intrinsic social values. Equality in rights, exemplifies our commitment to constitutional law, which in turn, is implied by the equal intrinsic worth and dignity of persons. Layered consequences thus take account of higher-order goals and of instrumental goals implicit in the ethos.

But unless something nonabstract, something empirical, enumerable, visible, fixed, or assessable is agreed upon as an indicator, taking into account the sub- and meta-goals—the secondary values—which justify a program, there is no way to know whether it is working. And policy programs, especially, in order to justify their existence and meet their budgets, must always be assigned enumerable evidence indicators. "Quality education" as a goal, for example, is often evidenced by the number of reports written, committee meetings called, money spent for note pads or ink bottles. "Affirmative action" is evidenced by quotas. Let us see how, in practice, such requirements are illogical.

Contradictory Evidence Is Generated by Contradictory Laws. If quotas are not stipulated to show empirically that compensatory goals have been reached, or that "good faith efforts" have been made and organizations are "in compliance," it is impossible to know whether a discriminatory policy like HEW's has achieved its mark. If it has not, then the secondary goals also cannot be met, since the entire tier of goals rests upon some numerical sub-structure of quantifiable data.

On the other hand, even the clear-cut positing of numerical quotas smudges our certainty that we have done all that we can do to remedy moral and legal errors. This is because, *at the same time that discriminatory orders are operant in the society, nondiscriminatory prohibitions are concurrently operant, each counteracting the evidence of the other.* Let us see how this confusion works.

Suppose, for example, that Company A is required to hire a predomi-nance of qualified women, using their sex as a legal justification. Suppose, however, that Company B, in keeping with *non*discriminatory employment practices, also required by law, hires qualified men and women indiscrimin-ately. Now, in order to find out whether policies are accomplishing their objectives, we set down rules of evidence that unequivocally describe which effects and how many such effects show that a program is working and also, often, what counts against its effectiveness. This is necessary in order to find out whether we ought to nullify a program that is not working or has unwanted side effects; to install some other better program that promises the effects we want; or perhaps to modify, instead, the original program in such a way as to help make it more effective. As HEW's Office for Civil Rights (OCR) puts it: "The best evidence of good faith is a good result." We saw, for example, that "quality education" is sometimes measured in terms of money spent for equipment. Money can be added up; arithmetical sums are hard and empirical when they represent supplies purchased, and they make good data. Although I believe that this is a mistaken criterion of quality education, it is often used as a substitute for our ignorance in matters of pedagogical excellence.

In the case of discriminatory favoring, effects may be measured in terms of some national figures or quotas to be met by a certain time. HEW and OCR have used, alternatively, a "proportion-to-population" rule, a "propor-tion-to-applicant" rule, and a "proportion-to-qualifiable-applicant" rule in order to get a numerical measure of results. If favoring is ultimately to be justified as a form of compensatory justice, then one must know how much reparation is to be paid, in what terms, by whom, by what time ("timetables" on the HEW program), and how much counterevidence will be tolerated before the program is declared ineffective (for example, men holding jobs that women could equally well perform). For example, will the program stop when the blacks have their 11 percent, their "proportion to population"? Yet how is such a figure to be sustained, over what period, and in what industries or educational establishments, exactly? It is also necessary to ascertain the marginal costs of effectiveness: what else of value could have been accomplished for the same costs, and what, exactly, is the relative value for "the public interest" in maintaining or financing this program instead of another?

Yet here begin the difficulties. Since, at the same time as the favoring programs are being acted upon, nondiscrimination laws are also in effect, how is one to know which effects count for what? For instance, what of several thousand women (and how many shall we require?) who are performing a certain job or enjoying a certain prestigious position—are they positive evidence of the effectiveness of the reverse discrimination program? Or are they positive evidence of the effectiveness of more rigidly upheld nondiscrimination between the sexes? Conversely, are they negative evidence of nondiscrimination; that is, do they represent more women in jobs because nondiscrimination has not been practiced? Or are they negative evidence of discrimination; that is, do they represent the number of women who might "naturally" be employed were discrimination not practiced?

When ad hoc programs contradict valid laws, it becomes logically impossible to tally up results. Therefore, it becomes logically impossible to know whether a program is effective; and hence it becomes logically impossible to know whether to rescind the program because it is not working or to insist upon more of the same because findings do not yet reveal that goals are being met. When the success of one and the failure of another incompatible program both require the same kind of evidence, it is logically impossible to know what evidence renders either of them effective, since it is impossible on principle to know whether that which results, the evidence, is due to the failure of, say, equal-treatment laws, or to the success of special-treatment programs—or perhaps neither. Perhaps it is a sign of voluntary choices resulting from public opinion and social pressure. If this is so, shall we repeal the equal-treatment law because applying special treatment nullifies its effects, or vice versa? Or shall we, rather, increase efforts to make special treatment (or, conversely, equal treatment) meet the stated needs better? Whichever way we turn, we cannot say: inevitable failure is entailed because, by definition, the evidence indicators of one negate the evidence indicators of the other.

A related problem now arises. Because it is impossible to ascertain what *kind* of evidence to count in judging that a program is effective, it is also impossible to know *how much* of a given kind of evidence to count before we know that it is effective, and how much counterevidence to subtract. Therefore, under equivocal legal directives, neither equal- nor special-treatment mandates can ever in principle be satisfied. We are led to the following destructive dilemma: Nondiscriminatory effectiveness does not require that more women be employed, but discriminatory effectiveness does require that more women be employed. Either more women are to be employed, or they are not. Therefore, either nondiscriminatory laws are not effective, or the discriminatory program is not effective.

Another related problem is that complaints by groups excluded by the discriminatory mandates can never be legitimately answered either, since their satisfaction runs counter to and logically negates evidence which could confirm that the favored group is being adequately favored. For litigatory law, the implications of eternal nonliability are egregious.

So much for the problem of evidence arising from the contradiction between just laws and unjust edicts. If confirming evidence cannot be made clear, we are without guidance as to how best to enjoy the kind of social life we believe we want, for we can never know by what instruments to obtain it. The solution, surely, is not to install any such programs as reverse discrimination, but to eliminate them altogether and get on with the business of not discriminating, and of punishing all violations of the equality which nondiscrimination legally secures. We already possess ample legal apparatus with which to maintain a just society: for example, the 1964 Civil Rights Act; the 1971 amendment forbidding sex discrimination in all public school courses of instruction and on athletic teams; the proposed amendment forbidding sexual discrimination; the Fourteenth Amendment (1868): " . . . nor shall any State . . . deny to any person . . . the equal protection of the laws"; the "equal treatment" and "equality in rights" entailments in the Preamble of the Constitution, the Declaration of Independence, and the Bill of Rights. And Article 6 of the Constitution reads: "This Constitution and the Laws of the United States . . . shall be the supreme Law of the Land." In these laws, therefore, reside this society's supreme intrinsic values. In consonance with them and in accordance with their explicit formulation, the only means by which to realize these values is equal treatment under law.

Time Lags Promote Further Uncertainty Regarding Effectiveness. An important precipitating factor in leading a society to believe that certain laws must be overhauled and overhauled quickly is the passing of time in which wanted changes appear not to be occurring after policies intended to effect them have been instituted. This is especially true with meta-principles, the superordinate systems of justification. Because of their relative abstractness, their logical distance from immediate evidence is often proportionate to the length of time that must pass before their realization is deemed complete. In the case of civil liberties and such superordinate constitutional principles as equality before the law, *no specified length of time must pass before their realization is complete; for their realization can never be complete or be intended to be.* They are regulative ideals, guides toward society's maintenance in keeping its order peaceable, civil, and just, and ever improving the liberties of all individuals. But people do not readily see what is invisible or ongoing, what is a tendency or a potential for improvement, or what are self-sustaining and enduring civil systems, without the mapped and graphic drama of a substantive consequence. Hence they do not readily see that such desirable values as higher quality of education, individual rights, equal opportunities, or nondiscriminatory employment are being actualized simply by being maintained and, when not, corrected. We look for evidence indicators to ground our expectations in what we can discern. It is correct that we should do so. But we forget that in the case of general and equal laws, the only indicators we are entitled to discover are corrected individual violations. Instead, we look for grosser and more dramatic signs. It is this that has led us to "affirmative action" and statistical quotas. But equal laws have no timetables.

The difficulties of social invisibility and time lag are compounded when people begin thinking that ineffective or undesirable legislation has already been enacted and that therefore all due haste is justified in abrogating it. And sometimes it is. Unfortunately, an ambiguous clause in our Constitution allows certain discriminatory state ordinances to be acted upon without their moral evil or legal injustice being called into question. This is indeed true racism, *using the force of government* to hurt members of disliked groups. When an unwanted phenomenon poses a threat or reflects a social crisis (as during the university and ghetto riots of the sixties), further haste in abrogating the enactment seems warranted. Further compounding the situation is intellectual error, not knowing to what to attribute the undesirable effects, as, when men did not see at the time of the Great Depression the economic nationalism that set the stage, they therefore rushed to manipulate the institutions that were only unfortunate symptoms, overlooking or reinstating the central causes (graduated taxes, artificially low interest rates, government credit expansion) that had led to catastrophe.

As an example of the time-lag problem, let us posit the installation of only one new mandate of the simplest possible sort. Let us say that Policy A (special-treatment discrimination) has been decreed but that its taking effect is slow or perhaps slower than expected. Since we saw that measuring the effects of discriminatory decrees is impossible, no clear-cut evidence can ever appear confirming the effectiveness of Policy A. Meanwhile, augmenting the ambiguous social condition, the effects of another and coeval law, Law not-A (nondiscrimination), is generating its own ongoing conditions, although we say that with equal general laws we cannot expect countable positive evidence but must, instead, keep a loose account, if we must, of successful indictments of violations. But not-A both empirically cancels out the effects of the new Policy A (every hired white male can be counted a failure of evidence of reverse discrimination) and logically confounds the computing of evidence that A is effective (since, as we saw above, we do not know into which of four categories of evidence to place the hiring of a white male). That is, we cannot tell whether a given effect (even if we can identify it) is a direct outcome of Law not-A or is, rather, the late-coming outcome of Policy A's doing its expected job of canceling out the effects of not-A. Meanwhile, as in any social order of complexity, other laws and programs keep on having parasitic, proliferating, and reinforcing effects on both A and not-A, some expected, some not expected, confuting coherent calculations of just which evidence is attributable to which program. The delay in evidence showing up while institutions gear themselves for compliance with the new mandate and carry it out confuses the issues further.

Now, the necessary justifying meta-principles obfuscate the situation still further. Nondiscriminatory laws, *in fact*, seem to have resulted in an economic and educational disbalance between the races and sexes. Yet the meta-principle of nondiscrimination is highly desirable and scarcely dispensable in our society, and for more than one reason. It enunciates the principle of equality of persons and the ideal, "Justice is blind," which we cannot abandon without distorting our national identity. It also tends to allow individuals an opportunity to go as far as their talents carry them (provided that others value their productive contribution); therefore, it promotes that precious diversity and excellence in the system which a machine-age society desperately needs. Witnessing, however, the aforementioned empirical disbalance, we quickly blame prejudice and racism; that is, we lay it exclusively to *illegal violations of nondiscriminatory laws* whose manifold proportions we correlate with the manifold proportions of the disbalance. What is the recommendation we come up with? Since violations are so many (that is, since evidence of nondiscrimination is so scanty), let us cancel nondiscriminatory laws by installing their contrary—discriminatory edicts. Thus will we even up the disbalance.

But it is not nondiscriminatory laws that causally produced the disbalance. We overlook 5,000 years of customary subjugation of peoples. We also overlook fundamental material conditions created by feudal and mercantile decrees and attitudes carried to this country, exciting and empowering easy violations and equivocal interpretations of equal laws. We overlook the feudal mentality of the serf-and-noble caste system that survived here in the seventeenth century, and also, in the eighteenth century, the mercantile mentality of the same economic nationalism that spawned colonialism and imperialism by postulating the ideology that one group can profit only at the expense of another. These attitudes are not pervasive in this country today. Without them, nondiscriminatory laws are freed from the subversive conditions that originally sullied their application.

Finally, we must accept that, *for a time yet,* equality in law may not rapidly increase economic equalities, bringing blacks into the middle class and women, if they wish it, into professional roles. This is because equal laws release only the prepared citizen to improve his position and thus contribute to the positions of others. Preparedness lies in attitudes reinforced by the ethnic and ethical tradition. The tradition of blacks may take a little longer to deliver its message. The traditional constraints of women are even older. But the voice of the public is helping to diversify our expectations.

Therefore, although there may be some evidence that Policy A, reverse discrimination, is directly observed to produce greater minority representation in favored statuses, still operative in the social order are the habits, expectancies, and securities associated with Law not-A, not to mention the backlash that may have set in upon confrontation with mandatory illogic. These psychological products of the passage of time frustrate the social body and subject it to cognitive discord which cannot so totally and in such short order alter its attitudes in accord with the outgo of not-A and the income of A. When it is not even clear why not-A should be rescinded, and when not-A, furthermore, coheres with fundamental constitutional law and tradition and their surrounding ethos, counterproductivity, destruction, and factional hostility must be the inevitable result.

We have this incredibly confusing situation: A society institutes Program A in order to effect wanted A-series empirical conditions, say, A_1 and A_2, and so forth. Conditions A_1 and A_2, and so forth are slow in making an appearance, or are not identified as following from Program A when they do appear. As time passes, what is the outcome? The society may not know whether A_1 and A_2 will ever occur, may need a longer time in which to occur, or can occur only in connection with, say, a parallel Program B (for example, some today are saying that early educational deprivation is not correctible unless an income-equality policy accompanies it). Society may not know whether A produces only C_1 and C_2, and so forth, or other unexpected effects and not all the wanted A-series effects; whether A can produce both the A-series effects and others, unwanted, as well; whether A-series effects are being voided by other laws or programs whose effects are difficult to disentangle; or whether another policy besides A might also produce A-series effects with fewer undesirable side effects. And so on.

Imagine the situation when, as is usually the case, more than one mandate is enforced at the same time or in quick succession, compounded by the erratic, inconsistent, or even partially enlightened annulment of laws already in effect. Now suppose that Program A, although on the whole deemed desirable, has also a number of undesirable side effects, some of which may be invisible until they multiply through time. If so, to the tangle of ignorance above must be added men's *evaluations* of what is to be tolerated and at what cost or loss, what is to be preferred and at what disutilities and for how long. For, given that Program A does not yield a utopia even though it may yield unmistakably desired conditions A_1 and A_2, men have to reckon with the possibility that another practice might have produced fewer or less undesirable social costs, or, to compensate, might have produced more A-series conditions. For alongside the time lag which elongates the agony of rational policy manipulation, ignorance of long-term or indirect effects remote in time and place from originating sources (or impatience in waiting for them to appear) is an equally significant element in leading a society into voiding good laws and installing less desirable ones. Or, sometimes worse, mistakes are aggravated by rescinding laws with such speed as to make it logically impossible ever to know of failure or success and hence to compound the same errors again. The sociology of social change also militates against short-term policy implants whose function is to coerce the correction of an observed economic imbalance. Social change comes about gradually, and the only laws that are economically feasible or morally tolerable are those laws that people are ready spontaneously to obey.

Comparative Merit Is Difficult to Evaluate. Suppose that a black is hired by a given firm both because he (or she) is qualified and also in conformity with a favoring program like HEW's. Both reasons are deemed necessary—neither alone is sufficient—for his being given an employment preference. Now suppose some time later the need arises to let some employees go—let us say that the employer is in financial straits—and suppose that the black's particular job is dispensable or that any number of other persons could equally perform it. Now on what grounds can he ever be fired? Four alternatives appear. All of them are in some way unsatisfactory. (1) Because his color was a consideration upon which he was hired, one might argue that he will have to be extraordinarily inefficient before he can be fired in order to offset the indeterminately sustaining validity of his color. But since his color alone is not sufficient to qualify him for the job—it is unrelated to the job— keeping an inefficient worker would be an economic drain on an already failing business. Or (2) the employer will have to claim either that color was not a necessary factor in hiring (which is untrue although nondiscriminatory) or that he may fire on grounds other than those on which he hired, which is illogical and unfair; for although he may claim that because of financial difficulties he has to let someone go, it does not explain why he chooses to let the black go. Or (3), if the black's efficiency drops, his color, by hypothesis, is not sufficient to sustain him on the job, since both conditions were necessary for hiring him in the first place. But this is noncompliance with discriminatory quotas. Or (4) the black will have to be let go because he is a black, and this is as immoral and illegal as hiring him because he is a black, and moreover contradicts one reason given for hiring him. Further, if discriminatory programs are in effect, the employer may not be allowed to let the black go even if he is unproductive. The only ground on which the black could be let go is if everyone is let go—the employer goes out of business.

The reasons that justify firing also justify hiring, barring the closing down of an institution altogether. If it is irrational and unjust and cruel to fire someone because he is a black or she is a woman—cases whose absurdity seems obvious—then it is equally irrational and unjust and cruel to hire someone because he is a black or she is a woman. To appreciate the parallel, one has only to remember that to hire X *because* of color is, ipso facto, *not* to hire Y because of color. When inscribed in law, this is racism.

When the institution involved is a university, the situation is crucial. An industrial concern may not put itself at a disadvantage by having equals on the job. This is why the Civil Rights Act makes some sense. But a university, to survive and fulfill its function, must seek and retain on its faculty the best it can get. Having nondiversified "equals" on the job is not an instrument of education. But OCR has ruled that "women or minority candidates must always be chosen over a man or nonminority candidate with 'equal' qualifications." The outcome is that female and minority applicants need qualify only better than the *least qualified* person presently employed by a department. If, then, a department "has just one professor far less competent than the rest, the department must hire only women or minority candidates until there is none available who is better qualified than that one, least common denominator."

These four examples of the effects of discrimination by law are not fanciful. Their counterparts are occurring now. The reason we ought to stop discriminating against blacks and whites and women and men and Indians and the poor and the rich is that when contradictory practices are construed as effects of laws instead of as violations of them, they seem to give us a warrant for enacting laws that allow them. This is disastrous, since to respond to a problem without understanding its causes is often to help create it.

The logical difficulties I have illustrated in this section are not peculiar to decrees that discriminate. They are endogenous in all kinds of legislation in which infractions of rights already inscribed in general law are not equally prohibited, or enjoyments of such rights are not equally allowed. Such difficulties may suggest that the science of society needs aeons of hard work to come up with an effective and unreason-avoiding method for implementing general and just law with policy implants that avoid conceptual confusion and social disorganization. But nothing is implied. What is desirable instead is to ease off from all legislation that requires the logically impossible collection of countable instances, as short-term empirical "results," to corroborate program effectiveness. In that way the tangled schemes presented above do not come into play. They remain unformulable.

3   THE SOCIAL CONSEQUENCES OF LEGAL DISCRIMINATION

I wish now to examine other consequences of legally required discrimination, consequences more overtly destructive of a social order in which justice can function as equal treatment.

Ultimately, the Favored Are Also Hurt. Unjust acts or judgments *in violation of law* diminish justice in an otherwise just society by the enormity of each separate act. But injustices *justified in law* diminish justice by pervading the entire order and the concepts embedded in its practices, arousing widespread and erratic vindictiveness. For a time, believing that such injustice in law is rightfully compensatory, assuaging their guilt and producing no visible effects of group favoring, some citizens may accept it as another instrument of social justice. Justified sympathies are tapped, utopian dreams are excited, the desire for instant rectification and an impatience with weighing or waiting for the longer-range results of nondiscriminatory legislation may cause the polity to assent to interest-group politics. The superficial resemblance to compensation in civil and criminal law conceals the tribal logic of group discrimination, and its theft of the lexicon of justice is for a time generally overlooked.

But the deception cannot last. The illogic of the system, the ineffectiveness of its procedures, and the increasing proximity of its disadvantages to persons discriminated against by its mandates eventually come home to the public. When that happens, both justice and special favoring occupy the same tumbril on the way to the guillotine. The soil is prepared for factional reaction and vengeance by a resentful populace.

Persons elevated in their class-related interests by being accorded special rights in law become objects of jealousy. When this happens, polarization precipitates class discord. Tolerance for the reparative nature of the reputed rights abates as new groups emerge demanding repair of *their* overlooked interests, and old forgotten groups, expecting the time for redemption to have passed, cry out again for evenness in the law. Anger explodes not only because offended groups reach their limit of toleration for groups irrationally defined and privileged, but also because the official dedication of politicians evaporates when popularity and power are no longer to be gained by courting the once fashionable preference. When another batch of politicians takes office, or when money to maintain the special agency runs out, blacks and women may be systematically severed from their services and benefits, or systematically uninvited to enjoy them any longer if their own efforts cannot maintain them against fair odds—or even if they do. Now the formerly favored group is discriminated *against*. Because expectations were aroused, because dependencies were generated that now must remain unsatisfied, and anger has mounted, the deprivation and suffering are greater. Sunny-weather beneficiaries are less prepared than before to cope with their chances when the promises of discriminatory decrees are broken.

We have already seen withdrawal symptoms in OCR and the muffling of its vetoes as various groups come to understand the implications of discrimination. The most effective voice, however, is seldom the voice of rational argument. More often it is a political power play, as the case for favored minorities subsides in indifference, and promises to those who threaten organized retaliation become attractive.

Discriminatory Mandates Institutionalize Economic Determinism. All legislation is divisive in which groups (or subgroups) within a unitary social order are identified by characteristics opposed to the legal and moral criteria of nondiscrimination and which it is physically impossible for others to share. Race and sex identifications are of such a kind. By stratifying they also factionalize classes, setting them up as adversaries of their logical opposites. By assuming opposing class interests etched along economically related lines (education, income, employment), preferential decrees covertly assume the premises of economic determinism, namely, that there is and ought to be one-way causal determination from independently objective class interests to edicts that will facilitate the development and satisfaction of those interests. Thus discriminatory edicts, by defining and favoring class interests, pit class against class in the paradigmatic class struggle. Since these classes are correlated with economic and political differentials in status, elective office, housing, and so forth, the lower status of the groups is held to be a reason for legalizing their preferential treatment. The only difference between this and feudalism is incidental: feudalism favored by law those with a high economic and political status. But the principle and the logic of the cases are the same. Now I shall try to show that the consequences are the same too.

Causation in social phenomena is not a one-way determination, but a bi-causation in which effects of certain social changes themselves serve as causes reinforcing and maintaining those same effects. Like operant conditioning in psychology, entrenched social forces, once identified and formulated in beliefs, are their own reinforcers; hence the built-in conservatism of social life and the slowness of social change inertly stabilizing its own self-preservation. Because people sometimes act on reasons, belief in antagonistic classes helps to create and continue their antagonisms, since belief in distinct class interests, observable independently of class-making legislation, lays down the conditions with respect to which people act. Hence by coercing social regulations through class-defined edicts that treat groups differently, a society helps to make economic determinism true.

A common example is poverty-creating legislation. Policies intended to relieve poverty actually create more poverty. Economic income, or wealth, is the everincrementing yield of individual work or entrepreneurial effort, of capital investment, consumer want, and resources productivity. It follows that income, or wealth, *legislatively redistributed* apart from work, investment, and productivity, reinforces the withholding of effort, capital investment, and resources. Less income or wealth is thus produced. Less income or wealth means more poverty. If the vicious cycle is continued, the existing national wealth is used up. Organized groups, therefore, latching onto political power, legislate to benefit themselves. Hence they help to create even more clearly economic classes—poor ones.

Social phenomena may exhibit the same vicious cycle that describes psychotic behavior. An individual believes himself to be weak and incompetent. He overreacts with a show of arrogant power. People are repulsed by his behavior. Failing to gain psychic security and acceptance by others, he believes himself to be even more weak and incompetent. He endlessly repeats the vicious cycle. The effect of which reinforces the originating cause. (Karen Horney, *The Neurotic Personality of Our Time*, 1964) Analogously, the more that economic and social circumstances determine the content and scope of enforced legalities, the more credibly economic determinism actualizes itself as an accurate rendition of the perspective we are impelled to take on social and legal issues.

When a current practice contradicts practices ultimately desired, counterproductivity inevitably results. If a university treats its students as if they were immature, the students react immaturely. Then the university retorts, "See, they *are* immature." Its reinforcing role is seldom recognized. Sometimes government treats the citizenry as if they were not sufficiently their brothers' keepers. Resentful, and seeing that charity is otherwise accomplished through taxation and income redistribution, citizens dry up their charitable giving. Then government retorts, "See, they *aren't* their brothers' keepers," failing to recognize the causal role of government—and the consequent problems of state welfare that we examined above begin to burgeon. Recently there has been a national proposal to defer traditional income-tax deductions for charitable giving. In time, the state will blame the people for what misinformed and unintelligent legislation has wrought.

A child is not made cooperative by slapping him into it; neither is a society made peaceable through war. So also a just society cannot be wrought by discrimination. In the social order at large, where affected interests are wide-scale and where knowledge of the future is indeterminable, a legal and therefore coercive stance against whole groups of people must lead to the institutionalization of the discriminatory vocabulary. When the *vocabulary* is institutionalized, justifications for more discriminatory policies will be formulated and acted upon, and we are on the way to a Hobbist state: "this war of every man against every man; this also is consequent: that nothing can be unjust. The notions of right and wrong, justice and injustice, have there no place."

These are not idle dialectical antics. They are examples from our current social life, and they illustrate the logical pattern of social events when illegal policies, like psychotic behaviors, intervene. All such maneuvers produce the opposite of what they aim at, since not only do conditions give rise to men's ideas, but men's ideas describe the conditions they try to effect in the social order. Hence the cycles of self-fulfilling prophecy continue. We can here, for a parallel, draw upon another well-established psychological regularity, the Yerkes-Dodson Law. Bad legislation is like an overly strong emotion; its coercive force destroys the wanted behavior. Voluntary favoring is like a mild emotion; choice facilitates the wanted behavior. *"The optimum level decreases as task complexity increases."* As the task of bringing minorities up to par increases in complexity, coercive force becomes less and less effective, since, in a task of complexity, innumerable refined adaptations have to be made which only on-the-spot individual choices of particulars can effect. One causal principle at work in the system of lawful discrimination seems to be that to try in law to satisfy the needs of an economic interest group is to create needs in other economic interest groups who define their interests as opposing. Since the interests we are concerned with here are economic, economic determinism and the class struggle begin to come true as soon as programs postulated on the economic provenance unjustly discriminate.

The choice of a law or policy is not a preference between preexisting options which will remain unchanged, like choosing a Buick over a Ford. Choosing social policies is *interpreting* the social order as being of such-and-such a kind because it is an engagement in maintaining the kind of social order which we believe desirable. To choose to discriminate, and to make it legally binding to do so, is therefore to recommend the maintenance of a society that discriminates, and that does so, moreover, on the basis of "qualities which its members could not help acquiring. This runs counter to the kind of society we have always believed in.

I have tried to show that unequal laws create class differentials. The self-reinforcing dialectic of social events, if locked into enforcement, defines classes; it then fails to satisfy the economic demands of the classes it created while increasing the differentials by new unequal laws, all of which chronically maintain the class struggle. The cost of opposing equal laws is the continual recreation of the problems which urged the corrective legislation upon us. Since there is often more than one solution to a problem, the only reasonable one is that which is compatible with the social order that we want to keep. Only nondiscriminatory laws can define what constitutes discrimination; therefore, their strict enforcement helps both to avert discrimination in advance and to serve as a corrective when such laws fail to avert discrimination. To renounce the generality and equality of law is to renounce the moral and legal justification for preventing and punishing that very discrimination.

If economic determinism were true, the following assertions should also be true: (1) Legal concepts in white-majority America discriminate in favor of whites. (2) There are no legal means in white-majority America to declare discriminatory laws, if there were such, unconstitutional, or to correct or abolish such laws. (3) There are no litigatory procedures which ever turn out in favor of those who are illegally discriminated against. (4) In white-majority America, there are no agencies or efforts like those of the NAACP or the Legal Defense Fund or the Civil Liberties Union to look to justice for the economically disadvantaged. But the foregoing assertions are all false.

Fixing the meaning, the moral legitimacy, and the causes of justice wholly to the nature of existing economic and social relations shows us the contemporary parallel of the feudal mentality. The requirement that citizens be materially defined before rendering them a certain kind of justice is a blatant repetition of feudal sociological jurisprudence. First serf, free-holder, and nobleman were identified by their economic and social status; then the justice due to each was measured accordingly. I believe it is not too far-fetched to compare the case before us with those execrable bills of attainder marking legal distinctions between the protected and the unprotected by hereditary birthright, and with feudal law of primogeniture in which inheritance passed to him who was favored by the contingencies of birth. For both the features we are discussing, color and sex, are *inherited contingencies— demarcating inheritable ranks!*

Since a person's economic position and aspirations are vitally important to him, surely it follows that laws ought to allow all individuals an equal chance to improve their positions or to change their aspirations if they so desire. This is what we have always meant by *equal opportunity*. We have meant legal access to such improvements in one's position as one may care to try for. Since education and employment affect one's social position and goals, legal access to employment and education must be nondiscriminatory, impartial for all. The economic determinism of reverse discrimination works to cover all cases, as a tautology always does. To establish on record discriminatory decrees that define and correspond to economic classes, deciding *for* people what should be their economic positions and goals, sets a dangerous precedent. Legal decrees fixing classes in order to favor a class believed disadvantaged can readily be used to favor a class believed advantaged.

4   CONCLUSION

Legalized Group Reparations Are Totalitarian. Arguments justifying special-treatment legal compensation are, at base, moral ones, and the deeper motives of sensitive persons are remonstrance and regret. Absence of sympathy or of the desire to correct racial and sexual abuses would be shocking; it would reveal us as a nation of moral primitives. But law, as law, can favor no special purposes, whether motivated by sympathy or anger. Principles can be violated or upheld by both good and malevolent wills, and laws as general reasons can reflect rational prescriptions in the interests of altruism and jealousy alike. As law, the law is indifferent to whether we use its power to compensate groups we feel contrite about or whether we use it to grant privileges to the friends of bureaucrats. It is for this reason that reverse discrimination works so well to entrench an organization of men whose powers may be difficult to eradicate. The nature of discretionary mandates like HEW's affirmative action requires decisions to be made at will, arbitrarily. Hence much authority has to be given to many men who form the power structures of the administering agencies. The consequences for the development of an authoritarian state based on legalized class differentials are too obvious to need further mention. Aristotle recognized the danger.

. . . The nature of reverse discrimination is, as I have tried to show, unintelligible—hence Reason cannot rule. Contradictions unresolvable by reason are often resolved by force. From the perspective of reason and consistency, to require men to favor a racial or sexual characteristic is no different from requiring men to disfavor a racial or sexual characteristic; the effect on the social order is the same. . . . Cicero said it in his *Laws:* "Law is the highest reason, implanted in Nature, which commands what ought to be done and forbids the opposite." In the sixth century B.C., Solon recognized equality of persons in his constitution for Athens, "for the noble and the base alike."

Voluntary Group Reparations May Be Morally Obligatory and Consonant with Legal Equity. It has taken this country almost two hundred years of moral and legal struggle to try to live up to a fundamental inscription in our Constitution that positively prohibits lumping people together into categories that are unrelated to them as moral persons, or that show disrespect for differences persons are born with. The outcome of this struggle is commitment to the belief that discrimination forced in law, and nondiscrimination violated in law, are evils when brought against contingencies that denote persons as members of social, religious, or economic ranks and ignore their shared humanity, their common moral obligations, and their common needs. Legitimate laws in this country therefore state that certain basic rights are secured to all individuals equally. To endorse reversals in such laws we must be sure that no other device will effect the changes we desire; namely, that persons will not stop discriminating so that the disadvantaged can enjoy equal opportunities to the good things in American life. It requires being sure that vigilant corrections in the practice of justice will not suffice; that present laws are ineffective or immoral; that nothing but immoral laws or ineradicable violations of law have caused the condition which we cannot approve; that the costs of reversal are, on balance, appreciably less than the costs of maintaining a just social order—that to continue class stratification is less damaging than to discontinue it—and that no evil will result. In this paper, I have tried to depict the evils that I think will result from reverse discrimination. I question whether even one of these requirements can be met by the employment of discriminatory mandates. I do not believe that any of them can be satisfied by reversals in justice which legalize the special treatment of special groups. Compensatory edicts are none other than that primitive, premoral *lex talionis* in disguise. When a member of one tribe injures another, an entire collectivity is revenged without regard to where responsibility falls. The Bible tells us that the sins of the fathers are visited upon the next generation. I had thought that an enlightened morality transcended this mystique. . . .

Twenty-four hundred years ago, eight generals were being tried for their failure to win the Athenians' battle of Arginusae against the Spartans. But they were not accused as individuals, each bearing his calculable degree of responsibility for the strategic error. They were tried and indicted en bloc. Six were condemned to die. Socrates was in the Assembly at the time of the iniquitous trial. He refused to add his voice. Socrates the constitutionalist recognized the injustice of departures from the rule of law.

Two thousand years ago, 960 Zealots took a last stand at Masada against the Romans whose incursions on the freedom of the Judean Jews had reached unbearable agony. The Zealots lost. But before they lost, they decided as a group to commit suicide. The decision was their own, that of a community of men and women acting in voluntary and spontaneous concert.

I have tried to show that the difference between the two cases of collective responsibility, one morally evil, one morally good, is supplied by legal coercion on the one hand, choice on the other. "You are all condemned" is a mandate with the most monstrous potential for evil when a corporate body is enabled to impose coercive sanctions upon whole groups of innocent people who are integral participants in that same corporate body. *Selach l'go Kodesh.* . . . *Chotonu Tsurainu; selach lonu Yotsurainu* ("O pardon an holy people. . . . We have sinned against thee, O our Rock; forgive us, O our Creator") is a moral achievement of the highest order. "We must all reform" is society as the Prodigal Son, redeeming itself through voluntary sacrifice, recognizing that whole groups of innocent people deserve to be compensated when individuals can be persuaded to fulfill their obligations.

Archibald Cox

Harvard College Amicus Curiae
DeFunis v. Odegaard

. . . We do not imply that in practice all applications are first put through the
step of winnowing out the unqualified, and that the qualified are thereafter
subjected to the step of selection. In practice, some applicants will immediately appear to be qualified in the first sense and to present an outstanding
case for selection in the second sense. In other instances, especially where
scholarly attainment is one of the major criteria for selection, it may quickly
appear that although an applicant is "qualified" in the first sense, his case
for actual admission, in terms of the criteria established for selection, is far
too weak to merit further consideration.

The distinction is important . . . because the criteria used for determining whether an applicant is qualified must not be confused with the
criteria for actual selection. At the first stage the criteria are chiefly intellectual: . . . Membership in a racial or disadvantaged minority group is relevant, if at all, only in adjusting test scores and other predictors of academic
success in order to compensate for correctible deficiencies in the previous
experience or education of particular students. . . . [T]he qualities which

Source: U.S. Supreme Court, *Oct. Term 1973, No. 73-235. Notes and citations
omitted in this edited version.*

admissions officers at a particular institution value in making actual selections may be the same as those to which they look in determining admissibility, but they may be different or they may be overlapping. The various predictors of academic success measured by grades on examinations and assigned papers may be the best measure in judging whether an applicant possesses the school's minimum qualifications, but neither logic nor law nor sound educational policy commands exclusive use of, or even any reliance upon, the predictors in making selections from among the qualified applicants at the second stage of admissions. Most institutions treat sufficiently great promise of academic success as ground for actual admission, using virtually the same predictors as are used in determining minimum qualification, but below that level such predictions may be treated as irrelevant, or the greater academic promise of one applicant may be judged less important than some quite different asset of another. The proportion of students selected because of academic promise alone differs from institution to institution. . . .

A given institution might wish simply to select students of the highest intellectual capacity, . . . in the belief that it should be exclusively concerned with challenging the intellect and increasing the formal learning of the student body, and with encouraging the students thus to challenge each other in these areas. Exclusive reliance on measured achievement might also be thought to introduce the highest form of equality and productive stimulus.

Another institution might conclude that education should be conceived more broadly and that, given minimum assurance of scholastic competence, all students are best served by selecting from the qualified applicants the entering class whose members have the most diverse social, economic and cultural backgrounds and the widest variety of talents and interests. In this view, diversity is a stimulus to the development of every student's personality and understanding as well as a preparation for the society in which he will live. Securing these non-discriminatory, educational objectives for the whole student body dictates evaluating a wide variety of personal characteristics, many of them utterly irrelevant in measuring ability to meet academic standards.

Still a third institution might wish to give substantial weight—say 40 percent—to superior intellectual qualifications in filling all the places in a class, but conclude that an equally marked superiority in other qualities judged to be important should be enough to offset them.

In the first case, neither race nor minority status would be relevant. In the second and third cases, membership in a minority race or other special ethnic group would be a relevant and often highly material consideration because of its significance in forming an entering class whose members will have the diverse characteristics, attachments and experience making them markedly stimulating to each other. Race, color or ethnic origin, like economic or cultural background, is one of the many characteristics that a student presents to his classmates as an individual does to the world—a characteristic which should carry neither invidious distinction nor arbitrary preference, which some treat as always and utterly irrelevant but which others may perceive as encouraging pride and a sense of identification in cultural origins and diversity without hostile connotation. Race, color, and ethnic origin also tend to identify forms of special experience, social and cultural background, outlook, interests and attachments which make important contributions to a student body. This is especially true at any institution which has been predominantly white for a long period.

... For the past 25 years Harvard College has received each year applications for admission that greatly exceed the number of places in the freshman class. The number of applicants who are deemed to be not "qualified" is comparatively small. The vast majority of applicants demonstrate through test scores, high school records and teachers' recommendations that they have the academic ability to do adequate work at Harvard, and perhaps to do it with distinction. Faced with the dilemma of choosing among a large number of "qualified" candidates, the Committee on Admissions could use the single criterion of scholarly excellence and attempt to determine who among the candidates were likely to perform best academically. But for the past 25 years the Committee on Admissions has never adopted this approach. The belief has been that if scholarly excellence were the sole or even predominant criterion, Harvard College would lose a great deal of its vitality and intellectual excellence and that the quality of the educational experience offered to all students would suffer. . . .

Ten or fifteen or twenty years ago, diversity meant students from California, New York and Massachusetts; city dwellers and farm boys; violinists, painters and football players; biologists, historians and classicists; potential stockbrokers, academics and politicians. The result was that very few ethnic or racial minorities attended Harvard College. In recent years Harvard College has expanded the concept of diversity to include students from disadvantaged economic, racial and ethnic groups. Harvard College now recruits not only Californians or Louisianans but also blacks and Chicanos and other minority students. Contemporary conditions in the United States mean that if Harvard College is to continue to offer a first-rate education to its students, minority representation in the undergraduate body cannot be ignored by the Committee on Admissions.

In practice, this new definition of diversity has meant that race has been a factor in some admission decisions. When the Committee on Admissions reviews the large middle group of applicants who are "admissible" and deemed capable of doing good work in their courses, the race of an applicant may tip the balance in his favor. . . . A farm boy from Idaho can bring something to Harvard College that a Bostonian cannot offer. Similarly, a black student can usually bring something that a white person cannot offer. The quality of the educational experience of all the students in Harvard College depends in part on these differences in the background and outlook that students bring with them.

In Harvard College admissions the Committee has not set target-quotas for the number of blacks, or of musicians, football players, physicists or Californians to be admitted in a given year. At the same time the Committee is aware that if Harvard College is to provide a truly heterogeneous environment that reflects the rich diversity of the United States, it cannot be provided without some attention to numbers. It would not make sense, for example, to have 10 or 20 students out of 1,100 whose homes are west of the Mississippi. Comparably, 10 or 20 black students could not begin to bring to their classmates and to each other the variety of points of view, backgrounds and experiences of blacks in the United States. Their small numbers might also create a sense of isolation among the black students themselves and thus make it more difficult for them to develop and achieve their potential. Consequently, when making its decisions, the Committee on Admissions is aware that there is some relationship between numbers and achieving the benefits to be derived from a diverse student body, and between numbers and providing a reasonable environment for those students admitted. But that awareness does not mean that the Committee sets a minimum number of blacks or of people from west of the Mississippi who are to be admitted. It means only that in choosing among thousands of applicants who are not only "admissible" academically but have other strong qualities, the Committee, with a number of criteria in mind, pays some attention to distribution among many types and categories of students.

The further refinements sometimes required help to illustrate the kind of significance attached to race. The Admissions Committee, with only a few places left to fill, might find itself forced to choose between A, the child of a successful black physician in an academic community with promise of superior academic performance, and B, a black who grew up in an inner-city ghetto of semi-literate parents whose academic achievement was lower but who had demonstrated energy and leadership as well as an apparently abiding interest in black power. If a good number of black students much like A but few like B had already been admitted, the Committee might prefer B; and vice versa. If C, a white student with extraordinary artistic talent, were also seeking one of the remaining places, his unique quality might give him an edge over both A and B. Thus, the critical criteria are often individual qualities or experience not dependent upon race but sometimes associated with it.

The explicit emphasis put on diversity at Harvard College is greater than in other parts of Harvard University. The range of relevant diversity is probably greater in undergraduate than graduate education; musical talent, for example, would surely be given greater weight by the Admissions Committee of Harvard College than by the committees at the Medical School or Law School. . . . Emphasizing a wide range of diversity, moreover, almost automatically ensures that Harvard College will help to open educational and career opportunities to young men—and through Radcliffe College, young women—from all parts of society and sections of the country.

Though the range of significant diversities may be less at some graduate or professional schools and relatively less weight may be placed upon them, all Harvard faculties recognize the educational importance of diversity of social and economic background, experience and resulting outlook in the class and seminar rooms, and in less formal discussions in the dormitories and commons. . . .

This Court has already affirmed in broader terms than we need advocate the right of school authorities to take account of race in forming and effectuating non-discriminatory educational policies. In *Swann v. Charlotte-Mecklenburg Board of Education*, 402 U.S. 1, 16 (1971) the Chief Justice wrote for the Court:

> School authorities are traditionally charged with broad power to formulate and implement educational policy and might well conclude, for example, that in order to prepare students to live in a pluralistic society each school should have a prescribed ratio of Negro to white students reflecting the proportion for the district as a whole. To do this as an educational policy is within the broad discretionary powers of school authorities. . . .

The efforts of counsel to distinguish the *Charlotte-Mecklenburg* case upon the ground that "[n]o student has a Constitutional right superior to any other student to attend a particular school in the system" mistake the situation . . . There is no greater "constitutional right" to a law school education than there is to assignment to a particular school in a single school system. In each case the student has a very real and important interest in his or her educational objective. The disappointments and adverse consequences of assignment to be bussed to a school out of one's own neighborhood may be as serious as those of denial of admission to a particular law school, for both parents and child. In some instances, denial of admission to a State university law school may, in conjunction with other individual circumstances, block access to legal education. In either event, the question is not one of relative hardship. If attention to race or color were barred under the Equal Protection Clause by any hard-and-fast rule, it would be as unconstitutional in the one case as the other.

Both State and lower federal court decisions also support the discretion of school districts to make school assignments with an eye to race in the interest of fulfilling the educational purpose of introducing racial pluralism into schools where segregation de facto formerly prevailed. . . .

Turning from precedent to principle, three simple truths delineate the only arguable issue:

(1) The Equal Protection Clause does not forbid pursuit of a selective admissions policy at a State institution of higher education. The state is not constitutionally obliged to provide higher education for those who appear to lack the intellectual and academic qualifications necessary to benefit. Nor is a State required to find the resources to provide places in its system of higher education for everyone who does have intellectual and academic qualifications giving promise of benefit. When the number of applicants qualified to benefit from the particular course of instruction is greater than the number of places available, the institution may, because it must, select some qualified applicants and turn away others.

(2) The Equal Protection Clause neither requires nor invites the judiciary to prescribe the standard of selection to be used by educators where the limited number of places forces them to select some qualified applicants for actual admission but to deny others despite the adequacy of their qualifications. Standards of selection that would not be constitutionally permissible in other contexts are acceptable in admissions to colleges and universities, both because the individual characteristics that may be educationally relevant are numerous and because, despite disappointments and hardships, selections must be made. . . .

A number of briefs urging reversal explicitly or implictly start from the premise that "intellectual competency and capacity," proved chiefly by academic performance and intelligence or aptitude tests, is the only permissible standard for selecting students for places in a law school unable to accept all its qualified applicants. . . . The use of intellectual merit as an almost exclusive standard has had enormous value in enhancing the quality of teaching and scholarship. It has been equally important in eliminating or reducing some forms of prejudice, first in higher education and then in the professions. It is surely plausible and may even be right to say that, in admissions to some kinds of graduate schools and other educational decisions, intellectual capacity and performance are still the ideal criteria even though they do less alone than when tempered with other criteria to meet the problems of racial and ethnic inequalities. Such questions are constantly under debate in higher education. That is where the debate belongs, for the issues are matters of educational policy, not constitutional law. The Fourteenth Amendment does not command the use of "intellectual competency and capacity" as the sole basis of selection for admission to every institution in whose activities a State is significantly involved. Here as elsewhere in the realm of ideas, variety and experimentation are the keys to greater understanding.

. . . Justice Powell referred to the "persistent and difficult questions of educational policy, another area in which this Court's lack of specialized knowledge and experience counsels against premature interference with informed judgments made at the state and local levels." Educational programs and the admissions policies and practices that affect them lie in the realm of ideas, where the highest importance attaches to academic freedom for both State and privately-endowed institutions. As Justice Brennan observed . . .

> Our Nation is deeply committed to safeguarding academic freedom, which is of transcendent value to all of us and not merely to the teachers concerned. That freedom is therefore a special concern of the First Amendment, which does not tolerate laws that cast a pall of orthodoxy over the classroom.

(3) It follows—putting such qualities as race or ethnic origin temporarily aside—that the Fourteenth Amendment generally permits an institution to make an applicant's probable contribution to the diversity of the student body the primary standard of selection once there is promise of satisfactory academic performance. . . . Given this relationship and the necessity of choice, comparing candidates in terms of talents, outlook, experience,

social, economic and cultural background and other like qualifications is within the discretion available to educational authorities under the Fourteenth Amendment even though distinctions made upon such grounds would be unconstitutional in such areas as taxation and criminal law. The constitutionality of such an approach to law school admissions was implicitly affirmed in *Sweatt v. Painter*, . . . where this Court observed:

> . . . although the law is a highly learned profession, we are well aware that it is an intensely practical one. The law school, the proving ground for legal learning and practice, cannot be effective in isolation from the individuals and institutions with which the law interacts. Few students and no one who has practiced law would choose to study in an academic vacuum, removed from the interplay of ideas and exchange of views with which the law is concerned.

. . . Given the necessity of preferring some qualified applicants over others and the permissibility of refined comparisons on the basis of very personal characteristics, does the Fourteenth Amendment nevertheless require admissions officers to blind themselves to what all the world knows: that the presence of members of minority races is one of the most valuable sources of diversity in any community, whether large or small, general or specialized?

Plainly, the words of the Constitution do not decree this form of colorblindness. Nor should its majestic generalities be so interpreted. The policy of the Equal Protection Clause looks to equal treatment of the members of the identifiable groups composing society, not to the elimination or disregard of the special characteristics of their members. In urging that admissions committees need not be blind to the opportunities for increasing diversity among the students in a class and thus improving their education *by including students from racial and ethnic minorities*, we do not suggest that race and ethnic origin may always be used as a basis of selection. To use race, color or ethnic origin *to exclude* members of an insular minority, impose a restrictive quota or enforce segregation is patently unconstitutional. . . .

It is argued that since a felt educational need for homogeneity within a classroom will not justify differentiations based upon race or color, they cannot be justified by a desire for diversity, because the one has no sounder educational claim than the other. The argument can be answered in educational terms, but the central fallacy is the assumption that the academic exclusion or segregation of minorities has the same psychological, sociological and political effects as their inclusion. In any society, the effects of including any defined group in opportunities and benefits will be different from the consequences of their segregation of exclusion. Professor Paul A. Freund puts a simple but revealing example:

> Compare a trust fund donated to a university, the income to be used for the education of the descendants of John Hancock, and an unrelated fund for the education of anyone except those descendents. It would not be surprising if the governing board of the university felt differently about the two preferences, and judges might be animated by the same sense of justice in applying the constitutional guarantee of equal protection of the laws. . . .

In the United States, as a result of the long years of slavery and Jim Crow policies any admissions policy that denies admission to black students, segregates them or limits their number not only carries the vice of exclusion but asserts the supremacy of the white race and the inferiority of others; and for that reason it constitutes "hostile" or "invidious" discrimination. On the other hand, there is no danger of "invidious" or "hostile" implication, whether in purpose or effect, when a predominantly white institution counts membership in disadvantaged racial or other minority groups as a factor favoring selection for admission from otherwise qualified candidates.

. . . A policy of promoting variety by including members of minority groups along with applicants of other diverse backgrounds and talents gives relatively little weight to minority status as such. To be sure, race, color or ethnic origin is one of the characteristics a student presents to his fellows as a man does to the world, and among those of limited experience a difference in these respects may arouse irrational prejudices that it is a function of education to dissipate. The real significance of minority status . . . is that it is a useful although not invariably reliable indicator of a kind of special social, economic or cultural background for which they [admissions officers] are looking because it is likely to carry its own important varieties of experience, perception, talent, outlook and interests. In addition, minority status is only one of many personal characteristics considered. . . .

Giving favorable attention to minority status in opening the doors to higher education to minority groups has the incidental effect of partially offsetting the severe inequalities in education and educational opportunities from which generally-disadvantaged minorities currently suffer. This point need not be advanced, however, to sustain the use of minority status as a factor which favors the admission of qualified minority applicants but is to be weighed among other indicia of applicants' diversely stimulating, individual characteristics in an effort to compose the student body offering the highest quality educational opportunities to all students. For in this situation no one group, majority or minority, is being preferred to any other. The objective of improving the education of all is non-discriminatory in every sense of the word. . . .

Counsel for the Anti-Defamation League of B'nai B'rith argue . . . that counting minority status as a factor favoring admission is "invidious" and "stigmatizing" to the students admitted because they suffer from the "uncommunicated realization that perhaps we were not authentic law students and the uneasy suspicion that our classmates [and certain members of the faculty] knew that we were not. . . . " This problem of the black student and students from other disadvantaged minorities is very real . . . but it arises from past racial injustices which have built a variety of inequalities into the whole structure of our society. To say that the individual black students, who are admitted to law school because of the weight given to their special background, outlook and talents and who may carry with them handicaps to high intellectual performance imposed from the past, are the victims of current stigmatizing and invidious treatment by the law school admitting them, flies in the fact of reality. First, the admitting law school does not create the feared intellectual handicaps. Second, the true comparison is not between attending law school with possible intellectual handicaps and without, but between attending with the possible handicaps and not attending at all. Third, all the law school does is to open an educational opportunity to the minority student which would otherwise be closed; the choice is the student's. Fourth, exclusive reliance upon tests of "intellectual competency and capacity" would long postpone eliminating the disadvantages in access to higher educational and career opportunities imposed upon minority groups by long years of society's hostile discrimination. . . .

. . . [I]t is also argued that giving favorable weight to minority status means that in the competition for the final place in an entering class members of the white race are put at a disadvantage because they may be passed over in favor of a black applicant whose other claims to selection are no greater than theirs; and imposing such a disadvantage in the comparison of A with B is said to be "invidious." The answer, we submit, is twofold: First, the comparison should not be perceived, and in truth is not made, in terms of race or color as such, but in terms of contribution to the richness and diversity of the contributions A and B respectively can make to the education of all students. Second, the risk that A will nonetheless perceive the distinction as mark of official bias towards the black race is too small to warrant subordinating the values promoted by allowing educational authorities thus to pursue non-discriminatory educational objectives.

In this connection, it is relevant to note that our submission does not require a ruling upon the constitutionality of fixed numerical target-quotas. . . . Such attention to numbers carries very different connotations from fixed minority target-quotas. The latter assert absolute concern for race, color or ethnic origins as such, without regard to other forms of diversity. Under a target-quota system, a black applicant, a Chicano and a native American Indian, for example, will each be admitted to fill the appropriate minority quota without looking to see what background, experiences, outlook and interests he is likely to bring to the class, and without comparing his probable total contribution with the probable total contribution of non-minority applicants competing for a place. . . .

Definition of community needs and choice of emphasis in filling them is a central aspect of educational policy-making at any institution of higher learning, whether privately-endowed or a State institution. . . . More often than not the choice of policy calls for special emphasis rather than total concentration. It is hard to imagine one law school devoting all its energies to training trial lawyers while another graduates specialists in the law of corporations and finance, but it is easy to visualize a faculty choosing to put special emphasis upon either. Furthermore, selective emphasis is often put upon particular objectives in undertaking specially oriented programs financed by State or federal government or a foundation.

An institution's criteria for selection of qualified students for an entering class or a particular program may be deeply influenced by its objectives. A medical school emphasizing the training of general practitioners may look for different qualities than one primarily concerned with higher levels of teaching and research. A school of education worried by the quality of teaching in the blighted areas of urban centers will hardly make its selections by the same criteria as one primarily concerned with educational administration.

In recent years many institutions of higher education have become gravely concerned about the disadvantages suffered by minority groups in access to higher education, business and professional opportunities, and professional services. Many kinds of obstacles face members of minority groups who might otherwise enjoy higher education: sheer prejudice, cultural barriers, language barriers, inferior schooling, economic obstacles, alienation and isolation, lack of incentives, and so forth. Many of the obstacles are the direct or indirect consequences of slavery, "white supremacy" and other historic prejudices leading to the poverty and isolation of disadvantaged groups. The barriers to entry into professional schools are also obstacles to entry into the professions. The lack of representative numbers of minorities in the professions not only deters successive generations of young men and women in minority groups from seeking higher education; it also narrows the membership and therefore the vision of the professions, and the availability of professional services. . . .

The benefits of removing those obstacles and hence increasing opportunities for disadvantaged minorities in the law schools and later at the bar fall under four headings: (1) increasing the individual's opportunities for challenge, satisfaction and advancement, (2) broadening the membership and therefore the understanding of the legal profession, (3) improving the access of minorities to understanding practitioners, and (4) improving legal education.

The United States prides itself as a Nation in providing open opportunity for success and satisfaction to all of its citizens. Law can be a wonderfully exciting and rewarding profession. Its challenge to human understanding and intellectual discipline is enormous. Its perquisites are often large both in terms of material wealth and social esteem. There is no reason to believe that, all other things being equal, minority members of society would wish any less than others to strive for and attain the status of attorney-at-law. Indeed, there were ten applicants for every one opening in the Council on Legal Education Opportunity (CLEO) program in the summer of 1973.

Surely, as membership in the legal profession becomes broader, so does its perspective. Collegial discussions and interactions with those who have first-hand knowledge of community and societal problems adds to the comprehension of the profession as a whole. Moreover, as membership becomes broader, understanding of the legal profession by larger segments of the population is also enhanced. What was heretofore only television knowledge is replaced by contact with friends and acquaintances who are lawyers in the same community. They may become role models for aspiring young men and women who had not previously appreciated their opportunities to practice law. Similarly, those once reluctant to seek legal advice may become less inhibited when they have access to attorneys with whom they are familiar, either personally or by reputation, within their own community. This is not to say that only a black attorney can represent a black client or that a Chicano must be represented by another Mexican-American. But it is myopic to believe that there is no difference in seeking representation from a person with whom one can identify as opposed to an "outsider."

. . . Law is an intellectual profession, but the law's concern is men and women, their daily lives, their joys and sorrows, their fears and aspirations, their mean pursuits and high adventures. Without sympathetic under-standing of life, perhaps without understanding the persons with whom he deals better than they understand themselves, a lawyer is scarcely worthy of the name. Diversity of experience, background, outlook and interests among law students matriculating together contributes to that understanding for all students, and may be indispensable for many. Although the interchange of ideas among very bright students who are all from similar backgrounds is usually intelligent, it may be so one-dimensional as to be more filling than fruitful. . . .

Earlier in this brief we explained our reasons for concluding that the Equal Protection Clause does not deny educational authorities discretion to elect to give favorable weight to membership in a minority race, among other criteria, . . . The legal analysis supporting that proposition is different in two respects from that required to support giving weight to race, or membership in another minority, as a way of reducing existing disadvantages in access to educational opportunities, career opportunities and sympathetic professional services. First, the objective of improving the quality of education, for all students can fairly be called "non-discriminatory" in every sense of the word. Second, if there is anything "invidious" about looking to race or other minor-ity status as a factor favoring inclusion in an entering class, the sting is mini-mal where such status is counted as an indication of some actual and more potential diversity in talents, background, outlook or interests (which are then examined further in each individual case) and weighted along with the many other personal attributes of all the qualified applicants. In contrast, the objective of reducing the existing disadvantages of minority groups is a racially, religiously, and ethnically conscious objective, and minority status as such becomes a factor favoring admission.

Despite these distinctions, the result in the latter case should be the same as in the former. The Equal Protection Clause does not prohibit all racially conscious government activity, but only that which is "hostile" or "invidious" towards minorities or else falls under the general constitutional ban upon arbitrary or capricious classifications. . . .

We are not unmindful of the fear that permitting consciousness of race to influence decisions to admit minorities now generally perceived as "dis-advantaged" not only reduces the opportunities of all others but *could* become the occasion for throwing the whole burden of the reduction upon other minorities not now seen as disadvantaged. Nothing in the decision below or our argument suggests that any form of racial, ethnic or religious characteristic may be given the slightest weight in excluding any applicant who would otherwise be admitted. Such use perhaps could not always be proved, but that would be true regardless of the ruling in this case. The risk of the revival of such prejudice would not be enhanced by affirmance of the State court's decision. . . .

From a constitutional standpoint, the difference between giving favorable but undefined weight to minority status and fixing a specific numerical target for the admission of at-least-minimally-qualified minority applicants may not be significant. But the differences are so important in terms of educational philosophy and fairness among individuals as to lead us to suggest that the question should be reserved. Even in an age seeking only to reduce the disadvantages which minority groups generally suffer as the ingrained consequences of earlier hostile official and private discrimination, the allocation of a fixed target-quota of places proportionate to the ratio of the minority in the population seems to assert a group entitlement based solely upon numbers. Fixed target-quotas for each minority close places to individual members of different groups regardless of any number or degree of relevant qualifications. They impart a quite different philosophy than a teaching that in the competition for a limited number of places some adjustment must be made for social objectives but they are to be weighed in individual cases along with other claims to the places available. Whether the differences have constitutional significance it is unnecessary now to decide. . . .

The judgment of the Supreme Court of Washington should be affirmed.

Archibald Cox
Attorney for Amicus Curiae

Justice William O. Douglas

DeFunis v. Odegaard, Dissenting Opinion (April 23, 1974)

I agree with Mr. Justice Brennan that this case is not moot, and because of the significance of the issues raised I think it is important to reach the merits.

1

... Applicants who had indicated on their application forms that they were either Black, Chicano, American Indian, or Filipino were treated differently in several respects. . . . [A]ll applications of Black students were assigned separately to two particular committee members: a first-year Black law student on the Committee, and a professor on the Committee who had worked the previous summer in a special program for disadvantaged college students considering application to law school. Applications from among the other three minority groups were assigned to an assistant dean who was on the Committee. The minority applications, while considered competitively with one another, were never directly compared to the remaining applications,

Source: U.S. Supreme Court, 416 U.S. 312 (1974). Notes and citations omitted in this edited version.

either by the subcommittee or by the full committee. As in the admissions process generally, the Committee sought to find "within the minority category, those persons who we thought had the highest probability of succeeding in law school." In reviewing the minority applications, the Committee attached less weight to the Predicted First Year Average "in making a total judgmental evaluation as to the relative ability of the particular applicant to succeed in law school." . . . In its publicly distributed Guide to Applicants, the Committee explained that "[a]n applicant's racial or ethnic background was considered as one factor in our general attempt to convert formal credentials into realistic predictions."

Thirty-seven minority applicants were admitted under this procedure. Of these, 36 had Predicted First Year Averages below DeFunis' 76.23, and 30 had averages below 74.5, and thus would ordinarily have been summarily rejected by the Chairman. There were also 48 nonminority applicants admitted who had Predicted First Year Averages below DeFunis. Twenty-three of these were returning veterans, . . . and 25 others presumably admitted because of other factors in their applications making them attractive candidates despite their relatively low averages.

It is reasonable to conclude from the above facts that while other factors were considered by the Committee, and were on occasion crucial, the Predicted First Year Average was for most applicants, a heavily weighted factor, and was at the extremes virtually dispositive. A different balance was apparently struck, however, with regard to the minority applicants. Indeed, at oral argument, the law school advised us that were the minority applicants considered under the same procedure as was generally used, none of those who eventually enrolled at the law school would have been admitted.

The educational policy choices confronting a University Admissions Committee are not ordinarily a subject for judicial oversight; clearly it is not for us but for the law school to decide which tests to employ, how heavily to weigh recommendations from professors or undergraduate grades, and what level of achievement on the chosen criteria are sufficient to demonstrate that the candidate is qualified for admission. What places this case in a special category is the fact that the school did not choose one set of criteria but two, and then determined which to apply to a given applicant on the basis of his race. The Committee adopted this policy in order to achieve "a reasonable representation" of minority groups in the law school. . . . Although it may be speculated that the Committee sought to rectify what it perceived to be cultural or racial biases in the Law School Admission Test or in the candidates undergraduate records, the record in this case is devoid of any evidence of such bias, and the school has not sought to justify its procedures on this basis.

Although testifying that "[w]e do not have quotas . . . " the law school dean explained that "[w]e want a reasonable representation. We will go down to reach if we can," without "taking people who are unqualified in an absolute sense. . . . " By "unqualified in the absolute sense" the Dean meant candidates who "have no reasonable probable likelihood of having a chance at succeeding in the study of law. . . . " But the Dean conceded that in "reaching," the school does take "some minority students who at least, viewed as a group, have a less such likelihood than the majority student group taken as a whole." . . .

It thus appears that by the Committee's own assessment, it admitted minority students who, by the tests given, seemed less qualified than some white students who were not accepted, in order to achieve a "reasonable representation." In this regard it may be pointed out that for the year 1969-1970—the year before the class to which DeFunis was seeking admission—the Law School reported an enrollment of eight Black students out of a total of 356. . . . That percentage, approximately 2.2%, compares to a percentage of Blacks in the population of Washington of approximately 2.1%.

2

The [LSAT] test purports to predict how successful the applicant will be in his first year of law school, and consists of a few hours' worth of multiple choice questions. But the answers the student can give to a multiple choice question are limited by the creativity and intelligence of the test-maker; the student with a better or more original understanding of the problem than the test-maker may realize that none of the alternative answers are any good, but there is no way for him to demonstrate his understanding. . . .

Those who make the tests and the law schools who use them point, of course, to the high correlations between the test scores and the grades at law school the first year. . . . Certainly the tests do seem to do better than chance. But they do not have the value that their deceptively precise scoring system suggests. The proponents' own data shows that, for example, most of those scoring in the bottom 20% on the test do better than that in law school—indeed six of every 100 of them will be in the top 20% of their law school class. And no one knows how many of those who were not admitted because of their test score would in fact have done well were they given the chance. There are many relevant factors, such as motivation, cultural backgrounds of specific minorities that the test cannot measure, and they inevitably must impair its value as a predictor. Of course the law school that admits only those with the highest test scores finds that on the average they do much better, and thus the test is a convenient tool for the admissions committee. The price is paid by the able student who for unknown reasons did not achieve that high score —perhaps even the minority with a different cultural background. Some tests at least in the past have been aimed at eliminating Jews.

The school can safely conclude that the applicant with a score of 750 should be admitted before one with a score of 500. The problem is that in many cases the choice will be between 643 and 602 or 574 and 528. The numbers create an illusion of difference tending to overwhelm other factors. . . .

Of course the tests are not the only thing considered; here they were combined with the prelaw grades to produce a new number called the Predicted First Year Average. The grades have their own problems; one school's A is another school's C. And even to the extent that this formula predicts law school grades, its value is limited. The law student with lower grades may in the long pull of a legal career surpass those at the top of the class. . . .

But by whatever techniques, the law school must make choices. Neither party has challenged the validity of the Predicted First Year Averages employed here as an admissions tool, and therefore consideration of its possible deficiencies is not presented as an issue. The law school presented no evidence to show that adjustments in the process employed were used in order validly to compare applicants of different races; instead it chose to avoid making such comparisons. Finally, although the Committee did consider other information in the files of all applicants, the law school has made no effort to show that it was because of these additional factors that it admitted minority applicants who would otherwise have been rejected. To the contrary, the school appears to have conceded that by its own assessment—taking all factors into account—it admitted minority applicants who would have been rejected had they been white. We have no choice but to evaluate the law school's case as it was made.

3

The Equal Protection Clause did not enact a requirement that Law Schools employ as the sole criterion for admissions a formula based upon the LSAT and undergraduate grades, nor does it proscribe law schools from evaluating an applicant's prior achievements in light of the barriers that he had to overcome. A Black applicant who pulled himself out of the ghetto into a junior college may thereby demonstrate a level of motivation, perseverance and ability that would lead a fairminded admissions committee to conclude that he shows more promise for law study than the son of a rich alumnus who achieved better grades at Harvard. That applicant would not be offered admission because he is Black, but because as an individual he has shown he has the potential, while the Harvard man may have taken less advantage of the vastly superior opportunities offered him. Because of the weight of the prior handicaps, that Black applicant may not realize his full potential in the first year of law school, or even in the full three years, but in the long pull of a legal career his achievements may far outstrip those of his classmates whose earlier records appeared superior by conventional criteria. There is currently no test available to the admissions committee that can predict such possibilities with assurance, but the committee may nevertheless seek to gauge it as best as it can, and weigh this factor in its decisions. Such a policy would not be limited to Blacks, or Chicanos or Filipinos or American Indians, although undoubtedly groups such as these may in practice be the principal beneficiaries of it. But a poor Appalachian white, or a second generation Chinese in San Francisco, or some other American whose lineage is so diverse as to defy ethnic labels, may demonstrate similar potential and thus be accorded favorable consideration by the committee.

The difference between such a policy and the one presented by this case is that the committee would be making decisions on the basis of individual attributes, rather than according a preference solely on the basis of race. To be sure, the racial preference here was not absolute—the committee did not admit all applicants from the four favored groups. But it did accord all such applicants a preference by applying, to an extent not precisely ascertainable from the record, different standards by which to judge their applications, with the result that the committee admitted minority applicants who, in the school's own judgment, were less promising than other applicants who were rejected. Furthermore, it is apparent that because the admissions committee compared minority applicants only with one another, it was necessary to reserve some proportion of the class for them, even if at the outset a precise number of places were not set aside. That proportion, apparently 15 to 20%, was chosen because the school determined it to be "reasonable," although no explanation is provided as to how that number rather than some other was found appropriate. Without becoming embroiled in a semantic debate over whether this practice constitutes a "quota," it is clear that given the limitation on the total number of applicants who could be accepted, this policy did reduce the total number of places for which DeFunis could compete—solely on account of his race. Thus, as the Washington Supreme Court concluded, whatever label one wishes to apply to it, "the minority admissions program is certainly not benign with respect to nonminority students who are displaced by it." . . . A finding that the state school employed a racial classification in selecting its students, subjects it to the strictest scrutiny under the Equal Protection Clause.

The consideration of race as a measure of an applicant's qualification normally introduces a capricious and irrelevant factor working an invidious discrimination, . . . Once race is a starting point educators and courts are immediately embroiled in competing claims of different racial and ethnic groups that would make difficult manageable standards consistent with the Equal Protection Clause. "The clear and central purpose of the Fourteenth Amendment was to eliminate all official state sources of invidious racial discrimination in the States." . . . The law school's admissions policy cannot be reconciled with that purpose, unless cultural standards of a diverse rather than a homogeneous society are taken into account. The reason is that professional persons, particularly lawyers, are not selected for life in a computerized society. The Indian who walks to the beat of Chief Seattle of the Muckleshoot Tribe in Washington has a different culture than Examiners at Law Schools.

The key to the problem is the consideration of each application *in a racially neutral way*. Since LSAT reflects questions touching on cultural backgrounds, the admissions committee acted properly in my view in setting minority applications apart for separate processing. These minorities have cultural backgrounds that are vastly different from the dominant Caucasian. Many Eskimos, American Indians, Filipinos, Chicanos, Asian Indians, Burmese, and Africans come from such disparate backgrounds that a test sensitively tuned for most applicants would be wide of the mark for many minorities.

The melting pot is not designed to homogenize people, making them uniform in consistency. The melting pot as I understand it is a figure of speech that depicts the wide diversities tolerated by the First Amendment under one flag. . . . Minorities in our midst who are to serve actively in our public affairs should be chosen on talent and character alone, not on cultural orientation or leanings.

. . . But . . . I think a separate classification of these applicants is warranted, lest race be a subtle force in eliminating minority members because of cultural differences.

Insofar as LSAT tests reflect the dimensions and orientation of the Organization Man they do a disservice to minorities. I personally know that admissions tests were once used to eliminate Jews. How many other minorities they aim at I do not know. My reaction is that the presence of an LSAT test is sufficient warrant for a school to put racial minorities into a separate class in order better to probe their capacities and potentials.

This does not mean that a separate LSAT test must be designed for minority racial groups, although that might be a possibility. The merits of the present controversy cannot in my view be resolved on this record. . . . I could agree with the majority of the Washington Supreme Court only, if on the record, it could be said that the law school's selection was racially neutral. The case, in my view, should be remanded for a new trial to consider, *inter alia,* whether the established LSAT tests should be eliminated so far as racial minorities are concerned. The reason for the separate treatment of minorities as a class is to make more certain that racial factors do not militate *against an applicant or on his behalf.*

There is no constitutional right for any race to be preferred. The years of slavery did more than retard the progress of Blacks. Even a greater wrong was done the whites by creating arrogance instead of humility and by encouraging the growth of the fiction of a superior race. There is no superior person by constitutional standards. A DeFunis who is white is entitled to no advantage by reason of that fact; nor is he subject to any disability, no matter his race or color. Whatever his race, he had a constitutional right to have his application considered on its individual merits in a racially neutral manner.

The slate is not entirely clean. First, we have held that *pro rata* representation of the races is not required either on juries, . . . or in public schools, . . . Moreover, . . . we reviewed the contempt convictions of pickets who sought by their demonstration to force an employer to prefer Negroes to whites in his hiring of clerks, in order to ensure that 50% of the employees were Negro. In finding that California could constitutionally enjoin the picketing there involved, we quoted from the opinion of the California Supreme Court, which noted that the pickets would "make the right to work for Lucky dependent not on fitness for the work nor on an equal right of all, but rather, on membership in a particular race. If petitioners were upheld in their demand then other races, white, yellow, brown, and red, would have equal rights to demand discriminatory hiring on a racial basis." . . .

> [t]o deny to California the right to ban picketing in the circumstances of this case would mean that there could be no prohibition of the pressures of picketing to secure proportional employment on ancestral grounds of Hungarians in Cleveland, of Poles in Buffalo, of Germans in Milwaukee, or Portuguese in New Bedford, of Mexicans in San Antonio, of the numerous minority groups in New York, and so on through the whole gamut of racial and religious concentrations in various cities.

The reservation of a proportion of the law school class for members of selected minority groups is fraught with similar dangers, for one must immediately determine which groups are to receive such favored treatment and which are to be excluded, the proportions of the class that are to be allocated to each, and even the criteria by which to determine whether an individual is a member of a favored group. There is no assurance that a common agreement can be reached, and first the schools, and then the courts, will be buffeted with the competing claims. The University of Washington included Filipinos, but excluded Chinese and Japanese; another school may limit its program to Blacks, or to Blacks and Chicanos. Once the Court sanctioned racial preferences such as these, it could not then wash its hands of the matter, leaving it entirely in the discretion of the school, for then we would have effectively overruled *Sweatt v. Painter,* 339 U.S. 629, and allowed imposition of a "zero" allocation. But what standard is the Court to apply when a rejected applicant of Japanese ancestry brings suit to require the University of Washington to extend the same privileges to his group? The committee might conclude that the population of Washington is now 2% Japanese, and that Japanese also constitute 2% of the Bar, but that had they not been handicapped by a history of discrimination, Japanese would now constitute 5% of the Bar, or 20%. Or alternatively the Court could attempt to assess how grievously each group has suffered from discrimination, and allocate proportions accordingly; if that were the standard the current University of Washington policy would almost surely fall, for there is no western State which can claim that it has always treated Japanese and Chinese in a fair and evenhanded manner. . . . This Court has not sustained a racial classification since the wartime cases . . . involving curfews and relocations imposed upon Japanese-Americans.

Nor obviously will the problem be solved if next year the law school included only Japanese and Chinese, for then Norwegians and Swedes, the Poles and the Italians, the Puerto Ricans and the Hungarians, and all other groups which form this diverse Nation would have just complaints.

The key to the problem is consideration of such applications *in a racially neutral way.* Abolition of the LSAT test would be a start. The invention of substitute tests might be made to get a measure of an applicant's cultural background, perception, ability to analyze, and his or her relation to groups. . . . There is, moreover, no bar to considering an individual's prior achievements in light of the racial discrimination that barred his way, as a factor in attempting to assess his true potential for a successful legal career. Nor is there any bar to considering on an individual basis, rather than according to racial classifications, the likelihood that a particular candidate will more likely employ his legal skills to service communities that are not now adequately represented than will competing candidates. Not every student benefited by such an expanded admissions program would fall into one of the four racial groups involved here, but it is no drawback that other deserving applicants will also get an opportunity they would otherwise have been denied. Certainly such a program would substantially fulfill the law school's interest in giving a more diverse group access to the legal profession. Such a program might be less convenient administratively than simply sorting students by race, but we have never held administrative convenience to justify racial discrimination.

The argument is that a "compelling" state interest can easily justify the racial discrimination that is practiced here. To many "compelling" would give members of one race even more than *pro rata* representation. The public payrolls might then be deluged, say, with Chicanos because they are as a group the poorest of the poor and need work more than others, leaving desperately poor individual Blacks and whites without employment. By the same token large quotas of Blacks or browns could be added to the Bar, waiving examinations required of other groups, so that it would be better racially balanced. The State, however, may not proceed by racial classification to force strict population equivalencies for every group in every occupation, overriding individual preferences. The Equal Protection Clause commands the elimination of racial barriers, not their creation in order to satisfy our theory as to how society ought to be organized. The purpose of the University of Washington cannot be to produce Black lawyers for Blacks, Polish lawyers for Poles, Jewish lawyers for Jews, Irish lawyers for the Irish. It should be to produce good lawyers for Americans and not to place First Amendment barriers against anyone. That is the point at the heart of all our school desegregation cases, . . . A segregated admissions process creates suggestions of stigma and caste no less than a segregated classroom, and in the end it may produce that result despite its contrary intentions. One other assumption must be clearly disapproved, that Blacks or browns cannot make it on their individual merit. That is a stamp of inferiority that a State is not permitted to place on any lawyer.

If discrimination based on race is constitutionally permissible when those who hold the reins can come up with "compelling" reasons to justify it, then constitutional guarantees acquire an accordionlike quality. Speech is closely brigaded with action when it triggers a fight, . . . as shouting "fire" in a crowded theatre triggers a riot. It may well be that racial strains, racial susceptibility to certain diseases, racial sensitiveness to environmental conditions that other races do not experience may in an extreme situation justify differences in racial treatment that no fairminded person would call "invidious" discrimination. Mental ability is not in the category. All races can compete fairly at all professional levels. So far as race is concerned, any state sponsored preference to one race over another in that competition is in my view "invidious" and violative of the Equal Protection Clause.

The problem tendered by this case is important and crucial to the operation of our constitutional system; and educators must be given leeway. It may well be that a whole congeries of applicants in the marginal group defy known methods of selection. Conceivably, an admissions committee might conclude that a selection by lot of say the last 20 seats is the only fair solution. Courts are not educators; their expertise is limited; and our task ends with the inquiry whether, judged by the main purpose of the Equal Protection Clause—the protection against racial discrimination—there has been an "invidious" discrimination.

We would have a different case if the suit were one to displace the applicant who was chosen in lieu of DeFunis. What the record would show concerning his potentials would have to be considered and weighed. The educational decision, provided proper guidelines were used, would reflect an expertise that courts should honor. The problem is not tendered here because the physical facilities were apparently adequate to take DeFunis in addition to the others. My view is only that I cannot say by the tests used and applied [that] he was invidiously discriminated against because of his race.

I cannot conclude that the admissions procedure of the Law School of the University of Washington that excluded DeFunis is violative of the Equal Protection Clause of the Fourteenth Amendment. The judgment of the Washington Supreme Court should be vacated and the case remanded for a new trial.

John Hart Ely

The Constitutionality of
Reverse Racial Discrimination

... If we are to have even a chance of curing our society of the sickness of racism, we will need a lot more black professionals. And whatever the complex of reasons, it seems we will not get them in the foreseeable future unless we take blackness into account and weight it positively when we allocate opportunities. But that must mean denying opportunities to some people solely because they were born white. Either way, it's no musical, and I confess I have trouble understanding the place of righteous indignation on either side of this wrenching moral issue.

On the surface at least, the constitutional issue is also quite troubling. We would not allow a state university to favor applicants because they are white, not even an iota, whether it called the adjustment a quota, affirmative action, or anything else. To allow it to favor applicants because they are black seems to be countenancing the most flagrant of double standards.

There is some authority, however, for the permissibility of "benign" racial classification. Closest to the mark, perhaps, is the Supreme Court's dictum in *Swann v. Charlotte-Mecklenburg Board of Education,* making

Source: University of Chicago Law Review *41 (1974). Reprinted by permission of the publisher. Notes and citations are omitted in this edited version.*

explicit its view that a local community may bus children according to race, if it wishes, to remedy school segregation caused by residential patterns. No obvious distinctions come to mind by which voluntary busing plans can be distinguished from other "benign" discrimination. First, although the contrary claim is voiced all too frequently, it is incorrect to say that no one is hurt by busing. Children can be hurt by busing, not simply by the inconvenience of the transportation process itself, but also by the transition from a school environment in which they have grown secure to strange surroundings in which they are likely to find themselves in a racial minority for the first time. Second, the argument that busing hurts neither race more than the other— which may or may not be true, depending on the particular plan—is foreclosed, and rightly so, by cases like *McLaughlin v. Florida* and *Loving v. Virginia*. The fact remains that busing hurts people precisely because of their color. Third, it might be contended that, busing or no busing, every child will go to some school, whereas a preferential-admissions program for a given law school will mean, after its effects have trickled down the entire law-school hierarchy, that someone will be completely denied the opportunity to go to law school because he is white. But even assuming this is so, it points to a difference in degree that probably should not go to the constitutional point. Places in desirable public schools are also scarce resources: an opportunity to attend some school is not the equivalent of an opportunity to attend the most desirable school in the area.

The problem in relying on precedent here is that the Court has never told us what the constitutional point is. Voluntary busing plans may, for all we know, be approved by the Court for any of four reasons: (1) the state's goal, racial integration, is a "compelling" one; (2) the use of a racial classification serves that goal perfectly and not approximately; (3) such plans are benignly motivated and therefore not "suspect" in the first place; or (4) the Court believes that even the most apparently "de facto" residential segregation has a bit of state action in its family tree, and that since busing has been imposed as a remedy for de jure segregation there would be no point in forbidding school boards to adopt similar methods. Or it may be—and the delayed dodge of *DeFunis v. Odegaard* strongly suggests this possibility— that the Court simply cannot agree about the significance of its constitutional precedents.

The standard constitutional defense of preferential treatment for blacks accepts the principle that racial classifications are suspect and therefore subject to special, or unusually demanding, scrutiny. But that does not mean, the argument continues, that racial classifications are necessarily illegal: they can be justified, but only on the basis of a compelling state interest. It is true that the imposition of a compelling state-interest requirement has generally been a prelude to invalidation. But surely, the argument concludes, the promotion of racial integration must be compelling enough. The words certainly flow in logical sequence, but simple assertions of relative importance can never wholly satisfy; one might again respond "double standard," were "no standard" not obviously more appropriate.

I shall argue that reverse racial discrimination can be constitutional, but for reasons quite different from those in the conventional account. Rather than asserting that the demands of "special scrutiny" can be met—an assertion neither the Court nor anyone else has given us criteria for evaluating—I shall suggest that "special scrutiny" is not appropriate when white people have decided to favor black people at the expense of white people. On one level there is a double standard here too: whites can do things to whites they could not do to blacks. But on another, the principle I propose is a neutral one: regardless of whether it is wise or unwise, it is not "suspect" in a constitutional sense for a majority, any majority, to discriminate against itself.

1

The unconstitutionality of all racial discrimination, malign and benign alike, is sometimes urged on the ground that the Fourteenth Amendment, although it does not mention race, was enacted largely to outlaw racial discrimination. But the express preoccupation of the framers of the amendment was with discrimination against blacks, that is, with making sure that whites would not, despite the Thirteenth Amendment, continue to confine blacks to an inferior position. That this is the amendment's history surely cannot conclude the matter; given the historical context, discrimination against blacks is all the framers would have been concerned about, and the equal-protection clause has rightly been construed to protect other minorities. But at the same time, the amendment cannot be applied without a sense of its historical meaning and function. Responsible inquiry must seek to determine the reasons why courts give unusually demanding scrutiny to classifications by which the dominant white majority has advantaged itself at the expense of blacks, and to what extent those reasons apply where the majority chooses to disadvantage itself in favor of blacks.

As a prelude, it may be useful to examine the manner and rationale of the ordinary ("rational relationship") review accorded ordinary ("nonsuspect") classifications under the equal-protection clause. Consider a familiar example: a state statute that permits optometrists, but not opticians, to duplicate lenses. Consider further the plea of an optician who wishes to demonstrate that, although it may be true that most optometrists are better qualified to duplicate lenses than most opticians, he is in fact as well or better qualified to duplicate lenses than a number of optometrists he could name. The proffered proof would be rejected, on the theory that legislative classification on the basis of admittedly imperfect comparative generalizations—stereotypes, if you will—must be tolerated: unbearable cost would result if the government were obligated to create procedures for deciding each and every case on its merits.

Pushed to this concession, our optician's next argument would be that although classifications rooted in comparative generalization are sometimes permissible, the unfairness that results to a number of individuals, himself included, from this classification is so great that it cannot be justified by the savings it effects. If the fit between classification and goal could be made tighter at no cost, the court might label the classification "irrational" and demand that it be made more discerning. But where, as in virtually every case involving real legislation, a more perfect fit would involve some added cost—either the cost to society of permitting some unqualified people to practice or the cost to the government of creating a case-by-case test of qualification—the court would refuse to second-guess the legislative cost-benefit balance. There is no reason to suppose, at least in an "ordinary" case like this, that legislatures are any more likely than courts either to undervalue the unfairness of a rough or undiscerning classification or to overvalue the cost of reducing the incidence of unfairness. . . .

Two factors often mentioned to account for the special scrutiny accorded racial classifications are that racial minorities have been subjected to legal disadvantage throughout our history, and that race is "generally . . . irrelevant to any legitimate public purpose." Neither factor alone can adequately account for extraordinary scrutiny. Some minorities (extortionists, for example) have been repeatedly disadvantaged by the law with good reason. And the fact that a characteristic is irrelevant in almost all legal contexts (as most characteristics are) need not imply that there is anything wrong in seizing upon it in the rare context where it does make a difference. Still, these two factors in combination add up to something significant. The fact that a group has repeatedly been disadvantaged in ways that no one could rationally defend should make us suspicious of any legislation that singles out that group for disadvantage. There is reason to suspect that the prejudices that generated the plainly irrational legislation of past eras are also partly responsible for the facially more palatable classifications of the present day. That suspicion in turn would seem to support the Court's disinclination to credit the usually sufficient imperfect-but-plausible statistical generalization in such contexts. For the usual mode of review assumes that legislatures can generally be trusted to appreciate the unfairness of a loose-fitting classification and objectively balance that unfairness against the savings it effects. Where there is unusual reason to suspect a legislative desire generally and irrationally to subjugate the group disadvantaged by the classification, however, this usual assumption seems an inappropriate basis for a system of review.

Of course, it cannot be said with assurance that all classifications by race that disadvantage minorities were intended to do so. The word, however, is *suspect*. The soundness of the Court's decision to treat these classifications with suspicion, irrespective of what can actually be proved about the legislature's underlying motivation, is corroborated by another point of distinction from the usual classification (to which the "rational-relationship" standard is applied). Racial classifications that disadvantage minorities are rooted in "we-they" generalizations and balances as opposed to "they-they" generalizations and balances. Few legislators are opticians; but few are optometrists either. Thus, although a decision to distinguish opticians from optometrists incorporates a stereotypical comparison of two classes of people, it is a comparison of two "they" stereotypes, namely, "*They* [opticians] generally differ from *them* [optometrists] in certain respects that we find sufficient on balance to justify the decision to classify on this basis." Legislators, however, have traditionally not only not been black; they have been white. A decision to distinguish blacks from whites therefore has its roots in a comparison between a "we" stereotype and a "they" stereotype, namely, "*They* [blacks] differ from *us* [whites] in certain respects that we find sufficient on balance to justify the decision to classify on this basis."

The choice between classifying on the basis of a comparative generalization and attempting to come up with a more discriminating formula always involves balancing the increase in fairness that greater individualization will produce against the added costs it will entail. But in we-they situations two dangers inherent in this balancing process are significantly intensified. The first is that legislators will overestimate the costs of bringing "them" into a position of equality with "us." But the balance is likely to be skewed in another, though related, way—through an undervaluation of the countervailing interest in fairness. It is no startling psychological insight that most of us are delighted to hear and prone to accept characterizations of ethnic or other groups that suggest that the groups to which we belong are superior to others. The second danger is therefore one of overestimating the fit of the proposed stereotypical classification. By seizing upon the positive myths about our own class and the negative myths about theirs, or for that matter the realities respecting some or most members of the two classes, legislators may too readily assume that not many of "them" will be unfairly deprived, nor will many of "us" be unfairly benefitted, by the proposed classification.

2

An understanding of why the Court has approached racial classifications that disadvantage minorities with suspicion unfortunately generates no bright-line test to determine whether other, nonracial minorities should receive similar protection. The implication of that understanding for the present discussion, however, seems obvious. When the group that controls the decision-making process classifies so as to advantage a minority and disadvantage itself, the reasons for being unusually suspicious, and, consequently, employing a stringent brand of review, are lacking. A white majority is unlikely to disadvantage itself for reasons of racial prejudice; nor is it likely to be tempted either to underestimate the needs and deserts of whites relative to those of others, or to overestimate the costs of devising an alternative classification that would extend to certain whites the advantages generally extended to blacks. The conclusion is corroborated by the realization, given eloquent voice in Justice Jackson's *Railway Express* opinion, that the function of the equal-protection clause is in large measure to protect against substantive outrages by requiring that those who would harm others must at the same time harm themselves—or at least widespread elements of the constituency on which they depend for reelection. But the argument does not work the other way around: similar reasoning supports no insistence that one cannot hurt himself, or the majority on whose support he depends, without at the same time hurting others as well.

Of course, there will be cases in which it will not be clear whether the legislative majority or the allegedly benefitted minority has ended up, on balance, with the comparative advantage—or, more to the point, whether the decision makers intended a greater benefit to the "we's" or the "they's." In these cases we should be suspicious. Furthermore, preoccupation with a majority-minority analytic framework should not obscure the fundamental premise that racial and related prejudices can properly give rise to suspicion.

Such prejudice could obviously generate a "they-they" classification, and for that matter a classification that facially disadvantages the legislative majority but was intended, and will function, as a de facto they-they classification. Thus, there might be reason to believe that a law that apparently favors blacks over whites was specifically intended to disadvantage a subset of whites that is both inadequately represented in the decision-making body and the object of unusual prejudice. But where there is no reason to suspect that the comparative disadvantage will not be distributed evenly throughout the "we" class, a we-they classification that favors the "they's" does not merit "special scrutiny"—though obviously the court should take a careful look to make sure that the case presented fits this description. Whether or not it is more blessed to give than to receive, it is surely less suspicious.

3

Even if one accepts this conclusion in a vacuum, its adoption and enforcement by the courts, particularly by the United States Supreme Court, would entail some difficulties and side effects that are troublesome at the least, and might even suggest that a prophylactic rule banning all racial classification is the better course. The concern may be that a preference for one minority may not operate to the undifferentiated disadvantage of the majority generally, but instead may cause disproportionate harm to a discrete, disfavored, and relatively powerless subset of the majority. This is not, of course, an argument invented for purposes of this discussion: just such a fear has prompted certain Jewish groups to voice strenuous opposition to preferential admissions for blacks. Somehow, the concern seems to run, most of those "black places" will be taken from Jews. I do not for a moment discount the reality of anti-Semitism in our society, nor can we consider the feared scenario "just one of the costs" of pursuing racial equality. It is an unacceptable scenario, and an unconstitutional one as well. An American state legislature, unlike, perhaps, the Israeli Parliament, cannot legitimately pursue the goal of reducing the percentage of Jewish lawyers. Whites generally, not Jews in particular, are a majority in our society, and consequently racial discrimination is unsuspicious only when it runs against whites in general.

It is questionable, however, whether this danger can form the basis for a constitutional argument against preferences for blacks or other racial minorities. A "discretionary" system of selection already leaves room for various sorts of indefensible prejudice to operate: no matter how one might feel about the comparative merits and dangers of such a system—my own feeling has never been very positive—a decision to extend preferences to blacks does not significantly alter the problem. Administrators who incline toward anti-Semitism in the one situation will very likely incline toward it in the other. The chances of catching them, of demonstrating the illegality of what they are doing, are no greater in the one than in the other. And if a preferential-admissions program for blacks should be accompanied by an unexplained disproportionate drop in the percentage of Jews, or even by a shift to a selection system that left more room for anti-Semitism—a more discretionary system or a ceiling on the number of students from New York City—the appropriate judicial response would be clear. There would be reason to suspect that the idea was to prefer one ethnic minority at the disproportionate expense of another for reasons of religious prejudice, and the scheme should be invalidated. Anti-Semitism is a danger—one that should, in any event, be combatted by every available tool, including constitutional litigation—but the danger is independent of a decision to extend preferences to blacks. Perhaps in other situations it will be impossible ever confidently to conclude that the dominant majority is not favoring blacks over some white minority for reasons of ethnic prejudice. But as long as there are situations where the two problems are separable—and this seems to be the case in the law-school situation in which *DeFunis* arose—an across-the-board ban on preferential treatment seems unjustified.

Some of us used to worry that any employment by the government of racial classifications for "benign" purposes—particularly with the Supreme Court legitimation—would retard public acceptance and enforcement of decisions like *Brown v. Board of Education.* . . . The concern might have carried the day so long as there was reason to hope that simply removing racial access barriers would result in genuine integration of society's various institutions. Although the barriers have not yet been entirely removed—heated debate on "benign" discrimination must not fool us into believing that malign discrimination is a thing of the past—we have enough experience to suggest that an "open door" is not sufficient, that if we are to have any hope of defeating racial prejudice we will have to take race into account for some purposes. And if that is the course we are to take, then that is the message we will have to project, difficult though it may be to expose the "contradiction" as only apparent. . . . The question is whether the negative educative effects of using racial criteria to overcome centuries of discrimination are so inevitable, and indeed so threatening, as to outweigh the good that such programs may accomplish. It is a difficult question, but the basis for an affirmative answer can hardly be secure enough to support an absolute declaration of constitutional impermissibility.

A credible **expl**anation of why "benign" racial classifications are not suspect, however, would require the Court to expose some of the considerations that have made malign racial classifications suspect, and that exposure poses arguable risks for the judicial process. Explaining that the Court has accorded special review to most racial classifications because they are often the product of irrational prejudice might prompt a charge that the Court builds its constitutional judgments on "sociology, not law." Even if the Court could sidestep that charge with an explanation phrased more in terms of the relative nonsuspiciousness of a group's decision to disadvantage itself in favor of another, it would still find itself in sensitive territory. The justices might feel awkward about publicly taking into account the racial or other composition of the decision-making body, or perhaps of its constituency, even assuming that the pertinent facts are obvious. . . .

Those who are troubled would be better advised to consider another alternative, eloquently elaborated in the earlier writings of Professor [Alexander] Bickel (indeed, "benevolent quotas" were one of the chief examples): denial of review. Powerful attacks have been mounted on the use of the "passive virtues" to avoid the invalidation of practices that are wrong on constitutional principle. The use suggested here is different, however, and is addressed to anyone who takes the (debatable) view that although the practice in question is not unconstitutional on principle, explaining why it is not would carry serious costs for the nation generally and the Court in particular.

By virtually inviting another *DeFunis* case, the Court seems to have indicated that it sees no great costs in writing the opinion, and I am inclined to agree. But that decision—and not the decision on the constitutional merits —is the hard one. Measures that favor racial minorities pose a difficult moral question that should, by one method or the other, be left to the states. There is nothing suspicious about a majority's discrimination against itself, though we must never relent in our vigilance lest something masquerading as that should in fact be something else.

Kent Greenawalt

Judicial Scrutiny of "Benign" Racial Preference in Law School Admissions

Racial preferences for blacks generate ambivalence in those who care about racial equality and also believe that individuals should be judged "on their own merits." This ambivalence is reflected in divergent "equal protection" values, the value of eliminating barriers to equality imposed on minority groups and that of distributing the burdens and benefits of social life without reference to arbitrary distinctions. It is hardly surprising, therefore, that after Marco DeFunis, Jr. challenged the constitutionality of racial preferences for admission to a state law school, the Supreme Court's resolution of the issue was awaited with intense interest and some trepidation. For the time being, the Supreme Court has avoided grappling with the substantive questions, but they give little promise of "going away." . . .

Although the University of Washington Law School may have been unusual in having a "minority" representation in its entering class that actually doubled the "minority" representation in the state, its substantial preference was typical of the policies of many public and private law schools throughout the country. These policies go well beyond tipping close choices in favor of

Source: Columbia Law Review 75 (1975). *Reprinted by permission of the author and publisher. Notes and citations are omitted in this edited version.*

members of minority groups and reflect definite decisions to have significant percentages of students from minority groups. Like the University of Washington Law School, most law schools do not have a fixed minimum quota for minority students, but as Justice Douglas indicates, there is no constitutional difference between using such a quota and using preferential policies to fill some approximate percentage of the class or to admit all minimally qualified minority applicants.

Washington's policy was apparently typical in two other respects which I shall also assume in my discussions: each member of the designated minorities was eligible for preference regardless of his own personal background; and members of some "racial" minorities, Chinese-Americans and Japanese-Americans, were not preferred. For the sake of simplicity in the body of this article, I shall concentrate on preferences for blacks, saving until the end analysis of whether the relevant justifications support preferences for other groups.

1   LEVELS OF REVIEW UNDER THE EQUAL-PROTECTION CLAUSE AND "BENIGN" RACIAL CLASSIFICATIONS

[In part one, which Professor Greenawalt has kindly summarized for this collection, he considers the appropriate standard for judicial review of "benign" racial classifications.]

Whether any classification will be accepted as consistent with the equal-protection clause of the Fourteenth Amendment depends in large part on the level of scrutiny with which the classification is reviewed. In "ordinary" cases, most notably those involving typical economic and social legislation, the Court asks only whether the classification bears a rational relationship to a permissible legislative purpose. Rather few classifications fail under this test, although in recent years the Court has applied the test in some areas, such as sex discrimination, with less leniency than is usual, and has struck down a number of challenged distinctions.

The alternative to the "rational-basis" test is "strict scrutiny." Under this approach the Court looks harder at whether a legitimate purpose exists and whether the classification serves that purpose. Even if the classification does serve a legitimate purpose, it may still be declared invalid unless it is "necessary" to a "compelling state interest." If the state interest is not deemed especially important or the interest could be served without the challenged classification, then the classification fails. Strict scrutiny is employed if the statute or administrative action uses a "suspect" classification, for example, one disadvantaging racial minorities, or a classification that burdens a fundamental right, for example, the right to travel.

The sharp dichotomy between rational-basis and strict-scrutiny review has been attacked on and off the Court. Justice Marshall has argued that the Court has in fact varied its standards of review in ways much more complex than the twofold categorization would imply, and has urged explicit acceptance of a sliding scale of review.

It is a crucial constitutional question for discrimination in favor of disadvantaged racial minorities what standard of review should apply. On the one hand, it is urged that all racial classifications are suspect, indeed perhaps so suspect that only the most urgent justifications, if any, could possibly support them; this is Justice Douglas' position in his dissent in *DeFunis*. On the other hand, it is argued that since the Fourteenth Amendment was passed to protect racial minorities, any discrimination in their favor need pass only the rational-basis test.

I conclude that an intermediate level of scrutiny is appropriate. Because discrimination in favor of blacks and other minorities gives an advantage to groups especially protected by the Fourteenth Amendment and is designed to promote long-run equality, which can be taken as one of the implicit values of the amendment, I think the Court should be more accepting of such discrimination than of classifications that disadvantage minority groups. Nevertheless, because benefits to particular racial groups encourage racial politics, because racially drawn lines tend to perpetuate thinking in racial terms by those directly affected and others, and because such lines require the state to stand ready to determine the race of someone applying for a benefit, benign racial discrimination does have severe drawbacks in terms of the values of the Fourteenth Amendment. The Supreme Court should accept a particular discrimination in favor of a racial minority only if it promotes a "substantial" interest and only if that substantial interest could not be promoted about as well and at tolerable administrative expense by a nonracial approach or a more narrowly tailored racial classification.

2   CONSTITUTIONAL EVALUATION OF JUSTIFICATIONS FOR PREFERENTIAL-ADMISSIONS POLICIES

The account I give of justifications for preferential policies coincides largely with that of James Nickel's thoughtful discussion [see pp. 324-347, herein]; what it adds to that discussion is analysis of the constitutional dimension.

Redress for Unwarranted Injury. One justification for preferential-admissions policies is that they redress unjust discrimination that blacks have suffered.

A. *Compensatory and Distributive Justice.* In his analysis, Professor Nickel makes use of the Aristotelian distinction between compensatory justice and distributive justice, between making a person whole for losses he has unjustly suffered and giving him the position in society he "deserves." Though it may be difficult to draw a precise line between these two kinds of claims, in many contexts the distinction is clear. The newly elected public official who argues that he should be paid more makes a claim of distributive justice on society's resources. A rich alcoholic "bum" who returns to society after ten years in jail on an unjust conviction and who is presently at least as well off as he would be if he had never been convicted has a claim of compensatory justice for the pain he has suffered. In the context of preferential programs for blacks, the distinction largely collapses in practice. The claim for distributive justice, like that for compensatory justice, rests on assertions of past injustice. If blacks had never been peculiarly subject to social injustice, there might be no constitutionally adequate reason to treat them as a "class" for determining if society's benefits are justly distributed. If it just happened that few blacks had inherent aptitude for law or an interest in being lawyers, the minute percentage of black lawyers would not reflect any distributive injustice. The main reason why a claim of distributive justice has force is that it is assumed that more blacks would now enjoy high positions if their race had not been held back by social injustice. If preferential benefits were subject to precise calculation, it is possible that claims for compensation would support greater benefits than distributive claims; but for purposes of constitutional law the distinction between claims of compensatory and distributive justice is so slender that in this context we may treat them together as claims for redress of injustices.

B. *Injustices the Government May Constitutionally Redress.* The government's duty to redress injustices is clearest when the government itself causes an injury that is illegal at the time it is caused, but its power to rectify injustice is hardly limited to these situations. It may compensate for injustices that it caused, say by the laws of slavery, that were legal at the time they were inflicted; and it may compensate for injustices suffered at the hands of private individuals, whether or not those injustices amount to a general social practice. It may, in fact, "compensate" for losses that are not the fault of either the government or other individuals, as when it establishes special relief programs for earthquake and flood victims.

The Supreme Court's approval of racial classifications to correct de jure segregation demonstrates that the government's interest in assuring redress of specific instances of illegal discrimination is great enough to justify some use of racial criteria. Since the government has the power to redress illegal discrimination indirectly as well as directly, and to redress injustices other than illegal discrimination, the person who claims that reliance on racial classifications in preferential-admissions policies is impermissible must argue that the government's interest here is less important than when it corrects illegal segregation, or that the particular hardships imposed by racially based preferential policies are unacceptable methods for redressing those injustices.

C. *Preferential Admissions and Social Injustice.* "Equal protection of the laws" would not have been denied to impoverished whites if in 1868 a state had made free land available to ex-slaves. If, instead, the state had made land available to all black adults within its borders, on the theory that few, if any, blacks had not suffered the effects of slavery or other state discriminations unique to blacks, it is hard to believe a court would have, or should have, found the program to be unconstitutional because all blacks and no whites were eligible for its benefits.

The constitutionality of modern programs to redress injustices to blacks is not as immediately apparent. I shall put aside for the moment the problem that the "burden" of many of these programs falls on excluded applicants, and assume that, as with the hypothetical grant of land, the burden falls on society generally. One or more of the three following theories might be used in support of a preference for a modern young black: (1) that he has been directly subjected to compensable discrimination; (2) that he has suffered the effects of discrimination against his forebears; or (3) that he should be compensated because of a special relationship to his forebears, whether or not he has suffered from wrongs done to them. We may deal briefly with the third possible theory as based on a dubious moral claim unlikely to be relied on extensively by thoughtful proponents of preferential admissions. Compensation to immediate survivors for harm done to others may have a place in the law of tort, since survival of actions helps to deter and penalize wrongful behavior and to compensate near kin for incalculable losses. Compensation to survivors may also be appropriate when a wrong is done to an ongoing entity like an Indian tribe, or when the perpetrators of a horrendous wrong wish to "purge" their guilt by compensating persons who have a significant relationship to the victims. But when the perpetrators and victims of social injustice are both dead, it is hard to explain why the government should prefer those who happen to be descendants of the victims, unless they have been affected by the injustice. Because two much stronger arguments exist for redressing injustices to blacks we need not explore this one further.

Since widespread discrimination against blacks continues in the United States, it is plausible to suppose that most young blacks have suffered from it in various ways and that government redress is appropriate. But a preferential policy designed for that purpose that includes all blacks and excludes all whites now has much more serious defects of underinclusiveness and over-inclusiveness than it would have had if adopted in 1868. It is not clear that most blacks suffer injustices significantly different in character from those inflicted on some whites. And some young blacks are members of families recently arrived from other countries, or of families so well situated that they have not been sharply touched by discrimination. One might try to answer the charge of overinclusiveness with the suggestion that discrimination against blacks is so pervasive that it has touched, or will touch, all blacks significantly. A more general response to the charge of imprecise classification would be that proof of discrimination is too uncertain to be handled administratively, and, further, that it would be undesirable for law schools to decide how much discrimination individual applicants have suffered. This is a close point, but I believe that law schools could assess reasonably well whether particular members of nonpreferred groups had suffered injustices similar to those imposed generally on the preferred group, and whether certain members of the preferred group had not suffered such injustices. I therefore think it doubtful that the Fourteenth Amendment should be interpreted to allow a straight racial preference where the only justification tendered is compensation to those directly injured by discrimination.

Benefits to young blacks may also be urged, however, on the ground that they continue to suffer the effects of discrimination against their parents and more distant forebears. Blacks victimized by discrimination have suffered educational, vocational, economic and psychological harms. Their ability to confer benefits on their children has been sharply impaired. No identifiable group of whites suffered injustice as extreme as that imposed on blacks under the American version of slavery. Not only were they deprived of virtually every kind of social good enjoyed by free men, they were also largely stripped of their culture. It would have taken several generations to wipe out the effects of slavery even if its end had meant instantaneous equal treatment. In fact, further systematic discrimination has perpetuated those effects. Most young blacks are undoubtedly still disadvantaged because of the direct effects of slavery and systematic racial discrimination against post-emancipation generations, and they have suffered from racial discrimination even if they have not all been personally subjected to racial bias.

It can be debated whether the young black has a greater claim on society's resources than a young white whose predecessors were equally ill-educated and destitute because they were persecuted in some other country or were lazy drunkards; but it is tenable to believe that a society has a special reason to eliminate the hardships stemming from its own injustices, and that this responsibility can survive the death of oppressors and direct victims, as long as ascertainable persons continue to suffer those hardships. This is not to say that rectifying the effects of injustice on subsequent generations is a typically desirable policy; it usually is not. It is only to say that a decision justified on that basis would not be evidently unsound.

If a reason for preference is to ameliorate the effects on this generation of injustice caused to past generations, then the use of an explicitly racial classification instead of a more individualized alternative is easier to defend than if the focus is on injustice to this generation. As to possible underinclusiveness, few whites have suffered from injustices like those inflicted on blacks by slavery and systematic discrimination, and the effects of any such injustices would be virtually impossible to trace.

Nor could possible overinclusiveness be cured by a study of black family histories to disqualify those few young blacks, if any, who may actually have benefited from slavery and the general discrimination against blacks. Neither their compensatory justification nor administrative necessity, however, would reach recent black immigrants from other countries.

We still have not faced the question whether the purpose of compensation is weighty enough to sustain a racial classification. It may be urged that society should be forward-looking in its policies, that society has survived intact despite the general failure to give government redress for injustices, and that a policy of compensation is of debatable wisdom and certainly does not reflect any paramount state interest. Proponents of preference can argue that social justice is among the most important aims of a social order, and that redress for blacks is both just and needed to relieve a sharp sense of injustice that most blacks feel. The need for redress may not be of undeniable urgency but the reasons that support compensation for most blacks reflect substantial government interests; if those reasons are accepted by legislators or administrators against competing arguments, they should be viewed by courts as important enough to sustain compensatory programs for blacks.

There remain two possible arguments for the impermissibility of pre-ferential-admissions policies as methods of redressing injustice, even if some more general compensatory program on racial grounds is acceptable. It might be thought that policies benefiting only a comparative handful of blacks directly cannot be justified on a compensatory basis. Three answers to this contention may be made. First, particular government institutions are not in a position to confer benefits generally; if compensation is to include vocational and educational positions, benefits crucially important to human fulfillment of which blacks have been unfairly deprived, each institution must be able to give redress in the manner appropriate for it. Otherwise, compensation would be possible only under a general legislative plan. Second, when law-school preferential-admissions policies are viewed in the context of other governmental preferential policies, the benefits are more general than they appear if one focuses only upon law schools. And preferences that produce more black lawyers and public leaders may indirectly help other blacks redress injustices. Third, whatever the average innate abilities of members of different races, social conditions in this country are the main determinant of differences in the average intellectual performances of blacks and whites. A state can reasonably assume that had it not been for discriminatory injustice, the percentage of blacks admitted to law school without preference would be much higher than it is. While it cannot be said that the very same blacks who are now reasonably well qualified and gain admission because of the preference would have been admitted without preference had there been no discrimination, it is plausible to suppose that many of these applicants would have been among the well-educated and intelligent blacks who would have been admitted. If one effect of discrimination is that fewer blacks can qualify without preference, then one proper form of compensation is to eliminate the effect of denial of admissions on those who would otherwise have qualified. The closest a law school may be able to come to identifying the class of those who in the absence of discrimination probably would have qualified without preference is to choose the best prepared blacks who now apply.

A more troublesome objection to preferential-admissions polices than the limited size of the class that directly benefits is the limited size of the class on whom the "burden" falls, and this is an objection that can be raised with respect to all the justifications given for preferential policies, not only the "compensatory" ones.

Unless a state expands facilities in order to accept more blacks, the burden of preferential-admissions policies falls squarely on excluded white applicants, not the people who have practiced discrimination or even society as a whole. That the burden of preferential policies falls on a few individuals rather than on society at large or the educational institution granting the preference may be a reason for closer judicial scrutiny of the preference, but it is not a major constitutional relevance. No white has a vested interest in a legal education. A white with high test scores and grades from an intellectual city family would have no substantial constitutional claim if he were denied admission to a state law school that decided to admit some "less qualified" applicants who had grown up on farms. Since applicants are vulnerable to being excluded in pursuit of any one of a number of possible policies, no special constitutional difficulty is caused because the burden of racial preference falls on them. Moreover, insofar as it makes sense to assume that without discrimination many more blacks would qualify without preference, a state might assume that borderline whites who are admitted in the absence of preferential policies are indirectly "benefiting" from discrimination of which they are completely innocent. If they are excluded because of preferential policies, they may be put in the position they would have been in if the discrimination had never occurred. Expansion of facilities and resources is not always a sensible option, or an option the relevant institution has the power to choose. While there may be some injustice in casting the burden of preference on excluded whites, the need to make certain kinds of very important benefits the subject of compensation renders that unfortunate effect constitutionally acceptable.

Preferential Admissions and Qualifications. A different kind of argument made for preferential admissions is that ordinary admissions procedures inadequately reflect the qualifications of minority-group members. Justice Douglas found some of these arguments persuasive in his dissent on the merits in *DeFunis*, though he rejected the appropriateness of outright racial preferences.

    A. *Qualifications for Law School Performances.* It is asserted that the law-school aptitude tests and college grades do not adequately indicate the probable law-school performance of blacks. Of course, exact predictions of performance are impossible, and even for white students predictions based on tests and grades do not correlate neatly with actual performance, but this argument assumes that these predictions are sufficiently reliable to be a weighty factor in the admission of whites. The contention is, however, that blacks are special because the law school aptitude tests are culturally biased and college grades also do not reflect the potential of those who are culturally disadvantaged.

    One problem with this argument is that predictions of law-school performance based on tests and grades are not significantly less accurate for black applicants than for other applicants. Perhaps the test is "culturally biased," but so also may be the law-school program and the practice of law, in the sense that they call for skills and attitudes developed in the dominant culture. Insofar as tests and grades are especially inaccurate predictors for most blacks, plainly this is not a result of race pure and simple. Presumably these standards of likely performance are not culturally biased for blacks who have well-educated parents and whose predominant contacts at home and school have been with whites. And the standards may very well be culturally biased for poor whites who were educated in culturally disadvantaged settings and whose predominant contacts have been with poor blacks. If there are special reasons why tests and grades do not accurately predict law-school performance for those from particular cultural backgrounds, it would not be very difficult administratively to make special exceptions from ordinary standards for whites from those backgrounds. Given the constitutional presumption against racial classification, this more particularized approach should be required as a less onerous alternative.

Another reason why this qualifications argument cannot support existing preferential policies is that whatever special dispensation might be given to blacks because of the special inaccuracy of the usual bases for prediction of law-school performance, no one can doubt that most law schools have gone far beyond that in their policies. They are admitting blacks who they are reasonably sure will not do as well in law school as white applicants denied admission.

B. *General Qualifications for the Legal Profession*. Only some of the skills lawyers need are tested in law school. Thus, there is a gap between qualifications for law-school performance and qualifications for legal practices. As difficult as it may be to identify the skills needed for good lawyering, a state law school could properly decide to admit those who would make better lawyers in preference to those who would make better law students. Perhaps there is some correlation between being black and having qualifications for legal practice that will not be reflected in law-school performance. Persons without educational advantages are much less likely to suffer with respect to some qualities lawyers need than with respect to the analytic precision and skill in written communication so important for law-school success. And deficiencies in writing and analytical skills are much more likely to be overcome in the course of an entire career than in the three years of law school itself. Nevertheless, as with predicting law-school performance, racial classification is much too imprecise a means if the underlying justification for preference is an attempt to gauge more accurately the general qualifications lawyers require.

C. *Job Placement and Qualifications*. Legal education fills a social need. Some legal jobs may be judged socially more important than others, and a state law school might decide to admit some "less qualified" students who are particularly likely to do socially valuable work in preference to "better qualified" applicants less likely to do such work. Again, even if one assumes that there is some correlation between being black and being likely to do socially valuable work, such as work for the poor and otherwise disadvantaged, it would be feasible administratively to make much "finer" guesses about an applicant's likely job orientation, based on his specific background, his previous activities and his expressed reasons for wishing to go to law school.

D. *Ability to Work with Blacks*. It can be argued that black lawyers are more likely to represent black people effectively because they can win their trust and understand them better. Commonality of background, vocabulary and attitude can be helpful for a lawyer's representation of his client. Of course, a rich white lawyer may do a superb job of representing a poor black defendant; and when a major legal issue is sharply presented, an expert lawyer's personal background makes little difference. But personal background may become much more important when one is counseling clients or trying to learn their story.

If a law school may permissibly aim to improve representation of segments of the community not now well represented, presumably it could give preference to applicants who speak Spanish or are from farming families or poor families, if it deems a firsthand knowledge of Spanish, farming, or poverty useful in representing groups or persons not now adequately served by the legal profession. Since blacks constitute about twelve per cent of the national population and less than two percent of the bar, and racial identity is certainly one relevant factor for easy understanding and communication in this culture, preference for blacks in order to improve representation for blacks is certainly rationally defensible. The Supreme Court's approval of preferences for members of Indian tribes for jobs in the Bureau of Indian Affairs was decided on narrow grounds, but it gives limited support to the notion that racial preferences for members of groups that have been disadvantaged are warranted by the need to give the most effective representation possible to those groups.

This "special-qualifications" argument is the only form of the "qualifi-cations" argument for preferences on explicitly racial lines that is plausibly consistent with the Fourteenth Amendment; my own conclusion is that even racial preferences based on this rationale should not withstand an equal protection attack. Racial identity is, at most, one small aspect of effec-tive representation. A more talented white lawyer will usually represent blacks better than a less talented black one. Moreover, many black lawyers will find themselves in jobs where they rarely represent black clients, so a general racial preference benefits many applicants for whom this argument will prove to be irrelevant. I believe that the Fourteenth Amendment policy against such racial classifications is stronger in terms of this argument than with respect to the compensation argument, because a governmental assumption that black lawyers can represent blacks more effectively implied-ly endorses racial ways of thought much more than a governmental assump-tion that blacks deserve compensation. It suggests that private citizens should take race into account in their dealings with lawyers. As Justice Douglas urged in his *DeFunis* dissent: "The purpose of the University of Washington cannot be to produce Black lawyers for Blacks, Polish lawyers for Poles, Jewish lawyers for Jews, Irish lawyers for the Irish." Perhaps if law schools made a more particularized effort to determine which applicants would be most likely to work on behalf of disadvantaged groups, they could take into account the possibility that black lawyers may be more effective in helping disadvantaged blacks than white lawyers. Perhaps also this special-qualifications argument, as well as the other qualifications arguments, can give slight added weight to the state's other interests in a general racial pref-erence in admissions; but the qualifications arguments, separately or to-gether, are not sufficient by themselves to sustain such a preference against constitutional attack.

Preferential Admissions and the Values of Diversity and the Amelioration of Attitudes That Hinder Equality of Opportunity. Some arguments for prefer-ential policies are based on claimed benefits to the general society if there are more black students in law school and black members of the bar.

A. *The Integrated Law School.* As the Supreme Court pointed out many years ago [in *Sweatt v. Painter*] and as Erwin Griswold stresses in his article, ["Some Observations on the *DeFunis* Case," *Columbia Law Review* 75 (1975)] one of the values of a legal education is the exposure to persons of diverse backgrounds and points of view. One might add that the benefits of diversity in the student body accrue to the faculty as well as the students. In order to enrich the education of all its students, a state law school may admit persons with unusual experience, say former schoolteachers or policemen, in preference to those who are slightly more "qualified" but who lack the special experience. Regrettable though it may be, race is a crucially important aspect of most people's experience; a white student who has never talked seriously with blacks will be unlikely to understand many very important things about life in the United States. While increasing understanding, such contacts may also eliminate or blur racial stereotypes that can inhibit one's effective functioning as a lawyer, judge, or administrator. If the diversity sought is diversity of racial experience, then obviously a preference in racial terms is precisely tailored to the aim.

If preferences are necessary to get a significant number of blacks into law school, the interest in a racially diversified student body is substantial enough to justify preferences for some blacks, since race is now such an important determinant of social perceptions, and so many problems with which lawyers and officials deal concern race. But it should not be assumed that because some preferential representation of a group is permitted to encourage diversity, members of that group can be admitted on a preferential basis until they constitute the same percentage of the student body as their percentage of the general population. It is not certain, for example, that relevant communication between blacks and whites will be much greater if the student body is 10 percent black than if it is 5 percent black. Of course, it may be unfair to impose on a small number of blacks the responsibility to communicate the "black experience" to a large number of whites; but a law school justifying its preferential policies in terms of law-school diversity should make some effort to decide how widely applicable racial preferences should be to achieve adequate diversity.

The proper degree of judicial review of a policy supported by a diversity justification is very difficult to determine, because it is much harder for judges to second-guess decisions about how much diversity is needed and how it can best be achieved than it is for them to deal with the questions of administrability of alternative standards raised by some compensation and qualifications arguments. It is hard even to conceive of the "evidence" a school might give to support a particular percentage of black representation. Nevertheless, given the general undesirability of racial classifications and the potential broad sweep of diversity arguments, it would be a mistake for the courts to accept a diversity claim as justifying whatever number of preferential admissions law schools choose to make. The courts should at least require a reasoned explanation by administrators of why they believe the actual number of preferences given will yield the desired diversity.

B. *The Amelioration of Racial Stereotypes.* Past discrimination has made it very hard for blacks to become professionals. The widespread assumption that blacks are more suited for menial jobs has affected the attitudes of whites toward blacks and the attitude of blacks toward themselves. If young blacks are to aspire to, and work toward, high vocational positions, it is important for them to see that significant numbers of persons with whom they identify are in those positions. And the perception of blacks in those positions will do much to vitiate possible feelings of racial inferiority among a much wider groups of blacks. If whites are going to accept blacks as equal, not only as a matter of religious or political philosophy but also on the intuitive level that so influences actual social relations, it is important that they deal with blacks as equals in the performance of social responsibilities.

A special reason why it is important to have black lawyers is that many lawyers become legislators and high administrators. Both blacks and whites need to see blacks in positions of community leadership, as well as to have a black perspective brought directly to bear on the resolution of many community problems.

Increasing the number of blacks in high vocational positions and as community leaders will not only raise the aspirations of young blacks and dissipate white racial stereotypes, but may also ameliorate some stereotypes blacks have about whites. No longer will it be so easy to distinguish "them" (the white power structure) from "us" (the black oppressed), because "them" will include many blacks. Other blacks will come more easily to see the constraints under which those with power operate and will abandon over-simplified notions of those in responsible positions as invariably "oppressors."

Given the pervasiveness of racial stereotypes in this society and their destructive effect on the quality of life, their dissolution is undoubtedly a proper public purpose. It may be a public purpose that draws implicit support from the Thirteenth and Fourteenth Amendments. The persistence of negative stereotypes about blacks can be argued to be an "incident" of slavery in the extended sense of a debilitating effect of slavery and also an "incident" in the narrower sense of a feature that accompanied slavery itself and continues to disadvantage blacks. As it has developed, the concept of equal protection in the Fourteenth Amendment implicitly condemns stereotypes based on race and class. It would be a denial of equal protection for the government purposefully to foster such stereotypes, and while attacking them may not be required, it is consistent with the spirit of the amendment.

If the purpose of preferential policies is to reduce racial stereotypes, then, of course, the racial classification fits its purpose exactly. So long as the superbly educated son of a black senator or the recent immigrant from Africa are identified as relevantly "black" by whites and other blacks, then this purpose of the preferential policy is served by admitting them.

Opponents of preferential policies argue that racial preferences will be unnecessary and even unhelpful in eliminating stereotypes, that the opening up of opportunities to blacks without preference will produce, as it has for many immigrant groups, enough professionals in a generation or two to undercut racial stereotypes, and that admission preferences for blacks will actually confirm stereotypes. I find neither contention persuasive enough to reject preferential policies; certainly neither is so evidently correct that a court should hold that a decision in favor of preferences is unsound. The average quality of black law students has increased quickly since the first years of preference, perhaps in part because law schools are now admitting many blacks who were admitted on a preferential basis to the best colleges. Most black law-school graduates perform competently, and whatever "gap" may remain at graduation from a given school between some of them and most white students is likely to be reduced during their careers. The "negative" stereotypes fostered by preferential admissions will be far outweighed by the positive effect of having blacks in important professional positions. The answer to the contention that preferences are unnecessary is twofold. Given the systematic historic discrimination against blacks and the more subtle and pervasive discriminatory attitudes that still exist and are particularly hard to eradicate because of the visibility of racial differences, genuine equality for blacks without preference may take much more than one or two generations. Second, the damage done to blacks by racial stereotypes now is so serious that any program that gives hope of altering stereotypes quickly is to be preferred to one that will work only over a longer term.

Whether the state's interest is put as the long run amelioration of racial stereotypes or the reasonably quick amelioration of these stereotypes, it is important enough to support preferential-admissions policies. Whether these policies are "necessary" to achieve these results may be debatable, but the debate is not one that can comfortably be resolved by the judiciary. Legislative or administrative judgments of the need for preferential policies should be accepted; and so long as the gap between the percentage of black professionals and the percentage of blacks in the population remains enormous, this justification for racial preferences will support almost any breadth of application for the preference.

The amelioration of racial stereotypes and compensation of blacks for injuries caused by present discrimination and the lingering effects of past injustices are the two justifications that are adequate to support outright racial preferences as extensive as those now being employed in many law schools.

Justificatory Arguments as Applied to Minorities Other Than Blacks. The purposes of this section are twofold. One is to outline a constitutional evaluation of existing preferences given to minorities other than blacks; the other is to consider the possible applicability of some of the justifications found substantial for preferences for blacks to preferential policies for other groups. The latter inquiry is important not only for its own sake, but also because of fears that if preferences may be given for blacks they may be given for all sorts of other groups, and that the end result may be a society splintered along racial, ethnic and religious lines, with each group having a proportion of desirable positions that matches its proportion of the population. If the justifications for preference do not extend to many other groups, these fears are not well founded.

The discussion in this section is summary; it is meant to sketch the major questions and lines of argument, not to provide a fully developed analysis of the issues.

A. *Groups Now Receiving Preferences in Some Law Schools.* While the historical treatment and present position of Indians are dissimilar to the treatment and position of blacks in important respects, "[I]t is . . . hard to say that the moral claim of the Negro is so much greater than that of the American Indian, who once ruled the continent and was slaughtered wholesale, deprived of his land, and penned up upon reservations." Undoubtedly, Indians have strong claims to redress of injustices and to the amelioration of social attitudes that hinder equality. The law-school diversity argument in one respect is stronger for Indians than for blacks, in another respect weaker. It is stronger in that many law students will have virtually no other contact with Indians; personal contact with Indians as fellow students may be even more important for understanding Indian perspectives. The diversity argument is weaker in that the problems and perspectives of Indians may now be less crucial for society as a whole than the problems and perspectives of blacks.

If preferences for Indians are viewed as preferences for members of tribes that enjoy a unique legal status and their descendants, and, as the Supreme Court has indicated, such preferences are not really racial, then they may be easier to defend in constitutional terms than preferences for blacks because the lines of inclusion and exclusion are not "suspect."

At the most straightforward level, preferences for Chicanos and Puerto Ricans are in terms of place of origin, but they have racial overtones because most Chicanos and Puerto Ricans are racially distinguishable from most "white" Americans in having some Indian or black forebears, and because their disadvantageous position in society is in part a consequence of "racial" discrimination. Arguments in terms of law-school diversity and amelioration of stereotypes are apt for these groups, at least in areas of the country where significant numbers of Chicanos and Puerto Ricans live. Redress of injustice arguments also are relevant, though their strength may depend in part on the section of the country. Insofar as lawyers need to be able to speak Spanish to service many members of these groups, a preference for applicants fluent in Spanish would be warranted, but a preference justified only on a linguistic basis would have to be extended to all those with the relevant linguistic skills.

Presumably similar arguments can be made about Philippine-Americans; their force would depend on premises about past and present treatment and about the effect of social stereotypes on opportunity for young Philippine-Americans. The basis for preference would have to be something more than the fact that applicants from a particular identifiable group have lower paper records than other applicants.

B. *Groups Defined in Terms of National Origin or "Ethnic" Characteristics.* It might be urged that immigrants of particular "ethnic" character or national origin were subjected to discrimination from which their descendants continue to suffer, that the experiences of descendants from each group would contribute to law-school diversity, and that each group needs graduates to ameliorate harmful stereotypes. Although these contentions are by no means ridiculous, they are much less powerful than similar claims by racial minorities.

Whatever stereotypes exist with reference to Italian-Americans or Polish-Americans do not seem seriously to block achievement by members of these groups or to impede social relations between them and others. Identification in terms of national origin is weaker for most people now than racial identification. For this reason, as well as because the original injustices were less severe than those inflicted on blacks, the present effects of earlier discriminations based on national origin are less apparent, and there is much more reason to suppose that those that remain will be ameliorated in the near future.

To promote diversity, a law school might give preference to some recent immigrants and children of immigrants, and perhaps might even be selective in terms of the particular cultures and forms of social organization of the relevant "mother countries." But there are too few social and legal problems on which a third-generation Greek-American is likely to have a different perspective than a third-generation German-American or an American of multiple national origins to warrant preferences on national-origin grounds for the sake of diversity.

A state does not have a substantial interest in preferences based simply on national origin. Since classifications in terms of national origin, like racial classifications, are suspect, even a benign classification of this type should fall if not supported by a substantial interest. We may now understand further why a higher level of scrutiny than "rational basis" is appropriate for "benign" preferences on ordinarily suspect grounds. Under the rational basis standard, a law school would be left free to divide much of the "pie" of places in the student body by preferences for a multiplicity of minority groups. In many parts of the country, a number of minorities make up the majority of the population. If each minority group were assured "proportional representation," the result would be much closer to a maximum quota for presently overrepresented groups than any existing preferential policies. The rational-basis approach would leave an applicant from an overrepresented group almost defenseless against this result; the requirement that the state must show a classification to be necessary in furthering a substantial state interest would provide some safeguards.

Like the term *racial*, the term *ethnic* is one of uncertain and shifting meaning. There are some "ethnic" groups, such as Slavs and Jews, that are not distinguishable from the majority of the population by "race," as that term is commonly used, and are classified in relation to some characteristic other than national origin. For the most part, what I have said about groups defined in terms of national origin is applicable to white "ethnic" groups; but it may be that some "ethnic" stereotypes are more virulent than national-origin stereotypes. Certainly in the past, widely shared stereotypes with respect to Jews have resulted in a great deal of discrimination against them in this country, and they continue to be subjected to considerable prejudice. Since Jews are overrepresented in academic life and the professions, however, it is unlikely that young modern Jews are suffering in relevant career opportunities because of past discrimination, and wholly implausible that preference in academic institutions is needed to multiply role models or improve the representation of Jewish views in the community.

C. *Minority Religious Groups.* Arguments based on past discriminations and present stereotypes might be made to support preferences for minority religious groups, but however persuasive such arguments might have been at earlier times in history, now most religious identifications seem no greater burden to social opportunity than national-origin identifications. Moreover, many religious stereotypes have little to do with the social status of members of the group subject to the stereotypes, so there is not much reason to suppose that improved opportunity for the group would have much effect on the stereotype. Since variant religious beliefs do lead to various perspectives on a spectrum of legal issues, the law-school diversity argument would be considerably stronger for admitting a few Catholics, religious Jews, or Jehovah's Witnesses on a preferential basis, than for admitting Polish-Americans.

Even if the arguments for religious preference were stronger, some special constitutional reasons would remain for hostility toward even "benign" religious classifications. Religious affiliation can be changed and falsified much more easily than race. One dominant principle of the religious clauses of the First Amendment is that the government should not encourage membership in one church rather than membership in another or in no church at all. Religious preferences would contravene this policy, as well as invite fraud and require government determinations of religious affiliation. Moreover, the dangers of religious politics were vividly apparent in Anglo-American history, and the religion clauses may well be read as a virtually absolute ban on public encouragement of political organization along religious lines.

D. *The "Culturally Disadvantaged."* Sometimes preferential-admissions policies are justified as directed at "culturally disadvantaged" or "culturally deprived" persons who have had relatively little social and educational opportunity to develop their talents. As we have seen, it can be asserted that standardized aptitude tests do not adequately measure the abilities of these applicants. Arguments in favor of preferences for them might also be formulated along the lines of redress of injustices and the amelioration of stereotypes with respect to poor persons. A preference in terms of "cultural disadvantage" is certainly permissible, especially since it is not "suspect" and therefore not subject to the higher level of scrutiny appropriate for racial classifications. But if the real aim is to help the "culturally disadvantaged," defined in nonracial terms, a state may not treat all minority-group members and no whites as "disadvantaged"; it must inquire into the "disadvantage" of each applicant.

The Constitutional Relevance of Nonpreference for Some Minority Groups. The University of Washington Law School did not prefer Japanese-Americans and Chinese-Americans, although these groups have certainly suffered discrimination, because it decided that enough applicants from these groups qualified without preference. Some Supreme Court cases have implied that when the legislature engages in reformatory efforts it can draw the lines of inclusion and exclusion almost as it chooses. Whatever the merit of this approach when bystanders are not harmed by benefits given to others, preferential-admissions policies actually disadvantage nonpreferred minorities as well as whites, and administrators should have to produce some reasonable basis for excluding one minority and including another, at least when a member of the excluded minority seeks preference. If an ample number of applicants do not "need" preference, that is a strong indication that members of the minority group are no longer suffering in educational competition from past injustice, that preference is not needed to ameliorate stereotypes, and that young members of the group do not need the extra professional role models preference could provide. Such an indication is a sufficient basis on which to exclude members of a minority group from preferences.

3   EVALUATION OF PARTICULAR JUSTIFICATIONS AND THE BROADER PROBLEM OF CANDOR

I have suggested that two of the asserted purposes for preferential admissions, the amelioration of harmful stereotypes and compensation for injustice, can support a policy of preference as broad as that employed by the University of Washington Law School in the *DeFunis* case. The purpose of law-school diversity does support an outright racial preference but perhaps only one of more limited application. Some other asserted purposes are not sufficient to support reliance on racial classifications in place of more particularized inquiries into the background and the personal qualities of each applicant.

Suppose a challenged program is defended on inadequate grounds when adequate ones could have supported it. Often the Court has sustained legislation with reference to a purpose that is not indicated in the legislation itself and was probably not in the minds of the legislators. An aspect of careful scrutiny, however, should be judicial assurance that those who have decided on classifications that are on the borderline of judicial permissibility have actually made the difficult judgments that such classifications are required. This is especially true if the classifications are administrative rather than legislative, for the courts can then ordinarily accept the defenses for the classifications made by the relevant administrators at the time of, or subsequent to, adoption; they need not probe the diverse motives of legislators. If a state law school defends a racial preferential-admissions policy on the basis of redressing "cultural disadvantage" or on the basis of integrating the law school itself, it should be told by the courts that the first purpose should be served by a more particularized mode of inquiry and that the second at least requires a serious judgment as to how many blacks really are needed to achieve diversity in the student body. It is, of course, conceivable that the administrators will reestablish the same admissions policy, now announcing adequate but spurious grounds, but we should not suppose that will usually happen. Most administrators want to comply in good faith with constitutional standards; they will either decide to tailor preferential policies differently or they will decide that independent reasons really do justify the racial classifications. Original judicial invalidation thus either will result in preferences that are less objectionable in light of the purposes they are designed to serve, or will result in more careful evaluation of the importance of purposes that may permissibly underlie racial preferences. Both are desirable consequences from the constitutional point of view.

If, as may be the most typical case, state authorities rely substantially on reasons for a racial preference that are adequate as well as some that are inadequate, a court should accept the preference, since it may suppose that the authorities would have reached the same decision even if they had realized some of their reasons were less weighty than they thought at the time of the decision.

Thus far I have assumed that an open weighing of constitutional values is to be desired in this area, as in most others. That is at least debatable. Consider the following position: Preferences for blacks are badly needed to alleviate black alienation and to create genuine equality of opportunity. But upper-middle-class liberal whites who make the decisions about preference will suffer a crisis of conscience if they have to admit they are favoring some racial groups at the expense of others and at the expense of criteria of individual merit. The poorer whites who have relatively few social opportunities will certainly resent such a policy very strongly. These effects can be partly avoided if an essentially racial preference is clothed in the polite language of "cultural disadvantage" and if the policy, whether explicitly racial or not, is based on the need for a "more sensitive assessment of qualifications" and a "diverse student body," politically the most noncontroversial justifications for preference. The broader harmful effects of announced and judicially approved racial preferences can be avoided if preference is accomplished under the cover of some apparently more open policy, or at least justified on the most noncontroversial grounds. There will be less encouragement to whites to think in racial terms; and blacks who enter law school may feel less that they are there because they happen to be black.

Given these powerful reasons for either avoiding approval of racial preferences altogether or avoiding heavy reliance on the compensatory and racial-stereotype justifications, a judge may be tempted to find a way out. In *The Least Dangerous Branch*, the late Alexander Bickel suggested that the Supreme Court should refrain from passing on the merits of benign discrimination. Justice Douglas' opinion in *DeFunis* provides another avenue of avoidance. For him, the Fourteenth Amendment permits no racial classifications and no judgments that members of one race are better qualified to be lawyers for other members of that race. But he is so skeptical of the value of traditional criteria of admission as applied to blacks and so willing to leave discretion over qualifications in the hands of law schools, that a law school could adopt a policy with virtually the same effects as that of the University of Washington Law School so long as it formulated it in racially neutral terms. A third, more limited, avenue of avoidance would be to sustain a racial preference but to do it on the less controversial, less defensible ground of "qualifications" or law-school diversity, or on some combination of all possible grounds, without any demand that administrators openly make the hard choices that my analysis suggests.

In response to the arguments for deception and evasion, it has been suggested that deceit and hypocrisy on this subject are particularly harmful, because blacks have been subjected to them so often. If so, then whatever pain honest and open analysis may cause may be less serious than the dangers of further covertness and delusion. Honest judicial confrontation with difficult legal issues is not always the best policy, but it *almost* always is; in the absence of an unanswerable argument for hypocrisy, the Court should proceed in this area, as in others, on the assumption that open evaluation of conflicting claims is its responsibility.

Terrance Sandalow

Racial Preferences in Higher Education: Political Responsibility and the Judicial Role

. . . Professors John Hart Ely and Richard Posner have established diametrically opposed positions in the debate. Their contributions are of special interest because each undertakes to answer the question within the framework of a theory concerning the proper distribution of authority between the judiciary and the other institutions of government.

. . . Professor Ely [see pp. 208-216, herein] defends the constitutionality of racial preferences, essentially on the ground that the equal-protection clause should not be read to prevent a majority from discriminating between itself and a minority only to its own disadvantage. The predicate for an active judicial role is lacking, . . . and, he concludes, resolution of the issue therefore ought to be left to the political process.

Professor Posner ["The DeFunis Case and the Constitutionality of Preferential Treatment of Minorities," 1974 *Supreme Court Review* 1], on the other hand, argues that the equal-protection clause should be read to prohibit "the distribution of benefits and costs by government on racial or ethnic grounds." Ironically, Posner defends this judicial limitation of legislative

Source: University of Chicago Law Review *42 (1975). Reprinted by permission of the publisher. Notes and citations are omitted in this edited version.*

power in part by arguing that a decision sustaining the constitutionality of minority preferences would intolerably augment the power of the judiciary to determine the direction of social policy. Courts must limit legislative power, as it were, in the service of democratic ideals.

Neither position, in my judgment, adequately confronts the problem of the judicial role in a democracy. The value choices . . . are inescapable if the equal-protection clause is to be employed as a measure of legislative power. Precisely because such choices are essential whenever the clause is used to limit legislative power, however, appropriate sensitivity to the values served by democratic decision-making requires courts to defer to legislative judgments unless they clearly transgress constitutional tradition. Nothing in American constitutional tradition requires courts to deny legislatures the power to authorize preferential-admissions policies for racial and ethnic minorities. The validity of such policies depends only upon a judgment that they serve the public welfare. . . .

The precise question posed by *DeFunis* and like cases, however, is not whether preferential-admissions policies are within the competence of a legislature, but whether they are valid when adopted by a university without explicit legislative sanction. There is, I shall argue, a significant difference between these questions, and because of that difference existing racial-preference programs draw no support from Ely's analysis. Although there is good reason to sustain preferential policies in any event, the grounds for such a judgment are far less compelling than they would be if the policies had received explicit legislative approval.

1   THE NORMATIVE BASIS OF EQUAL PROTECTION

A decision whether government may adopt a policy of explicitly preferential treatment of racial and ethnic minorities requires a painful choice between ideals to which American society has developed a deep commitment, deeper than many of its critics assume. On the one hand, such a policy seems inconsistent not only with the nation's rejection of racism but with concepts of individuality and merit that are even more deeply rooted in Western culture. A rejection of minority preferences, on the other hand, seemingly threatens both humanitarian and egalitarian ideals which also have deep roots in Western culture.

. . . The constitutional guarantee of "the equal protection of the laws," to begin at such a point, does not mean that everyone must be treated equally. . . . A prime function of law, indeed, is to mark out the bases for discrimination by government in its relations with the citizenry.

What the equal-protection clause does require, . . . is that government treat similarly all those who are similarly situated. But as the literature of moral philosophy articulates more clearly than the literature of the law, the principle of similar treatment for those similarly situated—Aristotle's principle of distributive justice—merely states a formal relationship. Standing alone, it is insufficient to decide any case because it does not indicate how to determine when individuals are similarly situated. All individuals are similar in some respects and different in others. . . . What is required, . . . is a material or substantive principle, a standard by which to determine when the differences among individuals justify treating them differently.

Now the principle of similar treatment of those similarly situated is merely a prescription for rational behavior and, in that sense, value-free. But the material principles which determine whether individuals are similarly or differently situated necessarily rest upon value choices . . . [and] cannot be made "without positing a certain scale of values, a determination of what is important and what is not. It is our view of the world, the way we distinguish what has value from what has none," [C. Perelman, *The Idea of Justice and the Problem of Argument* (1963)] that leads us to conclude whether individuals are similarly or differently situated. Controversy concerning the meaning of the equal-protection clause is a product of disagreement not only about those values, but about how and by whom they ought to be determined.

When the issue is whether the administration of law comports with equal protection, the demands imposed by the concept of equal protection are clear. The material principle is provided by the law. Equal protection consists of adherence to its terms. If, for example, the law prescribes a 10 percent tax on the income of all individuals, the principle of similar treatment for those similarly situated would be violated by a tax collector who levied a 15 (or a 5) percent tax only on blacks. The violation does not depend upon the use of a racial classification (either to the advantage or disadvantage of blacks), but upon the statute's stipulation that income differences alone are relevant to a determination of the taxes that individuals must pay. Thus, the principle of similar treatment for those similarly situated would also be violated if the tax collectors were to levy a tax greater (or less) than 10 percent upon the income of all individuals who have assets in excess of one million dollars. By stipulating that income differences are the only differences to be taken into account in determining taxes, the lawmaker has ruled out consideration of other differences, however much it might be wished that the tax collector were free to consider them. Wealth and race are equally irrelevant, not because either is in some sense intrinsically irrelevant to taxation, but because they have been made so by a particular material principle—the statute.

The meaning of the equal-protection clause is much less clear when the validity of legislation is at issue. A claim that legislation denies the equal protection of the laws is an assertion that the legislation treats differently individuals who are similarly situated. Since the individuals are in fact different and the legislation does distinguish among them, the claim must be that there is a principle extrinsic to the legislation in virtue of which the affected individuals must be deemed similarly situated. But since that extrinsic principle cannot be derived from the formal principle of similar treatment for those similarly situated, the claim must be that the equal-protection clause embodies one or more material principles from which it can be determined whether persons are similarly situated. Yet nothing in the language of the equal-protection clause suggests the values that ought to be given expression by a substantive reading of the clause.

... The absence of a textual foundation for whatever substantive principles are proposed to be read into those clauses diminishes the likelihood that the necessary value choices are rooted in constitutional tradition and thereby weakens whatever claim the judiciary might have for withdrawing those choices from the other institutions of government. I do not mean to suggest that a substantive reading of the due-process and equal-protection clauses can never be justified, but reasonable sensitivity to the values of democratic decision-making counsels that the courts proceed cautiously in reading those clauses to limit the choices available to government, especially the choices available to government in devising remedies for pressing social problems.

Perhaps because the justification for reading the equal-protection clause as enacting any particular material principle is so problematic, equal-protection analysis is often cast in terms that appear to obviate the need for such a principle. The Supreme Court has frequently stated, for example, that legislation offends the clause if there is no rational basis for the dissimilar treatment accorded different individuals. The emphasis upon rationality in this formulation may make it appear that there is no need for a material principle and, thus, that it is possible to determine the validity of legislation under the equal-protection clause without making the value judgments that inhere in such a principle. The appearance is deceptive. A determination whether there is a rational basis for the legislative classification involves precisely the same inquiry as the determination whether the affected individuals are differently situated. It would be irrational to decide differently two cases that are identical in all respects. But since no two cases are truly identical, the question of rationality is inseparable from the question of which differences are significant. Whether a legislative classification is rational depends upon a showing that individuals who are accorded different treatment are differently situated. And whether individuals are differently situated depends upon which differences are judged important in virtue of a particular material principle.

Judicial opinions are frequently written, nevertheless, to make it appear that the "rational basis" test can be employed without introducing an extrinsic material principle, simply by ascertaining whether the disparate treatment accorded individuals is justified by the purpose of the legislation. The implicit claim is that a material principle is provided by the purpose of the legislation and that the judicial role is confined to ascertaining whether the means chosen by the legislature is rationally related to its objective. . . .

The flaw in this approach is that it cannot explain any decision invalidating legislation without attributing to the legislature a purpose distinct from that revealed by the terms of the legislation it has enacted. When the cases in which the approach has been employed to invalidate legislation are fully analyzed, it is apparent that an extrinsic material principle implicitly underlies each of the decisions. . . .

. . . All legislature that raises equal-protection issues involves an accommodation of competing goals, each of which acts as a constraint upon the maximization of the others. None of the goals, standing alone, comprehends the purpose of the legislature, for that purpose is to achieve an optimal balance among competing goals. The potential multiplicity of legislative objectives means that it will always be possible to draw from the terms of a statute legislative purposes to which the statutory classification is rationally related. The burdens or benefits created by a statute suggest at the very least a purpose to burden or benefit all those who share the classifying characteristic. The statutory classification must be rationally related to that purpose because the purpose has been derived from the classification. "Legislative purpose so defined is nearly tautological. . . . " A conclusion that legislation offends the equal-protection clause cannot, therefore, be grounded solely upon a determination that the classifications employed in the legislation are not rationally related to the purpose of the legislation. . . .

The need for a principle is, however, a good deal more obvious than the warrant for any particular principle. Although the Supreme Court has in recent years frequently invoked the equal-protection clause to invalidate legislation, it has not carefully considered the problem of justifying the material principles upon which those decisions rest. Several members of the Court, led by Mr. Justice Marshall, have urged that material principles can be derived from values expressed by other constitutional provisions. A majority of the justices have rejected that position but have failed to advance any other. . . . [A] substantial number of the Court's recent equal-protection decisions rest upon material principles that cannot conceivably be drawn from other provisions of the Constitution. . . . [W]e lack a substantive theory of equal protection that would define the interests that the clause protects and thereby confine its reach.

. . . The desire for such a theory is readily understandable. In its absence, there seems no alternative to resting equal-protection determinations upon an assessment of the gains and losses resulting from the challenged legislation, with the judiciary exercising ultimate authority for determining what is a "gain" and what is a "loss." The opportunity thus conferred upon the judiciary to substitute its judgment for the legislature's on the relative merits of competing social goals is, after the past two decades, not simply a matter of conjecture. Yet, unless the courts are to abandon use of the equal-protection clause as a measure of the validity of legislation, a move toward which neither the Supreme Court nor its critics seems disposed, weighing the relative merits of competing social goals is an inescapable element of adjudication. There is no way, apart from choosing among such goals, that the courts can determine whether those who have received different treatment at the hands of the legislature are, for constitutional purposes, to be deemed similarly situated.

Nor is it feasible, over time, to confine the Court's role by adopting a theory which once and for all specifies the particular values that are to be accorded protection under the equal-protection clause. Social change is inevitably accompanied by change in social values. . . . The emergence of new values and the falling away of older ones leads to a continuous redefinition of the categories by which men perceive themselves and to continuous reassessment of the significance that they attribute to those categories. . . .

The means by which the Court can accommodate these democratic values with the need to recognize evolution in the values to be accorded constitutional protection is, of course, the great question of constitutional law, a question which is not uniquely posed by the equal-protection clause. In the concluding section of this paper, I want to suggest the beginnings—barely more than a hint—of an approach to that question. Before that, however, I want to show that constitutional tradition does not *require* that the equal-protection clause be read to prohibit state-supported colleges and universities from adopting an admissions policy that accords preferential treatment to racial and ethnic minorities.

2   RACIAL DISCRIMINATION AND CONSTITUTIONAL TRADITION

The "Legislative" History of the Equal-Protection Clause. The framers of the Fourteenth Amendment plainly did not intend to prohibit the states from employing a racial criterion to the advantage of the black population. Posner himself points out that "[s]o bizarre would discrimination against whites in admission to institutions of higher learning have seemed to the framers of the [f]ourteenth [a]mendment that we can be confident that they did not consciously seek to erect a constitutional barrier against such discrimination." Nor did they have the broader intention of prohibiting all consideration of race by government. Thus, "it is equally clear," as Posner concedes, "that the framers did not contemplate that the [a]mendment would compel equal treatment of blacks in public education"—or in a number of other areas either. The notion lately advanced by the Supreme Court and repeated by some commentators, that "[t]he clear and central purpose of the [f]ourteenth [a]mendment was to eliminate all official state sources of invidious racial discrimination in the States," is simply an anachronism—an attribution to the framers of the amendment of views that did not achieve currency until much later.

The idea that black and white are equal, . . . did not begin to gain ascendancy until well into the present century. Ideas that today would be labelled racist—the word did not exist in the nineteenth century—were during the nineteenth century the common property of the white population, North and South, educated and uneducated, slaveholder and abolitionist. . . . [T]he dominant sentiment of the time accorded race a significance that today, . . . seems almost beyond comprehension. Racial differences were perceived as fundamental, enduring and, almost always, reflecting the innate superiority of the white population.

In the intellectual milieu of the nineteenth century, the dominant question was not whether the races were different, but the significance of the fact that they were. During the years immediately following the Civil War, there was substantial sentiment, centered in the radical wing of the Republican Party, that whatever differences might exist between blacks and whites were not relevant to their equality before the law. . . . But, as the late Professor Alexander Bickel demonstrated in his study of the origins of the equal-protection clause, the radical Republicans were unable to carry their point. A rule that race was never to serve as a legally relevant category could not have gained the assent of the country, for it would have opened too wide a gap between the law and the understanding of the time.

The purpose of the clause was narrower, to gain for blacks equality with whites in respect of certain rights that were deemed necessary incidents of their status as free men. . . . Freedom, not equality, was the purpose of the equal-protection clause.

This "legislative" history does not require rejection of the principle proposed by Professor Posner; the point is rather that it does not require adoption of that principle. As Posner suggests, the provisions of the Constitution ought not to be confined to the precise meaning intended by their framers. But if it is undesirable to be governed by the past, it is worse to be ruled by a misconception of the past. And only a misconception of the past leads to the conclusion that it imposes upon government an obligation of "color-blindness."

. . . The framers of the Fourteenth Amendment accepted as an overriding value that blacks, solely by reason of their humanity, were entitled to be free. . . . But blacks and whites were not perceived as alike in all respects, nor were all relationships between citizens and government thought to involve the value of freedom. When freedom and its incidents were not involved, there were other values, such as the intelligent discharge of civic obligations, in respect of which blacks and whites were thought not to be similarly situated and in respect of which discrimination was, therefore, justified. The goals the framers sought to achieve thus determined for them when racial discrimination was to be permissible. Today, similarly, a decision about whether racial discrimination is permissible will be determined by what we seek to accomplish.

The Validity of Classification by Involuntary Characteristics. A second way of justifying a principle is to demonstrate that it can be derived from a more general and concededly valid principle. The only readily apparent principle from which Posner's principle might derive is the suggestion by several members of the Supreme Court that classification on the basis of characteristics that are adventitious and immutable is, if not necessarily invalid, at least constitutionally suspect. . . . It seems unfair that the burdens and benefits of social life, especially those distributed by government, should be apportioned among individuals on the basis of qualities over which they lack control. The denial of schooling to children because of their skin color or sex, the limitation of public office to certain families, and other familiar examples from history and literature suggest the force behind that idea. Ideally, these illustrations might be taken to suggest that distribution of the burdens and benefits of social life ought to bear some relationship to responsibility and merit. Yet, prevailing notions of responsibility and merit are intimately bound up with the opportunity for choice that is denied individuals when government classifies them on the basis of involuntary characteristics.

Professor Posner disclaims any reliance on this broader principle, however. . . . The situations are too numerous in which the values of our society call for attention to involuntary characteristics. Those values may require efforts to cultivate . . . the use of what are, in part, genetic characteristics, as when rewards or special training are given to the intellectually gifted or those of unusual physical prowess. Humanitarian considerations may suggest special consideration for the needs of those who suffer from an involuntary disability, say, by devoting a larger amount of resources to the education of handicapped children than to the education of other children. Surely, none of these policies would be held by a court to be beyond governmental competence, as recognized even in the opinions that suggest the illegitimacy of classification by adventitious, immutable characteristics. In such situations, it is explained, the classifying characteristic is relevant to a legitimate governmental purpose. But that formula, of course, is the test for the validity of all classifications, not merely those which rest upon adventitious and immutable characteristics. The accidental, unchangeable character of the classifying criteria adds nothing to the argument. . . .

Hostility to the use of involuntary characteristics to classify people may have a subtle historical explanation. Classification by such characteristics has frequently been used to perpetuate the dominant political, economic, or social position of certain groups. It thus seems reasonable to suppose that attitudes toward the use of involuntary characteristics have been colored by the fact that their use has often been at war with the egalitarian ideals that have dominated the modern age. The influence of egalitarian ideals upon our attitudes toward sorting people on the basis of adventitious circumstances is suggested also by the toleration for—perhaps insistence upon—such a sorting criterion when egalitarian ideals are served thereby. When life itself is at stake, for example, the fundamental equality of all humans—their equal dignity and worth—has at times seemed to require that the choice of who shall live and who shall die be left to chance. . . .

Now whatever other objections there may be to the preferences that recently have been accorded racial and ethnic minorities, it is obvious that those preferences do not serve to maintain a position of dominance for the preferred groups. Not only are the groups given preferential treatment among the least advantaged in the society in terms of political, economic and social status, but it is precisely their disadvantaged status that has provided the primary rationale for preferential treatment. . . .

Yet the objection of classification by involuntary characteristics does not seem to rest solely upon the use of such criteria to serve nonegalitarian objectives. Legislation that excluded left-handed children from kindergarten would, if unsupported by further justification, undoubtedly be universally condemned as unjust and invalidated by the Supreme Court as a denial of equal protection even though the classification neither perpetuated nor created long-term class consequences. The objection to such legislation would, I think, proceed somewhat along the following lines: one goal of a good society is to enlarge the opportunities of individuals to cultivate and express their individuality, to facilitate each individual's opportunity to pursue a personal conception of the good life. . . . Distribution of opportunities on the basis of involuntary characteristics is incompatible with that goal because the claim of each person to pursue his conception of the good life ought to be given similar consideration. Perhaps individuals who make a greater effort ought to receive greater consideration, but the fact that one individual differs from another by reason of race, sex, height, or another involuntary characteristic seems an insufficient reason for regarding him as more or less worthy of consideration. If opportunities are in short supply, it might thus be argued, they ought to be rationed on a basis that bears some relationship to the goal of enhancing the ability of individuals to develop their individuality. So, for example, if there are fewer vacancies in universities than applicants for admission, preference might be given to those applicants whose objectives would best be served by a university education or to those whose past efforts revealed a more intense desire to be educated. . . .

The obvious response to this argument is that . . . [n]o calculus exists for determining whether one person's or another's objectives would be better served by access to higher education. Nor are there adequate measures of relative intensity of desire or means by which to determine the extent to which differences in past performance are attributable to effort or to factors, such as native endowment, that are beyond individual control. Measurement is not the only difficulty, moreover. The relationship between adventitious characteristics and individual choice is uncertain. Past effort may be no more than a product of adventitious circumstances, a consequence not merely (and perhaps not at all) of individual will but of the family in which one chanced to be born and of natural endowment which offered promise that effort would be worthwhile. The same may be true of desire.

Thus, the same reasons offered to justify the conclusion that minority preferences are unjust may also be offered to support a conclusion that it would be equally unjust to admit to universities those applicants displaced by the minority preference: though race and ethnicity are adventitious, and hence irrelevant to desert, the same is true of natural endowment and childhood environment, important determinants of success on admission tests and in prior academic pursuits. If use of the former is to be viewed with suspicion because they ignore desert, it is not obvious why use of the latter ought not to be viewed with similar suspicion.

Pushed to the extreme, this line of reasoning threatens the premise with which we began. If individuals are solely a product of forces beyond their control, it is meaningless to posit as a social goal the enlargement of opportunities for them to develop their individuality. All individual goals, desires and efforts would be adventitious from the perspective of the unwitting individual. The determinism that underlies this view has, no doubt, played an important role in shaping modern attitudes, but it is certain that, in its extreme form, it does not command a consensus among Americans. Our legal system and political institutions, our moral conceptions and even the language we speak, reflect a belief that individuals make choices, that human will is a reality. . . . If that assumption has at times led to cruelty and injustice, its abandonment seems likely to be even more pernicious.

. . . The principle that classification by involuntary characteristics counts against the validity of a classification thus rests upon values that are central to our conception of the good society and therefore of the proper role of government.

All that has been established, however, is that the use of such criteria ought to count against the validity of a classification, not that they are always impermissible. There are numerous situations in which other values may call for discrimination by involuntary characteristics. At times, for example, the reward of desert is sacrificed to a social interest in the meritorious performance of certain tasks. Membership on the University of Michigan basketball team is not equally open to all. The men who have achieved it have, no doubt, demonstrated desire and effort. But no amount of desire and effort would yield a place on the team to the many individuals who lack the necessary physical attributes. We may regret the inability of the latter to fulfill their ambitions, even lament that "life is unfair," but the fact remains that we prize the ability to play basketball well more highly than the effort and desire to do so.

Now what is true of the University of Michigan's basketball team is also true of its law school, as it is of other law schools and of selective-admission higher-education programs generally. . . . Desert is thus sacrificed to a conception of social utility, the perception of a social need for highly competent lawyers and other professionals. If considerations of utility are sufficient to overcome reservations about the use of involuntary characteristics when competence is at stake, there is no apparent reason why similar considerations ought not to prevail in support of minority-admission preferences. Unless race and ethnicity are required (for some still unexplained reason) to be treated differently from other involuntary characteristics, the only question is whether social utility is served by minority preferences.

To the extent social utility is served, race and ethnicity may even be seen as measures of competence. Competence is the ability to perform a task in line with certain objectives. Those objectives, in the case of educational institutions, are typically defined with reference to some perception of social needs. Traditional academic admissions criteria reflect a particular perception of those needs—a need for students who will provide intellectual stimulation for other students, for lawyers with a high degree of analytic capacity, for physicians with an understanding of biochemistry, and the like. Undoubtedly, these intellectual needs are of critical importance and we depreciate them only at our peril. But they are not the only needs of the society, as educational institutions have occasionally recognized by tempering intellectual standards for admission with the use of geographic preferences. In the same way, special minority-admissions programs may serve particular social needs.

It is sometimes argued that even if social utility is served by such programs, they must nonetheless be held invalid because they impose upon the white applicants who would otherwise have been admitted too much of the cost that must be incurred to improve the conditions of minority groups. The fallacy of that argument should now be apparent. The burden upon the excluded applicant is real, but it is not different from the burden borne by applicants excluded under traditional criteria. Moreover, it is imposed for precisely the same reason, a judgment that the public welfare will be better served by the admission of someone else. In that respect racial and ethnic admissions criteria do not differ from traditional criteria that are unquestionably constitutional.

The principle that government may not distribute burdens and benefits on racial grounds cannot, therefore, be derived from a more general rule that classification by involuntary characteristics is either invalid or constitutionally suspect. . . .

Discrimination Against Minorities: The Question of Consistency. . . . . . . [I]f it could be shown that a constitutional role prohibiting classification on racial or ethnic grounds was necessary to support the line of decisions invalidating legislation that employs racial classifications to the disadvantage of blacks, adoption of the principle would be required. . . . Such a defense of the "color-blind" principle, if it could be established, would be not merely persuasive, but compelling. Consistency is not simply a matter of intellectual elegance as some students of the legal system appear to assume, but rather the critical test of whether decisions serve a coherent set of values.

. . . [But Posner acknowledges that] "discrimination against whites" is not "the same phenomenon as the sorts of discrimination involved in previous equal-protection cases involving members of racial or ethnic minorities . . . " because of the different social consequences of the current programs of minority preference and the discriminatory legislation that the Supreme Court has previously invalidated. The latter, served to perpetuate the dominant status of a preferred group . . . in a manner wholly incompatible with the nation's evolving egalitarian ideals. Minority preferences plainly are not subject to criticism on that ground.

. . . [T]he response . . . seems clear: whether or not the distinction has substance, the Supreme Court is not entitled to consider it in applying the equal-protection clause. A rule of constitutional law, Posner contends, must be "sufficiently precise and objective to limit a judge's exercise of personal whim and preference." A rule that requires an assessment of the consequences of discrimination in order to determine whether the discrimination is constitutionally permissible would, he argues, lack the necessary "precision and objectivity" and thus be no more than "a directive that the judges uphold those forms of racial and ethnic discrimination which accord with their personal values." . . .

. . . The purely personal references of judges, all would concede, are not adequate reasons for judicial limitation of legislative power. Something else is required. . . . The problem of identifying sources that will "limit as well as nourish" judgment is especially acute in fashioning law under the equal-protection clause . . . Absent a consensus concerning the appropriate sources of judgment, there is an inevitable risk that judgment will turn upon the personal preferences of the judges.

Precisely because that risk is unavoidable, however, its existence cannot be used . . . as a justification for selecting one rather than another material principle for giving meaning to the equal-protection clause. Value choices necessarily underlie the selection of one or another principle, and, absent societal agreement upon either the values or the source from which they are to be derived, there is no escape from the risk that the principle selected will reflect values personal to the judge. . . .

Posner himself comes close to recognizing this problem when he considers the question whether the principle he proposes "is itself subjective and arbitrary, because it does not explain why only race and ethnic origin, and not all immutable or involuntary characteristics" are to be held impermissible bases of classification. His response to that question is instructive. "There are," he writes, "two grounds of distinction:

> The first is one of necessity: if the constitutional principle were defined in terms of all involuntary characteristics, it would violate the requirement that a constitutional principle bind the judges. Since no one could argue that no involuntary characteristic should ever be used as a criterion of public regulation, the principle would give the judges interpreting it carte blanche to pick and choose among groups defined in accordance with one of the involuntary characteristics. Second, the grouping of people by an ancestral characteristic is surely not the same phenomenon as, say, grouping by sex or age. A rule forbidding blacks to work in mines, one forbidding women to work in mines, and one forbidding children to work in mines, may all be discriminatory, but one must strain to regard them as identical, in the sense that if one is invalid, so, obviously, are the others.

Neither reason is persuasive.

The second point merely calls upon our intuition that race, sex, and age differ from one another. Brief reflection will reveal, however, that whether or not they do depends upon the context in which the question arises. Race and sex differ from age in that neither of the former, in contemporary America, would be thought a permissible basis for differentiating among persons in determining the right to vote or in formulating compulsory school-attendance laws. Race differs from sex and age, however, when the issue is liability to compulsory military service: the latter, but not the former, would generally be considered appropriate bases for classification. None of these characteristics would be thought a permissible basis for determining liability to the thumbscrew: all persons would be equally exempt because their common characteristics, for this purpose, would be deemed more significant than their differences. . . . [T]he consequences of employing one or another of the criteria differ in different contexts, and it is by an appraisal of these consequences that we determine whether the criteria are permissible bases for sorting people.

. . . The idea that racial classifications are wholly forbidden by the Constitution apparently took root in the mid-1950s, in the effort to explain a series of per curiam decisions that extended the rule of the *School Segregation Cases* to all public facilities. Other principles that would justify those decisions were, no doubt, imaginable, but in the absence of any explanation by the Court, a principle requiring government to be "color-blind," as urged long ago by the first Justice Harlan, was both plausible and attractive.

. . . A principle forbidding government to classify by race would at least keep government out of so dirty a business and, by depriving it of an apparently vital support, perhaps end it altogether. Other values also seemed to be served by the principle. Its adoption appeared to promise significant improvement in the economically depressed condition of the black population, for it would require that governmental benefits, a significant form of wealth in modern society, be equally available to all, in fact as well as in theory. An end to enforced separation of the races offered the additional hope that traditional prejudices would be eliminated as blacks and whites came to know one another as individuals, a prospect viewed by many as desirable not only as a step toward realizing the cultural ideal of the "brotherhood of man," but as a means of further reducing the barriers to the economic and social advancement of the black population. . . .

To argue that constitutional principles must be formulated without regard to goals ignores the fact that it is precisely the consideration of those goals that suggested the "color-blind" principle. The altered perception of social reality over the past two decades—and the consequent need to reconsider the priority among our goals—is, indeed, a classic illustration of Perelman's observation that "[a]ny moral, political, or social evolution leading to a modification in the scale of values will at the same time modify the characteristics regarded as essential for the application of [the principle of similar treatment for those similarly situated]." It is one thing to maintain that people are similarly situated, notwithstanding racial differences, when the consequence of doing so appears to be the alleviation of suffering and the establishment of an integrated society. It is quite another to do so when the consequence appears to be precisely the opposite.

Professor Posner is right to point out that there are dangers associated with a principle that would permit race and ethnicity to be considered if the anticipated consequences seem desirable. "The necessary inquiries," he writes, "are intractable and would leave the field open to slippery conjectures." If this overstates the matter somewhat, the point is nonetheless important. Judicial freedom to examine the consequences of a racial or ethnic classification in determining its validity may also yield judgments disadvantageous to minorities. The risk is unavoidable. Yet it is difficult to understand Posner's conclusion that the "antidiscrimination principle is ... more compelling when it is divorced from empirical inquiries into the effects of particular forms of discrimination on the affected groups." Unless it is supported by an appraisal of such effects, an antidiscrimination principle is not even persuasive, let alone compelling. It is not, as we have seen, required by history, nor can it be derived from a more general principle of constitutional law.

3   THE ARGUMENT FOR A MINORITY PREFERENCE IN LAW-SCHOOL ADMISSIONS

... Legislation that classifies children by race to maintain racially segregated schools is impermissible. But classification by race is "within the broad discretionary powers of school authorities" if "in order to prepare students to live in a pluralistic society" those authorities wish to adopt a policy "that each school should have a prescribed ratio of Negro to white students reflecting the proportion for the district as a whole." The difference is not in the criteria employed to classify students, but in the Court's evaluation of the consequences of the two programs. The one leads to a racially segregated society, with all that that entails for the welfare of the black population; the other offers hope of a racially integrated society and of a time when at least one adventitious circumstance will have been removed as a barrier to the "pursuit of happiness."

The validity of preferential-admissions policies in institutions of higher learning, similarly, turns upon a judgment about whether the policies will contribute to or retard development of the kind of society we want. . . .

Any justification of racial and ethnic preferences must begin by recognizing that race and ethnicity are socially significant characteristics. Many Americans, and especially those who are members of the groups that have been the beneficiaries of preferential-admissions practices, live in communities and belong to organizations that are defined in racial and ethnic terms. The direction of their loyalties and of their sympathies is significantly determined by their racial and ethnic identifications. Whether, or to what extent, that is desirable is currently the subject of much debate; but whether it is good or bad, it is a reality with which the law must contend. . . .

. . . [T]he question whether blacks and other racial and ethnic minorities are substantially represented in law-school classes and at the bar assumes considerable importance. Gross underrepresentation of these groups has consequences quite different from those that would result from, say, the gross underrepresentation of men with one blue and one green eye or of lefthanded women. Individuals who share these latter characteristics do not identify with one another. Their associations are not significantly determined by their common trait. They do not share a distinctive cultural background which may make it easier for them to communicate with one another than with others. Governmental decisions do not affect them differently than they affect other persons, and, conversely, their views on issues of public policy are likely to be distributed in the same way as in the general population. In all these respects, individuals defined by these characteristics differ from the members of racial and ethnic minorities. And it is precisely because of these differences that gross underrepresentation of the latter in law school and the bar poses a significant social problem. . . .

Professor Posner develops at some length an argument that minority preferences cannot be justified by the desirability of a diverse student body. "For a diversity argument to be convincing," he correctly maintains, "it must identify a differentiating factor that is relevant to the educational experience." The only significance of race, he argues, lies in its strong correlation with other characteristics, like poverty, that arguably are relevant to diversity in the educational experience. "Race in this analysis is simply a proxy for a set of other attributes—relevant to the educational process—with which race, itself irrelevant to the educational process, happens to be correlated." The use of race as a proxy, Posner argues, may be "efficient" insofar as it reduces the costs of identifying individuals who have characteristics that are relevant to the educational process, but it is objectionable because it rests upon and thus "legitimizes the mode of thought and behavior that underlies most prejudice and bigotry in the United States." If race and ethnicity may be used as a proxy for desirable characteristics with which they are correlated, he concludes, the same interest in efficiency which justifies that use would permit them to be employed as a proxy for undesirable characteristics, thereby justifying discrimination against minorities.

The error of this argument lies in its failure to appreciate the social significance of race, quite apart from its statistical correlation with other attributes. Precisely because race itself is socially significant, students need knowledge of the attitudes, views and backgrounds of racial minorities. Posner is right to insist, although he overstates the point somewhat, that there "are black people (and Chicanos, Filipinos, etc.) . . . who have the same tastes, manners, experiences, attitudes, and aspirations" as many whites. What he ignores is that encountering that diversity is an important part of the educational process. Well-intentioned whites, no less than bigots, need to learn that there is not a common "black experience" and to appreciate the error of such statements as "blacks want (believe, need, etc.). . . . " Moreover, the distribution of attitudes among blacks is not the same as it is among whites. And that too is worth knowing. If the distribution of perceptions and views about politics, or crime, or family is different among blacks than among whites, that in and of itself may have important implications for public policy.

The educational objectives of a minority presence in law school, finally, encompass more than increased understanding of minority groups. There is also a need to increase effective communication across racial and ethnic lines. Many white students, for example, need to learn to be able to disagree with blacks candidly and without embarassment. I cannot imagine that any law teacher whose subject matter requires discussion of racially sensitive issues can have failed to observe the inability of some white students to examine critically arguments by a black, or the difficulty experienced by others in expressing their disagreements with blacks on such issues. Yet, these skills are not only a professional necessity, they are indispensable to the long-term well-being of our society. . . .

In a society in which racial and ethnic identities play an important role in everyday life, a lawyer's racial or ethnic background may have an important bearing on his ability to serve his client. Many of the tasks that lawyers perform for their clients require an understanding of the social context in which the client's problem arises. A brilliant and effective tax specialist is, for that reason, unlikely to be an effective representative in a labor negotiation. The reason is not simply that he is unfamiliar with the law of labor relations; it is also and perhaps primarily that he lacks an understanding of the practical problems of labor relations, of the customs that have developed in dealing with those problems, and of the style and manners of collective bargaining. To the extent that racial and ethnic groups form distinctive subcultures within our society, the representation of some of their members in connection with some of their legal needs may involve similar difficulties for the "outsider." The ability to "speak the language" of the client, to understand his perception of his problem, and to deal with others in the community on his behalf are qualities essential to being a "good lawyer." These qualifications are more likely to be found among lawyers who share the client's racial or ethnic identity, at least to the extent that the client's life is bound up in a community defined in these terms. . . .

Ely's premise is the familiar view that in determining the constitutionality of legislation, courts owe less than normal deference to legislative judgments when the interests of a minority are uniquely threatened. Although he is seemingly prepared to have the courts subject a legislative judgment to closer than a normal scrutiny whenever any minority is singled out for disadvantageous treatment, Ely employs the distinction primarily to explain why courts are justified in examining with special care legislation that employs a racial classification to the detriment of a minority. The reason, he argues, is that there is less basis than normally exists to have confidence in the legislature's assessment of the costs and benefits of the legislation. When the impact of legislation is broadly distributed through the society there is no reason to suspect inaccuracy in the legislature's measurement of costs and benefits. Similarly, when legislation distinguishes between two minorities . . . there is no reason to suppose that the legislature's assessment of costs and benefits has been inaccurate. When, however, the costs and benefits of legislation are differentially distributed between a (racial) majority, to which most members of the legislature belong, and a minority, the legislature's assessment of these costs and benefits is likely to be distorted. The legislature's exclusive identification with the group to which most of its members belong, Ely contends, will tend to distort its assessment in two ways: first, by leading it to overestimate the costs of treating the majority and minority equally, and, second, by causing it to undervalue the costs imposed upon the minority by the differential treatment. Both of these risks are enhanced by the existence of racial prejudice.

This analysis leads Ely to conclude that there is no reason for a court to view as constitutionally "suspect" a racial classification adopted by a majority "so as to advantage a minority and disadvantage itself." . . .

Ely's analysis and the conclusions he draws from it are troublesome . . . [I]n American politics majorities are rarely if ever monolithic. Typically, political majorities are coalitions of minorities which have varying interests in the issue presented for decision. The real dispute is not between a majority and a minority but between those minorities whose interests are most immediately affected. Resolution of the dispute depends upon which of the minorities is more successful in forging an alliance with those groups which are less immediately affected.

The issue whether state schools ought to adopt preferential-admissions policies is no exception. The immediate beneficiaries of these policies are the minorities which receive preferential treatment. But there is no reason to suppose that the costs of such policies are borne equally by subgroups within the white population. To the extent that they are not, the discrimination—though nominally against a majority—is in reality against those subgroups. The fact that the costs of racial and ethnic preferences are not equally or randomly distributed among the white majority is not, by itself, a basis for constitutional objection to the preferences. The costs of governmental policies often fall disproportionately upon subgroups in the society. In the absence of a constitutional norm insulating a group from that burden, there is no warrant for judicial intervention. The distribution of burdens and benefits is the central function of the legislative process.

The legitimacy of the legislative process does not depend upon the disinterestedness of the legislature, as Ely implicitly argues, but upon its political responsibility. Legislatures are, no doubt, not fully responsive to the wishes of the electorate—nor would we want them to be—but their political responsibility is crucial to the democratic ideal that governmental policies ought to respond to the wishes of the citizenry. The legislature's political responsibility serves that ideal in a number of ways. First, it provides a means by which government is made more sensitive to the impact of a policy upon the various segments of the society and thereby contributes to the calculation of gains and losses resulting from that policy. Second, since an appraisal of the consequences of policy involves not merely a measurement of gains and losses, but a judgment of what is to count as a gain or loss and how these shall be balanced, political responsibility helps ensure that government policy will not depart too far from the values of the citizenry. Finally, the political responsibility of the legislature creates an incentive for compromise and accommodation that facilitates development of policies that maximize the satisfaction of constituents' desires.

It is precisely these legitimating characteristics of the legislative process that lead to my doubts about the validity of existing preferential-admissions policies. Those policies are not the product of a politically responsible legislative body, but of decisional processes internal to the universities that have adopted them. Decisions to employ racial and ethnic preferences have either been made by faculties or by the governing bodies of the institutions. In either event, the process of decision and the character of the decision-making body are very different from those of legislatures, different in ways that ought to make the courts a good deal less confident about the propriety of those policies than would be justified if they had been adopted by a legislature.

A law-school faculty, for example, is not well situated to acquire information about the impact of its decisions upon persons outside the law-school community and the legal profession. Nothing in the relationship of the faculty to the public makes it likely that the faculty will learn whether a decision to grant preferences to certain racial or ethnic groups imposes unduly heavy costs upon other groups in the society or whether there are still other groups that might plausibly lay claim to a similar preference. . . . Faculties are, moreover, less constrained than legislatures by the need to obtain public consent for their actions, creating a danger that the choices they make will depart too widely from the values of the larger society. This danger is enhanced by the fact that, for all their diversity, faculties are relatively insular communities, subject to distinctive pressures and a tendency to form distinctive outlooks upon issues. Encompassing less diversity than the larger population, they are relatively more prone to fall victim to those enthusiasms and waves of passion that befall small groups and justify lodging decision-making authority in larger groups.

These considerations need not be a source of concern when, as will normally be true, faculty decisions are made within the framework of societal consensus, but they are a good deal more troublesome when, as in the case of racial and ethnic preferences, a consensus does not exist. The absence of a consensus is of particular concern because the question whether preferences shall be used poses major value choices for the society. Minority preferences may, as I have argued, serve deeply rooted societal values. But there is a risk, the dimensions of which cannot yet be fully understood, that they will do so at a significant sacrifice of other values.

One major area of concern is the impact preferential policies may have upon the relationship among racial and ethnic groups. It may be, as some have suggested, that "we can have a color-blind society in the long run only if we refuse to be color-blind in the short run." But there is a danger that the use of preferences will exacerbate existing tensions in the society, both by creating resentment against the preferred groups, and by buttressing existing identifications and loyalties. The current beneficiaries of preferential policies may have a compelling claim to them, but, given the incentives, other groups may be expected to come forward with claims that, to them at least, will seem equally compelling. Since groups that currently benefit from preferential policies are no more likely than the beneficiaries of other subsidies to relinquish them willingly merely because the needs by which they were originally justified have become less acute, the claims of other groups to similar preferences are likely to become increasingly justifiable over time. Significantly heightened racial and ethnic tensions would follow, as various groups in the society vied for their "rightful share" of university admissions and other social goods.

How seriously one takes these possibilities depends not only upon an estimate of the likelihood of their occurrence, but upon one's vision of the ultimate goal. All would agree that an intensification of racial and ethnic identifications and loyalties to the point where coexistence is threatened would be undesirable. Yet there is currently a good deal of disagreement about whether social policy should aim toward a fully integrated society—at the extreme, a society in which all racial and ethnic identity is lost—or a multiethnic, multiracial society in which the lives of many individuals would center upon their group identification. Adherents of one or another of these positions (or of some intermediate view) are, one suspects, likely to weigh the prospects of group conflict very differently.

More fundamentally, these positions reflect differing views about the desirable organization of society and the place of the individual in it. Movement toward a society organized along racial and ethnic lines may be seen as posing a serious threat to concepts of individuality that—though they have often been honored only in the breach—lie at the base of American beliefs and institutions. The extent to which the society will move in that direction will be primarily determined by forces other than those set in motion by preferential-admissions policies, but, given the importance of the universities in contemporary America, the policies they pursue are likely to be a factor in determining society's direction.

These considerations do not, in my judgment, disturb the earlier conclusion that the courts ought to reject a constitutional rule precluding legislatures from adopting racial and ethnic preferences. Balancing the dangers of these preferences against their potential gains is a delicate, and ultimately legislative, task. There is no warrant for the courts to draw the issue from the political forum. The *DeFunis* case, however, did not on its facts require a judgment about whether the courts should invalidate a legislative decision sanctioning minority preferences, nor is it likely that the next case to reach the Supreme Court will do so. Universities have adopted preferential-admissions policies without legislative sanction. The precise issue that is raised, therefore, is not whether such policies are valid when adopted by a broadly representative, politically responsible legislature, but whether they are valid when adopted by a university.

Now it may be argued that the source of authority for minority preferences is not relevant to the question whether they should be held to violate the equal-protection clause. The question whether law-school faculties are authorized to adopt preferential-admissions policies is, on this view, solely one of state law: the only federal question is whether the preferential policies violate the equal-protection clause, and courts must answer the latter question by proceeding as though the policies had been adopted by or received the express authorization of the legislature. It must be conceded that this is the conventional view of the matter and that there is support for it in Supreme Court decisions. The Court's decisions are, however, less clear on the point than might be supposed. The Court has at times indicated that the validity of action taken under the authority of the state may depend upon whether the legislature has made a deliberate and focused judgment that such action is an appropriate exercise of governmental power.

Although these decisions do not overrule the conventional view that the constitutionality of action by a state must be determined without reference to its source within the state, they are supported by more persuasive reasoning. The latter view is based upon the premise that the federal Constitution does not control the distribution of state legislative authority. The premise is sound, but it does not support the conclusion drawn from it. The issue is not whether state legislative authority can be delegated, but whether in determining the validity of state action that trenches upon constitutional values, the courts ought to consider whether the judgment under review is that of the legislature or of an agency that is less representative of the public and lacking direct political responsibility.

Minimally, whether challenged state action rests upon a legislative judgment ought to be relevant to the degree of respect shown by the court to the judgment. A commitment to democratic values requires considerable judicial deference to deliberate legislative judgments, rather more in my view than has been customary in recent years. But none of the reasons supporting judicial deference to legislative judgment support equal deference to the judgment of a police department or a law-school faculty. And only by ignoring all that we know about legislative behavior could it be supposed that a legislature's failure to limit the power of such bodies is equivalent to affirmative legislative approval of their decisions.

The notion that courts ought to respect all decisions taken under state authority as though they were the product of the most careful legislative deliberation, if consistently applied, would unnecessarily encroach upon constitutional values. Courts would be required to sustain the constitutionality of governmental action that, because of the political safeguards of the legislative process, might fail to receive legislative approval. Conversely, if judicial determinations of constitutionality are in reality influenced by an agency's lack of political responsibility, the failure of constitutional doctrine to acknowledge that fact candidly would lead to inappropriate restrictions on legislative power: a decision that certain action is unconstitutional when taken soley on the authority of a police officer will be taken to mean that such action would be unconstitutional even if sanctioned by the legislature.

. . . The blithe references to "constitutional values" in the preceding discussion ought not to obscure the fact that the values that receive constitutional protection change over time. Constitutional law evolves to reflect the changing circumstances and values of our society. Few would wish it otherwise. Yet, after nearly two centuries' experience, the courts have not succeeded in identifying sources of constitutional judgment that will, . . . "securely limit as well as nourish it." This failure stems from the tension between the institutional mechanism that has developed for giving meaning to the Constitution—judicial review—and the democratic ideal that politically responsible institutions should determine the direction of governmental policy. Quite possibly, that tension can never be completely eliminated. It might, however, be substantially reduced by the development of doctrines that place primary responsibility upon the legislature for making critical choices. When such choices must be made, the effort ought to be to draw from the legislature, as the most broadly representative, politically responsible institution of government, a focused judgment about the appropriate balance to be struck between competing values. Once the legislature has made such a judgment, courts ought to be extremely hesitant to upset it, for if the values to which law gives expression are to change over time, the legislature's warrant for making the necessary decisions is a good deal stronger than that of the courts. In the absence of such a judgment, however, democratic values require invalidating an exercise of state power that undermines values traditionally viewed as fundamental. The cause of democracy is not served by allowing a subordinate state agency to make such decisions.

These considerations frame the issues that are posed for the courts by current policies of racial and ethnic preferences in university admissions. There is no warrant for a judicially imposed rule foreclosing legislative authorization of such policies. The difficult question is whether those policies ought to be held to be within the competence of a university. If the analysis advanced here were to be adopted by the courts, the judicial answer to that question would only determine whether the proponents or opponents of minority preferences would bear the burden of seeking legislative action.

Ultimate authority over a critical issue of social policy would be consigned to the legislature as the most broadly representative, politically responsible institution of government. A judicial decision concerning the university's authority would, nevertheless, have considerable significance. Although neither proponents nor opponents of minority preferences lack the means to force serious legislative consideration of the issue, the difficulty of obtaining legislative action on so highly charged an issue would place the side bearing that burden at an important disadvantage. The question for the courts is which side ought to bear the burden.

The answer one gives to that question is likely to depend upon how one reads our constitutional tradition with respect to racial and ethnic discrimination. If that tradition is understood to flow primarily from egalitarian values, a concern that government ought not to contribute to the subjugation of minorities, there is little reason to deny universities the power to adopt preferential policies. Existing preferences seem likely to move the nation toward the goal of racial and ethnic equality. Such preferences are likely to be seen as contrary to constitutional tradition, however, if the tradition is understood to be rooted primarily in an ethic of individualism, a belief that each individual ought to be judged solely on his own merit. The difficulty, in my view, is that neither alternative is entirely accurate. Our constitutional tradition reflects both egalitarian and individualist values because, until recently, the two seemed entirely compatible. Now, for the first time, it appears (to many) that at least in the short run a choice may be required.

In the absence of a guiding constitutional tradition, I would conclude that two arguments call for a decision sustaining the power of universities to adopt preferential-admissions policies. The dispute over racial and ethnic preferences involves a conflict between values of a very high order. Such conflicts are never fully resolved. The practical question is how far the society will move in one direction or the other. Although the admissions policies of universities are not a negligible factor in determining that direction, their ultimate importance should not be overstated. There are many other points of decision within the society, including private enterprise and other government agencies. Moreover, the system of higher education is itself highly decentralized. When a value choice of such magnitude is posed, and especially when the need for choice has only recently become apparent so that its dimensions are not fully understood, there may be wisdom in allowing for a period of decentralized decision-making. Universities have, in fact, responded to the demands for increased minority enrollments in a variety of ways. Some have adopted racial and ethnic preferences. Others have adopted policies of preference for the disadvantaged without regard to racial and ethnic background. Still others have adopted policies of "open enrollment." Finally, some have maintained traditional "color-blind" standards. This diversity of approaches may generate a better understanding of the issues, permitting development of a consensus which is now lacking.

The most compelling reason for sustaining preferential-admissions policies is that they offer hope of ameliorating the nation's most enduring problem. The contrary arguments cannot be taken lightly; racial and ethnic preferences do involve serious dangers. In the end, however, a decision concerning their validity cannot avoid a judgment about whether they are likely to contribute to or retard development of the kind of society we want. In my own judgment, for reasons already explained, the former is more likely. It would be foolish to assert that judgment confidently, however. If the potential benefits are great, so too are the potential losses. But in the light of the seriousness of America's racial problem, the risk seems worth taking, however uncomfortable we may be with it.

So speculative and personal a judgment is a weak foundation for judicial interpretation of the Constitution. Yet, a contrary decision would necessarily rest upon predictions that are equally conjectural and, therefore, equally personal. If judges are uneasy about resting constitutional interpretation upon such foundations, the remedy is not to fashion principles that mask the underlying choices. The remedy, rather, is candidly to avow the choices that must be made and to develop doctrines that consign ultimate authority for those choices to the legislature, where in a democracy it rightly belongs.

Three: Value

Introduction

The selections in this part were generally written by and for philosophers. They deal with questions of the analysis of justice, morality, justification, consistency, and compensation. Generally we want to know if such and such were the case, in what would justice consist, what does morality require, and why? Part of the attraction of such pieces is the articulation of precise questions, the posing of answers, and the rapid response of opponents.

Bernard Boxhill takes the view that compensation is distinct from reparation, the latter looking backward, the former forward-looking, aiming to remove removable handicaps so as to give true equal opportunity.

Boris Bittker argues that to identify the proposed beneficiaries of any program of compensation for blacks involves conceptual difficulties that would require morally repugnant decisions leading to administrative nightmare. Claims and counterclaims would abound, with the ironic result that we would be forced to go back to the very racist criteria that movements for integration have always fought.

If racial discrimination is wrong because there is no moral basis for treating anyone in a particular way on account of his race, can it then be right to favor someone on the basis of that same morally irrelevant characteristic? James Nickel argues that the answer to this question is no, but that the question itself is misconceived. We do not compensate someone because of his race, but because he was discriminated against on account of his race. Therefore race is, and remains, a morally irrelevant characteristic.

L. J. Cowan replies that people who are injured deserve compensation. The difficulty arises over coupling individual histories with group traits and then claiming that the group as a whole deserves compensation. Once the two are separated, we see that only injury requires compensation.

In turn Philip Silvestri argues that Cowan is wrong because he fails to take into account that the correlation between being, say black, and receiving injury is so high that individual histories can be dispensed with.

Paul Taylor disagrees with both Nickel and Cowan. He argues first that blackness or femaleness are morally relevant characteristics, having been made so by the original evil social practice of discrimination. Second, it can consistently be construed as one for purpose of compensation. Third, there is an obligation to discriminate in favor of such persons, which falls upon society as a whole.

Michael Bayles argues that Nickel and Cowan are wrong because he can construct a parallel argument that would justify the original discrimination. But this is held by all to be immoral; hence the arguments they have framed must be unsound. Bayles suggests it is plausible to argue that there is no justifiable moral rule supporting discrimination against blacks, but that it does not follow that there is no justifiable rule supporting discrimination in their favor.

Are Taylor's claims as clear and compelling as he thinks? William Nunn argues that the notions of institutionalized injustice and compensation on which the argument turns are not explicated. Taylor's thesis is a prescription for continuing discrimination. Nunn contrasts cases in which compensation is a meaningful notion with those in which it is neither meaningful nor required. Compensating one group at the expense of another is not likely to end in justice for all.

Can groups logically, or even as a matter of fact, be the recipients of something? If not, the whole rationale of reverse discrimination must collapse. Roger Shiner argues that they can, and he constructs examples to prove his point. But he claims that the group/individual distinction is neither a barrier nor an aid in analyzing what people deserve. What is really necessary is the underpinning of a moral theory that entails certain connections between the way people are treated and what they deserve.

Nickel replies to Cowan, Taylor, and Bayles by distinguishing between a justifying and an administrative basis for a policy, arguing that the justifying basis would be the injurious discrimination, while the administrative basis must be some easily ascertainable ground upon which to identify the targets for compensation. The reader should compare this point with those in Bittker's article in this section. Nickel attacks Bayles' attempt to construct an argument parallel to the reparationist, but in defense of the racist, and addresses himself in detail to Taylor's brief claims about the place of compensatory justice in the scheme of John Rawls' *A Theory of Justice.*

Ought one to use an administrative basis for compensating large groups of people without examining it more closely? In reply to Nickel, Alan Goldman asks how high a correlation between injury and group membership would be necessary for us to agree to its use. Groups can be cut many ways: blacks, underpriviledged blacks, middle-class blacks, women, and so forth. The correlations will be quite different. (On this, see Sowell in Part I.) Goldman also argues that the operation of the market for talent will tend to give most help to those who need it least, under reverse discrimination.

Professor Nickel returns with a long and thoughtful essay ranging over goals and quotas, the justification of preferential policies in general, and the notion of compensation. He gives us a general scheme for analyzing preferential policies that can be relatively fair and feasible.

Professor Hardy Jones puts forward four aims that he would find compelling in favor of reverse discrimination were it not for the undesirable side-effects of that practice: to insure that discrimination ceases, to offer a symbolic renunciation of our racist past, to provide role models, to provide compensation. He then assesses five sets of objections to these goals and in each case attempts to get round them by outlining a method for minimizing their effect so that they shrink to manageable proportions.

Robert Hoffman argues that justice presupposes neither that all should be treated equally, nor that everyone have equal natural talents, and that all differentiation in the distribution of status, honors, and the like should be justified by individual merit or the common good. He holds that compensatory justice for groups is immoral if it contravenes what merit and the common good require, and that such programs are, in fact, being advocated.

Is it confused to argue that justice now requires favoring women and blacks since we disfavored them before? Lisa Newton thinks so. She distinguishes two notions of justice: one, the foundation and virtue of political associations—the rule of law is its pattern; the other, the ideal of equality for all—a moral ideal. Her argument is that it is a mistake to destroy the political for the sake of realizing the moral and that that is just what reverse discrimination does.

In my own contribution I claim that the balance of argument weighs heavily against reverse discrimination. There are flawed procedures for discovering its proposed beneficiaries; the consequences that flow from official sanction of race are very dangerous; there is no pattern of compensation or restitution nor any mechanism for implementing reverse discrimination; and its outcome is unjust toward both those it favors and those it disfavors.

Bernard Boxhill

The Morality of Reparation

In "Black Reparations—Two Views," [*Dissent*, July-Aug. 1969] Michael
Harrington rejected and Arnold Kaufman endorsed James Forman's
demand for $500 million in reparation from Christian churches and Jewish
synagogues for their part in the exploitation of black people. Harrington's
position involves two different points; he argues that reparation is irrelevant
and unwarranted because even if it were made, it would do little to "even up
incomes"; and he maintains that the *demand* for reparation will be counterproductive, since it will "divert precious political energies from the actual
struggle" to even up incomes. Now, though Kaufman seemed to show good
reason that, contra Harrington, the demand for reparation could be productive, I shall, in the ensuing, completely disregard that issue. Whether the
demand for reparation is counterproductive or not is a question the answer to
which depends on the assessment of a large number of consequences which
cannot be answered by philosophy alone.

In this paper I shall take issue with what I have distinguished as the first
of Harrington's points, namely, that reparation is unwarranted and irrelevant because it would do little to even up incomes. I assume that, by impli-

Source: Social Theory and Practice, *Vol. 2, no. 1. Reprinted by permission of the
author and publisher.* © *Social Theory and Practice, Florida State University, Talla-
hassee, Fla.*

cation, Harrington is not averse to special compensatory programs which will effectively raise the incomes of the poor; what he specifically opposes is reparation. By a discussion of the justification and aims of reparation and compensation, I shall now try to show that, though both are parts of justice, they have different aims, and hence compensation cannot replace reparation.

Let me begin with a discussion of how compensation may be justified. Because of the scarcity of positions and resources relative to aspiring individuals, every society that refused to resort to paternalism or a strict regimentation of aspirations must incorporate competition among its members for scarce positions and resources. Given that freedom of choice necessitates at least the possibility of competition, I believe that justice requires that appropriate compensatory programs be instituted, both to ensure that the competition is fair and that the losers are protected.

If the minimum formal requirement of justice is that persons be given equal consideration, then it is clear that justice requires that compensatory programs be implemented in order to ensure that none of the participants suffers from a removable handicap. The same reasoning supports the contention that the losers in the competition be given, if necessary, sufficient compensation to enable them to reenter the competition on equal terms with the others. In other words, the losers can demand equal opportunity, as well as the beginners can.

In addition to providing compensation in the above cases, the community has the duty to provide compensation to the victims of accident, where no one was in the wrong, and to the victims of "acts of God" such as floods, hurricanes, and earthquakes. Here again, the justification is that such compensation is required if it is necessary to ensure equality of opportunity.

Now, it should be noted that, in all the cases I have stated as requiring compensation, no prior injustice need have occurred. This is clear, of course, in the case of accidents and "acts of God"; but it is also the case that in a competition, even if everyone abides by the rules and acts fairly and justly, some will necessarily be losers. In such a case, I maintain, if the losers are rendered so destitute as to be unable to compete equally, they can demand compensation from the community. Such a right to compensation does not render the competition nugatory; the losers cannot demand success—they can demand only the minimum necessary to reenter the competition. Neither is it the case that every failure has rights of compensation against the community. As we shall see, the right to compensation depends partly on the conviction that every individual has an equal right to pursue what he considers valuable; the wastrel or indolent man has signified what he values by what he has freely chosen to be. Thus, even if he seems a failure and considers himself a failure, he does not need or have the right of compensation. Finally, the case for compensation sketched is not necessarily paternalistic. It is not argued that society or government can decide what valuable things individuals should have and implement programs to see to it that they have them. Society must see to it that its members can pursue those things they consider valuable.

The justification of compensation rests on two premises: first, each individual is equal in dignity and worth to every other individual, and hence has a right, equal to that of any other, to arrange his life as he sees fit, and to pursue and acquire what he considers valuable; and second, the individuals involved must be members of a community. Both premises are necessary in order to show that compensation is both good and, in addition, mandatory or required by justice. One may, for example, concede that a man who is handicapped by some infirmity should receive compensation; but if the man is a member of no community, and if his infirmity is due to no injustice, then one would be hard put to find the party who could be legitimately forced to bear the cost of such compensation. Since persons can be legitimately compelled to do what justice dictates, then it would seem that in the absence of a community, and if the individual has suffered his handicap because of no injustice, that compensation cannot be part of justice. But given that the individual is a member of a community, then I maintain that he can legitimately demand compensation from that community. The members of a community are, in essential respects, members of a joint undertaking; the activities of the members of a community are interdependent and the community benefits from the efforts of its members even when such efforts do not bring the members what they individually aim at. It is legitimate to expect persons to follow the spirit and letter of rules and regulations, to work hard and honestly, to take calculated risks with their lives and fortunes, all of which helps society generally, only if such persons can demand compensation from society as a whole when necessary.

The case for rights of compensation depends, as I have argued above, on the fact that the individuals involved are members of a single community, the very existence of which should imply a tacit agreement on the part of the whole to bear the costs of compensation. The case of reparation I shall try to show is more primitive, in the sense that it depends only on the premise that every person has an equal right to pursue and acquire what he values. Recall that the crucial difference between compensation and reparation is that whereas the latter is due only after injustice, the former may be due when no one has acted unjustly to anyone else. It is this relative innocence of all the parties concerned which made it illegitimate, in the absence of prior commitments, to compel anyone to bear the cost of compensation.

In the case of reparation, however, this difficulty does not exist. When reparation is due, it is not the case that no one is at fault, or that everyone is innocent; in such cases, necessarily, someone has infringed unjustly on another's right to pursue what he values. This could happen in several different ways, dispossession being perhaps the most obvious. When someone possesses something, he has signified by his choice that he values it. By taking it away from him one infringes on his equal right to pursue and possess what he values. On the other hand, if I thwart, unfairly, another's legitimate attempt to do or possess something, I have also acted unjustly; finally, an injustice has occurred when someone makes it impossible for others to pursue a legitimate goal, even if these others never actually attempt to achieve that goal. These examples of injustice differ in detail, but what they all have in common is that no supposition of prior commitment is necessary in order to be able to identify the parties who must bear the cost of reparation; it is simply and clearly the party who has acted unjustly.

The argument may, perhaps, be clarified by the ideas of a state of nature and a social contract. In the state of nature, as John Locke remarks [in his *Treatise of Civil Government*], every man has the right to claim reparation from his injurer because of his right of self-preservation; if each man has a duty not to interfere in the rights of others, he has a duty to repair the results of his interference. No social contract is required to legitimize compelling him to do so. But when compensation is due, that is, when everyone has acted justly, and has done his duty, then a social contract or a prior agreement to help must be appealed to in order to legitimately compel an individual to help another.

The case for reparation thus requires for its justification less in the way of assumptions than the case for compensation. Examination of the justifications of reparation and compensation also reveals the difference in their aims.

The characteristic of compensatory programs is that they are essentially forward looking; by that I mean that such programs are intended to alleviate disabilities which stand in the way of some *future* good, *however* these disabilities may have come about. Thus, the history of injustices suffered by black and colonial people is quite irrelevant to their right to compensatory treatment. What is strictly relevant to this is that such compensatory treatment is necessary if some future goods, such as increased happiness, equality of incomes, and so on, are to be secured. To put it another way, given the contingency of causal connections, the present condition of black and colonial people could have been produced in any one of a very large set of different causal sequences. Compensation is concerned with the remedying of the present situation however it may have been produced; and to know the present situation, and how to remedy it, it is not, strictly speaking, necessary to know just how it was brought about, or whether it was brought about by injustice.

On the other hand, the justification of reparation is essentially backward looking; reparation is due only when a breach of justice *has* occurred. Thus, as opposed to the case of compensation, the case for reparation to black and colonial people depends precisely on the fact that such people have been reduced to their present condition by a history of injustice. In sum, while the aim of compensation is to procure some future good, that of reparation is to rectify past injustices; and rectifying past injustices may not insure equality of opportunity.

The fact that reparation aims precisely at correcting a prior injustice suggests one further important difference between reparation and compensation. Part of what is involved in rectifying an injustice is an acknowledgment on the part of the trangressor that what he is doing is required of him because of his prior error. This concession of error seems required by the premise that every person is equal in worth and dignity. Without the acknowledgment of error, the injurer implies that the injured has been treated in a manner that befits him; hence, he cannot feel that the injured party is his equal. In such a case, even if the unjust party repairs the damage he has caused, justice does not yet obtain between himself and his victim. For, if it is true that when someone has done his duty nothing can be demanded of him, it follows that if, in my estimation, I have acted dutifully even when someone is injured as a result, then I must feel that nothing can be demanded of me and that any repairs I may make are gratuitous. If justice can be demanded, it follows that I cannot think that what I am doing is part of justice.

It will be objected, of course, that I have not shown in this situation that justice cannot obtain between injurer and victim, but only that the injurer does not *feel* that justice can hold between himself and the one he injures. The objection depends on the distinction between the objective transactions between the individuals and their subjective attitudes, and assumes that justice requires only the objective transactions. The model of justice presupposed by this objection is, no doubt, that justice requires equal treatment of equals, whereas the view I take is that justice requires equal consideration between equals; that is to say, justice requires not only that we *treat* people in a certain way, for whatever reason we please, but that we treat them as equals precisely because we believe they are our equals. In particular, justice requires that we acknowledge that our treatment of others can be required of us; thus, where an unjust injury has occurred, the injurer reaffirms his belief in the other's equality by conceding that repair can be demanded of him, and the injured rejects the allegation of his inferiority contained in the other's behavior by demanding reparation.

Consequently, when injustice has reduced a people to indigency, compensatory programs alone cannot be all that justice requires. Since the avowed aim of compensatory programs is forward looking, such programs *necessarily* cannot affirm that the help they give is required because of a prior injustice. This must be the case even if it is the unjustly injuring party who makes compensation. Thus, since the acknowledgment of error is required by justice as part of what it means to give equal consideration, compensatory programs cannot take the place of reparation.

In sum, *compensation* cannot be substituted for *reparation* where reparation is due, because they satisfy two differing requirements of justice. In addition, practically speaking, since it is by demanding and giving justice where it is due that the members of a community continually reaffirm their belief in each other's equality, a stable and equitable society is not possible without reparation being demanded and given when it is due.

Consider now the assertion that the present generation of white Americans owe the present generation of black Americans reparation for the injustices of slavery inflicted on the ancestors of the black population by the ancestors of the white population. To begin, consider the very simplest instance of a case where reparation may be said to be due: Tom has an indisputable moral right to possession of a certain item, say a bicycle, and Dick steals the bicycle from Tom. Here, clearly, Dick owes Tom, at least the bicycle and a concession of error, in reparation. Now complicate the case slightly; Dick steals the bicycle from Tom and "gives" it to Harry. Here again, even if he is innocent of complicity in the theft, and does not know that his "gift" was stolen, Harry must return the bicycle to Tom with the acknowledgment that, though innocent or blameless, he did not rightfully possess the bicycle. Consider a final complication; Dick steals the bicycle from Tom and gives it to Harry; in the meantime Tom dies, but leaves a will clearly conferring his right to ownership of the bicycle to his son, Jim. Here again we should have little hesitation in saying that Harry must return the bicycle to Jim.

Now, though it involves complications, the case for reparation under consideration is essentially the same as the one last mentioned: the slaves had an indisputable moral right to the products of their labor; these products were stolen from them by the slave masters, who ultimately passed them on to their descendants; the slaves presumably have conferred their rights of ownership to the products of their labor to their descendants; thus, the descendants of slave masters are in possession of wealth to which the descendants of slaves have rights; hence, the descendants of slave masters must return this wealth to the descendants of slaves with a concession that they were not rightfully in possession of it.

It is not being claimed that the descendants of slaves must seek reparation from those among the white population who happen to be descendants of slave owners. This perhaps would be the case if slavery had produced for the slave owners merely specific hoards of gold, silver or diamonds, which could be passed on in a very concrete way from father to son. As a matter of fact, slavery produced not merely specific hoards, but wealth which has been passed down mainly to descendants of the white community, to the relative exclusion of the descendants of slaves. Thus, it is the white community as a whole that prevents the descendants of slaves from exercising their rights of ownership and the white community as a whole that must bear the cost of reparation.

The statement above contains two distinguishable arguments. In the first argument the assertion is that each white person, individually, owes reparation to the black community because membership in the white community serves to identify an individual as a recipient of benefits to which the black community has a rightful claim. In the second argument, the conclusion is that the white community as a whole, considered as a kind of corporation or company, owes reparation to the black community.

In the first of the arguments sketched above, individuals are held liable to make reparation even if they have been merely passive recipients of benefits; that is, even if they have not deliberately chosen to accept the benefits in question. This argument invites the objection that, for the most part, white people are simply not in a position to choose to receive or refuse benefits belonging to the descendants of slaves and are, therefore, not culpable or blameable and hence not liable to make reparation. But this objection misses the point. The argument under consideration simply does not depend on or imply the claim that white people are culpable or blameable; the argument is that merely by being white, an individual receives benefits to which others have at least partial rights. In such cases, whatever one's choice or moral culpability, reparation must be made. Consider an extreme case: Harry has an unexpected heart attack and is taken unconscious to the hospital. In the same hospital Dick has recently died. A heart surgeon transplants the heart from Dick's dead body to Harry without permission from Dick's family. If Harry recovers, he must make suitable reparation to Dick's family, conceding that he is not in rightful possession of Dick's heart even if he had no part in choosing to receive it.

The second of the arguments distinguished above concluded that, for the purpose in question, the white community can be regarded as a corporation or company which, as a whole, owes reparation to the sons of slaves. Certainly the white community resembles a corporation or company in some striking ways; like such companies, the white community has interests distinct from, and opposed to, other groups in the same society, and joint action is often taken by the members of the white community to protect and enhance their interests. Of course, there are differences; people are generally born into the white community and do not deliberately choose their membership in it; on the other hand, deliberate choice is often the standard procedure for gaining membership in a company. But this difference is unimportant; European immigrants often deliberately choose to become part of the white community in the United States for the obvious benefits this brings, and people often inherit shares and so, without deliberate choice, become members of a company. What is important here is not how deliberately one chooses to become part of a community or a company; what is relevant is that one chooses to continue to accept the benefits which circulate exclusively within the community, sees such benefits as belonging exclusively to the members of the community, identifies one's interests with those of the community, and finally, takes joint action with other members of the community to protect such interests. In such a case, it seems not unfair to consider the present white population as members of a company that incurred debts before they were members of the company, and thus to ask them justly to bear the costs of such debts.

It may be objected that the case for reparation depends on the validity of inheritance; for, only if the sons of slaves inherit the rights of their ancestors can it be asserted that they have rights against the present white community. If the validity of inheritance is rejected, a somewhat different, but perhaps even stronger, argument for reparation can still be formulated. For if inheritance is rejected with the stipulation that the wealth of individuals be returned to the whole society at their deaths, then it is even clearer that the white community owes reparation to the black community. For the white community has appropriated, almost exclusively, the wealth from slavery in addition to the wealth from other sources; but such wealth belongs jointly to all members of the society, white as well as black; hence, it owes them reparation. The above formulation of the argument is entirely independent of the fact of slavery and extends the rights of the black community to its just portion of the total wealth of the society.

Boris Bittker

Identifying the Beneficiaries

A program to compensate children who were required to go to segregated schools before the Supreme Court's 1954 decision in *Brown v. Board of Education* would not raise any conceptual difficulties in identifying the beneficiaries. They would be the children who were enrolled in black schools in states with pre-1954 school-segregation laws. Just as a person who files a claim for social security or veterans' benefits must establish that he worked for the requisite period or served in the armed services, so a claimant under this hypothetical plan would have to establish that he attended a segregated school. Since benefits would be at stake, one would expect most of the program's intended beneficiaries to come forward with proof that they had been required to attend segregated schools. Their claims could be verified by school-attendance records, and records that were lost or destroyed could be reconstructed by affidavits or other supporting evidence. The administrative job would, of course, be monumental, but the ultimate question to be decided would be simple: Was the claimant required to attend a segregated school by the local authorities?

Source: Chapter 10 of The Case for Black Reparations. © *1973, Random House. Reprinted, with notes and citations omitted, by permission of the author.*

If the compensation plan provided that benefits could be inherited by the children of a deceased student, the administrative job would be enlarged, but it would not be unprecedented: when a person entitled to social security or veterans' benefits dies, the administrative agencies must pass on disputed issues of kinship and inheritance in deciding who inherits his rights. Another parallel is the German compensation program for victims of Nazi prosecution, which manages to cope with claims by hundreds of thousands of refugees and their heirs, scattered from Hong Kong to Buenos Aires, whose only evidence of entitlement to reparations may be a letter from a person who died in a concentration camp, a notation in Gestapo records seized by an Allied military unit, or the fading recollection of an elderly neighbor of the claimant's parents.

Though a reparations program confined to students who were required by law to attend segregated schools would entail a large administrative job, it would not raise difficult or painful questions of racial classification. Entitlement would depend exclusively on the fact that the student was assigned to a black school, regardless of his actual racial origin. Thus, a student who was required by the state to attend a Negro school would be entitled to benefits whether or not he was properly classified as "Negro"; conversely a Negro who covertly attended a white school would be excluded from benefits even though he would have been expelled if his racial makeup had been known to the authorities. Here again, I invoke by way of analogy the German compensation program, under which a person classified as a Jew by the Nazi authorities is entitled to compensation even if the classification was erroneous under the rules then in force in Germany, and needless to say, even if he would not have been so classified under the standards in vogue elsewhere.

But if, to take account of a broader range of racial discrimination, the circle of persons entitled to reparations is enlarged beyond those who were required to attend segregated schools, we quickly encounter the conceptual issue that I have previously sidestepped, namely, Who is black? An authoritative answer to this question would be required, for example, if reparations were to be paid for the humiliation caused by the Jim Crow system. Since it would not be feasible to require proof from each person of whether and how often he was forced to use the segregated entrance to a public building, or the segregated part of a bus, theater, railroad waiting room, park, and so on, a comprehensive reparations program would perforce have to rely on a set of rules (possibly augmented by rebuttable presumptions) in defining the class of beneficiaries. One possibility would be to include only those who were immediately subject to a legally enforced system of segregation, such as blacks who lived in states with Jim Crow laws or who served in the armed forces before the end of World War II. In view of the national fall-out generated by the Jim Crow system, however, it would be more realistic to embrace all blacks throughout the country. In either variation, such a program of individual reparations would require an official answer to the question, Who is black?

Racial classification is not, of course, a new art. Though geneticists and anthropologists agree that there is no scientific way to classify individuals, our society and others have long distinguished between whites and blacks. Moreover, the line has been drawn for legal purposes, not merely for such unofficial decisions as membership in social groups. For example, in reviewing the constitutional validity of a criminal conviction in American law, it is sometimes necessary to determine whether blacks were systematically excluded from jury service. Litigation in the school-desegregation area often requires federal courts to decide whether the racial makeup of a school is predominantly white or predominantly Negro. Similarly, government agencies and employers are sometimes asked for reports on the racial composition of their labor forces. These racial identifications, however, are made on a wholesale rather than retail basis and are customarily based on general impressions from looking at a sea of faces. Thus, federal agencies ordinarily employ a "visual census" to classify their employees for statistical purposes; if questionnaires are used, each respondent's self-identification is accepted automatically and without requiring that he swear to its accuracy.

American law has also sometimes required the official determination of an individual's race, for example, in the enforcement of school-segregation or antimiscegenation laws. These laws are now defunct, but there are some circumstances in which evidence of an individual's race might still be required. Thus, for example, if a defendant in a criminal case is not entitled to object to the systematic exclusion of Negroes from the jury unless he is himself a Negro, his right to make the objection might depend on whether he is "really" black or only an imposter. In the absence of official genealogies or expert evidence of the individual's genetic composition, the resolution of disputed cases depends on reputation, the jury's visual impression, or the testimony of observers . . . .

A racial test based on self-designation and reputation was evidently endorsed by a federal court in a recent desegregation case, when a Florida school board, in an obvious attempt to avoid compliance with a judicial decree, reported that it did not know how to classify its teachers and students by race, and then reported that they were all "Orientals." The court held, in this context, that a school board that had been able in the past to identify Negroes in order to segregate them should be able to identify Negroes "with similar ease" in desegregating the school system. It also quoted, with apparent approval, the Department of Health, Education and Welfare's definition of Negroes, namely, "persons considered by themselves, by the school or by the community to be of African or Negro origin."

A large-scale program of black reparations, however, could not be administered without a more formal set of eligibility rules. It would hardly be fair or constitutionally permissible to grant benefits if in the judgment of the administrator, a court, or a body of laymen the applicant "appears to have colored features," and to deny them if his appearance fails to meet this standard. There has been enough mating across racial lines in the United States to justify the prediction that hundreds of thousands, if not millions, of persons of debatable racial composition might apply for compensation if the benefits were worth pursuing. It has been estimated that over thirty-six million Americans classified as white in 1960 had "an African element in their inherited biological background." This means that the Africans brought to the United States have more "white" than "black" descendants.

It would be tempting to experiment with self-certification, allowing anyone identifying himself as black to receive reparations if he is willing to accept the public consequences of that classification. Recent experience with political pranksters, however, suggests that persons opposed to black reparations would not hestitate to file claims for benefits, knowing that whites masquerading as blacks for this purpose would not have to pay the price that society has imposed on genuine blacks; and these Abbie Hoffmans of the racial right might even win the admiration of their neighbors for outwitting or discrediting "the system." False claims might also be filed by persons with grievances, real or imagined, that in their own opinions entitle them to the status of "white niggers." These claims could not be denied, nor could the claimants be punished, without an officially sanctioned mode of proving that the applicant was not black. A useful analogy is the administration of the federal income tax, which commences with the taxpayer's own statement of his income and deductions. The return is provisionally accepted as accurate, but when it is audited by the Internal Revenue Service, the taxpayer has the burden of proving the propriety of all challenged entries. If a reparations program allowed the claimant to make a similar initial certification of his rights, the procedure could be protected against abuse only by penalizing false claims, and this safeguard would require an official code of racial classification to separate the sheep from the goats.

For guidance in this seemingly indispensable process of racial classification, the laws used by the Southern states to enforce their segregation and antimiscegenation laws could be resurrected; or, because these definitions conflicted with each other and were far from uniform, a panel of legal experts could be assembled and charged with the duty of extracting the "best" (or would it be the "worst"?) rule from this medley—the essence of racism, so to speak. If these sources are too provincial or antiquated for the modern temper, we could turn to the preeminent contemporary fountainhead: South Africa, whose scholars—heirs to both English and Roman-Dutch legal traditions—have explored every facet of this subject. Their work culminated in the enactment in 1950 of the Population Registration Act, under which every person's racial classification is recorded in a kind of Doomsday Book; unless successfully appealed to the courts, this classification is final and binding.

I venture to predict that the adoption of a formal code of racial classification, whether home-grown or imported, would have calamitous consequences for the United States. It would ease the way to more and more private, public, and official distinctions between black and white. It would put pressure on millions of persons of mixed blood to make an official declaration of their racial origin, instead of allowing their allegiance to remain private, ambiguous, submerged, neglected, or changeable. To be sure, they could protect their privacy by foregoing their benefits, but for many this would be an intolerable price. Some black nationalists might welcome official support for the process of racial identification, as would some white groups; but surely the legitimate objectives of groups seeking greater awareness of black history and a more intense racial pride can be served by the voluntary adherence of the persons to whom their messages are addressed. While the government should not build obstacles to the achievement of these objectives, it should be equally careful not to act as a recruiting office.

It may be said in response that we are already two societies, black and white, and that official racial classifications would do no more than accept the universe. But the theory that we are already so divided that no official action could increase the separation is as fatuous as the theory—so prevalent on college campuses in the spring of 1970—that official repression was already so total that no amount of reactionary backlash could make matters worse. In a dynamic world, governmental intervention is bound to push us one way or the other. The proposed code is more likely to reinforce and sharpen polarization than to reduce racial separation.

There is undoubtedly a bitter irony in arguing that a country that used racial classifications for many years should be wary of preserving or reviving them in a program of reparations. As pointed out earlier, however, it is one thing to permit persons who were required to attend segregated schools to recover damages under a corrective statute, such as Section 1983, which (like the German reparations program) simply accepts the past racial classification, whether "valid" or not, as a basis for corrective action. It is something else again to establish a bureaucratic apparatus to determine the race of persons who were never officially classified for such purposes as school segregation, especially since those who do not wish to submit to this process will have to sacrifice a financial benefit in order to preserve their privacy. Quite aside from persons of debatable racial ancestry who prefer ambiguity to clarification, there are surely many persons of undeniable black descent who will resent an official code of racial classification even though they acknowledge without cavil or proudly proclaim their *negritude*. The problems discussed here, to be sure, already exist in embryo in a variety of programs undertaken in recent years to counteract the effects of racial segregation and discrimination. School-desegregation plans, for example, sometimes permit a child who belongs to a racial majority in his school to transfer to a school where he will be in the minority; and preferential-employment and college-admissions plans may on occasion require a person of disputed racial ancestry to prove his classification. Given the fragmentary and experimental nature of these arrangements, it may be possible to administer them without elaborate administrative devices to resolve debatable racial claims; but they are hardly persuasive precedents for a comprehensive program of black reparations.

In addition to the dangers just canvassed, a code of racial classification could lead to a Balkanization of the racial map. South Africa, for example, uses the classifications "European," "Bantu," and "Coloured," the latter group being subdivided into "Cape Coloured," "Indian," "Malay," and four other categories. Similarly, in responding to claims by American Indians, we have indulged in some fine distinctions. For example, a recent Senate-approved bill relating to Alaskan natives provided that a person of one-quarter or more Indian, Eskimo, or Aleut blood would qualify for benefits, but that Tsimshian Indian blood would not count, nor the blood of any other Indian tribe that migrated to Alaska after 1867; and there is other legislation in force that distinguishes between "full blood" and "mixed blood" Indians. Rules of this type may be unavoidable in dealing with Indian tribes, since the very concept of a tribe implies a connection by blood among its members, but the extension of the process to other social groupings should not be undertaken lightly. The burgeoning of "ethnic studies" in schools and colleges suggests some of the possibilities in the official classification of individuals, initially in the compilation of statistics and then in the administration of remedial programs for their benefit. The process would be complicated still further by the ambiguity of the term *ethnic*, currently often used to denote groups characterized by national or regional origin, language, religion, or other traits, regardless of racial ancestry.

Even if confined to blacks, a racial code would invite distinctions—already familiar in American law—based on the individual's percentage of "African blood." This would, indeed, not be irrational in a system of black reparations, since the impact of discrimination depends in part on the degree to which a person is perceived as black by society, as well as on his self-perception. If a program of black reparations were to take account of these differences, however, it would ineluctably pit one subgroup against another in the race for benefits: should a mulatto get one-half the benefit of a full-blooded black, a quadroon one-quarter, and so forth?

At first glace, it might be thought that these problems would afflict only a program of individual reparations and could be avoided by shifting to group reparations. On examination, however, this strategy . . . proves to be unequal to the task, except at the cost of additional difficulties. The simplest case is a program confined to groups with black constituencies of their own, such as black universities and economic-development corporations. Since the legitimacy of their participation would depend upon the racial composition of their respective clienteles, these organizations would have to promulgate and apply their own racial codes to establish and preserve their credentials. As conduits for the flow of governmental benefits to their constituencies, however, they would at most disguise, without diluting public responsibility for their racial policies. Nor could Congress, if it empowered such an organization to administer a publicly financed program, wash its hands of the procedures used by its instrumentality to decide individual cases of disputed entitlement to participate in the benefits.

Thus, Indian tribes, despite their long-acknowledged "internal sovereignty," were subjected by the Civil Rights Act of 1964 to most of the constitutional restraints imposed on the federal and state governments by the first fourteen amendments. Had Congress not explicitly imposed these limitations on tribal self-government, it is quite possible that the federal courts would have moved in this direction on their own. The recent judicial tendency to require a wide variety of "private" organizations to conform to such constitutional concepts as "due process" and "equal protection" could hardly have been expected to take a detour around every Indian reservation in the country. The pressure would be even greater to impose similar requirements, by either legislative or judicial action, on organizations that lack the Indian tribe's historic and treaty-protected right to internal sovereignty. The organization's decisions to grant or deny government-financed benefits would surely rank high on any list of matters which could not be allowed to escape official scrutiny and revision.

The need for a racial code would dwindle, and its role would become less obtrusive, if the hypothetical program of group reparations embraced "black-managed" organizations, regardless of the racial composition of their audiences (for example, newspapers, radio and television stations, museums and galleries, training centers, and universities with racially mixed student bodies). A familiar American pattern is the voluntary agency that preserves a religious tinge at the trusteeship level while providing services without regard to the religious affiliation of the consumers, as for example, the YMCA, Notre Dame University, and Mount Sinai Hospital. However, if the group recipients of black reparations followed a similar open-door policy, the racial content of their programs would soon be only a symbolic vestige, or a vestigial symbol, of their history. Lovers of African music, soul food, and LeRoi Jones' plays would go to the Malcolm X Cultural Center, for example, in the same way that people who want to swim, lose weight, or learn karate go to the YMCA—without reference to their own religious affiliations and with equal disregard for the organization's historic roots. As an instrument of reparations, the organization would in time be no more distinctive than a national park, historic site, or museum of Negro history.

While reducing the need for a racial code, such a program of group reparations would require a host of ultimately arbitrary choices among the organizations that would clamor for participation. For example: should proof of a predominantly black constituency entitle an organization to receive benefits, regardless of its objectives? To illustrate the potential for conflict, assume that applications are filed by four organizations concerned with the geographical location of blacks, favoring (1) a back-to-African movement, (2) independent black nationhood for a group of American states, (3) emigration from inner cities to suburban areas, and (4) concentration in the inner city. If each group claims a monopoly on wisdom, asserting that its competitors are dominated by timidity, ignorance, servility, romanticisim, or selfishness, should the merits of each program be assessed, or should all four be regarded as equally deserving of assistance? In granting tax exemptions to nonprofit organizations, ideology ordinarily does not count; at the organizational level, this form of neutrality means that the group can keep whatever it can raise from its members and admirers without being burdened by taxes.

In theory, this approach could be employed in dispensing reparations by matching any contributions that the organization can attract from private sources (dollar for dollar or according to a more complex formula). Once begun, this procedure would be as self-executing as tax exemptions; but it would probably not command the support needed to reach the launching pad. This is because the largest black voluntary agencies are churches, fraternal lodges, and the NAACP; in this context, a reparations program consisting of matching grants would be hopelessly lopsided. Another source of difficulty is inherent in the vague concept of "black control." If this, rather than the racial composition of an organization's membership or clientele, is to determine the group's right to receive reparations, must its officers, directors, or staff be exclusively, predominantly, or significantly black? Would the Urban League, with its biracial board of directors, qualify; or Hampton University, with its biracial board and a growing percentage of white students; or the black-studies program of Cornell University; or the black-apprenticeship program of the United Automobile Workers?

The friction that would be caused by governmental answers to these and similar questions might be mollified by entrusting the decisions to a board of black representatives. To get this insulation, however, the government would first have to select these black notables, and unless they were constituted as a self-perpetuating body, it would have to pick their successors as well. . . . [T]his process would simultaneously proclaim that an aggregation of diverse individuals makes up a homogeneous collectivity, stir up justified resentment among those who were not selected for official recognition, and expose those who were selected to the charge of being official spokesmen despite their alleged representative character.

In conclusion, my inquiry into the problem of identifying the beneficiaries of a program of black reparations drives me to make two equally bleak observations: that compensation to individuals could not be administered without a racial code and a large-scale procedure for the racial classification of individuals; and that group reparations would mitigate or eliminate this hazard only to embrace the equally grave hazards of selecting, with no satisfactory guideposts, the black organizations to participate in the program or creating an official body of black "representatives" to make these decisions. It is the justice of reparations when viewed in the large, coupled with these perils of administering a program in the concrete that lead me to perceive this area as the locus of a second "American Dilemma."

James W. Nickel

Discrimination and Morally Relevant Characteristics

Suppose that a characteristic which should be morally irrelevant (for example, race, creed or sex) has been treated as if it were morally relevant over a period of years, and that injustices have resulted from this. When such a mistake has been recognized and condemned, when the morally irrelevant characteristic has been seen to be irrelevant, can this characteristic *then* properly be used as a relevant consideration in the distribution of reparations to those who have suffered injustices? If we answer this question in the affirmative, we will have the strange consequence that a morally irrelevant characteristic can become morally relevant if its use results in injustices.

The context in which this difficulty is likely to arise is one in which a group has been discriminated against on the basis of morally irrelevant properties, but in which this discrimination has been recognized and at least partly come to an end; and the question at hand concerns how the members of this group should now be treated. Should they now be treated like everyone else, ignoring their history, or should they be given special advantages because of past discrimination and injustices? There are a variety of consi-

Source: Analysis *32, no. 4 (March 1972). Reprinted by permission of the publisher.*

derations which are pertinent in answering this question, and I will deal with only one of these, the reverse-discrimination argument. This argument claims that to extend special considerations to a formerly oppressed group will be to persist in the mistake of treating a morally irrelevant characteristic as if it were relevant. For if we take a morally irrelevant characteristic (namely the characteristic which was the basis for the original discrimination) and use it as the basis for granting special consideration or reparations, we will be treating the morally irrelevant as if it were relevant and still engaging in discrimination, albeit reverse discrimination. And hence, it is argued, the only proper stance toward groups who have suffered discrimination is one of strict impartiality.

To state the argument in a slightly different way, one might say that if a group was discriminated against on the basis of a morally irrelevant characteristic of theirs, then to award extra benefits now to the members of this group because they have this characteristic is simply to continue to treat a morally irrelevant characteristic as if it were relevant. Instead of the original discrimination *against* these people, we now have discrimination *for* them, but in either case we have discrimination since it treats the irrelevant as relevant. Hence, to avoid discrimination we must now completely ignore this characteristic and extend no special considerations whatsoever.

The objection which I want to make to this argument pertains to its assumption that the characteristic which was the basis for the original discrimination is the same as the one which is used as the basis for extending extra considerations now. I want to suggest that this is only apparently so. For if compensation in the form of extra opportunities is extended to a black man on the basis of past discrimination against blacks (I do not mean to imply that we are in this situation, where discrimination against blacks is a thing of the past. We are not.) the basis for this compensation is not that he is a black man, but that he was previously subject to unfair treatment because he was black. The former characteristic was and is morally irrelevant, but the latter characteristic is very relevant if it is assumed that it is desirable or obligatory to make compensation for past injustices. Hence, to extend special considerations to those who have suffered from discrimination need not involve continuing to treat a morally irrelevant characteristic as if it were relevant. In such a case the characteristic which was the basis for the original discrimination (for example, being a black person) will be different from the characteristic which is the basis for the distribution of special considerations (for example, being a person who was discriminated against because he was black).

My conclusion is that this version of the reverse-discrimination argument has a false premise, since it assumes that the characteristic which was the basis for the original discrimination is the same as that which is the basis for the granting of special considerations. And since the argument has a false premise, it does not succeed in showing that to avoid reverse discrimination we must extend no special considerations whatsoever.

L. J. Cowan

Inverse Discrimination

The justice or injustice of "inverse discrimination" is a question of pressing social importance. On the one hand it is argued that when a morally irrelevant characteristic such as race, creed or sex has been treated as morally relevant and injustices have resulted, it is then proper to treat that characteristic as morally relevant in order to make reparations. On the other hand it is argued that if the characteristic in question is morally irrelevant, its use even in this manner would still constitute discrimination, discrimination now in favor of those possessing the characteristic and against those not, but unjust discrimination still.

Public discussion of this issue all too rarely goes far beyond the level of the arguments as given. Yet the logic of these arguments is murky, to say the least. It is therefore to be hoped that the analytical skills supposedly characteristic of philosophers might here play a valuable social role, and we are indebted to J. W. Nickel for beginning such a clarification. I should like here to try to continue it.

Nickel maintains that the argument against inverse discrimination given

Source: Analysis *33, no. 1 (Oct. 1972). Reprinted by permission of the publisher.*

above goes wide of the mark since the characteristic which is now operative is not actually the original morally irrelevant one. "For if compensation in the form of extra opportunities is extended to a black man on the basis of past discrimination against blacks, the basis for this compensation is not that he is a black man, but that he was previously subject to unfair treatment because he was black . . . in such a case the characteristic which was the basis for the original discrimination (for example, being a black person) will be different from the characteristic which is the basis for the distribution of special considerations (for example, being a person who was discriminated against because he was black)."

The problem is that Nickel does not make it entirely clear just what he is about here. He may simply be pointing out that if a person has suffered injustice through morally unjustified discrimination, then reparation to that person will be appropriate. But surely it was not against this relatively uncontroversial point that the original argument was directed. And Nickel's formulation leaves open the possibility that he is actually trying to support the far more questionable claim that was the original target of that argument.

"Being discriminated against because he was black" is clearly a complex predicate. What I would like to suggest is that the portion of it which was morally irrelevant in independence remains so within the complex and is thus mere excess baggage. The reason why he was discriminated against is not what should now ground reparation, but rather simply the fact that, and extent to which, he was unjustly discriminated against for whatever reason. Thus, assuming that the discrimination is otherwise the same, we would presumably not wish to say that Jones, who has been discriminated against as a black, should now be favored over Smith, who has been equally discriminated against as a woman or a Jew or whatever. We are therefore left without a moral relevance for blackness, and thus without a moral basis for inverse discrimination based on blackness, as opposed to discriminatory injustice per se.

Nickel's reasoning thus does not really, as it might be taken to do, provide any support at all for the kind of self-contradictory thinking the original argument was surely intended to rebut. This is the reasoning that since blacks, to retain this example, have suffered unjust discrimination we should now give them special treatment to make it up to them. Once again there is no problem insofar as this simply means that where individual blacks have suffered injustice it should, as with anyone else, insofar as possible be made up to those individuals who have so suffered. The fallacy arises when, rather than individuals, it is the group which is intended, and individuals are regarded merely as members of that group rather than in their individuality. This creates a contradiction since the original premise of the moral irrelevance of blackness on the basis of which the original attribution of unjust discrimination rests implies that there is and can be no morally relevant group which could have suffered or to which retribution could now be made. Thus those who would argue that since "we" brutally kidnapped "the" blacks out of Africa and subjected "them" to the abominations of slavery, or that since "we" have exploited and degraded "women" since Eve, "we" therefore now owe retribution to our neighbor who happens to be black or a woman, are involved in inextricable self-contradiction. Except to the extent he or she as an individual has unjustly suffered or will unjustly suffer from this history while we as individuals have unjustly profited or will unjustly profit there can be no such obligation.

Nickel's original formulation is thus ambiguous. "The context in which this difficulty is likely to arise is one in which a group has been discriminated against on the basis of morally irrelevant properties, but in which this discrimination has been recognized and at least partly come to an end; and the question at hand concerns how the members of this group should now be treated. Should they now be treated like everyone else, ignoring their history, or should they be given special advantages because of past discrimination and injustices?" Once the question is unambiguous the answer is clear. They should most certainly be treated like everyone else. But this does not mean "their" individual histories should be ignored. As with anyone else, injustices done "them" as individuals should be prevented or rectified insofar as possible. But past or future discrimination and injustice done "them" as a group and special advantages to them as a group are both out of the question, since in the moral context there is no such group.

Philip Silvestri

The Justification of
Inverse Discrimination

In answer to J. W. Nickel's claim that inverse discrimination is acceptable because the relevant characteristic is the fact that blacks were discriminated against and not just that they are black, J. L. Cowan has countered: "The reason why he was discriminated against is not what should now ground reparation, but rather simply the fact that, and extent to which, he was unjustly discriminated against for whatever reasons." Cowan claims that if prior discrimination is the basis it will apply to white and black, male and female, depending on the individual case, and inverse discrimination is replaced by a more conventional model of fairness.

It does seem to me, however, that Cowan is not giving the inverse-discrimination view its due. He has failed to consider the possibility of correlational factors. Suppose, which I think is the case, that blacks have been discriminated against to such a degree that one is on fairly safe ground in assuming that in repaying all blacks we are, with few exceptions, repaying fairly. In this kind of situation are we not justified in using, because of empirical correlation, a characteristic which, in itself, would lack moral relevance?

Source: Analysis *34, no. 1 (Oct. 1973). Reprinted by permission of the publisher.*

There might be two objections to this approach: (1) The extent of the correlation could be questioned. (2) It might be claimed that the use of this kind of correlation is just what we mean by improper discrimination. The first is, however, a criticism against this bit of inverse discrimination and not against the soundness of the procedure in general. The second presents more of a problem. In punishing and, in general, acting in a negative way towards categories of people we do not consider it proper to act even on high correlations; we feel each individual should be judged on his own merits. There are limits to this approach. There are always doubts about the individual. We never really know. Invariably we do act on correlation if it is very high. Yet in punishing we shy away from this kind of thing. The same does not apply to positive action, however. In giving we accept a much higher risk of unfairness respecting the individual case; we are less afraid of unjustly giving too much than of hurting the innocent. The considerations point, then, to the impropriety of coercing whites, for example, to give reparations to blacks; but voluntary reparations would be correct despite the unfairness (overpayment) in particular cases.

Paul W. Taylor

Reverse Discrimination
and Compensatory Justice

Two articles have recently appeared in *Analysis* concerning the apparent contradiction between:

> (1) At time t_2 members of group G have been discriminated against on the basis of a *morally irrelevant* characteristic C

and:

> (2) At time t_2 characteristic C is a *morally relevant* ground for making reparation to members of group G.

In the first article ("Discrimination and Morally Relevant Characteristics") J. W. Nickel presents what he calls the "reverse-discrimination argument" and offers a counterargument to it. The reverse-discrimination argument is that, if we grant as a matter of compensatory justice special advantages or benefits to persons who have been unjustly treated on the basis of a morally irrelevant characteristic (such as being a woman, being black, being a Jew,

Source: Analysis 33, no. 6 (*June 1973*). *Reprinted by permission of the publisher.*

and so forth), we are in effect using a morally irrelevant characteristic as if it were morally relevant and thus still engaging in an unjust treatment of persons. Hence if we are to be just we must avoid reverse discrimination. Nickel's counterargument is that the special treatment given to persons having characteristic C at time t_2 is not grounded on the (morally irrelevant) characteristic C, but on the (morally relevant) characteristic C´, namely, being a person who has been discriminated against because he was C.

In an article by J. L. Cowan ("Inverse Discrimination") Nickel is criticized for failing to realize that characteristic C´ is actually a complex predicate made up of a conjunction of two characteristics—C´´, namely: having been discriminated against (for whatever reason), and the characteristic C itself. Cowan's point is that C´´ is a morally relevant characteristic in matters of compensatory justice but that C remains morally irrelevant. He holds that reverse discrimination is wrong, since it involves giving people favorable treatment *because they are* C and hence using a morally irrelevant characteristic as a justifying ground for special treatment. Nevertheless, he concludes, special treatment should be extended to any *individual* who has been discriminated against (for whatever reason) in the past, that is, anyone who has characteristic C´´. For it is a requirement of compensatory justice that reparation be made to those who have been dealt with unjustly (for whatever reason).

In this paper I want to defend three views, all of which are inconsistent with the claims made by Nickel and Cowan. (1) With respect to the principle of compensatory justice, characteristic C has been *made* a morally relevant characteristic by those who engaged in a social practice which discriminated against persons because they were C. (2) Since C is a morally relevant characteristic at time t_2 with respect to the principle of compensatory justice, that principle requires reverse discrimination. (3) The reverse discrimination in question is aimed at correcting an injustice perpetrated at time t_1 by a social practice of discriminating against C-persons because they were C. Given this aim, the reverse discrimination must be directed toward the class of C-persons as such. Furthermore, the obligation to compensate for the past injustice does not fall upon any particular individual but upon the society as a whole. The society is obliged to establish a social practice of reverse discrimination in favor of C-persons. (It is assumed, of course, that this practice will be consistent with all other principles of justice that may apply to the action-types which are involved in carrying it out.) I offer the following considerations in support of these views.

1

Suppose there is a socially established practice at time t_1 of unjustly treating any person who has characteristic C, such treatment being either permitted or required on the ground that the person is C. For the purposes of this account I hold that the treatment in question is unjust because characteristic C would not be mutually acknowledged as a proper ground for such treatment by all who understood the practice and took an impartial view of it (in accordance with John Rawls' *A Theory of Justice,* Harvard University Press, 1971).

When a social practice of this kind is engaged in, the members of the class of C-persons are being discriminated against because they are C. By reference to the rules of this practice, having C is a relevant reason or ground for performing a certain kind of action which is in fact unjust (though not recognized to be so by the practice itself). In this context the characteristic C is not accidentally or contingently associated with the unjust treatment, but is essentially tied to it. For the injustices done to a person are based on the fact that he has characteristic C. His being C is, other things being equal, a sufficient condition for the permissibility of treating him in the given manner. Within the framework of the social practice of t_1, that someone is C is a ground for acting in a certain way toward him. Therefore C is a relevant characteristic of a person.

But is it *morally* relevant? The answer to this question, it seems to me, is that at time t_1 characteristic C is not morally relevant, but, if we accept the principle of compensatory justice, at time t_2 it is. The principle of compensatory justice is that, in order to restore the balance of justice when an injustice has been committed to a group of persons, some form of compensation or reparation must be made to that group. Thus if there has been an established social practice (as distinct from an individual's action) of treating any member of a certain class of persons in a certain way on the ground that they have characteristic C and if this practice has involved the doing of an injustice to C-persons, then the principle of compensatory justice requires that C-persons as such be compensated in some way. Characteristic C, in other words, has become at time t_2 a characteristic whose *moral* relevance is entailed by the principle of compensatory justice. In this kind of situation, to ignore the fact that a person is C would be to ignore the fact that there had been a social practice in which unjust actions were directed toward C-persons as such.

2

Given that characteristic C is morally relevant to how C-persons are to be treated if compensatory justice is to be done to them, it follows that reverse discrimination is justified. For this is simply the policy of extending social benefits, opportunities, or advantages to the class of C-persons as such. Contrary to what Nickel affirms, this is not selecting C-persons for special treatment on the basis of the complex characteristic C′, namely: being a person who was discriminated against because he was C. For even if the individual C-person who now enjoys the favorable compensatory treatment was not himself one of those who suffered injustice as a result of the past social practice, he nevertheless has a right (based on his being a member of the class of C-persons) to receive the benefits extended to all C-persons. This follows from our premise that reverse discrimination, directed toward anyone who is C because he is C, is justified by the principle of compensatory justice.

Cowan claims that compensatory justice does not require a policy of treating all C-persons favorably (other things being equal) because they are C. His argument is that, if the original unjust treatment of C-persons was unjust precisely because their being C was morally irrelevant, then "there is and can be no morally relevant group which could have suffered or to which retribution could now be made." My reply to this argument is that the moral relevance or irrelevance of a characteristic is not something that can be determined outside the framework of a set of moral principles. It is true that the principles of *distributive* justice were trangressed by the past treatment of C-persons precisely because, according to those principles, characteristic C is morally irrelevant as a ground for treating persons in a certain way. Nevertheless, according to the principle of *compensatory* justice (which applies only where a violation of other forms of justice has taken place), the fact that systematic injustice was directed toward a class of persons as being C-persons establishes characteristic C as morally relevant, as far as making restitution is concerned. For the same reason, it may be noted, characteristic C will become again morally irrelevant the moment all the requirements of compensatory justice with respect to the treatment of C-persons have been fulfilled. Thus justified reverse discrimination is limited in its scope, being restricted to the righting of specific wrongs within a given range of application. Once the balance of justice with regard to C-persons has been restored, they are to be treated like anyone else. The appropriate test for the restoration of the balance of justice (that is, fulfillment of the requirements of compensatory justice) is determined by the set of criteria for just compensation that would be mutually acceptable to all who understand the unjust practice and who view the matter disinterestedly (following Rawls, as before).

3

Does the foregoing view entail that, in the given society, *each individual* who is not a C-person has a duty to make reparation to *every* C-person he happens to be able to benefit in some way? This would seem to be unfair, since the individual who is claimed to have such a duty might not himself have intentionally or knowingly participated in the discriminatory social practice, and might even have done what he could to oppose it. It also seems unfair to C-persons, who would then be compensated only under the contingency that particular non-C individuals happen to be in a position of being able to benefit them. We must here face the questions: To whom is owed the compensatory treatment, that is, who has the right to reparation? And upon whom does the obligation corresponding to that right fall?

If we consider such compensatory policies as affirmative action and the equal-opportunity program to be appropriate ways of restoring the balance of justice, a possible answer to our questions becomes apparent. For such programs are, within the framework of democratic institutions, social policies carried out by organized agencies of a central government representing the whole people. They are not directed toward any "assignable" individual (to use Bentham's apt phrase), but rather are directed toward any member of an "assignable" group (the class of C-persons) who wishes to take advantage of, or to qualify for, the compensatory benefits offered to the group as a whole. The obligation to offer such benefits to the group as a whole is an obligation that falls on society in general, not on any particular person. For it is the society in general that, through its established social practice, brought upon itself the obligation.

To bring out the moral significance of this, consider the case in which an individual has himself treated a particular C-person unjustly. By so acting, the individual in question has brought upon himself a special obligation which he owes to that particular C-person. This obligation is above and beyond the duty he has—along with everyone else—to support and comply with the social policy of reverse discrimination being carried out by his government. For everyone in the society (if it is just) contributes his fair share to the total cost of that policy, whether or not he has, personally, done an injustice to a C-person. So the individual who commits such an injustice himself has a special duty, and his victim has a special right, in contrast to the general duty of everyone to do his share (by obeying laws, paying taxes, and so forth) in supporting the policy of reverse discrimination directed toward the class of C-persons as a whole, and in contrast to the general right on the part of any C-persons to benefit from such a policy if he wishes to take advantage of its provisions.

The issue of the justifiability of reverse discrimination does not have to do with an individual's making up for his own acts of injustice done to this or that person. It has to do with righting the wrongs committed as an integral part of an organized social practice whose very essence was discrimination against C-persons as such. In this sense the perpetrator of the original injustice was the whole society (other than the class of C-persons). The victim was the class of C-persons as a group, since they were the *collective target* of an institutionalized practice of unjust treatment. It is for this reason that Cowan's concluding remarks do not stand up.

At the end of his article he makes the following statements regarding the present members of a group which has been discriminated against in the past: "They should most certainly be treated like anyone else. But this does not mean 'their' individual histories should be ignored. As with anyone else, injustices done 'them' as individuals should be prevented or rectified insofar as possible. But past or future discrimination and injustice done 'them' as a group and special advantages to them as a group are both out of the question since in the moral context there is no such group." But there is such a group. It is the group that was, as it were, *created* by the original unjust practice. To deny the existence of the group is to deny a social reality—a reality which cannot morally be ignored as long as the wrongs that created it are not corrected.

Cowan's position assumes that compensatory justice applies to the relations of one individual to another, but not to organized social practices and whole classes of persons with respect to whom the goals and methods of the practices are identified and pursued. This assumption, however, completely disregards what, morally speaking, is the most hideous aspect of the injustices of human history: those carried out systematically and directed toward whole groups of men and women *as groups*.

My conclusion is that society is morally at fault if it ignores the group which it has discriminated against. Even if it provides for compensation to each member of the group, not qua member of the group but qua person who has been unjustly treated (for whatever reason), it is leaving justice undone. For it is denying the specific obligation it owes to, and the specific right it has created in, the group as such. This obligation and this right follow from the society's past use of a certain characteristic or set of characteristics as the criterion for identification of the group, membership in which was taken as a ground for unjust treatment. Whatever duties of justice are owed by individuals to other individuals, institutionalized injustice demands institutionalized compensation.

Michael D. Bayles

Reparations to Wronged Groups

If a group of people (blacks, women) has been wronged by its members' being discriminated against on the basis of a morally irrelevant characteristic, is it morally permissible to use that characteristic as a basis for providing special considerations or benefits as reparations? It is frequently argued that since the characteristic is morally irrelevant, its use as a basis for providing reparations must also constitute wrongful discrimination.

James W. Nickel contends that such reparations are not wrong because they are not based on the morally irrelevant characteristic. Being black, for example, is a morally irrelevant characteristic for discriminating against or for a person. However, Nickel claims that if a black man receives special consideration as reparation for past discrimination the basis is not the morally irrelevant characteristic of his being black. Instead, it is the morally relevant one of his having been "subject to unfair treatment because he was black."

J. L. Cowan criticizes Nickel for even including the morally irrelevant characteristic as part of the complex predicate on the basis of which repara-

Source: Analysis *33, no. 6 (June 1973). Reprinted by permission of the publisher.*

tions are given. It is not a man's having been subject to unfair treatment because he was black which is the basis of reparation, Cowan contends, "but simply the fact that, and the extent to which, he was unjustly discriminated against for whatever reason." We would not, Cowan points out, wish to favor a person who has been discriminated against for being Jewish. He further claims that the problem of using a morally irrelevant characteristic as the basis for reparation "arises when rather than individuals it is the group which is intended, and individuals are regarded merely as members of that group rather than in their individuality. This creates a contradiction since the original premise of the moral irrelevance of blackness on the basis of which the original attribution of unjust discrimination rests implies that there is and can be no morally relevant group which could have suffered or to which retribution could now be made."

The solution of the problem proposed by Nickel and Cowan, that the reparation is based on a characteristic other than the morally irrelevant one, is spurious. By parallel reasoning it can be argued that the original discrimination was not on the basis of a morally irrelevant characteristic. Racists do not discriminate against blacks simply because they are black. Rather they claim that blacks as a class are inferior in certain relevant respects, that is, they lack certain abilities and virtues such as industriousness, reliability and cleanliness. Thus, reasoning similarly to Nickel and Cowan, racists could contend that they do not discriminate on the basis of a morally irrelevant characteristic, but the morally relevant ones which are thought to be associated with being black. Further, a reformed racist could contend that he was mistaken to believe blacks lacked such abilities and virtues. But, since it was a *mistaken* belief which was the basis of his discrimination, he was not responsible and owes no reparations. In short, if being black is not the basis for reparations, it was not the basis for the original discrimination.

However, there need be no contradiction involved in claiming that being black is both morally irrelevant for discriminating against people and morally relevant in discriminating in favor of people to provide reparations. One may simply hold that there is no justifiable moral rule which, when correctly applied, supports discriminating against blacks, but there is one which supports discriminating in favor of them. One may hold that people have an obligation to give reparations to groups they have wronged. By using the characteristic of being black as an identifying characteristic to discriminate against people, a person has wronged the group, blacks. He thus has an obligation to make reparations to the group. Since the obligation is to the group, no specific individual has a right to reparation. However, since the group is not an organized one like a state, church, or corporation, the only way to provide reparations to the group is to provide them to members of the group.

Being black can, thus, become morally relevant in distinguishing between those individuals who are members of the group to whom reparations are owed and those who are not. But being black is only derivatively morally relevant. It is not mentioned as a morally relevant characteristic in the rule requiring one to provide reparations to groups one has wronged. Instead, it becomes relevant by being the identifying characteristic of the group wronged. The way in which it is an identifying characteristic here differs from the way in which it is an identifying characteristic for the racist. Being black is an identifying characteristic for the racist only because he thinks it is contingently connected with other characteristics. But being black is not contingently connected with the group one has wronged. Rather, it is logically connected as the defining characteristic of members of the group.

Cowan has failed to distinguish the relevance of being black as applied to groups and individuals. One may hold that one owes reparations to the group, blacks, not because the group is the group of blacks, but because the group has been wronged. But with respect to individuals, one may, as reparation, discriminate in their favor on the basis of their being black. One discriminates in favor of individuals because they are black, but one owes reparations to the group, blacks, because it has been wronged. Nor does such a position commit one to favoring individual blacks over individuals who belong to another wronged group, for example, women. One has a morally relevant reason to favor each on the basis of their being black and female respectively. It does not follow that either should be preferred over the other.

Nothing has been said to support accepting any moral rules or principles applying to groups. (As a matter of fact, most people appear to accept one such rule, namely, that genocide is wrong.) Nor has anything been said to support accepting the rule that one has an obligation to provide reparations to groups one has wronged. These remarks have only indicated how being black can derivately be a morally relevant characteristic for discriminating in favor of individuals if such a role is accepted.

William A. Nunn III

Reverse Discrimination

In his recent article supporting the policy of reverse discrimination, Paul W. Taylor argued, roughly, that when a certain group of persons within a given society is discriminated against because of some nonmoral characteristic (that is, skin color), and such discrimination is essentially tied to a pervasive social practice, the characteristic upon which the discrimination is based takes on a moral quality; consequently it becomes the moral duty of the society to make reparation to that group. Although I find it difficult to disagree with the allegation that in some sense institutionalized injustice demands institutionalized compensation, I think that Taylor's argument contains two fundamental flaws. First, he has not concerned himself with the task of making reasonably clear some of the essential terms he employs—among them "institutionalized injustice" and "institutionalized compensation." Secondly, a consistent application of his thesis to a given society is more likely to perpetuate than eliminate the injustices of discrimination.

Source: Analysis *34, no. 5 (April 1974). Reprinted by permission of the publisher.*

1

There are a good many different kinds of organized social practices in every society, most of which in one way or another are discriminatory. Certain religious groups, for example, either forbid or actively discourage inter-marriage between their members and those of other religious groups. Although I think it unlikely that this sort of discriminatory practice could be justified by disinterested observers who understood it, it is on quite a different level from, say, a governmental prohibition against interracial marriage in the form of an antimiscegenation statute. Both of these social practices embody a form of discrimination which is both institutionalized and unjust. Yet it is arguable that no society has the right to interfere with the former, whereas the latter ought not to be tolerated by any society. Again, the policy of not a few social and professional organizations excluding certain persons from membership solely on the basis of race, sex, or other nonmoral criterion is clearly not on all fours with an overt or covert sanction of discrimination by a government on the same grounds. The difficulty, then, is to determine which discriminatory social practices fall under Taylor's concept of institutionalized injustice and which do not. Once that problem is resolved, we may turn our attention to the nature and scope of the required compensation—a subject he dismisses with a vague reference to the "restoration of the balance of justice."

Clearly a democratic government, in its capacity of representing all the people, has a duty to rectify discriminatory legislation and enforcement of the law. It may also have a duty to abolish certain forms of private discrimination in which it has a compelling interest. It is not clear that private organizations have a duty to abolish and make reparation for their discriminatory practices. Nor is it clear that in every case of unjust discrimination some form of compensation is either desirable or possible. The appropriate compensation for an unjust tax might include a refund with interest; or for the unjust taking of private property a restitution of the property itself or, that not being possible, an award of damages for its value. But it is doubtful whether the concept of compensation is at all meaningful in the case of an antimiscegenation statute. The appropriate remedy for the last form of discrimination is repeal—not an award of damages (how would damages be measured?) or the enactment of a statute requiring that henceforth all marriages be interracial.

Taylor has not offered a clue as to whether he thinks all unjust social practices must be abolished or, if not all, how to differentiate between those that should and those that need not be abolished. Nor has he demonstrated the necessity or even possibility of compensation in such cases. The vagueness of his use of these important terms gives rise to a suspicion that the phrase, "institutionalized injustice demands institutionalized compensation," may be little more than a high-sounding but vacuous slogan.

2

Assuming *arguendo* that the meaning of the terms discussed above is reasonably clear and that there are no logical difficulties involved in their application, compensation for past discrimination is nevertheless unjustifiable if it incorporates reverse discrimination. By *reverse discrimination* I refer to a policy of according favored treatment to a group of persons unjustly discriminated against in the past because of some nonmoral characteristic C possessed by each member of the group (hereafter the C-group), and corresponding unfavored treatment to a group of persons no member of which possesses the characteristic C (hereafter the C'-group). As Taylor correctly argues, individual moral desert is not relevant to the application of such a policy. It is both justifiable and necessary, he believes, even though it is possible (indeed probable) that not every C-person suffered and there are C'-persons who neither caused, condoned, practiced, nor benefited from the initial discrimination. The reason it is justifiable, he explains, is that the original discrimination created the C-group's right to reparation—not as individuals, but as a class—and the existence of that right entails reverse discrimination. In short, the C-group must be compensated at the expense of the C'-group.

In applying the policy, it seems to me that whatever good is accomplished by compensating members of the C-group for past wrongs is vitiated by the corresponding denial of benefits to the C'-group. Where before the entire C-group was victimized for the benefit of individual C'-persons, now the entire C'-group has been substituted as a victim for the benefit of individual C-group persons. The criterion for discrimination is no longer C but C'. Thus while certain C-persons are compensated for the wrongs done them or other members of the C-group, the C'-group is unjustly discriminated against as a class. It follows that a right to reparation is created within the C'-group— not as individuals, but as a class—and the existence of this right entails what we might call *reverse discrimination*. It is not difficult to see where this path leads.

The theory of compensatory justice, as explained by Taylor, will not do insofar as it incorporates reverse discrimination. The best way of avoiding the injustices of discrimination is to avoid unjust discrimination in the first place. The second-best method is to avoid making the same mistake twice.

Roger A. Shiner

Individuals, Groups and Inverse Discrimination

Many morally sensitive people find themselves faced with the following
dilemma. On the one hand, they are persuaded by the argument that if being
black, for example, is morally irrelevant, then it is morally irrelevant and no
more justifies favorable inverse discrimination than it justifies unfavorable
discrimination. On the other hand, this move seems to open the way to
neglect, whether benign or malign, of genuine social injustices. James W.
Nickel and J. L. Cowan have done much to bring the logic of this situation to
the surface. I shall not resist their general strategy of showing that the above
is a false dilemma. My concern is with Cowan's diagnosis of the trouble as
consisting in the illegitimacy of the thought that blacks *as a group* deserve
inverse discrimination. His view is that one cannot argue that blacks as a
group deserve retribution without also implying that blackness as such is a
morally relevant characteristic. This is false.

In the first place, it simply is not true that sense can never be made of
the thought that a group as such deserves inverse discrimination. Consider
these cases. (1) The Illyrians, through the incompetence of their negotiators,

Source: Analysis *33, no. 6 (June 1973). Reprinted by permission of the publisher.*

entered the European Economic Community under extremely unfair conditions. Later on, an EEC Council member argues, "We ought now to give the Illyrians especially favorable consideration," and recommends inverse discrimination. (2) Form 3B is not allowed to go on the school outing because there are thirty-five in the class—or so they are told, and this is not a matter of the school bus size or the tickets available. The form master argues later, "3B should be given special consideration," and recommends inverse discrimination.

The objection might be raised that Form 3B is not really a group in a sense relevant to the problem at issue. It is an individual member of the group "classes in elementary schools," and an individual school class may deserve inverse discrimination because of unfair treatment in the same way as an individual black or woman. However, there are many educators who argue that a disproportionate amount of money has been spent in recent years on secondary and postsecondary education, and that we now need to spend an equally disproportionate amount of money on elementary schools and schoolchildren as a group. But my argument need not turn on the accuracy of this remark, for the Illyrians are not a closed, formally defined group as is Form 3B, nor are they members of some wider group.

Now it might be said that statements about Illyria or the Illyrian nation are reducible without remainder to statements about individual Illyrians. So I still have not presented a counterexample to the thesis that a group as such cannot deserve inverse discrimination. But this is a highly contentious philosophical thesis, and the debate about whether it is true remains unresolved. It cannot be that the present question about inverse discrimination is simply this old chestnut in a new guise, and indeed Cowan does not talk as though this is what he has in mind. Those who wish to support inverse discrimination draw on the stock of available collective nouns, and frequently speak of the black/Indian/Jewish nation/race/people and of the female sex.

These points show, then, I submit, that talk about groups deserving inverse discrimination, as opposed to similar talk about individuals, cannot be simply ruled out as nonsensical, nor will it do to rule it in purely on the basis of some reductionist theory about nations. If we are to get at what is peculiar about the thought that blacks as a group deserve inverse discrimination, we must try a different tack.

Consider these remarks—(3) "My car ought to go in for repair, because it is a 1970 Ford"; (4) "George deserves inverse discrimination, because he is black." Cowan and Nickel are upset about (4), because it is logically of a piece with (5) "George deserves to be discriminated against, because he is black," and we want to reject that inference, on the grounds that the feature mentioned is irrelevant. But why should my car's being a 1970 Ford and just exactly that mean that it ought to go in for repair? We explain a case like (3) by treating it as an elliptical argument, with a missing premise (3*) to the effect that all 1970 Fords have been recalled by the maker and ought to go in for repair. We can then underpin (4) in the same way, by supplying a premise (4*) to the effect that all blacks have been discriminated against unjustly in the past and deserve discrimination now.

This is pretty clearly the kind of point Cowan wants to make, but to show that (4) won't do unless underpinned with (4*) is not to show what, if anything, is wrong with (4′) "Blacks as a group deserve inverse discrimination," still less that it is the introduction of the notion of a group deserving inverse discrimination that is problematic. As I have implied, to get from the need for (4*) to the illegitimacy of (4′), we will at least need to grapple with the reductionist position outlined above.

Nonetheless, the need for (4*) will enable us to get a correct picture of the peculiarity of the bold inference (4). Compare (3)/(3*) and (4)/(4*) with (6) "This figure is a rectangle, because it has equal diagonals." (6) to the same degree seems to need (6*) "All figures with equal diagonals are rectangles." However, although the (3) and (4) sets and the (6) set are in this respect structurally similar, there is an important difference in their content. (3*) and (4*) are, if true, then a posteriori, true. (6*), on the other hand, is true and moreover a priori true. Thus, the arguments constituted by the (3) set and the (4) set will only be sound as well as valid if (3*) and (4*) are as a matter of empirical fact true. The difference between the (6) set and the (3) set and (4) sets is that there is an a priori and conceptual connection between being a rectangle and having equal diagonals, whereas there is *no* a priori and conceptual connection between being a 1970 Ford and needing to go in for repair, nor between being a black and deserving inverse discrimination.

This, then, I take to be the fundamental point about the moral irrelevancy of the characteristic of being a black. It is not a matter of whether it is a group or an individual that is held to have the characteristic. It is instead a matter of the kind of link that exists between the possession of that characteristic and the possession of some other moral characteristic. The moral irrelevancy of being a black is a matter of the absence of the appropriate a priori link. Contrast (7) "Fred deserves inverse discrimination, because he is socioeconomically disadvantaged," and the corresponding (7*) "The socioeconomically disadvantaged deserve inverse discrimination." In this case, many philosophers would be prepared to concede that, if (7*) were part of a plausible moral theory, for example, a la Rawls, (7*) would state a conceptual connection.

In short, my thesis in this paper is that, if we want to get clear why being a black is morally irrelevant though blacks deserve inverse discrimination, then the individual/group distinction is a red herring. We need instead the a posteriori connection/a priori connection distinction. The absence of the latter connection means that any claim to the effect that blacks, whether as a group or as individuals, deserve inverse discrimination must stand, not simply on their being blacks, but on the facts of history. If, that is to say, blacks as a group deserve inverse discrimination, it will be because some claim like (4*) is true. But if (4*) is true, then one can reasonably argue that blacks as a group deserve retribution *without* also implying blackness as such is a morally relevant characteristic. I suspect the facts of history can stand the weight thus put on them.

James W. Nickel

Should Reparations Be
to Individuals or to Groups?

The discussion occasioned by my note, "Discrimination and Morally Relevant Characteristics" has helped to clarify some of the available positions on
the justification of special benefits for victims of discrimination. J. L. Cowan
agrees that the justification for special help lies in the fact that one has been
wronged, not in the fact, say, that one is black. But he thinks that it is important to emphasize that the special benefits which are due to many blacks are
due only because they are individuals who have been wronged, not because
of any fact relating to their race. On his view, "reparations for blacks" must
be understood as "reparations for wronged individuals who happen to be
black." P. W. Taylor and M. D. Bayles criticize my approach from the
opposite direction. They think that my approach pays insufficient attention
to the moral status of wronged groups. In what follows I shall attempt to
point out some weaknesses in my critics' positions and to elaborate further
my own.

The "reverse-discrimination argument" alleges that special benefits for
blacks are unjust because they continue to base special treatment on an ir-

Source: Analysis *34, no. 5 (Apr. 1974). Reprinted by permission of the publisher.*

relevant characteristic (namely, being black) and hence continue to discriminate. The counterargument that I offered has two premises:

P_1 : For differential treatment to be discriminatory (and unjust for that reason) it must be based on a morally irrelevant characteristic.

P_2 : Differential treatment of blacks for purposes of reparations is not based on an irrelevant characteristic (as it would be if it were based on race instead of the fact of having been wronged).

From these premises I drew the conclusion that differential treatment of blacks for purposes of reparations is not unjust on account of being discriminatory.

Cowan's criticism is that the formulation of the argument is ambiguous because it fails to make clear whether it is defending special help to individuals or special help to groups:

> Nickel's reasoning thus does not really, as it might be taken to do, provide any support at all for the kind of self-contradictory thinking the original argument was surely intended to rebut. This is the reasoning that since blacks . . . have suffered unjust discrimination we should now give them special treatment to make it up to them. Once again there is no problem insofar as this simply means that where individual blacks have suffered injustice it should, as with anyone else, insofar as possible be made up to those individuals who have so suffered. The fallacy arises when rather than individuals it is the group which is intended, and individuals are regarded merely as members of that group rather than in their individuality.

But it was indeed my intention to provide support for the kind of thinking that Cowan finds contradictory. I intended to suggest that since almost all American blacks have been victimized by discrimination it would be justifiable to design and institute programs of special benefits for blacks. Such programs, which are probably the only effective and administratively feasible way to provide reparations to blacks, would be justified in terms of the injuries that almost all of the recipients have suffered—not in terms of the race of the recipients. To make this clearer one needs to distinguish between the justifying and the administrative basis for a program. The justifying basis for such a program would be the injuries that many blacks suffer and the special needs that many blacks have because of discrimination. The administrative basis for distributing the program's benefits might be the presence in an individual of these needs and injuries, but it is more likely that it would be some other characteristics (such as race and present income) which were easier to detect and which were highly correlated with the justifying basis. My assumption here is that it is sometimes justifiable for reasons of administrative efficiency to use as part of the administrative basis for a program of benefits a characteristic such as race which would be implausible as a justifying basis. Cowan argues that special advantages to blacks as a group are "out of the question since in the moral context there is no such group." I agree with the premise that there is no such group insofar as this means that race or ancestry can never be a justifying basis for differential treatment. But I do not agree that race or ancestry can never serve as a morally acceptable administrative basis for a program of differential treatment which provides compensation for past wrongs, and hence I reject the unqualified conclusion that special advantages to blacks as a group are out of the question.

Bayles and Taylor want to go further than this. They want to give direct moral status to the defining characteristics of wronged groups, and argue that special help to blacks as a group can be justified in terms of a principle requiring reparations to wronged groups. They hold the view, paradoxical but not contradictory, that although race is irrelevant in a context where persons of a given race are being unjustly harmed, it is not irrelevant in a context where the obligation to give reparations to wronged groups is being met. Bayles, unlike Taylor, does not offer positive grounds for his own view; he simply offers it as an alternative to my approach—which he thinks can be discredited by refutation by analogy. In response to my claim that having been wronged rather than being black is the justifying basis for special help, he says:

> By parallel reasoning it can be argued that the original discrimination was not on the basis of a morally irrelevant characteristic. Racists do not discriminate against blacks simply because they are black. Rather they claim that blacks as a class are inferior in certain relevant respects, e.g., they lack certain abilities and virtues such as industriousness, reliability and cleanliness. Thus, reasoning similarly to Nickel and Cowan, racists could contend that they do not discriminate on the basis of a morally irrelevant characteristic, but the morally relevant ones which are thought to be associated with being black.

Bayles' complaint is that if those who favor reparations can use this argument, then so can racists. He thinks that if it works for the one then it will work for the other. And since it is obvious that it won't work for the racist as a way of showing that he doesn't discriminate, he concludes that it won't work for those who favor reparations.

One response to this complaint is to argue that the second premise of my counterargument to the reverse-discrimination argument would not be true when used by the racist. The racist's version of the second premise would be:

RP$_2$: My differential treatment of blacks is not based on an irrelevant characteristic (as it would be if it were based on race instead of the fact of being
lazy, unreliable and unclean).

In most cases this would not be, I submit, a true claim. It would, rather, be a
self-serving rationalization. In B. A. O. Williams' words, the racist is "paying, in very poor coin, the homage of irrationality to reason." Most racists
could not use this defense of their differential treatment of blacks because its
premise about their real reasons would not be true.

But to avoid being doctrinaire about this we must allow that some
racists might be able to make this claim about their real reasons without
falsehood and rationalization. And Bayles is right in suggesting that this
possibility requires me to modify or give up my counterargument. Bayles'
approach is to give up this defense and use a much stronger principle about
reparations to wronged groups to defend programs of reparations to blacks
from the charge of unjust discrimination. But before adopting Bayles'
approach we will do well, I think, to consider modifying the first premise of
my counterargument. This premise holds that for differential treatment to
be discriminatory (and unjust for that reason) it must be based on an irrelevant characteristic. But it should be changed to one which holds that for differential treatment to be discriminatory (and unjust for that reason) it is
necessary that it be based on an irrelevant characteristic *or* on a false claim
about the correlation between characteristics. This is, in effect, to modify
one's definition of *discrimination*. When this modification is made, the
defender of reparations is not able to move directly from the fact that preferential treatment was not based on an irrelevant characteristic to the conclusion that it was not unjustly discriminatory. To get to this conclusion, he
would also have to show that there was in fact a very high correlation between
being an American black and being a victim of discriminatory and harmful
treatment. I think that the defender of reparations can do this, but the racist
cannot make the analogous move. He cannot show that there is in fact a high
correlation between being black and lacking industry, reliability and cleanliness, and hence his actions are based on false beliefs about correlations
between characteristics and can—under the modified premise—be condemned as discriminatory. Hence the defender of reparations can use this
defense without making an equally good defense available to the racist.

Taylor agrees with Bayles' claim that the justification of special benefits
to blacks requires us to appeal to a moral principle about compensation for

wronged *groups*. He formulates this principle as follows: "The principle of compensatory justice is that, in order to restore the balance of justice when an injustice has been committed to a group of persons, some form of compensation or reparation must be made to that group." When there has been institutionalized discrimination against persons who have a certain morally irrelevant characteristic, the effect of this principle is to *make* this characteristic relevant for purposes of reparations. Taylor insists that in such a case reparations are due to the group, not just to those of its members who were harmed by the discriminatory practice. Since the characteristic which defines the group was essentially involved in the discriminatory practice, reparations must be made available to all those who have this characteristic.

An interesting aspect of Taylor's paper is his suggestion that principles of compensatory justice can be chosen from the perspective which John Rawls advocates for choosing principles of distributive justice. If it can be argued plausibly that persons in the Rawlsian original position would choose compensatory principles which include a principle providing benefits directly to wronged groups, then any lingering suspicion that Taylor's principle is ad hoc and has been invented specifically to deal with the issue of special benefits for blacks could be laid to rest.

Rawls has very little to say about compensatory and retributive justice in *A Theory of Justice*, but the principles of distributive justice which he thinks would be chosen in the original position would themselves require a good deal of compensatory activity on the part of government. These principles embody a general conception of justice which holds that "all social values . . . are to be distributed equally unless an unequal distribution of any, or all, of these values is to everyone's advantage" (*A Theory of Justice*, p. 62). A consequence of this is that heavier-than-average burdens are unjust unless they can be justified by showing that even the person who suffers the most from bearing the burden would be worse off if that kind of burden were shifted or compensated. But it will be impossible to show this with regard to many types of burdens, and hence these will have to be shifted to others with lighter loads or compensated. Since it is often impossible to shift such burdens (for example, a heavy work load resulting from skills which are much in demand, or disabilities resulting from an accident), compensation in the form of balancing benefits will be required in many cases by Rawls' principles of distributive justice. This applies to all unjustifiable burdens, no matter what their origin, and would include unequal burdens resulting from discrimination. The latter, being unjustifiable, would have to be shifted or compensated. It appears, therefore, that Rawls' principles of distributive justice by themselves would take us some distance towards remedying the effects of discrimination.

Since the compensation of unjustifiable burdens would be required by Rawls' principles of distributive justice, it is not entirely clear that *any* distinct principles of compensatory justice would be chosen by persons in the original position. From the Rawlsian perspective, such principles would not be chosen merely because it was thought to be "fitting" that wrongdoers should repay their victims. They would be chosen only if their use would maximize the life prospects of those who would live in the projected society.

But assume, for purposes of argument, that persons in the original position would choose to have compensatory principles among their principles of justice. These principles would require persons and institutions to compensate the victims of their wrongdoing and negligence, and would require government to provide compensation when the wrongdoer was financially unable. The question, then, is whether persons in the original position would also choose a principle which would compensate *groups* as such for injuries suffered by their members as members. Since the members of these groups could obtain compensation as individuals under the other reparations principles, would there be any reason to provide compensation to groups as such?

I am unable to think of any such reason, and I think that the reason that Taylor presents is unsound. He contends that a program of reparations which is justified by reference to the wrongs suffered by individuals "completely disregards what, morally speaking, is the most hideous aspect of the injustices of human history; those carried out systematically against whole groups of men and women *as groups.*" If Taylor is right in claiming that providing reparations to groups as groups is the only alternative to ignoring these hideous injustices, then persons in the original position would have a reason for choosing principles requiring such reparations. One function of requiring the performance of acts of reparations is to provide a symbolic denunciation of the evil that was done and to provide the wrongdoer with an opportunity to declare in a concrete and meaningful way his turning away from that evil. Perhaps it is this element that those, like Taylor, who demand reparations to blacks as a group feel would be missing in any approach to reparations which proceeded on an individual basis. A person of strong moral feeling may hold that such an approach allows America to bury its racist past rather than to confront it and repent of it. A symbolic denunciation of racism is desired, and it is held that only a program of reparations to blacks as a group can do this.

But surely Taylor presents us with a false dilemma when he suggests that compensation to groups as such is the only alternative to disregarding the injustices of institutionalized discrimination against groups. We can give great emphasis to the injustices involved in such discrimination through means other than those of imitating the structure of such injustices in our compensatory mechanisms. We can denounce such practices, teach our children to notice their silent but sinister operations and avoid them, make them illegal and provide effective enforcement mechanisms, and provide to their victims reparations that are justified—but not necessarily administered—on an individual basis. If we succeed in doing these things then it can scarcely be said that we have disregarded the most hideous aspects of institutionalized discrimination against groups. Direct compensation to groups, of the sort advocated by Taylor, is not the only effective way of demonstrating our aversion to this kind of injustice.

The upshot of this is that there do not seem to be any reasons why the life-prospects of persons in the original position would be bettered by their choosing a principle requiring reparations to wronged groups. Furthermore, there is at least one reason for thinking that these prospects would be worsened. This is that there might well be cases in which the result of following Taylor's principle would be to waste resources on substantial numbers of persons who were completely unaffected by discrimination directed against a group to which they belonged. Suppose that there was a group which was evenly distributed throughout the country but which was subject to discriminatory treatment in only some sections, and as a result of this half of the members of this group were completely unaffected by this discrimination— even though it was based on a characteristic which all of them shared. Would we be willing to agree with the conclusion of Taylor's principle that all of them should receive compensation whether they had been harmed or not? This problem does not arise in the case of American blacks since all, or almost all, of them have suffered significantly from discrimination, and hence there is no great unfairness or waste of resources if benefits are provided for all. But in dealing with a group in which only a portion of the members had been affected by the discrimination, it is far from clear that a principle requiring compensation to all would be desirable.

Alan H. Goldman

Reparations to Individuals or Groups?

James Nickel bases his latest argument for reparations to groups upon a distinction between the justifying and administrative basis for a program of reparations. I have argued against compensatory hiring for groups elsewhere, but had not considered this most recent argument. Its novelty lies in the shift from abstract or ideal principles of compensatory justice to the necessity in practice of balancing claims so as to maximize (imperfect) justice. The justification for favored treatment for groups, according to Nickel, derives from the administrative feasibility of such a program by comparison with the high cost and impracticality of administering compensatory justice in this area on an individual basis. Thus while there is only a high correlation between being black, for example, and having been discriminated against and so deserving compensation (justifying basis), so that preferential treatment for the group will occasionally result in undeserved benefits for individuals, the balance of justice in practice favors such treatment. The viable alternatives seem to be either award of deserved compensation in the great majority of cases and occasional undeserved benefit and hence injustice

Source: Analysis *35, no. 5 (Apr. 1975). Reprinted by permission of the publisher.*

to white job applicants, or compensation on an individual basis, which would require demonstration of past injustice in court or before a special administrative body, so that the cost and difficulty of the operation would result in far fewer awards of deserved reparation. It is better, the argument holds, to have compensation which is only almost always deserved than a program which in practice would amount to almost no compensation at all, so that a policy which would not be accepted in an ideally just world (a world which became ideally just after compensation was paid) becomes best in the present situation.

In reply, one would first of all like to ask how high the correlation between group membership and past discrimination, and hence the proportion of deserved to undeserved compensation, must be. Presumably a ratio of fifty-one to forty-nine will not do, since in the case of preferential-hiring policies, there are two injustices involved in every case of undeserved compensation: first the payment for the undeserved benefit made by society in accepting less efficient service (since the candidate will not be as competent if hired only because of preferred treatment), but, more important, the injustice to the white male applicant who is best qualified. The correlation is presumably not as high in the case of women as a group as in the case of blacks, and not as high for middle-class as for lower-class blacks. The latter compensation suggests narrowing the specification of the group so as to maximize the correlation, but of course at the limit of such narrowing is a program administered on an individual basis.

Thus far it still seems we must balance ideal theory against practice, but the far more serious point completely forgotten in Nickel's argument is the effect of the operation of market criteria upon hiring, even within a compensatory program of preferential treatment. Since hiring within the preferred group still depends upon relative qualifications and hence upon past opportunities for acquiring qualifications, there is in fact an inverse ratio established between past discrimination and present benefits, so that those who benefit most from the program, those who actually obtain jobs, are those who least deserve to. Given that those individuals will always be hired first who have suffered least from prior discrimination, this effect of competence requirements completely destroys the rationale of arguing by correlation unless the correlation is extremely close to perfect, for as long as there are some members in the market who have not unfairly lost opportunities, they will be the ones getting the jobs. But the establishment of such high correlation for a specific group, or the narrowing of specifications for group membership until virtually all members have been treated unjustly, amounts to administering a program on an individual basis. It will have to be determined for each individual whether he belongs to the narrowly specified group and have to be determined for individuals within that group whether virtually all have been discriminated against and thereby suffered harm. These two steps, when the group is sufficiently narrowly specified, will, I suspect, be as difficult as handling cases on an individual basis from the beginning.

Since Nickel's argument wrongly assumes that the majority of compensation cases will tend to be fair if the correlation of past injustice to group membership is above 50 percent, it is unsound. Nor can the practice of hiring by competence itself be blamed or held therefore unjust. If efficiency is Nickel's basis for arguing for group compensation, he cannot condemn a general practice which in the long run results in more goods for all in favor of some less efficient alternative. It would at least be strange to recommend hiring the least competent as a general practice within some preferred group, and in this case efficiency would be gained, not lost, by moving away from a group program. In order then not to create a policy which in practice singles out for benefits within a generally unjustly treated minority just that minority which has not been unjustly treated, and thus does treat unfairly members of the "majority group" applying for jobs, a compensatory program of preferential hiring must be administered on an individual basis. Where there are significant departures from this toward preferential treatment for loosely defined large groups, we must suspect further injustice not only to "majority-group" members, but to members of the minority who have suffered previous injustice and are now passed over in favor of other members who have at least suffered less. There are surely degrees of injustice, and the market here will invert the ratio of past injustice to present compensation if the program is directed toward a group.

James W. Nickel

Preferential Policies
in Hiring and Admissions:
A Jurisprudential Approach

This article discusses some of the troublesome policy issues that arise in connection with preferential policies that are designed to assist blacks and other victims of hardship and discrimination. In dismissing the case of Marco DeFunis, Jr., on mootness grounds, the Supreme Court disappointed those who had hoped for a definitive ruling on these matters and insured that the issues involved would be discussed for a while longer. There is still much to be said.

Preferential hiring [for linguistic economy I will take *hiring* to include matters of promotion and retention, although I recognize that preference in promotion and retention may involve different issues] and admissions policies give an advantage in competition for jobs or places in educational institutions to members of particular groups. The most common use of preferential policies in the United States has been to provide special educational and employment opportunities for veterans, but the recent controversy over preferential policies has to do with their use in recent years to provide special opportunities to blacks and members of other disadvantaged groups. The

Source: Columbia Law Review 75, no. 3 *(April 1975). Reprinted by permission of the author and publisher. Notes and citations are omitted.*

advantage conferred on the preferred group may be very small (as it is when the policy is to give preference to a member of the group only when he or she is as well qualified as any other candidate), or it may be very large (as it is when persons who are not members of the group are not even considered for the position). To hire or admit a person on a preferential basis is to do more than to use special investigative measures to determine, in a case where an applicant has an unusual history or culture, how well his qualifications and potential measure up to that of other applicants. It is rather to use a lower standard in his case which will make it easier for him to succeed.

The use of preferential policies is sometimes accompanied by the use of quotas, and what I have to say about preferential policies will apply in part to quotas as well. A quota, in this context, is a numerical goal or requirement for the hiring or admission of members of specified groups within a certain time or until a certain percentage is reached. Quotas can be used independently of preferential policies in order to provide stimulus for and evidence of nondiscrimination—for example, if the only action required to meet the quota is to stop discriminating and hire the best candidates. Although quotas are sometimes used in these ways, they are more typically used in connection with preferential policies, and this is one of the main reasons why many find quotas objectionable. Hence, if one succeeded in providing a defense of preferential policies, one would thereby succeed in eliminating one of the main objections to quotas. Insofar as quotas involve additional problems such as inflexibility or a threat to institutional autonomy, the following discussion will not provide a defense of their use.

It is important to recognize that preferential policies need not be used in combination with racial or other classifications based on inherent characteristics. One might apply them, for example, to all persons who are on welfare or who have an income below a certain level. Hence, after discussing some justifications for using preferential policies, I will divide my discussion of objections to preferential policies into two parts. The first part will discuss objections to preferential policies that have nothing to do with the use of racial or ethnic classifications to define the preferred groups, and the second part will discuss objections that focus on the use of racial (and ethnic) classifications. My approach, put broadly, is that of a defender of preferential policies, but I hope that my analysis of the issues involved will be helpful even to those who disagree. By making needed distinctions, by exposing important premises and inferences to scrutiny, and by illustrating how important policy considerations conflict in this area, it may be possible to make discussions of these matters more rational.

1   JUSTIFICATIONS AND CONCEPTIONS

It is a commonplace of political life that people often support social programs for different reasons and consequently have varying conceptions of the proper purposes of a program. Programs which use preferential policies to increase the educational and employment opportunities available to the poor or to disadvantaged minorities are no exception to this. Although such programs are often called *compensatory*, they are not necessarily designed to meet the requirements of compensatory justice by providing compensation for past wrongs. To compensate is merely to counterbalance, and the counterbalancing of disadvantages can be done for reasons other than those of compensatory justice. One may advocate the counterbalancing of disadvantages with special opportunities because doing this would eliminate inequities in the distribution of income—a justification in terms of distributive justice—or because it would promote the public welfare by reducing poverty and its attendant evils, bringing about a better utilization of our human resources, or providing personnel who will provide needed services to the poor —justifications in terms of utility or public welfare. The fact that programs which use preferential policies can be conceived as means to these different ends, and hence be advocated on different grounds, complicates discussion of the merits of such programs. Although some people may be willing to accept more than one of these justifications, others may be bitterly opposed to any conception of the purposes of these programs other than their own. A person who favors the use of preferential policies on grounds of utility to provide special educational and employment opportunities to members of disadvantaged minorities may be strongly opposed to doing this in the name of compensatory justice, perhaps because he thinks that this would involve some admission of guilt that he is unwilling to make, even though the actual operation of the program is amenable to either conception. This is not to say, of course, that the exact character of such programs is never affected by which conception is dominant—and I will try to trace out some of these differences—but in practice many "compensatory" programs admit of all these interpretations.

The situation is further complicated by the fact that two people who would be able to agree in most cases on which particular individuals ought to receive special opportunities may nevertheless disagree hotly over whether racial classifications can be used in dispensing these special opportunities. As a means of clarifying these matters, I will discuss the different sorts of justifications that might be offered for programs that use preferential policies, and the difficulties with each. Depending on the justification used, different groups will benefit by preferential policies, and racial, ethnic, or sexual classifications will be used with greater or lesser defensibility.

Compensatory Justice. To argue that programs which use preferential policies to provide greater opportunities to members of disadvantaged minorities are justifiable on grounds of compensatory justice is to argue that either the actual recipients or the persons that one thinks *ought* to be the recipients deserve compensation for wrongs they have suffered. Compensatory justice requires that counterbalancing benefits be provided to those individuals who have been wrongfully injured which will serve to bring them up to the level of wealth and welfare that they would now have if they had not been disadvantaged. Compensatory programs differ from redistributive programs mainly in regard to their concern with the past. Redistribution is concerned with eliminating present inequities, while compensatory justice is concerned not only with this but with providing compensation for unfair burdens borne in the past. Considerations of compensatory justice can justify a person's getting more in the present than would be fair if his past losses were not considered. For a person who has been unable to get any decent job because of discrimination, it may be feasible to make up for his past losses by using preferential policies to provide special employment opportunities. Similarly, persons denied adequate educational opportunities by racist school systems can perhaps be brought up to the level they would otherwise have reached if special educational opportunities are provided. Similar steps have often been taken to compensate veterans for opportunities lost, injuries suffered, and services rendered during wartime.

There are a number of difficulties involved in using considerations of compensatory justice to justify programs that use preferential policies to assist the disadvantaged. These include: (1) questions about whether compensatory benefits are owed only to those particular individuals who have been harmed substantially by discrimination and hardship or to all members of those groups that have been frequent targets of discrimination; (2) questions about whether a person who was once harmed by discrimination but who has overcome his losses through his own efforts still deserves compensation now; (3) questions about whether governments, companies, institutions, and individuals have obligations to compensate losses they did not cause; and (4) questions about how far back into the past the view of compensatory justice should extend. Although I cannot undertake here the extended discussion that would be needed for an adequate exploration of these questions, the first one must be given some attention since it is crucial to how justifications in terms of compensatory justice are conceived.

It is sometimes maintained that in addition to compensatory principles that apply to individuals there are compensatory principles that create obligations between groups when one group injures another group or is unjustly enriched at the other group's expense. Paul W. Taylor, for example, argues that there is a principle of compensatory justice which requires that "[w]hen an injustice has been committed to a group of persons, some form of compensation or reparation must be made to that group." In Taylor's view, a group's right to compensation does not derive from the right to compensation of individuals in that group and cannot be satisfied by only compensating those within the group who as individuals deserve compensation. Furthermore, a member of a wronged group who has not personally been wronged may have a right to compensation as a member of the group. Taylor's approach offers a basis for giving preference to all members of wronged groups without regard to their personal histories. Group rights to compensation are not rights against particular wrongdoers but are against society as a whole: "The obligation to offer such benefits to the group as a whole is an obligation that falls on society in general, not on any particular person. For it is society in general that through its established social practice brought upon itself the obligation." Finally, Taylor thinks that "affirmative-action" programs are an appropriate way for a government to discharge society's obligation to wronged groups.

Although compensatory principles that apply directly to groups are frequently advocated, I personally do not find them appealing. Although there may well be moral principles that apply directly to groups, I find the principle that Taylor advocates implausible because it would unnecessarily duplicate many of the rights and obligations created by compensatory principles that apply to individuals, and would provide compensatory benefits to persons who personally have sustained no injury and therefore need not be made whole. It may be desirable to offer special opportunities to, say, all young blacks, whether or not they have personally been significantly harmed by discrimination, but the justification would have to be based on considerations of redistribution, utility, or administrative convenience, not on the claim that all blacks, whatever their situation, have a *right* to such benefits on grounds of compensatory justice. Another reason to avoid reliance on compensatory principles for groups in attempting to justify the use of preferential policies is that invoking such principles is likely to be question begging. Since such principles do not have established noncontroversial applications in other areas, a person who is not already committed to the desirability of compensatory programs and who is told that such programs are desirable because they satisfy the requirements of such a principle is likely to find the principle as much in need of justification as the programs it supposedly supports.

Any approach in terms of compensatory justice is likely to be controversial and problematic, but it seems to me that the least problematic approach along these lines is to suggest that the ones who have a right to compensation are those who have personally been injured by discrimination, and who have not yet been able to overcome this injury.

Distributive Justice. Programs using preferential policies are also conceived as a means of promoting the redistribution of income and other important benefits. This approach would claim that the justification for such programs lies in the reduction of distributive inequities that they bring about. Since good educations lead to good jobs, and good jobs provide income, security, and status, altering the ways in which educations and jobs are distributed so as to give a bigger share to the previously deprived is one way of bringing about redistribution. A concern with distributive justice is a concern with whether people have fair shares of benefits and burdens. Distributive justice does not require that all people have the same income or equally good jobs, the requirement is rather that benefits and burdens be distributed in accordance with relevant considerations such as the rights, deserts, merits, contributions and needs of the recipients. Thus, if both Jones and Smith have had adequate opportunities for self-development, and if Jones is qualified for a desirable and prestigious job as a director of an art museum, while Smith is only qualified for janitorial positions, then there will be no injustice in hiring Jones as the director and Smith as the janitor. One who advocates redistribution on grounds of distributive justice must argue that in spite of the fact that it is possible to justify many inequalities in terms of relevant differences, there are nonetheless many inequalities in our society that cannot be justified. Although it is often difficult to pinpoint these inequalities and to discern the extent to which they reveal discrimination rather than reflect relevant distinctions, it is clear that many distributive injustices exist in our society and that it would be desirable to eliminate them. Many people will allow that some persons are undeservedly poor, others undeservedly rich, and that it would be a good thing—on grounds both of justice and of utility—to reduce poverty. But advocates of preferential policies may not be content to merely increase the opportunities available to those now in poverty. A person may be getting an unjustly small amount of income even though he is above the poverty line, and hence one might advocate the use of preferential policies to help groups that contain many persons who are not justly rewarded for their contributions.

Those who take this approach are likely to point to large statistical differences between the incomes of blacks and whites or men and women as evidence of unjustifiable inequalities. It is beyond doubt that there has been and still is discrimination in employment against blacks and women, and that blacks and women have had fewer opportunities to develop qualifications. The difficulty, however, in arguing from such statistics is in distinguishing the extent to which the differences derive from discrimination rather than from other factors which may vary in strength between sexes and among groups. When there are groups which have different histories and cultures and emphasize different personal goals, it is unlikely that their members will uniformly utilize the same opportunities, go into the same areas of employment, and have the same attitudes towards vocational achievement. The ideal of having all groups represented at all levels of income and achievement in proportion to their numbers in the country's population may therefore be unrealistic, and perhaps even unappealing. This ideal, which might be called the ideal of proportional equality, has been criticized by many of those who are opposed to preferential policies for women or blacks, but the case for the use of preferential policies does not stand or fall with its acceptance or rejection.

Utility. Redistribution of important benefits may also be advocated because it is believed that the public welfare, on the whole and over the long term, can be promoted by reducing poverty and inequality. On this approach a program using preferential policies to increase educational and employment opportunities would be seen as one means of promoting the public welfare by eliminating poverty and its attendant evils and by eliminating the sort of economic inequality that leads to resentment and strife. Extreme poverty is objectionable to one who is concerned with utility because of what it involves, namely unmet needs and suffering, and because of what it leads to, namely crime, family strife, lack of self-respect, and social discontent. Economic inequality of the sort that we currently have, with wide extremes of income and wealth and with some groups largely concentrated at the bottom of the economic ladder is objectionable under this view because it perpetuates stereotypes, deprives people in low-income groups of role models, fosters lack of self-respect, and makes understanding and cooperation between groups more difficult. As long as there are, for example, few black doctors, lawyers, or executives, it will be easy for people, blacks included, to believe that blacks generally lack the abilities to fill these positions, and the maintenance of such belief can only perpetuate inequality with its untoward consequences.

Considerations about unmet needs and suffering may only require the elimination of extreme poverty, but consideration about the bad effects of economic inequality—especially the sort that sees some groups concentrated at the lower levels—suggest stronger measures to facilitate upward mobility for those at lower levels. Hence, moving towards proportional representation might be desirable on grounds of utility even if it is not required by distributive justice.

A much-emphasized connection between utility and the use of preferential policies is found in the need of disadvantaged minorities for persons who can and will provide them with legal and medical services. Thomas Nagel puts this as follows:

> Suppose for example that there is a need for a great increase in the number of black doctors, because the health needs of the black community are unlikely to be met otherwise. And suppose that at the present average level of premedical qualifications among black applicants, it would require a huge expansion of total medical school enrollment to supply the desirable absolute number of black doctors without adopting differential admissions standards. Such an expansion may be unacceptable either because of its cost or because it would produce a total supply of doctors, black and white, much greater than the society requires. This is a strong argument for accepting reverse discrimination, not on grounds of justice but on grounds of social utility. (In addition, there is the salutary effect on the aspirations and expectation of other blacks, from the visibility of exemplars in formerly inaccessible positions.) (Nagel, "Equal Treatment and Compensatory Discrimination," *Philosophy and Public Affairs* 2 [1973], p. 361.)

This kind of argument is sometimes attacked on the grounds that it falsely supposes that only black doctors or lawyers can serve blacks effectively, that only Chicano doctors or lawyers can serve Chicanos effectively, and so forth. But one who uses this argument does not need to make this strong supposition; all he need assume is that blacks who become doctors or lawyers are *more likely* to help meet the medical needs of the black community than whites who become doctors or lawyers. It is clear, for example, that there would be no impassioned outcry if a state medical school in Nebraska gave preference to natives because they are more likely to stay in the state to practice, or to persons who promise to practice in an area with a shortage of doctors. The objection to increasing the availability of needed medical and legal services through preferential policies ends up simply being an objection to giving such preferences on the basis of race: it would not work against preferences given on the basis of where one was from, on the basis of an agreement to serve in a particular area, or on the basis of particular skills such as an ability to speak Spanish fluently.

I have discussed some of the utilitarian benefits which are thought to follow from the use of preferential policies to increase the educational and employment opportunities available to disadvantaged minorities, but on any utilitarian approach these benefits must be balanced against the accompanying costs. Taking money or other benefits away from those who have much in order to promote the public good by giving these benefits to the disadvantaged is not without its costs. The rich person who has some of his money taken to finance job programs, or the young person who finds it difficult or impossible to get into professional school because of programs designed to increase the number of economically disadvantaged persons applying or accepted will not normally be made happier or better off as a result. There may also be attendant social costs, for the rich person may have invested the appropriated money in a way that would have benefited more people, or the young professional-school applicant may have been more qualified. These costs cannot be ignored; utilitarian advocates of preferential policies must claim that they are outweighed by greater benefits. This is probably true in many cases, but judgments about this depend on particular facts and must be made in particular cases.

Comparisons. In practice, at least, the differences between programs which take compensation for past wrongs as their goal and programs which take creation of a more equitable distribution or promotion of utility as their goal are not likely to be very apparent. The point at which differences are most likely to appear is in the criteria that are used to determine which applicants are eligible for preference. If the criteria pertain to the discrimination and wrongful treatment that the applicant suffered, the inequitable position that he presently is in, or the good that would be done by increasing his opportunities, then the program could be seen to be, respectively, compensatory, redistributive, or utilitarian. But preferential programs typically select recipients on the basis of gross criteria such as having a low income or membership in a disadvantaged group. Since the groups selected by these gross criteria overlap substantially, but not completely, with those who have been harmed by discrimination, or who are in an inequitable position, or whose betterment would promote utilitarian objectives, the primary goal of programs based on preferential policies is often not apparent from the selection criteria they use.

One useful way of comparing the different conceptions of the goals of preferential programs is in terms of whether they can justify, and if so, how they justify, giving preference to *all* applicants who are members of specified disadvantaged groups. If one accepted a compensatory principle that applied directly to wronged groups then one would probably be willing to advocate, for example, preferences for all black applicants regardless of their personal histories. If, however, one held that compensatory principles applied only to individuals then one would advocate preference only for those black applicants who had personally been harmed by discrimination. On this latter approach, preference for all black applicants would be harder to justify, and could only be done on the basis of a claim that nearly all black applicants have been harmed by discrimination and that it is therefore administratively efficient and not intolerably unfair simply to prefer all black applicants.

A similar contrast can be drawn between an approach which holds that the ideal of proportional representation expresses the requirements of distributive justice—and which correspondingly requires that *any* member of an underrepresented group should be preferred, whether or not he personally is in an inequitable position—and an approach which holds that inequities should be recognized and dealt with only in individual cases. The latter approach in terms of distributive justice would find it more difficult to justify preferring *all* female applicants, for example, and could do this only on the basis of a claim that the vast majority of female applicants have been subject to distributive injustices and that it is therefore administratively efficient and not intolerably unfair to prefer all female applicants.

If one is not inclined to accept compensatory principles that apply directly to groups or to believe that proportional equality is required by distributive justice, one will then have to justify preferences for all members of disadvantaged groups in terms of the administrative advantages of doing so. It may be somewhat easier, however, to justify preference for all members of disadvantaged groups on the utilitarian approach. If progress toward proportional equality is desirable on utilitarian grounds, even if not required by distributive justice, the conferral of a preference to all applicants (or all promising applicants) from groups that are substantially underrepresented at higher levels of income and achievement may be justifiable. If the utilitarian approach, however, concentrated on poverty, unmet needs, and serving the needs of the poor, rather than on inequality per se, then to qualify for preference one would have to be poor. Approaches which emphasize proportional representation (whether they do so on grounds of distributive justice or utility) will sometimes conflict with approaches that emphasize the elimination of poverty and unmet needs. In law school admissions, for example, those who are concerned with proportional representation for blacks in the legal profession may want to admit middle-class black applicants on a preferential basis because they often have better educational backgrounds and hence may have a better chance of succeeding in law school and as lawyers. Those who are concerned with poverty and unmet needs, however, may be opposed to extending preferences to these applicants and want to restrict preferences to low-income blacks or to low-income applicants generally.

An interesting difference between the approaches in terms of justice and the approach in terms of utility is in the nature of the recipient's claim to preference. Viewed as a matter of justice, the preference is claimed as something that satisfies the recipient's right to compensation or his right to a fair share. Viewed as a matter of utility, the claim is not that the recipient personally has a right to preference; it is rather that the public good can be promoted by preferring him in awarding opportunities.

2   GENERAL OBJECTIONS TO PREFERENTIAL POLICIES

In this section and the next I discuss two quite different sorts of objections to preferential policies. The objections discussed in this section apply to any sort of preferential policy for anyone—whether it be for blacks and other minority-group members, veterans, or persons with physical handicaps. The objections discussed in the next section go to preferential policies that define the target group in racial, ethnic, or sexual terms.

Problems of Incompetency. The use of preferential policies to achieve important social goals rests on the recognition that the distributive effects of hiring and admissions practices are very important in determining the character of the overall distribution of benefits and burdens, and on the recognition that these practices can be altered slightly in order to bring about more desirable results. Preferential policies utilize and alter the distributive practices and effects of existing institutions. In a similar way, special home-loan programs altered the distributive effects of the housing market in favor of veterans, and special scholarship programs altered the distributive effects of the educational system in favor of veterans. But preferential hiring and admissions policies do more than provide the money needed to enter the competition; they alter the rules of the competition so that veterans have a better chance of success. And that is why they are more controversial.

Insofar as the use of preferential policies led to the admission or hiring of unqualified persons, significant reductions in the efficiency and productivity of companies and institutions would be likely to follow. Those who are opposed to preferential policies often raise the specter of illiterate students, highway patrolmen who do not know how to drive, teachers who cannot handle children, and surgeons who remove tonsils by cutting throats. Although these dangers are easily exaggerated, the importance of competent personnel to institutional efficiency must be recognized, and it can be readily conceded that preferential policies should be restricted to those who are adequately qualified, or who, with the training provided, can become adequately qualified for the position sought. This will mean that if a person is unable to perform the task adequately, then preferential policies will not apply to him with respect to the position. Although there will be cases in which it will be difficult to decide the degree of competence that is adequate, I think that the criterion of adequate competence can serve as a useful general limit for preferential treatment. A narrower limit may be required with regard to jobs where small differences in competence within the range of adequate competence can make a great deal of difference in the level of performance, and hence in the level of institutional efficiency. For gardeners, postal clerks, X-ray technicians, and sales personnel, adequate competence may be sufficient; but in the case of surgeons, professional athletes, and airline pilots, small differences in competence can make a great difference, respectively, in lives saved, games won, or crashes averted, and hence the scope allowed to preferential policies should be more restricted. One advantage of the minimal preferential policy—hire the preferred person only when he or she is as well qualified as any other candidate (a policy that only serves when a tie-breaker is needed)—is that it does not lead to the selection of a less qualified candidate.

Problems of Unfair Burdens. A second objection is that preferential policies unfairly place the burden of helping those who are preferred on those who are thereby excluded. Thus, it might be argued that putting the burden of helping to compensate and meet the needs of veterans on those who are excluded from government jobs by policies which prefer veterans is an unfair way of distributing the cost of a legitimate goal. A well-qualified nonveteran who had hoped to get a government job but who was denied it because of a policy which gives veterans an advantage may feel that too much of the cost of helping veterans was placed on him. This person may feel that providing benefits from taxes—where the cost can be spread among many taxpayers—is preferable as a means of helping veterans to programs which impose the burden on a few people whose opportunities are reduced by preferential policies.

The problem here is one of justice in the spreading of burdens rather than one of total costs. A policy which prefers veterans does not result in any more persons being excluded than a normal policy; the only difference is in who is excluded. The complaint of those excluded will have to be that it is somehow worse to exclude them and to reduce their opportunities than to do the same to the veterans who would not have gotten the job were it not for the preferential policy.

If we assume that preference is only given to adequately qualified candidates, and hence that both preferential and nonpreferential policies are compatible with the requirements of efficiency, what is it that makes it worse when those excluded are persons who are better qualified than some of those hired? An answer to this question will obviously refer to the better qualifications of the persons excluded by the preferential policy, but why is it worse to exclude better qualified persons than to deprive less qualified candidates of preferences indicated by considerations of compensation, distributive justice, or utility? One possibility is to say that better qualifications confer upon their holders a prima facie right to be chosen in preference to anyone who is less qualified. This claim is plausible because, other things being equal, the best way of distributing jobs is to give them to the best-qualified candidate. Although this is normally the best way, it does not seem to be the only permissible way. If in a case where small differences in competence had little impact on institutional efficiency a company chose to save money and effort by hiring the first adequately qualified person who applied or to select among the adequately qualified candidates by lot, no one would have good grounds for complaint. It is unclear whether these cases show that there is no right to be hired in preference to less qualified candidates, or simply that this right is one that can be overridden by considerations of efficiency in some cases, but these cases do at least show that the policy of selecting in accordance with the best qualifications is not sacrosanct.

Suppose, however, that one recognized a prima facie right to be hired in preference to all less qualified candidates. To recognize such a right would be to recognize an obligation on the part of hiring officers to award, other things being equal, jobs to the best-qualified candidates. The question then arises whether things are equal in the case of veterans—that is, whether there are other considerations that can override this obligation. If there are such considerations, they would pertain to the special needs that veterans have, to the utility of a smooth reintegration of veterans into the economy, and to the fact that many veterans deserve compensation for their services and sacrifices. These are considerations which personnel officers do not normally consider, but the question is whether they should be considered.

A proper judgment on this issue depends, I think, on the recognition that when one awards a good job, more is usually at stake than finding a capable employee. One is also awarding or denying a strategic benefit that often has great consequences for a person's long-term levels of income, security, and status. Since the decisions of personnel officers often have this effect, it may be appropriate for them to consider matters that are relevant to the proper distribution of income, security, and status. When two or more benefits tend to go together—for example, a job and a good and secure income—to consider only those matters that are relevant to whether a person should get one of these is to award or deny one of the benefits on the basis of an incomplete consideration of all of the relevant factors. When a society succeeds in providing many paths to good and secure incomes, then personnel officers may be justified in generally ignoring the distributive effects that their decisions have and concentrating on job qualifications. But in cases where a denial of a job, or a pattern of denying jobs, is likely to have very bad consequences for the individual or for society, it may be desirable for personnel officers to take these broader consequences into account.

My presupposition here is that hiring officers, and those who create the policies that guide them, are morally obligated to promote desirable social goals when this can be done at slight institutional cost. I think that this applies to both private and public institutions, but one who disagrees with this can still allow that there is such an obligation for public institutions and for those private institutions that are committed to serving the public good— and this will cover most of the institutions where questions about the desirability of preferential policies have arisen. It is not uncommon in any institution for considerations other than those of qualifications to be taken into account in awarding jobs. Such considerations come into play when it must be decided whether to retain an older employee who has ceased to be very useful to the company but who would find it very difficult or impossible to find another source of income. These considerations also come into play when it must be decided whether to give a job to a qualified handicapped person or to an equally qualified applicant who is not handicapped. Knowing that the scarcity of such jobs may make denying the job to the handicapped person tantamount to denying him a good income and a basis for self-respect, personnel officers are likely to take this into account. In public employment, legislation has dictated that this be done with regard to disabled veterans. The Veterans Preference Act of 1944 gave disabled veterans a ten-point advantage in competition for some jobs, and superpreference in others.

Similar considerations apply with regard to nondisabled veterans, but with somewhat less force. In a postwar period, jobs are likely to be scarce because of production cutbacks in war-affected industries in the face of an oversupply of labor due to the many returning veterans and the workers who have been laid off in those industries. In these circumstances, a veteran who spent several years as a soldier when he might otherwise have been getting an education or job experience may have special difficulties in getting a good job and the good income that goes with it. Denying such a person a job may be tantamount to denying him a decent income for a period. Not only are veterans likely to have difficulty in getting decent jobs and decent incomes in the period after a war, they are also likely to have a special claim to such benefits because of their services and sacrifices. These are considerations which hiring policies and hiring officers may appropriately take into account.

Even if it is allowed that it is sometimes appropriate for personnel officers to take the special needs and claims of veterans into account, one may continue to hold the view that to place the burden of helping veterans on the nonveterans whose opportunities are reduced by a preferential policy is to place the cost of a legitimate objective on too small a group. Because jobs are such strategic benefits, unfairness in the allocation of job opportunities must be taken seriously. Although one might argue that the excluded nonveterans owe something to veterans because of the services and sacrifices of the veterans, or because of the opportunities that nonveterans had and which veterans missed, this is also true of other nonveterans—not just those who happen to be now competing for jobs—and hence it provides no justification for putting a burden on only some of the nonveterans.

One way to reduce the force of this charge of unfairness would be to combine preferential policies with measures that will increase the total number of jobs available, thereby increasing job opportunities and reducing the loss of opportunities that nonveterans suffer because of preferential policies for veterans. This could be done, for example, by using tax money to create more government jobs, to increase jobs in the private sector, and to provide retirement benefits that will encourage early retirement. Preferential policies might also be restricted to a certain percentage of the jobs or promotions in a given department or bureau so as to insure that nonveterans will not be at a disadvantage with regard to all opportunities within that agency.

Even if all these policies were followed there would probably still be some unfairness in the allocation of the cost of helping veterans. Rather than trying to deny this, it is probably more plausible to argue that the fact that there is some unfairness in the distribution of this burden does not settle the question of whether using preferential policies is acceptable or wise. In order to meet its obligation to veterans, society imposes a greater part of the cost of doing this on some individuals than on others. It is not that these nonveterans owe more than other nonveterans; it is rather that society requires them to live with reduced opportunities in order to meet its obligations. Many wise and acceptable policies involve placing burdens on individuals where similar burdens are not placed on all individuals or even on all individuals who are similar in relevant ways. Fighting a war, building a dam or highway, and protecting public access to a beach through zoning restrictions are all activities that inevitably place heavier burdens on some individuals than on others. Weaker but more equitable means are preferable if they will do the same job in the same time, but this is seldom the case. The advantage of preferential policies is that they are fast and effective as a means of shifting patterns of distribution, and this, no doubt, is the key to their appeal in the instant context of the use of such policies for blacks and other disadvantaged groups.

3   OBJECTIONS TO PREFERENTIAL POLICIES THAT USE RACIAL, ETHNIC, OR SEXUAL CLASSIFICATIONS

Much of the discrimination that blacks have suffered in this country can be viewed as the result of preferential policies that prefer whites, and hence many people are likely to hold the view that using preferential policies in combination with racial classifications is a very dangerous business. The focus of this section is on the objections that are likely to be made by people who feel that racial, ethnic, and sexual preferences are dangerous. In order to make the discussion concrete and to avoid the repeated use of lists such as "blacks, women, Chicanos, and Indians," I will take as my example preferential policies for blacks.

Race as an Irrelevant Characteristic. When a black person is preferentially awarded a job, and a nonblack person is thereby denied it, both the award and the denial seem to be on the basis of an irrelevant characteristic, namely the race of the candidates. Awarding and denying benefits on the basis of such an irrelevant characteristic seems to be no different in principle —even though the motives may be more defensible—from traditional sorts of discrimination against blacks and in favor of whites. Preferential hiring or admissions policies for blacks are therefore likely to be charged with being discriminatory, even though they are done in the name of rectifying discrimination and other evils. If one condemns the original discrimination against blacks because it was based on an irrelevant characteristic, and hence was unreasonable, one is likely to be charged with inconsistency if one now advocates policies that award and deny benefits on the basis of the same characteristic.

The defect in this charge is that it mistakenly assumes that race is the justification for preferential treatment. This is only apparently so. If preference is given to blacks because of past discrimination and present poverty, the basis for this preference is not that these people are black but rather that they are likely to have been victimized by discrimination, to have fewer benefits and more burdens than is fair, to be members of an underrepresented group, or to be the sorts of persons that can help public institutions meet the needs of those who are now poorly served. Being black does not itself have any relevancy to these goals, but the facts which are associated with being black often do in the present context.

Administrative Convenience as Inadequate Justification. When this defect is pointed out, the person arguing that racially based preferential policies are discriminatory may formulate a new version of his objection. This version recognizes that the *justifying basis* for preferential policies is discrimination, injustice, unmet needs, and so forth, but it notes that being black is often a necessary condition for receiving preference and therefore forms the *administrative basis* for preferential programs. Those who defend the use of race as part of the administrative basis allow that race in itself is irrelevant, but they assert that the use of racial classifications in administering preferential policies is justified by the high correlation between being black and having the characteristics that form the justifying basis. Having noted this, the critic of preferential policies using racial classifications is likely to point out that a similar claim was and is made by racists. Racists claim that they do not treat blacks worse than whites simply because they are black, but rather because blacks are lazy or untrustworthy or have some other characteristic that makes them undeserving of good treatment. Like the advocates of preferential policies for blacks, racists deny that they base differential treatment on an irrelevant characteristic such as race. They claim that the justifying basis for their differential treatment of blacks is something relevant such as being lazy or untrustworthy, not something irrelevant such as race. Race only forms, the racist might say, the administrative basis for his policy of treating blacks worse than whites. The critic of preference on the basis of racial classifications will argue, therefore, that an approach to the justifications of preferential policies which distinguishes between the justifying basis—for example, having been harmed by discrimination—and the administrative basis—for example, being a low-income black—makes the same mistake as the racist since the form of reasoning is exactly the same. Thus, the objection continues, if the advocates of preferential policies can use this distinction between the justifying and the administrative bases to show that he is not practicing invidious discrimination, then so can the racist. But since this defense will not work for the racist, neither will it work for the defender of preferential policies.

But there is a way of distinguishing these cases, and it can be seen by comparing the premises that are used to connect being black with having a relevant characteristic. When these premises are compared, it becomes apparent that for the racist to defend his position, he has to make claims which can be proven to be erroneous about the correlation between being black and having some relevant defect such as being lazy or untrustworthy, while the defender of racially administered preferential policies can make a plausible case without using erroneous premises. Hence, one important way of distinguishing justifiable from unjustifiable uses of racial classifications is in terms of the soundness of the alleged correlation between race and a relevant characteristic.

It is possible, however, that there are cases in which a racist can find genuine correlations between race and a relevant deficiency that will serve his exclusionary purposes. He might claim that blacks are more likely than whites to have a criminal record, no high-school diploma, or chronic health problems. But a higher percentage of some relevant deficiency in a particular group does not ordinarily justify excluding all members of that group without considering whether a member personally has that deficiency. Excluding all members of a group on the basis of a correlation between membership and having a relevant deficiency would be justifiable only if (1) the correlation between membership and having the deficiency was very high, and (2) it was so difficult to check for the relevant deficiency itself in individual cases that it would be unacceptably wasteful and inefficient to do so. These conditions are seldom met, and they are certainly not met with regard to correlations between race and characteristics such as having a criminal record, no high-school diploma, or chronic health problems—both because the correlations are not high enough and because the relevant deficiencies themselves are not difficult to identify.

Suppose, however, that a racist was able to show that his policy of excluding all blacks was in fact based on a genuine correlation between race and a difficult-to-identify relevant deficiency. Would we than say that his practice of excluding all blacks on that basis was justifiable? To make this even clearer (and even less likely to occur), suppose that there was no question about whether the correlation was high enough or about whether having the relevant deficiency was always sufficient to disqualify one for the position. The question, then, would be whether it would be permissible to exclude all blacks because of a deficiency that statistical sampling revealed, say, 90 percent of them to have.

One might reply that the exclusion of all blacks would not be permissible because it would be unacceptably wasteful and inefficient to use the difficult-to-identify characteristic itself as the criterion. In *DeFunis*, Justice Douglas dismissed the objection to the administrative inconvenience of the individualized admissions procedures he prefers: "Such a program might be less convenient administratively than simply sorting students by race, but we have never held administrative convenience to justify racial discrimination." Were the racist to use individual tests or investigations to exclude only the 90 percent that had the relevant deficiency, then he would exclude all unqualified blacks without unnecessarily excluding the qualified 10 percent. In the same way, the objection runs, the advocate of preferential policies could achieve all of his desired results if he were to predicate preference in education and employment directly on relevant characteristics, such as having been harmed by discrimination, being unjustly poor, or having unmet needs. By doing this he would give preference to only those persons who had these characteristics. This practice would have the advantage not only of excluding blacks without these characteristics, but also of including nonblacks who had them.

The question, then, is whether the price of excluding that 10 percent of the blacks who are qualified for the job that the racist is awarding, and of excluding those nonblacks who also ought to get preference is too high a price to pay for administrative efficiency. Efficiency in administering large-scale programs requires that detailed investigations of individual cases be kept to a minimum, and this means that many allocative decisions will have to be made on the basis of gross but easily discernible characteristics. By giving preferences to all applicants who are members of certain disadvantaged groups, administrative costs can be kept to a minimum. The alternative is to investigate on an individual basis. The expense of such investigations might be reduced by inviting applicants to provide information about their personal history as part of their application materials if they think they deserve special consideration because of past discrimination, hardships, injustice, or present need. But this would merely reduce, not eliminate, the costs of investigation because some check on the authenticity of these claims would be needed. An approach of this sort might be workable and desirable in some circumstances, but would be expensive both for the applicant and for the institution processing the applications. For this reason, there are considerable advantages in using gross indicators, including racial, ethnic, and sexual ones, as indicators of the presence of the characteristics that provide the justifying basis.

Problems of Stigmatization and Loss of Self-Respect. One might argue that it is permissible to use gross indicators such as being an honorably discharged veteran, but not ones such as being black. This, no doubt, is Justice Douglas' position, since he has often expressed his willingness to allow legislatures considerable latitude, outside of the racial and First Amendment areas, in designing classifications for dealing with complex problems. Given our history of evil uses of racial classifications, there are good reasons, both moral and constitutional, for being very cautious in their use, even for good ends. Hence, we should be reluctant to use them to effect a small gain in administrative efficiency. But the consequences of using racial classifications are not always the same as when they were used to stigmatize and exclude blacks, and their likely nonpejorative impact in the present context ought to be taken into account in balancing their use against less efficient procedures. Using racial classifications which place a burden on whites is probably less dangerous than using classifications that put a burden on blacks, since there is little likelihood that whites will ever be an isolated and mistreated minority in this country. The kind of self-hatred and belief in one's own inferiority that sometimes resulted from discrimination against blacks is not likely to result among white applicants who have their opportunities reduced by preferential programs, since such programs carry no implication of white inferiority.

It may be the case, however, that the use of racial classifications in preferential programs favoring blacks confirm a sense of inferiority among black recipients, since the presupposition of such programs is that blacks deserve or are in need of such assistance. Justice Douglas offered an argument of just this sort: "A segregated admissions process creates suggestions of stigma and caste no less than a segregated classroom, and in the end it may produce that result despite its contrary intentions. One other assumption must be clearly disapproved, that Blacks or Browns cannot make it on their individual merit. That is a stamp of inferiority that a State is not permitted to place on any lawyer."

Although special admissions procedures for blacks may, if misunderstood, be taken to imply black inferiority and thereby to stigmatize blacks, it seems to be an exaggeration to say, as Justice Douglas does, that programs designed to remedy injustices and overcome handicaps nevertheless stigmatize blacks no less than policies that required blacks to attend segregated schools. Indeed, if the stigmatizing effect of preferential programs were as great as that of segregated schools, one would expect to find blacks avoiding such programs, black organizations opposing them, and black leaders denouncing them. In practice, however, one finds nothing of the sort and indeed finds the opposite.

Making predictions about the consequences of using racial classifications is a risky and difficult business, but it seems to me that the use of such classifications in remedial programs is not likely to have the bad consequences that resulted from using them to exclude and segregate blacks. Condemnations of discrimination, it seems to me, should not go so far as to prohibit all uses of racial classifications; they should rather condemn those that are based on false beliefs of high correlations between race and relevant characteristics, that can be avoided without great loss of efficiency through the use of nonracial classifications, or that result in a group's being stigmatized and subject to loss of self-respect.

4   A FRAMEWORK FOR ANALYZING PREFERENTIAL POLICIES THAT USE RACIAL, ETHNIC, OR SEXUAL CLASSIFICATIONS

It will be helpful to begin by introducing some general considerations about the use of gross criteria—characteristics which, although irrelevant in themselves, are useful as statistical indicators of relevant characteristics. For a gross criterion C to be perfectly correlated with a relevant characteristic R, it must be the case that *all* and *only* C's are R's. Thus, for ". . . is black" to be perfectly correlated with " . . . has been harmed by discrimination," it would have to be the case that all and only blacks have been harmed by discrimination. If it is not the case that all American blacks have been harmed by discrimination, then the gross indicator would be overinclusive since it would select some individuals who do not have the relevant characteristic. And if it is not the case that only blacks have been harmed by discrimination—as it clearly is not—then the gross indicator would be underinclusive since it would not select some individuals who have the relevant characteristic. Most classifications used in legislation are both over- and underinclusive to some extent, and the importance of having clear boundaries that are administratively workable requires that some looseness be tolerated. Hence, the requirement cannot be perfect correlation but must rather be something like high correlation (in a case where one is distributing something as important as educational and employment opportunities, and where one is using racial classifications to do so, one would probably want to say that there must be a very high correlation). When a gross criterion is overinclusive, one way to remedy this is to add additional characteristics to the indicator until one includes only the desired smaller group. Thus, if the gross criterion " . . . is black" is overinclusive because most blacks with a personal income of over $20,000 a year do not have the relevant characteristic of having been harmed by discrimination, then the overinclusiveness could be reduced by adding "with an income of less than $20,000 a year" to the gross criterion. The cost of adding characteristics to the gross criterion is the loss of efficiency that may result from having to verify the presence of more characteristics. When a gross criterion is underinclusive, this can be remedied either by substituting another that has wider scope (for example, substituting " . . . is a member of a disadvantaged minority group" for " . . . is black"), or by using a disjunctive clause to include another gross criterion (for example, substituting " . . . is black *or Chicano*" for " . . . is black"). In the former case, the cost of remedying underinclusiveness would be a loss in efficiency because a vague general classification is likely to be difficult to verify in individual cases, while in the later case, there is ordinarily no significant additional cost.

The extent to which the criteria used by a preferential program are over- or underinclusive will depend on which relevant characteristics one selects as the justification for awarding preference. It is clear, for example, that there are now more blacks who are not in poverty than there are blacks who have not suffered from discrimination, and hence a program which attempted to reduce poverty by giving money to all blacks would be more overinclusive than one which compensated victims of discrimination by giving money to all blacks. If cases of overinclusion are frequent, serious objections can be made on grounds of justice and efficiency. If, for example, a black was hired in preference to a better-qualified white, and if this particular black person had not been harmed by discrimination, was not unjustly poor, did not have unmet needs, was not likely to be upwardly mobile if given special opportunities, could not serve as a role model, and could not help to provide needed services to blacks, then a less-qualified person was hired, and a better-qualified person excluded, without achieving any counterbalancing goal. Although it may be possible to reduce overinclusiveness by adding characteristics to the gross criterion which restrict its scope, it would be pointless to do this if it would reintroduce the need for individual investigations that the use of racial classifications was designed to avoid. Since family income can be checked without too much difficulty, restricting preference to group members with a family income below a certain level may be an effective means of reducing overinclusiveness with regard to some conceptions of the proper goals of preferential programs.

Underinclusiveness is probably a greater problem, since one of the most divisive aspects of preferential programs has been the nonpreferential treatment of disadvantaged persons who are not members of groups that are now deemed to be disadvantaged. Assuming that there is sufficient similarity between the situations of the latter persons and that of blacks to justify similar treatment, these programs are clearly underinclusive. Although some latitude must be allowed those who create such programs in experimenting with small groups, in meeting different problems with different means, and in beginning with programs for those with the greatest needs, none of these considerations can justify a long-term policy of using administrative classifications which provide benefits to some while ignoring others with similar claims for preferential treatment. Although underinclusiveness can sometimes be remedied by adding disjunctive clauses, and hence one could offer benefits to anyone who is black *or* Chicano *or* Puerto Rican *or* Filipino *or* American Indian, this solution will result in groups being either entirely included or excluded and therefore generate intense political pressures on behalf of excluded groups who have some members with the relevant characteristics and perhaps many others who are borderline cases. Justice Douglas accurately senses this problem:

> The reservation of a proportion of the law school class for members of selected minority groups is fraught with similar dangers, for one must immediately determine which groups are to receive such favored treatment and which are to be excluded. . . . There is no assurance that a common agreement can be reached, and first the schools, and then the courts, will be buffeted with the competing claims. The University of Washington included Filipinos, but excluded Chinese and Japanese; another school may limit its program to Blacks, or to Blacks and Chicanos.

The prospect of controversies of this sort is one reason for switching to a general, nonracial criterion, but the appeal of this alternative will depend on the justification for preferential programs. If one is trying to compensate victims of discrimination or to provide legal and medical personnel for poorly served groups, such a general criterion will be less appealing than if one is trying to reduce poverty and inequality. Since there are many poor persons who are poor for reasons other than that of having been harmed by discrimination, selecting persons for a program designed to help victims of discrimination on the basis of a low income would involve much overinclusion. If no nonracial criteria were found suitable, one might reduce the underinclusiveness of preferential programs that use lists of groups as selection criteria by allowing persons who do not belong to any of the listed groups but who think they have the characteristics that justify preference to apply for preference by presenting a documented claim. This would still require individual investigations in these cases, but not in the cases of persons who qualified on the basis of membership in one of the listed groups. If one utilized this approach, one could construct a criterion for awarding preference that would be acceptable in regard to over-and underinclusiveness and which would retain considerable administrative efficiency. It would have the following form:

> Preference will be awarded to persons who have a family income of less than ___(specify amount)___ dollars per year, *and* who are members of any of following groups ___(list groups)___ . Persons who do not qualify in accordance with the above criterion but who believe that they have the characteristics which justify preferences such as ___(list relevant characteristics)___ may apply for preference by presenting evidence for their claim on forms available from the admissions (or personnel) officer.

This kind of scheme, even though it employs racial, ethnic, and sexual classifications, is not underinclusive with regard to entire groups, and hence relatively well-off groups who have some disadvantaged members would not need to fight to get on the list. This kind of criterion would be overinclusive only to the extent that having a low income and being a member of one of the listed groups was insufficient to exclude persons who lacked the characteristics that can justify preference.

Hardy E. Jones

On the Justifiability
of Reverse Discrimination

The topic of reverse discrimination in hiring excites strong passions on all sides. It is a complex issue, the difficulty of which is reflected in divisive, often volatile debates. In the following discussion I shall consider whether and why preferential treatment for members of certain groups is permissible. I assume that discrimination against females and blacks is wrong and unjust. The issue is whether employment discrimination against white males in favor of less-qualified persons of another sex or color is morally justifiable. Another crucial assumption is that employers are able and willing to use objective standards for determining relevant qualifications—that they have access to, and can follow, nonsexist and nonracist criteria.

I shall adumbrate four aims in view of which a comprehensive social program of reverse discrimination may be justified. These are worthy goals which, were there no serious countervailing considerations, should surely be sufficient to justify preferential treatment.

1. *To ensure that past discrimination against females and blacks does*

Source: This is an original paper.

not continue. It takes some societies a long time to cease, finally and completely, patterns of injustice that have prevailed for generations. Legislative acts and constitutional amendments often simply do not do the job. A comprehensive, tightly administered social program involving reverse discrimination in hiring would help bring past and continuing injustice to a halt. Blacks and females may feel, quite understandably, that in order for them not to be discriminated *against* they must be discriminatingly *favored*.

2. *To offer, officially and explicitly, a symbolic denunciation of our racist and sexist past.* A program of reverse discrimination, suitably touted and carefully advertised, might serve well as such a symbol. Among other benefits, such a program could have the salutary effect of encouraging victims to work hard to offset the often sadly debilitating consequences of injustice. Further, this gesture might represent a confession of past wrong and a resolution to be more just. Employers might be encouraged voluntarily to stop discriminating against blacks and females.

3. *To provide role models for victimized blacks and females.* One good way for persons to shake off the shackles of past injustice is to become aware of others, relevantly similar to them, who have good jobs. By noting quite directly that these others are succeeding in respectable positions, persons may be encouraged to proceed vigorously in pursuit of satisfying careers for themselves.

4. *To compensate victims of discrimination by preferring them over beneficiaries of injustice.* It seems only just to give those who have been treated unjustly extra benefits and, in this way, to make some effort toward "evening the score." Those to benefit directly from the preferential treatment may not have been discriminated against, but they may have suffered from previous unjust acts toward their ancestors. The effects of past discriminatory acts may have deprived them of the wealth, education, health, and employment essential to equal-opportunity competition. The white males to be discriminated against may not have perpetrated the injustices, but many have greatly benefited from them. So it seems proper that they now be deprived of still further fruits, in the form of jobs, of past acts of unjust discrimination. This position may be buttressed by reflection on how people have come to have the qualifications they possess. The better-qualified white males might have been far less qualified had they not reaped the benefits of an unjust system which favored them at every turn. And the now lesser-qualified blacks and females might have been much better qualified if they and their ancestors had received equal, fair treatment from the start. The meritocratic views holds that persons deserve jobs on the basis of merit or ability—

whatever their qualifications now happen to be. The position set out here rejects this "meritocracy of present qualifications." What is also relevant is how people have gotten qualifications and what their qualifications would have been if certain crucial aspects of their histories had been different.

The notion employed here may be thought of as "counterfactual meritocracy." On this view, people are deserving, at least within certain limits, of jobs on the basis of what their qualifictions would have been if they had been neither victims nor beneficiaries of past injustice. In principle there is nothing wrong with a fair meritocracy. What makes the usual meritocracy pernicious is its allowance of past injustice to penetrate, or spill over into, the present by refusing to factor out the unjust causes of present qualifications. The fair counterfactual meritocracy, whatever its defects, is not subject to this criticism. There is also a forward-looking feature of the basic position. The future qualifications of job applicants, as well as present and "what would have been" qualifications, are relevant. If a presently lesser-qualified person, a victim of past injustice, can increase his level of competence by being offered the position, then there is some reason for preferring him to a beneficiary of past injustice whose future qualifications will become no higher.

All of these appear to be eminently good reasons for instituting a compensatory program of reverse discrimination. But there are serious objections that must be conscientiously confronted. I shall state the difficulties with reverse discrimination, assess their relative strengths, and suggest how they might be resolved.

1

Perhaps the most nearly devastating objection to a scheme based on the notion of "counterfactual meritocracy" is that it requires vastly more knowledge about individual cases than we have any reasonable prospect of obtaining. If we do not know that the particular white male to be passed over (in favor of the lesser-qualified black or female) has benefited from past injustice in obtaining his qualifications, then we run the risk of unfairly discriminating against him. And there is surely a very strong, widely shared intuition that "two wrongs do not make a right"—that we cannot rightly rectify past injustice by committing further injustices. It is very difficult to know the truth of counterfactual claims about what a white male's qualification would have been without the benefits of injustice, of what a black person's qualifications would have been without the liabilities of injustice.

We might be tempted just to throw up our hands in frustration and say "Who knows?" Recognizing the lack of special favors and facing more severe competition, the white male might have worked harder to obtain high qualifications. Being confronted with less formidable obstacles to overcome, the black might have felt less of a challenge and might never have worked as hard to obtain his qualifications. And without injustice many other factors could have worked differently in the lives of both. So how could one ever know where either would have ended up when it came time to apply for a job? The perfect working of the counter-factual meritocracy would seem to require the existence of an ideal social observer, in possession of all knowledge as to how individuals have benefited and suffered from injustice—and how things would have been in a just world. Not having this sort of God's-eye-view, we seem destined to lack enough knowledge to implement a fair program of reverse discrimination. Furthermore, even if human means of obtaining the requisite knowledge were developed, their use might be very costly—so costly that everyone in the society would suffer.

The objection is a serious one, and I do not have a fully satisfactory answer. Three points, however, seem noteworthy. First, the risk of unfair treatment of white males can be greatly reduced by establishing small minimal differentials between the better and lesser qualifications. A black female could get the job if she were slightly less qualified. If the difference between the two is very small at present, then it would seem likely that without past injustice the black female would have acquired much better qualifications. Only a cursory knowledge of racist and sexist injustice in American history is necessary to know that discrimination has been widespread, touching the lives of virtually everyone to some degree.

This point suggests a second reply. Lacking the knowledge of a godlike social observer, we are not totally ignorant either. We know a lot about how injustice has affected many individuals. And we can learn more through extensive interviews with individuals and inquiries into the social conditions of their childhood environments. The program could involve setting up hearings for this purpose. In cases in which only a small fraction of the needed knowledge is obtainable, the job could standardly go to the presently more qualified. The program need not be entirely scrapped for lack of complete knowledge of all the cases that may arise.

The third reply is based on an analogy with the administration of criminal justice. In many cases it is very difficult to get enough evidence to know whether an accused person is guilty or innocent. There are great risks involved in a trial system with an attached schedule of punishments. Some innocent people will be found guilty and punished for crimes they did not commit, some guilty persons will be found not guilty and escape the punishment they deserve. We are aware of these uncertainties; yet we are not thereby deterred from implementing a system of indictments, trials, and punishments. Apparently it is thought that the risks of committing injustice are worth taking. If we are reasonable in proceeding with this sort of system, then we would not be obviously unreasonable to institute a program of reverse discrimination with its attendant risks of unfair treatment of white male applicants. Indeed, the injustice of not hiring a deserving white male seems far less serious than the injustice of punishing an innocent person. The latter may happen less often, but when it does occur we countenance something akin to tragedy. With the generally better opportunities most white males have, it does not seem tragic to prefer unfairly some black female for a particular job. Furthermore, more injustice may result from not having a program of reverse discrimination than from having one. For if we hire solely on the basis of present qualifications, then it is likely that many "counter-factually deserving" but actually less-qualified females and blacks will lose out in favor of white males. Not having a program of reverse discrimination runs the risk of more extensively victimizing persons already unfairly treated. Such a risk seems far more serious than that of unfairly preferring blacks or females to white males who have thus far not been victimized.

The three replies go a way toward meeting the first objection to my scheme to counterfactual meritocracy. In the absence of perfectly adequate knowledge of the individual cases, we must rely on certain roughly reliable indices of past injustice. For purposes of implementing the program initially, rather crude indicators would probably have to be used. "Being black" would be taken as an index of being a victim of past discrimination, and "being a white male" an index of being a beneficiary of past injustice. As knowledge progresses and as we gain experience with the workings of the system, more complex and refined indices could be introduced.

2

Another cluster of objections relates to the administration of the program on a class or group basis. There are serious problems in offering preferential treatment to persons because they are members of a group most of whose members are victims of injustice, and in discriminating against persons because they are members of a group in which most of the members are beneficiaries of injustice.

One of these difficulties is simply that not everyone who deserves compensation will get it. Only a segment of the group of black persons (or female persons) can be given jobs within a preferential-hiring scheme. The appropriate reply here is that reverse discrimination is only *one* way of compensating *some* victimized persons for some of the wrongs done to them. It cannot rectify all past injustice to members of unfairly treated minority groups. There are many other ways to provide compensation, and the operation of a program of reverse discrimination in hiring does not preclude their being tried. Perhaps some more broadly based program could compensate all victims more fairly and efficiently than the more limited program of preferential hiring. However, without such a program, it is surely unobjectionable to compensate as many as possible within our unfortunate limitations. The fact that we cannot compensate everyone does not justify us in compensating no one. The civil-law system of compensating negligently injured persons does not work perfectly so as to insure that every victim receives his due. Still, in the absence of a fairer and more efficient system, the present one is worth keeping. A well-designed system of preferential hiring would seem to be analogous.

But there is a still more serious problem. The programs based on the notion of a counterfactual meritocracy would presumably allow market criteria to determine which members of the groups get jobs (and thus receive compensation). The members must still compete for positions, and the best qualified will obtain them. One result will be that those who have suffered most lose out to those who have suffered least. The better qualified are those mostly likely to have suffered less from past injustice, and those who are most victimized will be the lesser qualified. So those who are less deserving of compensation will receive it at the expense of those who are more deserving. The compensation will not be distributed in proportion to the degree of liabilities resulting from injustice. [A discussion of this problem is found in Alan Goldman's article, pp. 321-324 herein.]

A partial answer to this objection has already been suggested. The proposed system is very imperfect, but in the absence of a better one it seems worth pursuing. If the amount of injustice rectified is greater than that incidentally committed, the program would seem to be worthwhile. Furthermore, other types of compensation could be provided to those victimized persons who lose out in the competition for jobs. As our knowledge of degrees of victimization grows, such information can be incorporated so as to dispense positions proportionately to past injustice. Though extremely important, the objection does not appear to be devastating.

3

The next major difficulty may be labelled the "efficiency objection." It is arguable that, even with knowledge that would allow perfect correlations between being a certain sort of person and being deserving of a certain degree of compensation, the program would be a social disaster. The counterfactual meritocracy, administered comprehensively and assiduously, would drastically reduce efficiency and productivity. To maintain these at acceptable levels, jobs must be allocated on the basis of *actual* qualifications rather than hypothetical "what would have been" qualifications. Everyone in the society will suffer if too many of the lesser qualified are given job preference over better-qualified applicants. Those who are already victims probably will suffer even more than the rest. Poorer, more disadvantaged students, for example, have the greatest need of the very best instructors in their schools. Again, some of what has already been said is applicable here. Other compensatory programs may be useful in making up for the losses suffered by some members of minority groups as a result of the effort to aid the others. Reverse discrimination in hiring is not the only viable method of providing compensation.

Unless the losses in efficiency and productivity are so great that they produce injustice, a trade-off between efficiency and fairness seems justified. Surely the society can afford to tolerate some reduction in efficiency for the sake of rectifying past injustice. It would also be possible to build into the program methods of minimizing inefficiency. One way to do this would be to establish a "threshold of minimal qualifications" viable from job to job. No applicant could fall below this standard and still be hired, and no one would be hired if he were clearly unqualified. But the very best qualified might be passed over without unacceptable losses of efficiency. Another efficiency-conserving device is a "maximum differential of qualification," again varying perhaps from job to job. This would insure that a lesser qualified black or female applicant would not be hired if that person were far less qualified than someone else. The differential would have to be small enough so as to minimize inefficiency, yet large enough so that at least some victimized, lesser-qualified persons are given preference. These suggestions are rather vague, even amorphous; but they at least indicate how the efficiency issue could be handled.

4

At least as serious is the "white male objection." The program of preferential hiring works so that white male applicants, new candidates for new or newly available positions, bear the major burden of providing compensation. They are the ones who primarily suffer from this rectification of past injustice. Though most whites males have probably benefited from discrimination against others, they are by no means the only ones who have done so. Though some have actually perpetrated injustices against blacks and females, different individuals are more largely responsible for the unfair treatment. And though many whites males have tolerated injustices, virtually everyone else has also. Such facts make a commonly asked question especially pressing. Why must young white males be the ones to make the heavy sacrifices imposed by a program of compensatory justice? The costs of rectification would seem to be unfairly shared among members of a large group of beneficiaries of past injustice.

The ultimate force of the objection hinges on just how much injustice would be committed by the program as compared with how much can be rectified by its implementation. Not having a program of reverse discrimination and running the society on the model of an actual meritocracy brooks injustice by allowing the effects of past unfairness to penetrate into the future. The failure to have compensatory treatment is a failure to rectify injustice; but it also allows former injustices partially to prevail and to remain infused in our present society. So, all things considered, the amount of injustice tolerated without reverse discrimination may exceed that involved in making white males bear the burden. Such a conclusion is admittedly distasteful and unsatisfying.

There is a more utopian, vastly less realistic way of viewing the matter. Those white males who already have jobs have probably benefited more from past injustice than have the new applicants for newly available positions. Some evidence for this consists in the fact that the former have (and in many cases have had for a long time) secure, satisfying, often lucrative positions. Many of these positions were acquired during the days when there was not ever the pretense of fair treatment and equal opportunity for blacks and females. Also, many of these well-entrenched individuals are actual perpetrators, not mere beneficiaries, of injustice to members of minority groups. As a group they are probably much more "guilty" than the young white males who confront the dismal job market for the first time. It seems only fair that those who presently have jobs share the burdens of rectification. One way to do this might be to legislate a heavy tax, a "beneficiary of injustice" tax. The money could be spent to create new jobs and to provide needed social services to victims of unfair discrimination. These points are also suggestive of a more tantalizing, potentially very alarming vision. All jobs in the society could simply be subject to being vacated and then refilled. Everyone (well-entrenched, formerly secure veterans as well as hopeful new candidates) would have to apply for the jobs. The positions would then be filled— of necessity on a gradual, piecemeal basis—in accordance with criteria of justice and merit. A general redistribution of jobs could be accomplished. This would provide the proper rectification of past injustice in such a way that no particular group is unfairly treated.

This scheme is subject to the objections already discussed. The "knowledge objection" and the "efficiency objection" would become especially acute. Very complicated procedures and criteria would have to be devised so as to provide much knowledge about degrees of benefit and victimization. And it would become difficult to determine the appropriate balances between justice and efficiency. As difficult as they are, such problems are not clearly insurmountable. I should emphasize that this proposal is highly speculative. There is virtually no chance of its being very seriously considered and tried. Members of our society will not be willing to institute it. But this program ideally could become the most practically feasible, the most fair, and the most intellectually fascinating means of rectifying the gross injustices of the past.

5

I conclude with the "self-respect objection." If blacks and females know that they have been given jobs because of their group membership and that they have been chosen over better-qualified individuals, they may suffer severe losses of self-respect. Whereas if a person knows he deserves his job in virtue of his merit, ability, and prospects for success, then he will have a strong feeling of dignity and self-worth. Reverse discrimination would be counterproductive with regard to the purposes of having a job. At least one main motivation in seeking a position is the enhancement of one's self-esteem. Such an aim is defeated if persons are not hired solely because of their possession of the very best qualifications.

It is too easy to exaggerate the importance of this difficulty and thus to de-emphasize the benefits of a program of compensatory hiring. The problem could possibly be avoided by deceiving job-seekers and making them believe that only the best qualified are hired. This is not likely to be a very workable solution. It would be difficult to carry out the deception on a massive scale, and those who discover the truth may suffer even greater losses of self-respect from having been lied to. Another way of dealing with the problem would be both more sincere and more effective. One could emphasize to persons given the preferential treatment that they would have been best qualified if they had not been victims of injustice. If this is correct and if the central claims of this paper are sound, then people selected for jobs can have the appropriate and secure feeling that, whatever detractors may say, they are getting what they deserve.

Robert Hoffman

Justice, Merit, and the Good

This paper has three main theses: first, that although justice neither requires treating everyone equally nor presupposes that their natural powers are equal, whatever inequality obtains in the distribution of strongly desired offices, statuses, honors, commodities, opportunities, and so forth should be justified by individual merit or the common good, and may not rest upon the mere interest of some favored person or group; second, that so-called compensatory justice in behalf of ethnic, racial, or sexual groups or their members as such is immoral if it contravenes what merit and the common good warrant; and third, that actual large-scale compensatory policies that are being applied in some domains, where merit and the common good are ascertainable, are immoral.

Let us begin with the principle of formal justice, that is, that relevantly similar cases be treated similarly and relevantly dissimilar cases be treated differently in direct proportion to the relevant differences between them. One is tempted to say that the principle is a moral principle, for it usually concerns moral justice. (There are, of course, other kinds of justice, indicated by

Source: This is an original paper.

such phrases as 'doing justice to an argument by stating it clearly or to a piece of music by performing it expressively' and 'doing justice to oneself by fully developing one's talents'.) But it would be wrong to yield to the temptation. For it is the justice that is moral, not the principle. Rather, the principle is a feature of the logical and categorical structure of thinking itself. This principle functions in our thinking much as the principle of sufficient reason functions. This principle, that is, that for every contingent fact there is a reason why the fact is so and not otherwise (though the reason need not be conclusive), is one that we presuppose in thinking about the world and that we apply extensively in all domains of inquiry. It does not seem to be either a necessary truth or a contingent truth, yet its denial seems implausible to the point of absurdity. It is a constitutive principle of thought.

So also is the principle of formal justice. Consider its application in three different domains: the mathematical, the empirical, and the moral. First, consider the formula for the area of a square, a^2, where a is the length of one of its sides. Given that we understand the relevant mathematical concepts, it would be absurd to treat any square differently from others by contending that the area of that square cannot be determined by applying the formula. Second, consider two liquid solutions, each of which is pH4. To treat one but not the other as an acid would be nonsensical. Third, consider identical twins who commit an identical offense in identical circumstances: they take cookies from their pantry in circumstances in which they know themselves to have been forbidden to take them. (Throughout this paper, I use *identical* in the sense in which two numerically distinct things are qualitatively identical and therefore qualitatively indistinguishable.) It would be absurd to punish one twin by denying him cookies for a day *and* to punish the other by denying him cookies for a week. Apart from any complaint about being denied the cookies, the second twin probably would protest that he is being treated unfairly in having a seven times longer term of deprivation imposed for the same offense. What he would thereby focus upon is not the severity of his punishment per se, but its inconsistency with respect to his twin's punishment. What he would object to is that he is being unfairly discriminated against when compared with the treatment accorded his twin. His objection is not that he is not receiving his due (injustice *in se*), but that relevantly similar cases are being treated differently, that is, as though they were not relevantly similar cases.

The squares and liquids of the first two examples raise no moral issue, because neither geometrical figures nor volumes of liquid are the sorts of things that have an interest; and morality presupposes interest. The moral objection of the third example arises because the protesting twin has an interest in being treated just as the other twin is treated; and, in not being treated that way, he is harmed. Morality, then, does not inhere in the principle of formal justice, but attaches to it when it is applied to interactions that affect human interests.

The principle, of course, applies to benefits as well as to deprivations; and assuming that our twins behave themselves and therefore are not deprived of cookies, we should give them the same number of cookies. Were they not to receive the same number, the twin who receives fewer would rightly complain of favoritism toward the other twin. And if we further vary the case to deal with two children who are not identical but who have different intensities of appetite or one of whom conforms his conduct to the rule against taking cookies from the pantry whereas the other violates the rule, then we should be justified in treating them differently by giving one of them more cookies than we give the other. Notice, however, that if the difference between two children, other things being equal, is that one has brown and the other blue eyes, then no difference in the apportionment of cookies is warranted. Accordingly, the question arises, "What kind of difference is relevant to an application of the principle of formal justice?"

When relevant, a difference warrants dissimilar treatment. But there are different kinds of warrant; and before inquiring into relevance, I want to discuss some of these. Let us consider the distribution of some benefit with respect to two people, A and B, who desire it. The benefit may be an office, a status, an honor, a commodity, an opportunity, and so forth.

First, A may be eligible for a benefit, whereas B is not. To say that someone is eligible for a benefit is to say that he satisfies all preliminary necesssary conditions for receiving it. Thus, someone is eligible for the United States' presidency only if he is a natural-born citizen of the United States, is at least thirty-five years old, has resided in the country for at least fourteen years, and so forth. If A satisfies these conditions but B does not, then A is eligible to be president but B is not. Eligibility does not admit of degree: either one satisfies the relevant conditions or not. The conditions themselves are specified by institutional rules and procedures, in this instance by the United States Constitution and congressional legislation.

But to be eligible for a benefit is not necessarily to qualify for it. The person who satisfies all the preliminary conditions to be president may be corrupt or stupid or emotionally unstable, and so forth. Although his claim to office cannot be voided on these grounds, as it can be nullified by his failure to satisfy the aforementioned conditions, he plainly would be unqualified to hold the office if he were, say, stupid. An excellent example of someone's being eligible for an office for which he is unqualified is to be found in Shakespeare, *Macbeth,* IV. iii. 50-103, where Malcolm's self-condemnation of his lack of "the king-becoming graces" elicits Macduff's denunciation that Malcolm is not fit to live, much less to govern.

Even to be eligible and to qualify for some benefit is not necessarily to be entitled to it. Beyond the preliminary necessary conditions and the qualifying conditions of the presidency, for instance, the further conditions of receiving a majority of the electoral votes and of taking the oath of office must be satisfied. Entitlement, like eligibility, is determined by institutional rules and procedures. In some circumstances, entitlement can be legally determined by a court (for example, regarding contractual obligations); and in other circumstances, in which it cannot be so determined, we can appeal to specific social institutions (for example, promising or competition for prizes) that rest upon socially, but not legally, sanctioned demands that a particular sort of interest be guaranteed.

Someone who is eligible and qualified for something to which he is entitled may nevertheless not deserve it. To say that he deserves it is to introduce yet another consideration, that of worthiness, for example, natural capacity, moral merit, artistic excellence, and so forth. Thus, for A to deserve to be president and B not to deserve it is determined, other things being equal, by A's having and B's lacking certain virtues: amplitude of intellect, zeal for the interests of the state, capacity for moral discrimination and dispassion, talent for command, and so forth. The conditions for qualification differ from those for desert in that the former are only minimal.

Finally, there is what I shall call a *plenary right*, a valid claim that someone has to some benefit by virtue of being both entitled to and deserving of it. If he is denied the benefit in ordinary circumstances, then he has a legitimate ground for making a demand upon someone else to remove the impediment to his attaining or enjoying it. His demand may or may not succeed; but even if it does not, the plenary right is his. This right, of course, differs from a legal right, for the latter need not have anything to do with desert and the former may not be guaranteed by law. Thus, if a footrace, in which injury plays no part, is run fairly, then the rules of sport entitle the winner to the prize for which he and the other runners compete, and the fact that his speed alone determined the outcome makes him deserving of the prize: he has a plenary right to it. But someone who discovers oil beneath the land that he owns but bought without any notion whatever of there being oil beneath it has a legal right *in rem* to the oil, although there is no question of his deserving to have the oil or not.

These five concepts, namely, eligibility, qualification, entitlement, desert, and plenary right, fall into two groups, depending upon whether they are merely institutionally grounded or whether they depend partly upon some standard of value that is independent of the institutional grounding, if any. Since institutions may presuppose incorrect, improper, or unseemly standards, I shall ignore eligibility and entitlement, except insofar as they enter into decisions about qualification, desert, or plenary right.

We may now consider the notions of merit and the common good. First, merit. Some people contend that merit cannot be ascertained and that, accordingly, it cannot be adduced as a (good) reason for treating people differently. The contention strikes me as nonsensical.

A skill is a capacity to do well or proficiently something that is inherently technically difficult. Some actions exhibit skill and are, indeed, the exercise of a skill. Such actions are good of their kind. Thus, performing on the violin is a skill, and any individual performance that exhibits the skill is to that extent a good performance. Plainly, moreover, there are standards of proficiency for performances that exhibit skill; and the standards vary with the kind of action. Thus, we do not look for the same things in a good performance by a violinist as we look for in a good performance by a football player. Accurate pitch has nothing to do with playing football well, and passing a football accurately has nothing to do with playing the violin well. Given that we are considering someone merely as a violinist or merely as a football player, we know what sort of proficiency is relevant to his performance; and knowing what is a skillful performance in each activity, we can appraise the performer. This is so even though a skillful performance of Bach differs in some respects from one of Bruch, and a skillful performance by a quarterback differs in some respects from one by a halfback. And it is so whether the appraisal be an instance of grading, that is, evaluation merely with respect to an ideal, or of ranking, that is, comparative evaluation of one performer with another in the light of relevant standards. Each of these alternatives includes an instance of merit according to standards that are relevant to a worthwhile kind of action.

To be sure, there are skills not worth having and actions not worth performing even if one performs them well, for example, the skill of a confidence man that enables him to deceive and thereby to exploit his victim. Even skills that do not serve immorality may not be worth having, for example, the skill that enables someone to thread a needle with his tongue (although he can far more easily thread it with his hands). Having a skill is meritorious if, and only if, it characteristically serves some worthwhile objective.

Given, then, that merit can be ascertained by judging performances of a worthwhile kind of action according to standards inherent in the action, it follows that in principle some people have greater merit than others with respect to a particular kind of action. I shall not trouble the reader with an argument that purports to establish that some people *actually* have greater merit than others in a given respect. Rather, I simply remind him of the gap between Shakespeare and lesser poets, Bach and lesser composers, Gauss and lesser mathematicians, Cardozo and lesser jurists, and Pelé and lesser soccer players.

Now consider goods or benefits. They may be private or public: they may relate to a specific person(s) only, or they may concern any member of a given community without distinction. Green ink, for instance, is a private good for people who letter posters; and adequate (public) health facilities is a public good for the community at large. Mindful of the distinction between public and private goods, we shall find it useful also to speak of the *common interest* as the net interest of a large and unspecifiable group in contradistinction to an opposing *special interest* of some significantly smaller group or some specific person. The good with respect to the common interest is the common good.

Merit and common good, I suggest, are two things that are relevant to different treatment.

Let us now contemplate some discriminative universes. (To discriminate is to perceive and to appraise differences between things. It has nothing to do with acting on the basis of prejudice.) Each is discriminative by virtue of having some of its members treated differently—whether justly or not—with respect to the distribution of some benefit because they are thought to differ in some relevant respect.

Discriminative Universe 1. This universe consists of a major symphony orchestra, its conductor, its audience of music lovers, and three candidates for the post of concertmaster. Candidate A is not a technically proficient enough violinist for the orchestra's repertory; candidate B is technically proficient enough for it, but not proficient enough to distinguish himself when called upon for solo performance (as in Rimsky-Korsakov's *Scheherezade*), and he also lacks a sense of ensemble playing; and candidate C is a superb soloist who has an excellent sense of ensemble playing. Otherwise, they do not differ. The orchestra and its conductor choose C. They reject candidate A because he is unqualified; he does not meet the minimal requirements for holding the post. They reject candidate B because, although he meets the minimal requirements, he lacks the artistic excellence of candidate C. And they choose candidate C because his (relevant) superiority merits the post. They do justice by proportioning the value of his fate, insofar as they determine it, to the excellence of his skill. The benefit that they award is due him. And given that candidate C is entitled to the post by the authority of the orchestra and its conductor, C has a plenary right to be concertmaster.

Discriminative Universe 2. Let us modify Discriminative Universe 1 by supposing that the candidates are seen only after they somehow have been auditioned unseen and that C is a member of some visually discernible minority against which the orchestra and its conductor are prejudiced, although their prejudice would not affect the quality of their performance were they to choose C. Their bias, however, causes them to reject him and to choose B, knowing full well that C is superior to B in all relevant respects. B is entitled to the post by the authority of the orchestra and its conductor even though he does not deserve it; and although C does deserve it, he is not entitled to it.

Notice, moreover, that the same result would obtain if prejudice *for* B rather than *against* C were to cause the former to be chosen.

In Discriminative Universe 2, we can distinguish several disvalues to which either prejudicial choice gives rise: there is the intrinsic injustice of not giving C his due; there is the comparative injustice of giving B what is due C; there is the contributive disvalue of making the orchestra's performances less good aesthetically than they would alternatively be; there is the instrumental disvalue of frustrating the other musicians; and there is the instrumental disvalue of displeasing the audience. In Discriminative Universe 2, even apart from the intrinsic injustice to C, the distribution has unfortunate consequences. Concern for the common good and concern for giving C his due both militate against the choice.

Discriminative Universe 3. Let us modify Discriminative Universe 2 by supposing that the audience, in its nonmusical activities, have prejudicially discriminated against members of the visually discernible minority of which B is a member and against B himself, although neither the orchestra nor its conductor has prejudicially discriminated against either. Plainly, the concertmaster post is due C; and since the prejudicial conduct against B was nonmusical, he cannot reliably claim that his musical inferiority to C was caused by that conduct.

Discriminative Universe 4. Let us modify Discriminative Universe 3 by supposing that the orchestra, as constituted, and its conductor have prejudicially discriminated against members of the visually discernible minority of which B is a member, but not against B or anyone personally known to him. The latter alternative is included because it is not unreasonable to believe that B's knowledge of such an injustice would impair his audition performance. The concertmaster post still is due C. Neither B himself nor anyone personally known to him was ever prejudicially discriminated against by either the orchestra or its conductor, and they therefore do not now owe him anything other than a fair audition.

Discrimination Universe 5. Let us modify Discriminative Universes 3 and 4 by supposing that the orchestra and its conductor have prejudicially discriminated against all members of B's visually discernible minority, except B, and that the audience has prejudicially discriminated against all the members of that minority, including B, both musically and nonmusically. In this universe, it is not unlikely that B has not had an opportunity equal to C's to attain equal proficiency at the violin, even if equally endowed with musical talent.

An opportunity is a state in which someone may choose whether or not to perfom some effortful act(s) that he considers desirable in themselves or a means to something desirable in itself. Equality of opportunity consists in equally good opportunities being open to all without unfair discrimination, *insofar as such opportunities can reasonably be provided.* This qualifying clause calls attention to a common but misguided tendency to think of equality of opportunity as requiring the same opportunity to be provided to all, which is an unrealizable and therefore an unreasonable demand.

To be born to different parents is to be born with different genetic endowment, to live in a different place, and therefore to have different experiences. Candidate A, for instance, may have been born with a lesser genetic endowment than candidate C; or, having an equal genetic endowment, A may have had the misfortune to be born to parents who had no music in their souls, or the misfortune to live where there is no first-rate music school, and so forth. Nature does not act; and injustice can be ascribed only to (human) action, to allocations or states of affairs that are deliberately determined by people. When we speak of nature's "distributing" or "allocating" things, we talk metaphorically. Mindful of this, we should recognize, further, that nature is spontaneously idiosyncratic in distributing genetic benefits and disadvantages (and much else); and although the result may be undesirable, it cannot meaningfully be said (literally) to be unjust, even though nature may (metaphorically) be said to prejudice the outcome of human effort. Accordingly, we should distinguish what is the outcome merely of human effort from what is the outcome of human design. Whereas the former can be lucky or unlucky, the latter can be just or unjust.

People, moreover, can be correctly charged with injustice, rather than ignorance or stupidity, only with respect to such consequences of their action as they can reasonably be expected to foresee. Intelligent attempts to redress injustice are commendable but should not be confused with efforts to secure a just "distribution" in the natural order, which efforts cannot aim at redressing *injustice*, since nature's distribution is not the product of human design. Rather, they aim at controlling chance, which, being independent of human design, cannot be controlled. Necessarily failing to "equalize" nature, those who have this unrestrained passion for equality direct their coercive power against the people whom they regard as privileged and in behalf of the people whom they regard as disadvantaged. And in doing this, they turn from a social system that is predicated upon belief in the desirability of restraining government from infringing upon individual effort to a social system that is predicated upon belief that the government should limit and direct people's behavior in whatever sphere of action allegedly needs to be controlled to produce the equality that nature does not grant. Theirs is the way to totalitarian government. An interesting example of an infringement that moves in this direction is *Guidelines for Creating Positive Sexual and Racial Images in Educational Materials* (New York: Macmillan, 1975); see my "Petty Despotism: Macmillan Publishing Company on Sex and Race," *The Occasional Review* 4 (Winter 1976).

Whether or not one agrees with what I have just written, there remains the moral claim implicit in the description of Discriminative Universe 5, which is a model of our actual society. Surely past injustice in the United States includes systematic prejudicial discrimination against members of various racial, religious, and ethnic groups and against women, so that disproportionately many members of these groups were denied the opportunity to develop their talents. People who were prejudicially preferred to them received benefits that they (the preferred) did not deserve. By this initial treatment and by similar treatment subsequently, it is alleged, descendants of the original victims of bias and descendants of the original beneficiaries of bias have had unequal opportunities to attain the qualifications and merit by which one now deserves the benefits for which they now compete. Accordingly, runs the argument, the descendants of bias victims should now be prejudicially preferred to the descendants of bias beneficiaries so as to provide compensation for past injustice. This practice is called *reverse discrimination* and its (alleged) justification is called *compensatory justice.* Advocates of compensatory justice apparently believe that it is a *moral right* of the victim's, in the sense that, all things considered (that is, whether or not he is entitled to or deserving of the benefit), he *ought* to receive it.

The defense of the position has been argued with admirable clarity by Taylor.* He believes that institutionalized compensation is owed to groups whose members have formerly been prejudicially discriminated against by society. He contends that (1) the fact that a morally irrelevant characteristic C has been the basis for discriminating against members of a group G at time t_1 entails (2) that C has been *made* a morally relevant characteristic at t_2 with respect to the principle of compensatory justice, and that (2) entails (3) that some form of reverse discrimination is required at t_2, aimed at correcting an injustice perpetrated at t_1 by a social practice of discriminating against C-persons because they were C. This aim entails (4) that the reverse discrimination be directed toward the class of C-persons as such. Taylor adds (5) that the obligation to compensate for the past injustice does not fall upon any particular individual but upon society as a whole, which is obliged to establish a social practice of reverse discrimination in favor of C-persons, and (6) that this practice should be consistent with all other principles of justice that may apply to the action-types that are involved in carrying it out.

To simplify matters, let us consider two groups, G and H, that were prejudicially discriminated against and for, respectively, with respect to a particular characteristic, C.

My first objection to Taylor's system (and to similar systems) is that its conditions are not mutually consistent. Consider a paradigm of compensatory reverse discrimination: the practice of hiring members of G by virtue of their being C, as Taylor would advocate. But, also, according to Taylor, the obligation to compensate for past injustice should not fall upon any particular person(s), but upon society as a whole. In the paradigm, however, the compensation is paid only by those non-C persons who are discriminated against by the favoritism to a C person. No non-C person who does not apply for the position given to the C person pays any compensation. Accordingly, the burden of compensation falls unequally upon non-C persons.

This defect, moreover, is not limited to the paradigm. All affirmative-action programs suffer from an identical limitation with respect to *who* makes compensation. In no instance, does *everyone* in society (that is, every non-C person) contribute a "fair share" to the total cost of the compensatory policy. Rather, in every instance, particular persons pay a share and others

* P. W. Taylor, "Reverse Discrimination and Compensatory Justice," *Analysis* 33, no. 6 (1973), pp. 296-302 herin.

pay nothing, which makes the share an unfair payment. This defect is a necessary feature of Taylor's justification, for no set of circumstances finds every non-C member of society applying for what some C person gets by an act of reverse discrimination.

Second, why should not *anyone* who was prejudicially discriminated against receive prejudicially preferential treatment now, including members of H? "Equally a victim in the past, then equally a beneficiary now" seems to be what the principle of formal justice requires here. But if it does, then an H who in particular was prejudicially discriminated against, although H's in general were improperly favored, deserves so-called compensatory justice. And the difficulty here is that if we agree to this—and the principle of formal justice supports it—then Taylor's system commits us to something morally unacceptable, namely, the denial of preferential treatment to someone who deserves to receive it.

Of course, Taylor does not explicitly deny that the H deserves to receive it; he focuses upon groups rather than individuals. But, in fact, it is only some persons who benefit from the policy. And it does not follow logically that if some group members are justly compensated, then the group is justly compensated, for the benefit is conferred only upon those who apply for it.

Third, justice requires that dissimilar cases be treated differently in direct proportion to the relevant differences between them. Accordingly, whoever benefited from prejudice is now to lose by it proportionately, that is, to make compensation for his earlier illegitimate gain. But how he gained is an important consideration that Taylor seems to overlook. Surely there is something immoral in punishing someone for something that happens to him in contradistinction to something that he does. Suppose that an H who indirectly benefited from the bias of some past H has himself been a just and good person. The benefit that he enjoyed, for example, better schooling than that offered to an equivalent G, is not something that he could have avoided. He was lucky in being born an H and in being raised by H's, rather than a G who was raised by G's, which is a matter of nature, not human design. All that it would be moral to ask him to do with his good fortune (when he recognizes it) is that he undertake to gain from it only if he thereby also aims at improving the condition of those who have not been favored. But it is morally absurd to penalize him for an evil that he could not have prevented.

If Taylor replies that his position requires that the obligation to provide benefits to the formerly victimized group falls on society in general, not on particular people, my rejoinder is that since the benefits to G's are provided artificially, they must arise from artificially induced disadvantages or deprivations to H's. If someone is to get more than his (equal) share of something, then someone else must get less than his (equal) share of it.

Taylor also may reply that an H who would be hired if there were no reverse discrimination is not being unjustly discriminated against even if adversely affected, since the rules of the practice do not aim at discriminating against anyone.* This reply strikes me as an appeal to the principle of double effect: when someone produces a morally forbidden effect, X, that he rightly foresees to be the inevitable, although undesired and unintended, consequence of some morally permissible (or morally desirable) act, Y, the evil of X is not morally imputable to him, because he aimed at doing Y but did not will X.

There are two objections to this position. First, its proponent needs to justify his contention that there is a conceptual difference between someone's intending to do something and his bringing it about as a rightly foreseen inevitable consequence of his doing something else, which he does intend to do. And second, insofar as preferential hiring is concerned, prejudicially discriminating in favor of a G vis-à-vis an H is not to deny the job to the H *as a consequence of favoring* the G, but to deny it to him in favoring the G. The prejudicial award and the prejudicial denial are correlative aspects of one act. The prejudicial discrimination is a comparative judgment about the two people. Accordingly, the principle of double effect, even if morally defensible, simply does not apply to preferential hiring.

I leave Taylor's defense of reverse discrimination and compensatory justice, and consider a related matter. Justice, it is agreed, requires that dissimilar cases be treated differently in direct proportion to the relevant differences between them. But under actual affirmative-action programs, the preferential hiring is permitted to occur partly according to principles of the free economic market, that is, spontaneous ordering that is determined by individual purposes rather than by organized pursuit of a specific predetermined goal. Accordingly, the actual practice of preferential hiring does not compensate G's in proportion to their (alleged) desert, which presumably is computed in terms of the severity of the harm that past bias has done them. Although the principle of reverse discrimination requires that compensation be proportional to past harm, preferential hiring introduces additional injustice by giving some G's more and some less compensation than they (allegedly) deserve. The G who has been most incapacitated by past bias is virtually

---

* P. W. Taylor, in a private communication with the author.

certain to be awarded an inferior job to that given a G who has been less incapacitated by past bias. There are two rules of reverse discrimination: that those who were prejudicially discriminated against are now to be prejudicially favored, and that the benefits awarded them be proportional to the harms previously done them. The actual practice of preferential hiring violates the second rule. Hence, the practice would be an improper means to effect compensatory justice, even if the latter were otherwise defensible.

The guidelines of the Department of Health, Education, and Welfare are all the more absurd because, having stated its intention to compensate groups for past injurious bias, HEW then prejudicially discriminates the groups that are to receive this benefit, ignoring Jews and Chinese, for instance. Moreover, in the domains in which it meddles, HEW uses mere statistical parity to general population ratios as a test of bias, although the lack of such parity is not even prima facie evidence of bias until qualification or merit, historical or cultural interest, age, marital status, family role, and so forth are examined.

There is an even greater evil in reverse discrimination than its inherent injustice. Earlier in this paper, I wrote of the common interest and the common good. The reverse discrimination of HEW's affirmative-action programs is an innovation that it imposed upon institutions of various kinds. Among these are institutions of higher learning, professional schools, and the professions themselves. Reverse discrimination applied to these not only generates (alleged) compensatory justice, but changes the institutions. The change, however, is inimical to the common interest.

Consider professional schools. Under governmental and group pressures, some law schools have admitted unqualified G students, that is, students who could not reasonably have been judged capable of adequately completing the work for a degree, when judged by the current standards. When a disproportionately high ratio of G students subsequently failed to qualify for their degree, that fact alone was said to establish continued prejudice by the schools or the continued effects of their past prejudice. Accordingly, degree requirements were eased for some of the G students. But then a disproportionately high ratio of these students failed the state bar examination. Again the charge of prejudice was raised. There the matter rests. But suppose that the requirements for admission to the bar are eased for some of these students. Subsequently, they will lose a disproportionately high ratio of cases, charge prejudices, and demand that courts prejudice themselves in favor of G lawyers. Now, any policy that allegedly aims at promoting justice in society, but that has this consequence, is incoherent.

More than that, however, it conflicts with the common good by decreasing the adequacy of the legal services that are in the interest of all.

The same difficulty arises with any other institution that is similarly predicated upon merit and similarly connected with the common good. A professor at the Harvard Medical School recently charged that academic standards in the nation's medical schools have fallen in consequence of the increased enrollment of minority students*. Were the result not so unpleasant to contemplate, one might amuse himself with the *reductio ad absurdum* that when a disproportionately high ratio of G doctors' patients fail to recover or they die, that result establishes that nature is prejudiced.

In instances in which the possibility of merit (capacity to perform well, good performance itself, and so forth) inheres in an activity or in which non-meritorious or a fortiori incompetent performance is detrimental to the common interest, attempts to promote reverse discrimination are immoral. *Fiat* (compensatory) *justitia, ruat coelum* is an extremely foolish maxim. Compensatory justice, if desirable, is not the only value; and to sacrifice to it such important values as respect for excellence and the professional competence necessary to certain institutions if they are to promote the common good, is very shortsighted indeed. There certainly is no moral right to reverse discrimination that aims at compensatory justice, for in these instances the policy is immoral.

Confusion about its morality derives, I think, chiefly from two sources. First, strongly motivated people often decide empirical matters on a priori grounds. Thus, it is not known whether the self-esteem of G people in general will be enhanced if some of them have unmerited benefits conferred upon them, or whether their self-esteem will thereby be further damaged by their coming to believe that they are not good enough to merit the benefits. But both those who commend and those who condemn reverse discrimination adduce the "appropriate" answer (that is, that it will be enhanced, or that it will be damaged) as evidence for the soundness of their appraisal. But neither the proponents nor the opponents know.

Second, confusion about the morality of reverse discrimination derives from failure to distinguish the categories that I differentiated earlier in this paper: eligibility, qualification, entitlement, desert, plenary right, and moral right. If one fails to distinguish them, the ambiguities of ordinary usage lead to confusions such as the following. In common usage, to say that someone is entitled to something may mean that he is eligible for it, that he is qualified

* *The New York Times*, May 13, 1976, p. 14.

for it, that he has a legal right to it, that he deserves it, that he has a plenary right to it, or that he has a moral right to it. Accordingly, it is easy to fall into errors that depend upon confusing the categories, and easy also deliberately to generate the errors. When "X is entitled to benefit B" means merely that some legal directive enjoins us to provide the benefit to X, it is a serious error to believe that the statement means that X has a moral right to the benefit. This kind of confusion, however, is rife.

I conclude by emphasizing that institutions whose activities are inherently meritarian and that impinge upon the common interest, for weal or woe, should be kept free of reverse discrimination. I have no recipe for redressing the wrongs of a remote past, if indeed we should try to redress them; but I do have a last thought to offer those who are passionately persuaded that we should and who support reverse discrimination as the means by which to do it. The French historian, Renan, declared (in 1882) that racial theory was "a very great fallacy whose dominance would ruin European civilization . . . According to this theory the Germans have the right to take back the scattered members of the German family, even if these members [do not wish it]. Thus one creates a primordial right analogous to that of the divine right of Kings. . . . Will the Germans, who have raised the banner of ethnography so high, not see one day the Slavs [follow their example and reclaim the lands] of their ancestors? It is good for all of us to know how to forget."* My thought is that Renan's conclusion applies to the kinds of institutions that I have been discussing.

* Quoted, as bracketed, by Hans Kohn in "Nationalism," *International Encyclopedia of the Social Sciences*, ed. David L. Sills (New York: Macmillan Co., 1968), II.

Lisa H. Newton

Reverse Discrimination
as Unjustified

I have heard it argued that "simple justice" requires that we favor women
and blacks in employment and educational opportunities, since women and
blacks were "unjustly" excluded from such opportunities for so many years
in the not so distant past. It is a strange argument, an example of a possible
implication of a true proposition advanced to dispute the proposition itself,
like an octopus absent-mindedly slicing off his head with a stray tentacle. A
fatal confusion underlies this argument, a confusion fundamentally relevant
to our understanding of the notion of the rule of law.

Two senses of justice and equality are involved in this confusion. The
root notion of justice, progenitor of the other, is the one that Aristotle (*Nich.
Ethics* 5.6; *Politics* 1.2; 3.1.) assumes to be the foundation and proper virtue
of the political association. It is the condition which free men establish
among themselves when they "share a common life in order that their association bring them self-sufficiency"—the regulation of their relationship by
law, and the establishment, by law, of equality before the law. Rule of law is
the name and pattern of this justice; its equality stands against the inequali-

Source: Ethics *83, no. 4 (July 1973). Reprinted by permission of the author and the U.
of Chicago Press.*

ties—of wealth, talent, and so forth, otherwise obtaining among its participants, who by virtue of that equality are called "citizens." It is an achievement—complete, or, more frequently, partial—of certain people in certain concrete situations. It is fragile and easily disrupted by powerful individuals who discover that the blind equality of rule of law is inconvenient for their interests. Despite its obvious instability, Aristotle assumes that the establishment of justice in this sense, the creation of citizenship, was a permanent possibility for men and that the resultant association of citizens was the natural home of the species. At levels below the political association, this rule-governed equality is easily found; it is exemplified by any group of children agreeing together to play a game. At the level of the political association, the attainment of this justice is more difficult, simply because the stakes are so much higher for each participant. The equality of citizenship is not something that happens of its own accord, and without the expenditure of a fair amount of effort it will collapse into the rule of a powerful few over an apathetic many. But at least it has been achieved, at some times in some places; it is always worth trying to achieve, and eminently worth trying to maintain, wherever and to whatever degree it has been brought into being.

Aristotle's parochialism is notorious; he really did not imagine that persons other than Greeks could associate freely in justice, and the only form of association he had in mind was the Greek *polis*. With the decline of the *polis* and the shift in the center of political thought, his notion of justice underwent a sea change. To be exact, it ceased to represent a political type and became a moral ideal: the ideal of equality as we know it. This ideal demands that all men be included in citizenship—that one Law govern all equally, that all men regard all other men as fellow citizens, with the same guarantees, rights, and protections. Briefly, it demands that the circle of citizenship achieved by any group be extended to include the entire human race. Properly understood, its effect on our associations can be excellent: it congratulates us on our achievements of the rule of law as a process of government but refuses to let us remain complacent until we have expanded the associations to include others within the ambit of the rules, as often and as far as possible. While one man is a slave, none of us may feel truly free. We are constantly prodded by this ideal to look for possible unjustifiable discrimination, for inequalities not absolutely required for the functioning of the society and advantageous to all. And after twenty centuries of pressure, not at all constant, from this ideal, it might be said that some progress has been made. To take the cases in point for this problem, we are now prepared to assert, as Aristotle would never have been, the equality of sexes and of persons of different colors. The ambit of

American citizenship, once restricted to white males of property, has been extended to include all adult free men, then all adult males including ex-slaves, then all women. The process of acquisition of full citizenship was for these groups a sporadic trial of half-measures, even now not complete; the steps on the road to full equality are marked by legislation and judicial decisions which are only recently concluded and still often not enforced. But the fact that we can now discuss the possibility of favoring such groups in hiring shows that over the area that concerns us, at least, full equality is presupposed as a basis for discussion. To that extent, they are full citizens, fully protected by the law of the land.

It is important for my argument that the moral ideal of equality be recognized as logically distinct from that condition (or virtue) of justice in the political sense. Justice in this sense exists *among* a citizenry, irrespective of the number of the populace included in that citizenry. Further, the moral ideal is parasitic upon the political virtue, for "equality" is unspecified—it means nothing until we are told in what respect that equality is to be realized. In a political context, *equality* is specified as "equal rights"—equal access to the public realm, public goods and offices, equal treatment under the law— in brief, the equality of citizenship. If citizenship is not a possibility, political equality is unintelligible. The ideal emerges as a generalization of the real condition and refers back to that condition for its content.

Now, if justice (Aristotle's justice in the political sense) is equal treatment under law for all citizens, what is injustice? Clearly, injustice is the violation of that equality, discriminating for or against a group of citizens, favoring them with special immunities and privileges or depriving them of those guaranteed to the others. When the southern employer refuses to hire blacks in white-collar jobs, when Wall Street will hire women only as secretaries with new titles, when Mississippi high schools routinely flunk all black boys above ninth grade, we have examples of injustice, and we work to restore the equality of the public realm by ensuring that equal opportunity will be provided in such cases in the future. But of course, when the employers and the schools *favor* women and blacks, the same injustice is done. Just as the previous discrimination did, this reverse discrimination violates the public equality which defines citizenship and destroys the rule of law for the areas in which these favors are granted. To the extent that we adopt a program of discrimination, reverse or otherwise, justice in the political sense is destroyed, and none of us, specifically affected or not, is a citizen, a bearer of rights—we are all petitioners for favors. And to the same extent, the ideal of equality is undermined, for it has content only where justice obtains, and by destroying justice we render the ideal meaningless. It is, then, an ironic paradox, if not a contradiction in terms, to assert that the ideal of equality justifies the violation of justice; it is as if one should argue, with William Buckley, that an ideal of humanity can justify the destruction of the human race.

Logically, the conclusion is simple enough: all discrimination is wrong prima facie because it violates justice, and that goes for reverse discrimination too. No violation of justice among the citizens may be justified (may overcome the prima facie objection) by appeal to the ideal of equality, for that ideal is logically dependent upon the notion of justice. Reverse discrimination, then, which attempts no other justification than an appeal to equality, is wrong. But let us try to make the conclusion more plausible by suggesting some of the implications of the suggested practice of reverse discrimination in employment and education. My argument will be that the problems raised there are insoluble, not only in practice but in principle.

We may argue, if we like, about what "discrimination" consists of. Do I discriminate against blacks if I admit none to my school when none of the black applicants are qualified by the tests I always give? How far must I go to root our cultural bias from my application forms and tests before I can say that I have not discriminated against those of different cultures? Can I assume that women are not strong enough to be roughnecks on my oil rigs, or must I test them individually? But this controversy, the most popular and well-argued aspect of the issue, is not as fatal as two others which cannot be avoided: if we are regarding the blacks as a "minority" victimized by discrimination, what is a "minority"? And for any group—blacks, women, whatever—that has been discriminated against, what amount of reverse discrimination wipes out the initial discrimination? Let us grant as true that women and blacks were discriminated against, even where laws forbade such discrimination, and grant for the sake of argument that a history of discrimination must be wiped out by reverse discrimination. What follows?

First, are there other groups which have been discriminated against? For they should have the same right of restitution. What about American Indians, Chicanos, Appalachian whites, Puerto Ricans, Jews, Cajuns, and Orientals? And if these are to be included, the principle according to which we specify a "minority" is simply the criterion of "ethnic (sub) group," and we're stuck with every hyphenated American in the lower-middle class clamoring for special privileges for *his* group—and with equal justification. For be it noted, when we run down the Harvard roster, we find not only a scarcity of blacks (in comparison with the proportion in the population) but an even more striking scarcity of those second-, third-, and fourth-generation ethnics who make up the loudest voice of Middle America. Shouldn't they demand *their* share? And eventually, the WASPs will have to form their own lobby, for they too are a minority. The point is simply this: there is no "majority" in America who will not mind giving up just a bit of their rights to make room for a favored minority. There are only other minorities, each of which is discriminated against by the favoring. The initial injustice is then repeated dozens of times, and if each minority is granted the same right of restitution as the others, an entire area of rule governance is dissolved into a pushing and shoving match between self-interested groups. Each works to catch the public eye and political popularity by whatever means of advertising and power politics lend themselves to the effort, to capitalize as much as possible on temporary popularity until the restless mob picks another group to feel sorry for. Hardly an edifying spectacle, and in the long run no one can benefit: the pie is no larger—it's just that instead of setting up and enforcing rules for getting a piece, we've turned the contest into a free-for-all, requiring much more effort for no larger a reward. It would be in the interests of all the participants to reestablish an objective rule to govern the process, carefully enforced and the same for all.

Second, supposing that we do manage to agree in general that women and blacks (and all the others) have some right of restitution, some right to a privileged place in the structure of opportunities for a while, how will we know when that while is up? How much privilege is enough? When will the guilt be gone, the price paid, the balance restored? What recompense is right for centuries of exclusion? What criterion tells us when we are done? Our experience with the civil-rights movement shows us that agreement on these terms cannot be presupposed: a process that appears to some to be going at a mad gallop into a black takeover appears to the rest of us to be at a standstill. Should a practice of reverse discrimination be adopted, we may safely predict that just as some of us begin to see "a satisfactory start toward righting the balance," others of us will see that we "have already gone too far in the other direction" and will suggest that the discrimination ought to be reversed again. And such disagreement is inevitable, for the point is that we could not *possibly* have any criteria for evaluating the kind of recompense we have in mind. The context presumed by any discussion of restitution is the context of rule of law. Law sets the rights of men and simultaneously sets the method for remedying the violation of those rights. You may exact suffering from others and/or damage payments for yourself if and only if the others have violated your rights; the suffering you have endured is not sufficient reason for them to suffer. And remedial rights exist only where there is law: primary human rights are useful guides to legislation but cannot stand as reasons for awarding remedies for injuries sustained. But then, the context presupposed by a discussion of restitution is the context of preexistent full citizenship. No remedial rights could exist for the excluded; neither in law nor in logic does there exist a right to *sue* for a standing to sue.

From these two considerations, then, the difficulties with reverse discrimination became evident. Restitution for a disadvantaged group whose rights under the law have been violated is possible by legal means, but restitution for a disadvantaged group whose grievance is that there was no law to protect them simply is not. First, outside of the area of justice defined by the law, no sense can be made of "the group's rights," for no law recognizes that group or the individuals in it, qua members, as bearers of rights (hence *any* group can constitute itself as a disadvantaged minority in some sense and demand similar restitution). Second, outside of the area of protection of law, no sense can be made of the violation of rights (hence the amount of the recompense cannot be decided by any objective criterion). For both reasons, the practice of reverse discrimination undermines the foundation of the very ideal in whose name it is advocated; it destroys justice, law, equality, and citizenship itself, and replaces them with power struggles and popularity contests.

Barry R. Gross

Is Turn About Fair Play?

Men born to freedom are naturally alert to repel invasion of liberty by evil-minded rulers. The greatest danger to liberty lurks in insidious encroachment by the men of zeal, well-meaning but without understanding.——Louis D. Brandeis

No rule on the subject recommends itself so strongly to the primitive and spontaneous sentiment of justice as the *lex talionis,* an eye for an eye and a tooth for a tooth. Though this principle of the Jewish and Mohammedan law has been generally abandoned in Europe as a practical maxim, there is, I suspect, in most minds, a secret hankering after it; and when retribution accidentally falls on an offender in that precise shape, the general feeling of satisfaction evidenced bears witness how natural is the sentiment to which its repayment in kind is acceptable.——John Stuart Mill

The balance of argument weighs against reverse discrimination for four interrelated sets of reasons. First, the procedures designed to isolate the discriminated are flawed. Second, the practice has undesirable and dangerous consequences. Third, it fails to fit any of the models of compensation or reparations. Fourth, it falls unjustly upon both those it favors and those it disfavors. I conclude that if to eliminate discrimination against the members

Source: Journal of Critical Analysis *5, no. 4 (Jan./April 1975). Reprinted by permission of the publisher.*

of one group we find ourselves discriminating against another, we have gone too far.

Sociologically, groups are simply not represented in various jobs and at various levels in percentages closely approximately their percentage of the population. When universities in general and medical schools in particular discriminated heavily against them, Jews were represented in the medical profession in far greater percentages than their percentage of the population. At the same time, they were represented in far lower percentages in banking, finance, construction, and engineering than their percentage in the population, especially the population of New York City. A similar analysis by crudely drawn group traits—Jew, Roman Catholic, WASP, Irish, and so forth— of almost any trade, business or profession would yield similar results.

But the argument from population percentages may be meant not as an analysis of what is the case, but as an analysis of what ought to be the case. A proponent might put it this way: It is true that groups are not usually represented in the work force by their percentage in the population at large, but minority C has been systematically excluded from the good places. Therefore, in order to make sure that they get some of them, we should now systematically include them in the good places, and a clear way of doing it is by their percentage in the population. Or we might conclude instead: therefore, in order to make up for past exclusion, they should be included in the good places as reparation, and an easy way to do it is by their percentage in the population.

If the definition of a minority discriminated against is ipso facto their representation in certain jobs in percentages less than their percentage in the general population, then one has to remark that the reasoning is circular. For we are trying to prove: (1) that minority C is discriminated against.

We use as a premise (3) that minority C is underrepresented in good jobs. Since (1) does not follow from (3) (mere underrepresentation not being even prima facie evidence of discrimination), it is necessary to insert (2) that their underrepresentation is due to discrimination. But this completes the circle.

A critic might reply that we know perfectly well what is meant. The groups discriminated against are blacks, Puerto Ricans, Mexican-Americans, American Indians, and women. He is correct, though his answer does not tell us *how to find out* who is discriminated against. This critic, for example, left out Jews and Orientals. If he should reply that Jews and Orientals do well enough, we point out that the question was not "Who fails to do well?" but rather, "Who is discriminated against?" This argument shows that the mechanisms for identifying the victims of discrimination and for remedying it are seriously deficient.

Even if we allow that the percentage of the group in the work force versus its percentage in the population is the criterion of discrimination, who is discriminated against will vary depending upon how we divide the groups. We may discover that Republicans are discriminated against by our literary or intellectual journals—*New York Review, Dissent, Commentary.* We may also discover that wealthy Boston residents are discriminated against by the Los Angeles Dodgers, that women are discriminated against by the Army, and that idiots (we hope) are discriminated against by universities.

What employment or profession a person chooses depends upon a number of variables—background, wealth, parents' employment, schooling, intelligence, drive, ambition, skill, and not least, luck. Moreover, the analysis will differ depending upon what group identification or stratification you choose. None seems to have priority over the others. Every person can be typed according to many of these classifications. It seems, therefore, that the relevant analysis cannot even be made, much less justified.

In addition, some proponents of the population-percentage argument seem to hold: (4) From the contingent fact that members of the group C were discriminated against, it follows necessarily that they are underrepresented in the good positions. They then go on to assert (5) if members of group C were not discriminated against they would not be underrepresented, or (6) if they are underrepresented, then they are discriminated against.

But clearly (4) is itself a contingent, not a necessary truth. Clearly also neither (5) nor (6) follows from it, (5) being the fallacy of denying the antecedent and (6) the fallacy of affirming the consequent. Lastly, neither (5) nor (6) is necessarily true. The members of a group might simply lack interest in certain jobs (for example, Italians in the public-school system are in short supply). Could one argue that, even though neither (4), (5), nor (6) is *necessarily* true, the mere fact of underrepresentation in certain occupations does provide evidence of discrimination? The answer is no—no more than the fact of "overrepresentation" in certain occupations is evidence of favoritism.

At most, underrepresentation can be used to support the contention of discrimination when there is *other* evidence as well.

FAIR PLAY: OUGHT WE TO DISCRIMINATE IN REVERSE?

There are at least three difficulties with reverse discrimination: first, it is inconsistent; second, it licenses discrimination; third, it is unfair.

If we believe the principle that equal opportunity is a right of everyone, then if members of group C are excluded from enjoying certain opportunities merely because they are members of group C, their right is being abrogated. They are entitled to this right, but so is everybody else, even those persons who presently deny it to them. If both are made to enjoy equal opportunity, then both are enjoying their right. To give either oppressors or oppressed more than equal opportunity is equally to deny the rights of one or the other in violation of the principle of equal opportunity.

Proponents of reverse discrimination seem to be caught on the horns of a dilemma: either discrimination is illegitimate or it is not. If it is illegitimate, then it ought not to be practiced against anyone. If it is not, then there exists no reason for *now* favoring blacks, Puerto Ricans, Chicanos, Indians, women, and so forth over whites.

Two strategies present themselves. Either we can analyze one disjunct with a view to showing that distinctions can be made which require compensation or reparations in the form of reverse discrimination to be made to wronged individuals or groups; or we can try to soften one of the disjuncts so as to make a case for exceptions in favor of the wronged. The first appeals both to our reason and our sense of justice. The second appeals to our emotions. I shall argue that neither strategy works.[1]

Now reverse discrimination can take several forms, but I think that what many of its proponents have in mind is a strong form of compensation—a form which requires us to discriminate against non-C members and favor C members even if less qualified. One may well wonder whether there is not a little retribution hidden in this form of compensation.

THE "SOFTENED" GENERAL PRINCIPLE

The argument for construing reverse discrimination as compensation or reparation has a great appeal which can be brought out by contrasting it with another approach. One might agree that as a general rule reverse discrimination is illegitimate but that it need not be seen as universally illegitimate. In particular, in the case where people have been so heavily discriminated against as to make it impossible for them now to gain a good life, there is no possibility of their having a fair chance, no possibility of their starting out on anything like equal terms, then and only then is it legitimate to discriminate in their favor and hence against anyone else.

Against this "softened" general principle I shall urge two sorts of objections which I call respectively "practical" and "pragmatic." Against the reparations type of argument, I shall urge first that there is some reason to think the conditions for exacting and accepting them are lacking, and second that, owing to the peculiar nature of the reparations to be exacted (reverse discrimination), the very exaction of them is unreasonable and unfair to both parties—exactors and exactees.

I mention briefly two sorts of practical objections to the "softened" general principle. First, it is simply the case that when discrimination is made in favor of someone regardless of his qualifications, there is the greatest possible danger that the person getting the position will not be competent to fill it. Second, when a person is placed in a position because of discrimination in his favor, he may come to feel himself inferior.[2] This may easily lead to the permanent conferral of inferior status on the group, an inferiority which is all the stronger because self-induced. Its psychological effects should not be underestimated.

The pragmatic objection to the "softened" general principle is much stronger. Discrimination in any form is invidious. Once licensed, its licenses rebound upon its perpetrators as well as others. Principles tend to be generalized without consideration of restrictions or the circumstances to which they were intended to apply. Students of the Nazi movement will have noticed that in licensing the discrimination, isolation, persecution, and "final solution" of the Jews, the Nazis (foreign and German) licensed their own. (Hitler's plans for extermination included political groups, for example, the Rohm faction of the SA, as well as other racial groups, for example, Slavs and Balts who fought on the German side.) It is necessary to be quite careful what principles one adopts. In view of the long and bloody history of discrimination, one ought to be very chary of sanctioning it.

COMPENSATION, REPARATIONS, AND RESTITUTION

Because it escapes most of these objections, the reparations argument becomes very attractive. What is more obvious than the principle that people ought to be compensated for monetary loss, pain and suffering inflicted by others acting either as agents of government or as individuals? From the negligence suit to reparations for war damage, the principle is comfortable, familiar, and best of all, legal. For victims of broken sidewalks, open wells, ignored stop signs, the conditions under which damages are awarded are quite clear. (1) There is specific injury, specific victim, specific time and place. (2) A specific individual or set of individuals must be found responsible either (a) by actually having done the injury, or (b) by failing to act in such a way (for example, repairing the sidewalk, sealing the well) so as to remove a particular potential source of injury on their property. (3) A reasonable assessment of the monetary value of the claim can be made. In such cases no moral blame is attached to the person forced to pay compensation.

But reparations are somewhat less clear. How much does Germany owe France for causing (losing?) World War I? Can we say that *Germany* caused the war? Can we say that Germany *caused* the war? Germany did pay, at least in part, based upon rough calculations of the cost of the Allied armies, including pensions, the loss of allied GNP, indemnities for death and for the destruction of property.

Besides the ability to calculate the indemnities, reparations between countries require at least three other conditions to be met: (1) Responsibility for the events must be able to be assigned and accepted. (2) There must be governments or government-like agencies between which the transfer of goods and services and money takes place. (3) There must be a *modus agendi* worked out. The transfer of vast amounts of goods, money, and services is immensely complicated. In the end Germany could refuse to pay and the Allies to accept large parts of the reparations. Part of the Allied refusal is instructive. Britain, for example, simply could not absorb the payments without extreme economic dislocation.

The meaning of *reparations* was extended to cover payments to Israel and payments to individuals both in and out of Germany who suffered losses through the actions of the Third Reich. The payments to Israel, which did not exist during the war, were to reimburse that state, as the representative of the Jewish people, for the expenses incurred by Jewish organizations during the war in resettling persons uprooted by persecutions and made victims of "unspeakable Nazi crimes." [3]

German payments to individuals were called *Wiedergutmachung* (restitution). *Wiedergutmachung* was awarded not merely for damages or injuries but in order to restore a person to his former position in life. It was calculated on a precise basis. You could be indemnified for: (1) loss of property; (2) loss of income; (3) loss of family; (4) length and type of imprisonment; (5) what you would have earned based upon a reasonable calculation, if you were young and had not yet begun a career. To qualify for indemnities, one had to produce, respectively, proof of ownership and value of property, a calculation of the difference between what one earned as a refugee and would have earned, proof of loss of family, proof of imprisonment.

INAPPLICABILITY OF THESE PARADIGMS

Can reverse discrimination be construed to fit any of these paradigms? Can favoring blacks, Chicanos, Indians, women, and so forth over whites or males be seen as compensation, reparations, or restitution? The answer is no for two general reasons and for several which are specific to the various paradigms. The general reasons are, first, that responsibility for discrimination past and present and for its deleterious consequences is neither clearly assigned nor accepted. Some seem to think that the mere fact of its existence makes all whites (or males in the case of antifeminism) responsible.[4] But I do not know an analysis of responsibility which bears out this claim. Second, there is a great difficulty, if not an impossibility, in assigning a monetary value to the damage done and the compensation allegedly owed—that is to say, reverse discrimination.

If we turn to the negligence paradigm, all the conditions seem to fail. *Specific* injury is lacking, *specific* individual responsibility is lacking, and there is no way to assess the monetary value of the "loss." Indeed, in the case of reverse discrimination it is not monetary value which is claimed but preferential treatment. Under the large-scale reparations paradigm two conditions beyond responsibility are lacking. There are no governments or government-like agencies between which the transfer could take place, and there is no *modus agendi* for the transfer to take place.

Where the transfer is to be of preferential treatment, it is unclear how it is even to be begun. So we come to the third paradigm: individual restitution. This is much closer, for it deals with compensating individual victims of persecution. Again, however, it fails to provide a model, first, because reverse discrimination cannot be looked at in monetary terms, and second, even if it could, the restitution is designed to bring a person back to where he was before the deprivation. In the case of the minorities in question, there can be no question of restoring them to former positions or property. Precisely, the point of the reparation is to pay them for what they, because of immoral social practices, never had in the first place.

But doesn't Condition 5 under *Wiedergutmachung* seem ready-made for the purpose here? Does it not require calculation of what the person would have earned had his life not been blighted? If A was a doctor, lawyer, office manager, beginning a career, or even a mere student, you could get a rough estimate of what he might earn based upon his family position, the average earnings for that occupation, and so forth. But suppose A is young, uneducated, unskilled, unemployed, from a broken home; what might he have been had circumstances been different? Anything. And that is the tragedy. But how can you calculate his earnings on that basis, and how can you translate them into reverse discrimination?

JUSTICE

Finally, if we ignore all that has been said and simply go ahead and discriminate in reverse, calling it reparation, it remains to ask whether it would be either reasonable or just? I think the answer is no. It is possible to hold that in some set of cases, other things being equal, compensation is required and yet to argue either that since other things are not equal compensation is not required, or that even if some compensation is required it ought not to take the form of reverse discrimination. Certainly, from the fact that some form of compensation or reparation must be made it does not follow that any *specific* form of compensation is in order. If X is discriminated against in awarding professorships because he is a member of C group, it scarcely follows that if compensation is in order it *must* take the form of his being discriminated in favor of for another professorship, at least not without adopting the principle of "an eye for an eye" (and only an *eye* for an eye?). Consider X being turned down for an apartment because he is a C member. Must compensation consist just in his being offered another ahead of anybody else? Even if he has one already? To go from the relatively innocuous principle that where *possible* we ought to compensate for damages, to sanction reverse discrimination as the proper or preferred form of redress, requires us to go beyond mere compensation to some principle very much like "let the punishment mirror the crime." But here the person "punished," the person from whom the compensation is exacted, is often not the "criminal." Nor will it help to say that the person deprived of a job or advancement by reverse discrimination is not really being punished or deprived, since the job did not belong to him in the first place. Of course it didn't; nor did it belong to the successful candidate. What belonged to both is equal consideration, and that is what one of them is being deprived of.[5]

There is an element of injustice or unfairness in all reparations. The money derived from taxes paid by all citizens is used for reparations regardless of whether they were responsible for, did nothing about, opposed, or actually fought the policies or government in question. Yet we say that this is the only way it can be done, that the element of unfairness is not great, and that on the whole it is better that this relatively painless way of appropriating money from Jones, who is innocent, be used than that the victims of persecution or crime go uncompensated. But the consequences of reverse discrimination are quite different, especially when it is based upon group membership rather than individual desert. It is possible and is sometimes the case that though most C members are discriminated against, Y is a C member who has met with no discrimination at all. Under the principle that all C members should be discriminated in favor of, we would offer "compensation" to Y. But what are we compensating him *for*? By hypothesis he was no victim of discrimination. Do we compensate him for what happened to others? Do we pay Jones for what we buy from Smith? We seem to be compensating him for being a C member, but why? Do we secretly hold C members inferior? Some claim that society as a whole must bear the burden of reparation. But then reverse discrimination will hardly do the trick. It does not exact redress from the government, or even from all white (responsible?) citizens equally, but falls solely against those who apply for admissions, or jobs *for which blacks or other minorities are applying at the same time.* By the same token, it does not compensate or "reparate" all minority persons equally but merely those applying for admission, jobs, promotions, and so forth. Those whose positions are secure would not be made to pay, and those who do not apply for anything would not be paid. A white person who fought for civil rights for blacks may be passed over for promotion or displaced, a victim of reverse discrimination, while a Ku Klux Klan man at the top of the job ladder pays nothing. This would be a laughably flawed system if it were not seriously advocated by responsible people, and partly implemented by the government. Surely, it violates the principles of both compensatory and distributive justice.

NOTES

1. For examples of these strategies, see the articles by J. W. Nickel, L. J. Cowan, and Paul Taylor herein.

2. *Contra* this objection see Irving Thalberg, "Justifications of Institutional Racism," *The Philosophical Forum,* Winter 1972.

3. See the text of the reparations agreement in Rolf Vogel, *The German Path to Israel* (Dufour Editions, 1969), pp. 56 ff.

4. See Thalberg. For an interesting catalogue of "irresponsible uses of 'responsibility'" see Robert Stover, "Responsibility for the Cold War—A Case Study in Historical Responsibility," *History and Theory,* 1972. For a clear-cut analysis that more than mere presence on the scene is required to show responsibility, see S. Levinson, "Responsibility for Crimes of War," *Philosophy and Public Affairs,* Spring 1973.

5. See Gertrude Ezorsky, "It's Mine," *Philosophy and Public Affairs,* Spring 1974.

Bibliography

Abrams, Charles. Foreword to *Equality*. New York: Pantheon, 1965, i-xiv.

Abrams, Eliot. "The Quota Commission." *Commentary,* Oct. 1972.

Alevy v. Downstate Med. Center, N.Y.S. Court of Appeals, Apr. 8, 1976.

Alexander & Alexander. "The New Racism: An Analysis of the Use of Racial and Ethnic Criteria in Decision-making." 9 *San Diego L. Rev.* 190 (1972).

America, Richard. "A New Rationale for Income Redistribution." *The Review of Black Political Economy* 2 (1972).

Askin. "The Case for Compensatory Treatment." 24 *Rutgers L. Rev.* 65 (1970).

——— "Eliminating Racist Inequality in a Racist World." *Civil Liberties Review* 2 (1975).

Askin and Cohen. (Debate) "Preferential Admissions in Higher Education: Should We Support or Condemn It?" *Civil Liberties Review* 2:95-116 (1975).

Barasch, Frances. "H.E.W., the Universities, and Women." *Dissent,* Summer 1973.

Bard, Bernard. "College for All: Dream or Disaster?" *Phi Delta Kappan* 56 (1975).

Bayles, Michael. "Compensatory Reverse Discrimination in Hiring." *Social Theory and Practice* 2, 3.

——— "Reparations to Wronged Groups." *Analysis* 33, 6.

Becker, Gary S. *The Economics of Discrimination.* Chicago: U. of Chicago Press, 1957.

Bedau, H. A. "Compensatory Justice and the Black Manifesto." *The Monist* 56, 20 (1972).

Bell, Derrick A. "Black Students in White Law Schools: The Ordeal and the Opportunity." 1970 *Toledo L. Rev.* 539.

——— "In Defense of Minority Admissions Programs: A Reply to Professor Graglia." 119 *U. of Pa. L. Rev.* 264 (1970).

——— "Racism in American Courts: Cause for Black Disruption or Despair?" 61 *Calif. L. Rev.* 165 (1973).

Benson, Robert S. & Harold Wolmen, eds. *Counterbudget: A Blueprint for Changing National Priorities 1971-1976.* New York: Praeger, 1971.

Bickel, A. "The Original Understanding and the Segregation Decision." 69 *Harv. L. Rev.* 1 (1955).

Bittker, Boris. *The Case for Black Reparations.* New York: Random House, 1973.

——— "The Case of the Checker-Board Ordinance: An Experiment in Race Relations. 71 *Yale L. Jl.* 1887 (1962).

Black, Virginia. "The Erosion of Legal Principles in the Creation of Legal Policy." *Ethics.* 84, 2.

Blumenrosen, Alfred. *Black Employment and the Law.* New York: Rutgers U. Press, 1971.

——— "The Crossroads for Equal Employment Opportunity: Incisive Administration or Indecisive Bureaucracy?" 49 *Notre Dame Law* 46 (1973).

——— "Quotas, Common Sense, and Law in Labor Relations: Three Dimensions of Equal Opportunity." 27 *Rutgers L. Rev.* 675 (1974).

——— "Strangers in Paradise: Griggs v. Duke Power Co. and the Concept of Employment Discrimination." 71 *Mich. L. Rev.* 59 (1975).

Boulding, Kenneth. "Social Justice as a Holy Grail." (unpublished).

Boxhill, Bernard. "The Morality of Reparations." *Social Theory and Practice* 2, 1.

Brown, Dee. *Bury My Heart at Wounded Knee.* New York: Bantam, 1971.

Browne, Robert A. "The Economic Basis for Reparations to Black America." *The Review of Black Political Economy* 2 (1972).

Buek, Alexandra & Jeffrey H. Orlean. "Sex Discrimination—A Bar to a Democratic Education: Overview of Title IX of the Education Amendments of 1972." 6 *Conn. L. Rev.* 1 (1973).

Bunzel, John H. "The Politics of Quotas." *Change,* Oct. 1972.

Burke, Armand. "Another View of Reverse Discrimination." *Philosophical Exchange* 1, Summer 1974.

Cabrabes, "Careers in Law for Minorities: A Puerto-Rican's Perspective on Recent Developments in Legal Education." 25 *Jl. Legal Ed.* 447 (1973).

Carter, Robert L. *Equality.* New York: Pantheon, 1965.

Cochran. "Some Thoughts on American Law Schools, the Legal Profession, and the Role of Students." 1970 *Toledo L. Rev.*

Cohen, C. "Race and the Constitution." *The Nation* 1975.

Coleman, Jules. "Justice and Preferential Hiring." *Jl. of Critical Analysis* V, 1.

Comment: "Are Sex-Based Classifications Consritutionally Suspect?" 66 *N. W. L. Rev.* (1971).

Consalus. "The Law School Admission Test and the Minority Student." 1970 *Toledo L. Rev.* 501.

Cooper, G. & R. B. Sobol. "Seniority and Testing Under Fair Employment Laws: A General Approach to Objective Criteria of Hiring and Promotion." 82 *Harv.*

L. Rev. 1598 (1969).

Countryman, Vern, ed. *Discrimination and the Law.* Chicago: U. of Chicago Press, 1965.

Cowan, L. J. "Inverse Discrimination." *Analysis* 33, 1.

———"Group Interests." 44 *Va. L. Rev.* (1958).

Crandel, John C. "Affirmative Action: Goals and Consequences." *Philosophical Exchange* 1, Summer 1974.

Davis, Bernard D., M.D. "Of Doctors and Quotas." letter, *The New York Times,* 16 April 1976.

DeFunis v. Odegaard, Amicus Curiae Brief for the Anti-Defamation League of B'Nai B'Rith, Theodore Bickel and Philip Kurland.

DeLoria, Vine. *We Talk, You Listen.* New York: Macmillan, 1970.

"Developments in the Law, Equal Protection." 82 *Harv. L. Rev.* 1065 (1969).

Diamond, Esther E. *Issues of Sex Bias and Sex Fairness in Career Interest Measurement,* Washington, D.C.: 1975.

"Disadvantaged Students and Legal Education—Progress for Affirmative Action." 1970 *Toledo L. Rev.* 277.

Duncan, Otis Dudley. "Inheritance of Poverty or Inheritance of Race." *On Understanding Poverty: Perspective from the Social Sciences,* ed. D. P. Moynihan. New York: Basic Books, 1969.

Dworkin, R. "The DeFunis Case: The Right to Go to Law School." *The New York Review of Books,* Feb. 5, 1976.

Edwards, A. "New Role for the Black Law Graduates—A Reality or an Illusion?" 69 *Mich. L. Rev.* (1971).

Edwards, H. T. & B. L. Zaretsky. "Preferential Remedies for Employment Discrimination." 74 *Mich. L. Rev.* (1975).

Elden, Gary. "Forty Acres and a Mule, with Interest: The Constitutionality of Black Capitalism, Benign School Quotas, and Other Statutory Racial Classifications." 47 *Journal of Urban Law* 591 (1969).

Ely, John Hart. "The Constitutionality of Reverse Discrimination." 41 *U. of Chi. L. Rev.* 723 (1974).

Equal Opportunity Commission and the City of New York v. Local 28 of the Sheet Metal Worker's International Association, U.S. District Court, Southern District of N.Y., Fall 1975.

Ezorsky, Gertrude. "The Fight Over University Women." *The New York Review of Books,* May 16, 1974.

———"It's Mine." *Philosophy & Public Affairs,* Spring 1974.

——— Exchange of Letters, *The New York Review of Books,* Oct. 19 & 31, 1974, & April 3, 1975.

Fairfax-Brewster School, Inc. v. Ganzales, U.S. 75-66.

Fiss, Owen. "A Theory of Fair Employment Laws." 38 *U. of Chi. L. Rev.* 235 (1971).

——— "The Charlotte-Mecklenberg Case—Its Significance for Northern School Desegregation." 38 *U. of Chi. L. Rev.* (1971).

———"Groups and the Equal Protection Clause." *Philosophy & Public Affairs,* Winter 1976.

———— "The Fate of an Idea Whose Time Has Come: Anti-Discrimination Law in the Second Decade After *Brown v. Board of Education*" 41 *U. of Chi L. Rev.* 742, (1974).

Fleming and Pollack. "The Black Quota at Yale Law School: An Exchange of Letters." *The Public Interest* 19, 1970.

Forman, Irving. "Discrimination in Employment." *N.Y.U. Law Forum,* 1960.

Frank and Munro. "The Original Understanding of 'Equal Protection of the Laws.'" 50 *Colum. L. Rev.* 131 (1950).

Fredreckson, *The Black Image in the White Mind.* New York: Harper & Row, 1971.

Freund, P. *On Law and Justice.* Cambridge: Harvard U. Press, 1968.

Fried, Marlene G. "In Defense of Preferential Hiring." *Philosophical Forum* V, 1-2.

Galanter, Marc. *Equality and Compensatory Discrimination in India.* forthcoming.

Gellhorn, E. "The Law Schools and the Negro." 1968 *Duke L. Jl.* 1069.

Ginger, Ann Fajan, ed. *DeFunis v. Odegaard and the University of Washington: The University Admissions Case, the Record.* Oceana Publications, 3 vols.

Glazer, Nathan. *Affirmative Discrimination.* New York: Basic Books, 1975.

———— "A Breakdown in Civil Rights Enforcement?" *The Public Interest,* Spring 1971.

Glennerster & Hatch, eds. *Positive Discrimination. Fabian Research Series* 314.

Goldman, Alan. "Affirmative Action." *Philosophy & Public Affairs,* Winter 1976.

———— "Justice & Hiring by Competence." *American Philosophical Quarterly,* forthcoming, Jan. 1977.

———— "Limits to the Justification of Reverse Discrimination." *Social Theory and Practice* 3, 3.

———— "Reparations to Individuals or Groups?" *Analysis* 33, 5.

———— "Reverse Discrimination and the Future: A Reply to Thalberg." *Philosophical Forum* II, nos. 2-3.

Golightly, Cornelius L. "Justice and 'Discrimination For' in Higher Education." *Philosophical Exchange* 1, Summer 1974.

Graglia, Lino A. "Special Admissions of the 'Culturally Deprived' to Law School." 119 *U. of Pa. L. Rev.* 351 (1970).

Green, Mark. "Reparations for Blacks." *Commonweal,* June 13, 1969.

Greenawalt, Kent. "Judicial Scrutiny of 'Benign' Racial Preference in Law School Admissions." 1975 *Colum. L. Rev.* 559.

Greenberg, Jack. "Affirmative Action, Quotas, and Merit." *The New York Times,* "Op. Ed. Page." 7 Feb. 1976.

Griggs v. Duke Power Co., 401, US 424 (1971).

Griswold. Erwin. "Some Observations on the DeFunis Case." 75 *Colum. L. Rev.* 512 (1975).

Gross, Barry R. "Is Turn About Fair Play?" *The Journal of Critical Analysis* V, 4, 1975.

———— letter, *The New York Times,* 12 April 1975.

———— Review of O'Neil, *Discriminating Against Discrimination* and Glazer, *Affirmative Discrimination,* in *The Humanist,* Nov.-Dec. 1976.

Gunther, Gerald. "Forward: In Search of Evolving Doctrine on a Changing Court: A

Model for a Newer Equal Protection, The Supreme Court, 1971 Term." 86 *Harv. L. Rev.* 1 (1972).

Harrington, Michael & Arnold Kaufman. "Black Reparations—Two Views." *Dissent*, 1969.

Hill, Herbert. letter, *The New York Times*, 16 May 1972.

——— "New Judicial Perception of Employment Discrimination—Litigation under Title VII of the Civil Rights Act of 1964." 43 *U. Col. L. Rev.* (1972).

——— "Affirmative Action and The Quest for Job Equality." Delivered at the tenth anniversary of the U.S. Equal Employment Opportunity Commission, The Law School, Rutgers, Nov. 28, 1975.

Hook, Sidney. "Discrimination, Color Blindness, and the Quota System." *Measure*, Oct. 1971.

———"H.E.W. Regulations—A New Threat to Educational Integrity." *Freedom at Issue* 10, 1971.

——— "The Road to a University Quota System." *Freedom at Issue*, Mar.-Apr. 1972.

——— "The Bias in Anti-Bias Regulations." (Review of Lester, below) *Measure*, Summer 1974.

——— "A Quota is a Quota is a Quota." *The New York Times*, " Op. Ed. Page" 13 Nov. 1974.

Horowitz. "14th Amendment Aspects of Racial Discrimination in 'Private' Housing." 1*Cal. L. Rev.* (1964).

Hughes. "Reparations for Blacks?" 43 *N.Y.U. L. Rev.* 1063 (1968).

Hughes, McKay & Winograd. "The Disadvantaged Student and Preparation for Legal Education: The New York University Experience." *Toledo L. Rev.* 701 (1970).

Johnson, Sheila K. "It's Action, But Is It Affirmative?" *The New York Times Magazine*, 11 May 1975.

Jones, J. E. "The Bugaboo of Employment Quotas." 1970 *Wis. L. Rev.* 341.

——— "Federal-Contract Compliance in Phase II—The Dawning of the Age of Enforcement of Equal Employment Obligations." 4 *Ga. L. Rev.* 756 (1970).

Kahn v. Shevin, 416 U.S. 351 (1974) Brennan, J. dissenting

Kain, J. F. *Race and Poverty: The Economics of Discrimination*. Englewood Cliffs: Prentice-Hall, 1969.

Kaplan. "Equal Justice in an Unequal World: Equality of the Negro—The Problem of Special Treatment." 61 *N.W. U.L. Rev.* 363 (1966).

Karst & Horowitz. "Affirmative Action and Equal Protection." 60 *Va. L. Rev.* 955 (1974).

Katzner, Louis J. "Is Favoring Women and Blacks in Employment and Educational Opportunities Justified?" in *Philosophy of Law*, eds. Feinberg & Gross, New York: Dickenson Publishing Co., 1975.

Kaufman, Arnold. *The Radical Liberal.* 1968

Kempton, Murray. "The Black Manifesto." *The New York Review of Books*, July 10, 1969.

Kenneth Hupart, *et al.* v. The Board of Higher Education of New York City, *et al.* 75 civ. 178, 75 civ. 915, 75 civ. 2117.

Kilson, Martin. "The Black Experience at Harvard." *New York Times Magazine*, 2 Sept. 1973.

Kirkland and Hayes v. N.Y.S. Department of Correctional Services, U.S. Court of Appeals for the second circuit, Sept. 1974

Kraft, Ivor. "DeFunis v. Odegaard: Race, Merit and the Fourteenth Amendment." Sacramento, 1976.

Kurland, P. "Egalitarianism and the Warren Court." 68 *Mich L. Rev.* 629 (1970).

————*Politics, The Constitution, and The Warren Court.* Chicago: U. of Chicago Press, 1971.

Kuttner, Bob. "White Males and Jews Need Not Apply." *The Village Voice*, 31 Aug. 1972.

Lester, Richard. *Anti-Bias Regulation of Universities.* New York: McGraw-Hill, 1974.

Lichtman, Richard. "The Ethics of Compensatory Justice." 1 *Law in Transition Quarterly* 76 (1964).

Lusky. "Stereotype: Hard Core of Racism." 13 *Buff. L. Rev.* 450 (1964).

Lyon, Catherine D. and Terry Saario. "Woman in Educational Administration." *UCEA Review*, Sept. 1974.

McCrary v. Runyon————U.S.————75-306 (1970)

McDonald v. Sante Fe Transportation Co.————U.S.————75-260

McDonnell Douglas Corp. v. Green 411————U.S.————792 (1973).

McGary, Howard Jr. "Reparations and Inverse Discrimination." *Dialogue* 17, 1, (1974).

McGuire, Joseph W. & Joseph A. Pinchler, eds. *Inequality: The Poor and the Rich in America.* 1969.

McPherson, "The Black Law Student: A Problem in Fidelities." *Atlantic,* April 1970.

Making Affirmative Action Work, a report of the Carnegie Commission on Higher Education, San Francisco: Jossey-Bass. 1975.

Marcuse, P. "Benign Quotas Re-examined." *Jl. Intergroup Relations* 3 (1962).

Margaret Kohn v. Royall, Koegel and Wells, U.S. District Court, Southern District of New York, 72 Civ. 2705

Marketti, Jim. "Black Equity in the Slave Industry." *The Review of Black Political Economy* II, 2 (1972).

Martin, Michael. "Pedogogical Arguments for Preferential Hiring and Tenuring of University Teachers." *Philosophical Forum* V, 1-2.

Martinez, Suzanne. "Affirmative Action and Public Education: Some Preliminary Issues and Questions." *Youth Law Center*, Sept. 1975.

Morris. "Equal Protection, Affirmative Action and Racial Preferences in Law Admission: DeFunis v. Odegaard." 49 *Wash. L. Rev.* 1 (1973).

Nagel, Thomas. "Equal Treatment and Compensatory Discrimination." *Philosophy & Public Affairs,* Summer 1973.

Newton, Lisa. "Reverse Discrimination as Unjustified." *Ethics* 83, 4 (1973).

Nickel, James. "Classification by Race in Compensatory Programs." *Ethics* 84, 2 (1974).

———— "Discrimination and Morally Relevant Characteristics." *Analysis* 32, 4.

———— "Preferential Practices in Hiring and Admissions: A Jurisprudential

Approach." 75 *Colum. L. Rev.* 534 (1975).

——Review of Bittker, Boris. *The Case for Black Reparations,* in *Ethics* 84, 2 (1974).

——— Review of O'Neil, Robert M., *Discriminating Against Discrimination,* in *The Chronicle of Higher Education,* forthcoming.

———"Should Reparations Be Made to Individuals or Groups?" *Analysis* 34, 5.

"Note: Constitutional Law and Reverse Discrimination." 41 *Cin. L. Rev.* 250 (1972).

"Note: Constitutionality of Remedial Minority Preferences in Employment." 56 *Minn. L. Rev.* 842 (1972).

"Note: Decline and Fall of the New Equal Protection: A Polemical Approach." 58 *Va. L. Rev.* 1489 (1972).

"Note: Racial Bias and the LSAT: A New Approach to the Defense of Preferential Admissions." 24 *Buff. L. Rev.* 439 (1975).

Nunn, William III. "Reverse Discrimination." *Analysis* 34, 5.

O'Krueger, Anne. "The Economics of Discrimination." *Journal of Political Economy* 72 (1963).

O'Neil, Robert M. *Discriminating Against Discrimination.* Bloomington: Indiana U. Press, 1975.

——— "Preferential Admissions: Equalizing Access to Legal Education." 1970 *Toledo L. Rev.* 281.

——— "Racial Preference and Higher Education: The Larger Context." 60 *Va. L. Rev.* 925 (1974).

——— "After DeFunis: Filling the Constitutional Vacuum." 27 *U. Fla. L. Rev.* 315 (1975).

Ornstein, Allan. *Race & Politics in School Community Organizations.* Englewood Cliffs: Goodyear, 1974.

——— "Are Quotas Here to Stay in Minority Hiring?" *National Review,* 26 April, 1974.

——— "What Does Affirmative Action Affirm? A Viewpoint." *Phi. Delta Kappan,* Dec. 1975.

——— "Affirmative Action and The Education Industry." in Ornstein & Muller, eds. *Policy Issues in Education.* Lexington: D.C. Heath, 1976.

Paulson, Monrad. "DeFunis: The Road Not Taken—Introduction." 60 *Va. L. Rev.* 917 (1974).

Peck, C. J. "Remedies for Racial Discrimination in Employment: A Comparative Evaluation of Forums." 46 *Wash. L. Rev.* 455 (1971).

Pelikan, Jaroslav. "Quality and Equality." *The New York Times,* 29 March 1976.

Plessy v. Fergeson, 163, US 537 (1896), Harlan, J. dissenting.

Pollitt, D. H. "Racial Discrimination in Employment: Proposals for Corrective Action." 13 *Buff. L. Rev.* 59 (1963).

Pollock, Mordeca Jane. "On Academic Quotas." *The New York Times* "Op. Ed. Page" 4 March 1975.

Posner, R. A. "DeFunis case and the Constitutionality of preferential treatment of of racial minorities" 1974 *Sup. Ct. Rev.* 1.

"Preferential Treatment and other Improper Procedures . . . " pamphlet submitted to the secretary of H.E.W. by six Jewish organizations, Apr. 8, 1972.

Raphael, D. D. "Equality and Equity." *Philosophy* 21 (1946).

Redish, "Preferential Law School Admissions and the Equal Protection Clause: An Analysis of the Competing Arguments." 22 *U.C.L.A.L. Rev.* 343 (1974).

"Report of the AAUP Committee on Discrimination." *AAUP Bulletin,* June 1973.

Robinson, J. B. "Housing—The Northern Civil Rights Frontier." 13 *W.R.L. Rev.* 101 (1961).

Rothbard, Murray. "The Quota System, in short, must be repudiated immediately." *Intellectual Digest,* Feb. 1973.

Runyon V McCrary 75-62 ———U.S.———(1976).

Saario, Terry. "Title IX: Now What?" in Ornstein & Muller, *Policy Issues in Education.* Lexington: D.C. Heath, 1976.

Sandalow, Terrence. "Racial Preferences in Higher Education: Political Responsibility and Judicial Role." 42 *U. of C. L. Rev.* (1975).

Schucter, Arnold, *Reparations.* Philadelphia: Lippincott, 1970.

Seabury, Paul. "H.E.W. and the Universities." *Commentary,* Feb. 1972.

Seligman, Daniel. "How 'Equal Opportunity' Turned into Employment Quotas." *Fortune,* March 1973.

Sher, George. "Justifying Reverse Discrimination." *Philosophy & Public Affairs,* Winter 1975.

Sherman, Malcolm. "Affirmative Action and the AAUP." *AAUP Bulletin,* Winter 1975.

Shiner, Roger. "Individuals, Groups and Inverse Discrimination." *Analysis,* June 1973.

Shrader and Pitcher. "Predicting Law School Grades For Black American Law Students." *Educational Testing Service Report,* 1973.

Silvestri, Philip. "The Justification of Reverse Discrimination." *Analysis* 34, 1.

Simon, Robert. "Preferential Hiring." *Philosophy & Public Affairs,* Spring 1974.

Smith, Donald R. *India as a Secular State.* Princeton: Princeton Univ. Press, 1963.

Southern Independent School Assn. v. McCrary, 75-278, ———U.S.——— (1976).

Sowell, Thomas. *Black Education: Myths & Tragedies.* New York: McKay, 1974.

——— *Affirmative Action Reconsidered,* pamphlet. American Enterprise Institute For Public Policy Research, 1975.

——— "Affirmative Action Reconsidered." *The Public Interest* 42, Winter 1975 (a shorter version).

——— "A Black Conservative Dissents." *The New York Times Magazine,* 8 Aug. 1976.

Spiess, Hardy and Roantiec v. C. Itoh & Co., U.S. District Court for the Southern District of Texas, Judge Bue, presiding.

Steinbach, Sheldon. "Fighting Campus Job Discrimination in Higher Education." *Change* 5, Nov. 1973.

Streibergh, Fred. "Troubled Times with A.A." *Yale Alumni Magazine,* Apr. 1973.

Summers, "Preferential Admissions: An Unreal Solution to a Real Problem." (1970). *Toledo L. Rev.* 377.

Swann v. Charlotte-Mecklenburg, Board of Education, 402, US 1 (1971).

Sweatt v. Painter, 339 US 629 (1950).

Taylor, Paul. "Reverse Discrimination and Compensatory Justice." *Analysis,* June 1973.

Thalberg, Irving. "Reverse Discrimination and the Future." *Philosophical Forum* V, 1-2.

———"Visceral Racism." *The Monist* 56, (1972).

Thomson, Judith Jarris. "Preferential Hiring." *Philosophy & Public Affairs,* Summer 1973.

Thurow, Lester. *Poverty and Discrimination.* The Brookings Institution, 1969.

Tittle, Carol K. *Women and Educational Testing.* Princeton: Princeton U. Press, 1974.

Todorovich, Glickstein exchange. *Civil Rights Digest.* Spring 1975.

Todorovich. Testimony 8/20/75, for the Committee on Academic Non-discrimination. 444 Park Ave. So.

Transcript of the hearings of the O'Hara Committee.

Tussman & Ten Broek. "The Equal Protection of the Laws." 37 *Calif. L. Rev.* 341 (1949).

U.S. Commission on Civil Rights. *Federal Civil Rights Enforcement Effort.* Washington, D.C., 1970.

Vieira, Norman. "Racial Imbalance, Black Separatism and Permissible Classification by Race." 67 *Mich. L. Rev.* 1553 (1969).

Wade, John W. *Cases and Materials on Restitution,* 1966.

Washington, Mayor of Washington, D.C. *et. al.* v. Davis 74-1492,———U.S.——— (1976).

Wasserstrom, Richard. "The University and the Case for Preferential Treatment." *American Philosophical Quarterly* 13, April 2, 1976.

Weaver, Robert. "Integration in Public Housing." *Annals* 86 (1956).

"What do you people want?" *Harvard Business Review* March-April, 1969.

"Where we stand: Quotas and goals." Pamphlet from the American Jewish Congress. May 12, 1972.

Woodruff, Paul. "What's Wrong with Discrimination?" *Analysis* 36, March 3, 1976

Yarmolinsky, Adam. letter, *The New York Times,* 16 April 1976.

List of Contributors

F. K. BARASCH teaches English at Baruch College of The City University of New York.

MICHAEL D. BAYLES teaches Philosophy at the University of Kentucky. He has published articles in *Ethics and Social Philosophy*.

BORIS I. BITTKER is Stirling Professor of Law at Yale. He has written books and articles on taxation and on political and civil rights.

VIRGINIA BLACK teaches Philosophy at Pace University in Westchester.

BERNARD BOXHILL teaches Philosophy at U.C.L.A.

L. J. COWAN teaches Philosophy at the University of Arizona. He has published articles on ethics and the philosophy of mind.

ARCHIBALD COX is Wilston Professor of Law at Harvard. He has served in many government posts, most recently as Director of the Watergate Special Prosecution Force. He is the author of books on labor policy and the Warren court, among others.

WILLIAM O. DOUGLAS is a retired Associate Justice of the United States Supreme Court and the author of many books.

JOHN HART ELY is Professor of Law at Harvard University.

NATHAN GLAZER is Professor of Education and Social Structure at Harvard. He is the coeditor of *The Public Interest*, and the author of books and articles on American society.

HOWARD GLICKSTEIN is Director of the Center for Civil Rights at the

University of Notre Dame. He was formerly Director of the United States Commission on Civil Rights.

ALAN H. GOLDMAN teaches Philosophy at the University of Idaho. He has published papers on epistemology, the philosophy of mind, and ethics.

KENT GREENAWALT is Professor of Law at Columbia University.

BARRY R. GROSS teaches Philosophy at York College of the City University of New York. He has published books and articles on analytic philosophy, philosophy of mind, and social problems.

ROBERT HOFFMAN teaches Philosophy at York College of the City University of New York. He is the author of many articles on epistemology aesthetics, philosophy of religion, and philosophy of mind, as well as a book on epistemology.

SIDNEY HOOK is Emeritus Professor of Philosophy at New York University and Senior Research Fellow at the Hoover Institution on War, Revolution, and Peace. Among his most recent books are *Revolution, Reform, and Social Justice,* and *Pragmatism and the Tragic Sense of Life.*

HARDY E. JONES teaches Philosophy at the University of Nebraska. He writes on problems in ethics and social philosophy.

LISA H. NEWTON teaches Philosophy at Fairfield University in Connecticut. She has written on social and political problems.

JAMES W. NICKEL teaches Philosophy at Wichita State University. He has published articles on ethics, social problems, and the philosophy of law.

LEE NISBET was formerly Assistant Professor of Philosophy at Alfred University and is now Executive Editor of *The Humanist* magazine.

WILLIAM NUNN, III teaches law at the Washington Law School of American University.

ROBERT M. O'NEIL is a lawyer and Vice President of the Bloomington Campus of Indiana University. He has written books on free speech and civil liberties.

J. STANLEY POTTINGER was the Director of the Office of Civil Rights of H.E.W. from 1970-73. He is currently Assistant Attorney General in the Civil Rights Division of the United States Department of Justice.

TERRANCE SANDALOW is Professor of Law at the University of Michigan.

PAUL SEABURY teaches Political Science at the University of California at Berkeley. He has written many books, the most recent of which is *The Great Détante Disaster.*

ROGER A. SHINER teaches Philosophy at the University of Alberta. He writes on epistemology and social and political philosophy.

PHILIP SILVESTRI teaches Philosophy at Lehman College of the City

University of New York.

THOMAS SOWELL is Professor of Economics at U.C.L.A., adjunct scholar at the American Enterprise Institute in Washington, D.C. and a Fellow of the Hoover Institution on War, Revolution, and Peace.

PAUL W. TAYLOR is Professor of Philosophy at Brooklyn College of the City University of New York. He has written numerous articles on ethical problems.

MIRO M. TODOROVICH teaches physics at Bronx Community College of the City University of New York. He is coordinator of the Committee on Academic Non-Discrimination and Integrity. He has edited books on social and educational problems.